Songs on the Death
of Children

Songs on the Death of Children

Selected Poems from Kindertotenlieder

FRIEDRICH RÜCKERT

Translated and Annotated by DAVID BANNON

Foreword by Cornelia Kallisch

Jefferson, North Carolina

All Scripture quotations, unless otherwise indicated, are taken from the Holy Bible, New International Version®, NIV®. Copyright ©1973, 1978, 1984, 2011 by Biblica, Inc.™ Used by permission of Zondervan. All rights reserved worldwide. www.zondervan.com The "NIV" and "New International Version" are trademarks registered in the United States Patent and Trademark Office by Biblica, Inc.™

Scripture quotations designated CJB are taken from the Complete Jewish Bible by David H. Stern. Copyright © 1998. All rights reserved. Used by permission of Messianic Jewish Publishers, 6120 Day Long Lane, Clarksville, Maryland 21029.

Scripture quotations designated ESV are taken from The ESV® Bible (The Holy Bible, English Standard Version®), copyright © 2001 by Crossway, a publishing ministry of Good News Publishers. Used by permission. All rights reserved.

Scripture quotations designated NLT are taken from the Holy Bible, New Living Translation, copyright ©1996, 2004, 2015 by Tyndale House Foundation. Used by permission of Tyndale House Publishers, Inc., Carol Stream, Illinois 60188. All rights reserved.

Scripture quotations designated NRSV are taken from the New Revised Standard Version Bible, copyright © 1989 the Division of Christian Education of the National Council of the Churches of Christ in the United States of America. Used by permission. All rights reserved.

Scripture quotations taken from the (NASB®) New American Standard Bible®, Copyright © 1960, 1971, 1977, 1995, 2020 by The Lockman Foundation. Used by permission. All rights reserved. www.lockman.org.

All translations in this book are by the author, David Bannon, unless otherwise indicated in the reference and translation notes. Translation copyright © 2015–2022 by David Bannon.

Please refer to the Acknowledgments for more copyright information.

ISBN (print) 978-1-4766-9042-1
ISBN (ebook) 978-1-4766-4894-1

LIBRARY OF CONGRESS AND BRITISH LIBRARY
CATALOGUING DATA ARE AVAILABLE

Library of Congress Control Number 2022055311

© 2023 David Bannon. All rights reserved

No part of this book may be reproduced or transmitted in any form or by any means, electronic or mechanical, including photocopying or recording, or by any information storage and retrieval system, without permission in writing from the publisher.

Front cover image: © hxdyl/Shutterstock

Printed in the United States of America

Toplight is an imprint of McFarland & Company, Inc., Publishers

Box 611, Jefferson, North Carolina 28640
www.toplightbooks.com

When I close my eyes I feel them near:
in my heart's holy silence I see my children.
—Friedrich Rückert, 1834

Translator's dedication:
for Jessica

Contents

Foreword by Cornelia Kallisch	1
Overture	3
Songs on the Death of Children	23
Supplemental Poems	138
Coda	145
Abbreviations	149
Translator Notes	150
Acknowledgments	168
Notes	171
Bibliography	189
Index of First Lines in English and German (from *Songs on the Death of Children*)	209
Index of First Lines and Authors (Not Part of *Songs on the Death of Children*)	212
Index of Bible Verses	213
Index	214

Foreword
by Cornelia Kallisch

Gustav Mahler's music, especially his setting of Friedrich Rückert's *Songs on the Death of Children* (*Kindertotenlieder*), had a profound effect on my life as a vocalist and ultimately influenced my initial decision to become a singer. My early musical education ended with Beethoven, with brief excursions into Robert Schumann's *Scenes from Childhood* (*Kinderszenen*). It wasn't until shortly before graduating from high school that I was introduced to the third song of Mahler's *Kindertotenlieder*, "When your mother." A substitute teacher had brought in this "unheard-of" music.

The sounds were thrilling and absolutely new. They pierced my heart. In a way, the song struck me as an answer to questions that I had not known I was asking. The allure was almost magical.

Another decisive experience with Mahler's music was a dress rehearsal of the "Resurrection" symphony, his second, with Claudio Abbado in Munich. A student at the time, this was my first exposure to the power and diversity of a symphony orchestra, with its wide range of voices and colors. It dawned on me that I could understand music, its "language," free of translation, simply as it is.

Suddenly I had a growing desire to make the music my own, "to put the words in my mouth," as the saying goes. I wanted to feel it from within, entrust my breath and body to it, adapt to it, live in it.

And so my troubles began. My voice was not yet developed to meet the demands of such music. I needed experience and training in operatic and orchestral settings.

Mahler's corpus was my guide: his symphonies, vocal settings, his singers, his world of ideas. *Kindertotenlieder* in particular became my constant companion and the measure of my progress as a vocalist. Still—and I'm not fishing for compliments here—I've never quite sung them the way I hoped they would sound.

I was always faced with the challenge of balancing my sense of compassion with the objective task of expressing despair in a manner that was not awkward or overly emotional, overly sentimental, overly dramatic.

Not getting in the way is one of the keys in interpreting *Kindertotenlieder*.

There is beauty in these songs, and simplicity, but it must be worked through. This requires us to experience the entire mourning process, overcoming all delusions and self-recriminations, before we arrive at the incomprehensible conclusion of the last song in *Kindertotenlieder*. It is one of the most calming endings I have ever heard: "they rest as in their mother's house."

The fourth song tells us that "we will catch them up on the hills." No longer. Here in the fifth and final song the strain of effort ebbs, the tempo slows, a D major asserts itself, and Mahler instructs us that the music should be performed "slowly, like a lullaby" and "quietly to the end." Something remarkable happens. You stand having sung the words, the orchestra spreads like a blanket and peace returns. All has been said. The children are safe in their mother's house. All is well.

The children. These songs are not about the pain in Franz Schubert's *Winter Journey* (*Winterreise*), nor the loss that Orpheus laments; no, they are about children who have gone before us.

Rückert's only means of coping with his loss was through poetry, poem after poem, song after song. This must have resonated with Mahler. Through his settings they have achieved one of the inexplicable wonders of music—a form of immortality.

Beauty plays a special role in *Kindertotenlieder*. An ineffable role, actually. How can we sing of such overwhelming pain? Remaining silent seems more reasonable: endlessly grieving, weeping, keening. No. This is art, creation, transformation. And that is the most demanding challenge for anyone who dares the high-wire act of *Kindertotenlieder*. In the end it must remain a creative expression—through which the greatest suffering, the most intense pain, is given its own voice and its own beauty.

There may be some solace in that.

Cornelia Kallisch is a three-time Grammy-nominated mezzo soprano and world-renowned interpreter of Gustav Mahler's musical setting of Songs on the Death of Children (Kindertotenlieder).

Overture

Luise Rückert eased into her familiar pew in a parish church outside of Coburg. The winter had been relatively mild but this spring was unseasonably cold, wet and windy. The meadows along the Itz River had not yet started to bloom. It was Easter Monday, 31 March 1834.

This was the first time Luise had attended church in three months—since her youngest children, Ernst and young Luise, had died of scarlet fever, the pandemic of their age. "As we sang the hymn," the grieving mother wrote, "the full weight of everything that had happened this last quarter-year settled on my heart; I feared my violent weeping might force me out of the chapel."[1]

Only thirty-six years old, Luise had already lost three children. Her son, Karl Julius, had been born on 6 January 1832 and died three days later. Luise's daughter and namesake, three-year-old Emilie Therese *Luise*, took ill on Christmas Day, 1833. The doctor arrived on Boxing Day, which was also the parents' twelfth wedding anniversary.

Luise and her husband, scholar and poet Friedrich Rückert, had been wed on 26 December 1821. They had five surviving sons: Heinrich, Karl, August, Leo and *Ernst* Wilhelm Moriz. Young Luise was their only daughter and an adored little sister to her brothers: "our throng of boys,"[2] as Friedrich called them in one of the most poignant poems in his collection of laments, *Songs on the Death of Children* (*Kindertodtenlieder*).[3]

Three-year-old Luise lasted barely six days, dying at two-thirty in the morning on 31 December 1833. Her closest brother, four-year-old Ernst, could not attend her funeral, held four days later. He too was ill. The boy turned five on 4 January and died on 16 January 1834.

At first, the grieving parents had resisted the consolations of clergy and pious friends. Their words seemed callous and unhelpful; their promises and glib platitudes rang false. Luise's husband dealt with the Easter holiday in his own way, writing that spring:

Christmas—fresh and healthy,
surrounded by siblings;
New Year—mouth pale,
Epiphany—in the dirt.
So we marked the feast days:
bound to death and the grave.
This wound lasted through *Easter*
and will not heal by Pentecost.

Luise decided to attend the Easter Monday service alone. "While I was wracked with tears," she wrote, "I prayed that God might bless the pastor with a word of comfort for me."[4] The clergyman read verse 25 from chapter 19 of the Book of Job. It is one of the most famous in the Bible, often offering solace to the bereaved: "I know that my redeemer liveth, and that he shall stand at the latter day upon the earth."[5] Luise was stunned. "The message, a proper resurrection sermon," she wrote, "was an answer to my prayer."[6]

But she did not hear the famous phrase from the King James Version that we know today. She heard something quite different. This change meant far more to the grieving mother. The Holy Bible commonly used across Germany in 1834, known as the Luther Bible, contained a uniquely consoling variation of Job 19:25. This comes as no surprise. The verse has puzzled rabbinical scholars for centuries.

Harry Orlinsky, editor-in-chief of the New Jewish Publication Society translation of the Torah, called the passage "impossible of textual solution." Other linguists cite "corruption," "ambiguities," and "emendations," complaining of the "uncertainties and difficulties of this verse being so great" that the "line is altogether obscure and uncertain!"[7]

No wonder, then, that the Luther Bible read by Luise was so different. Yet it was this precise variation that spoke to her wounded heart, as it had to German mourners since early modern times.[8] "The passage has often consoled me since," Luise wrote, quoting the 1834 edition: "'I know that my redeemer lives and he will *raise me up from the earth.*'"[9]

***

My daughter, Jessica, died on 16 January 2015 of a fentanyl-laced heroin overdose. She was twenty-six. I am not surprised that a message of reunion and resurrection resonated with Luise in her sorrow on that long-ago Easter Monday, nor am I shocked that Friedrich's poems are steeped in love, pain, guilt, memory, tears, unexpected joys and prayer.

We who mourn seek no false hope, no easy assurances. When we pray for a word of comfort, we ask only to know that our loved ones are safe, that death is not the end, that we will be with them again. Luise found that solace nearly 200 years ago in a small church along the Itz River. She and Friedrich rest in the cemetery there.

> Joy is a partnership,
> Grief weeps alone;
> Many guests had Cana,
> Gethsemane had one.
> —Frederic Lawrence Knowles,
> "Grief and Joy"[10]

Friedrich Rückert

Friedrich Rückert was a modest man. Visitors often commented on his self-effacing nature, enthusiasm, guilelessness, whimsy and gentle humor.[11] Many of his *lieder*, or songs, were set to music by the great composers of the day. But for three decades Friedrich hid from view his most personal work.

Rückert was born on 16 May 1788 in Schweinfurt, Franconia, Germany. At the age of seventeen, in 1805, he enrolled in college to study law and philology in Würzburg, then later in Jena. By 1811, he was lecturing on Greek and oriental mythology. These classes may have contributed to his fascination with creating a modern German identity based on medieval perceptions of valor. This in turn led to his working with the Swabian minister Karl August Freiherr von Wangenheim to draw up a controversial constitution for the newly founded Kingdom of Württemberg.

In 1817–18, Friedrich toured Italy. There he discovered his passion for poetry and the cultures of the world. By the early 1820s, he was immersed in the study of languages—Persian, Arabic, Sanskrit, Hebrew and Chinese. He married Anna *Luise* Magdalene Witthaus-Fischer in 1821. They had three boys in quick succession: Heinrich (1823); Karl (1824); and August (1825).

Rückert's appointment as chair of Oriental languages at the University of Erlangen came none too soon. They moved to Erlangen in 1826. The city was an intellectual hub, producing some of the world's finest Christian scholarship of the 19th century, along with Göttingen, Tübingen and Marburg.[12] The family had barely settled into their small house when more children arrived: Leo (1827); Ernst (1829); and young Luise (1830).

Then scarlet fever struck. By the winter of 1833/1834, the disease was rampant in Erlangen. Scarlet fever epidemics plagued Germany throughout the 19th century. The spread was particularly lethal in Göttingen, Jena, Wittenberg and Leipzig.[13] Doctors did not know what caused the disease, but they saw its devastating effects. They referred to it as "pestilential," "insidious and deceptive."[14] At a time when about half of all deaths were children below the age of six,[15] the pandemic made matters worse. Scarlet fever's mortality rate ranged from 16.7 percent to 33.3 percent, with the most deaths occurring among those three to five years old, precisely the ages of Luise and Ernst.[16]

The first of the Rückert children to contract the disease was nine-year-old August, on 18 December 1833. A week later, Luise, just three and one-half years old, fell ill. It was Christmas Day. She was followed by six-year-old Leo, who showed signs of scarlet fever on 30 December, the day before Luise died. On New Year's Day, the fever struck four-year-old Ernst. He died fifteen days later.

Karl, seven years old, was also suffering from the illness. It is unclear when his symptoms first showed, but by his brother Ernst's fifth birthday, 4 January 1834, Karl was able to get up from bed. August suffered badly but recovered. Leo and Karl's symptoms were slightly milder.[17] The eldest, Heinrich, was staying with his maternal grandparents in Neuses, some 46 miles (75km) away. He was unaffected by the disease that killed Luise and Ernst.[18] "This has been a cruel, terrible winter...," Friedrich wrote in April of that year. "My two dearest children died suddenly and the others, my wife included, were in mortal danger for some time."[19]

Over the first six months of 1834, Rückert composed some 500 poems on loss and mourning. He turned forty-six that May. His grief over Ernst and Luise would remain unassuaged for the rest of his life. "That I should drink and eat, eat and drink," Friedrich wrote, "forgetting all the while that you are lost to me.... Spare me these delights! They cannot fool my heart, adding grief to

A friend of the Rückert family, Carl Barth, painted these portraits of Luise (age three) and Ernst (age four) in the fall of 1833. Friedrich kept them with him until the day he died. They still hang in Coburg-Neuses. Courtesy Christel and Klaus Rückert, Rückert-Gedenkstätte Neuses.

grief." He averaged two to three poems each day. These pieces make up what was published posthumously as *Songs on the Death of Children*. It has never been out of print in Germany.

"Things have been terrible here," Friedrich wrote a friend. "I lost my two youngest, dearest, most precious children to scarlet fever, with nothing left to console me other than two rather unsuccessful portraits by Barth, whom you know, and unspeakable stacks of laments."[20] In the autumn of 1833 Friedrich had asked his friend, Carl Barth, to paint pastels of Luise and Ernst. Unsuccessful or not, he kept them with him until the day he died. The portraits still hang in the Rückert house in Coburg-Neuses.[21]

Rückert did not date his *unspeakable stacks of laments*. He scribbled them during his walks, sitting in his office: wherever he happened to be on whatever scraps were at hand. In June of 1834, he handed the jumble of notes to his wife, Luise. Some are his finest, others less so; none was intended for publication. He and Luise agreed on that. "I could not win him over to making it accessible to a wider audience through publication," wrote their eldest son Heinrich, "as often and as urgently as the desire was expressed."[22]

Friedrich probably wrote a few more in 1835[23] and occasionally revisited the laments over the years, but on his death in 1866, Heinrich inherited the haphazard collection with no hint of their intended order. He then organized them under loose thematic headings, beginning with a poem titled "Preface" as an explanation of why consolation poetry has value to the bereaved. This was surely based on personal experience: Heinrich had lost his younger siblings, a grief of great intensity, as well as witnessing his parents deal with the deaths.

Rückert's path of personal cultivation and enlightenment[24] provided him with a rich store of knowledge to call upon in his grief. For years his lyric poetry and translations gave him a huge following among educated middle-class Germans. Such praise was not limited to Europe. Rückert was also popular in America, where his songs were quickly rendered in English and widely distributed. This lasted throughout his lifetime and well after his death.[25]

Friedrich produced the first poetic translation of the Qur'an,[26] large quantities of Sanskrit, Farsi, Arabic and Chinese verse, as well as passages from the Bible.[27] His familiarity with Hebrew and Greek complemented his knowledge of the Luther Bible that his family kept in their home. In this lament, Friedrich references Paul's letter to the Galatians, "nor is there male and female, for you are all one in Christ Jesus."[28]

Reunion

Your children are lost now
but you will see them again;
they were born to you, they
cannot be lost.

No doubt you sense that
you will see them in time;
though you can't quite
grasp how that will be.

Not as children: would you
keep them tiny for eternity?
Not changed: would you see
yourselves so estranged?

Distinctions that seem at odds
here are meaningless there:
"nor is there male and female,"
nor is there old and young.

***

Biblical scholar Paul de Legarde wrote of his mentor Rückert, "it is incomprehensible that he thought of himself as German at all since it is difficult to imagine a more consistent cosmopolitan."[29] Friedrich's multilingualism not only benefited his cognitive abilities, but it also expanded his perception of the world around him.[30] For example, traditional ties with the sacred dead from Eastern beliefs

Friedrich Rückert in the fall of 1833, a few months before the deaths of Luise and Ernst. Published in the *German Muses Almanac of 1834* (December 1833).

informed his growing sense of a continuing bond with Ernst and Luise.[31]

When the family moved to Neuses in 1836, their social life returned to the usual bustle that Friedrich's wife enjoyed. Luise was fond of entertaining. "Our home enjoyed a colorful, extremely stimulating social life at the time," Heinrich recalled years later. "When you consider that Stockmar and Wangenheim were the kinds of guests we had every day, you get a sense of the comings and goings back then."[32] Heinrich was speaking of Christian von Stockmar, personal physician and advisor to Leopold I of Belgium, Queen Victoria and Prince Consort Albert, and Baron Karl August von Wangenheim, former Minister of Culture of the Kingdom of Württemberg. The family's list of houseguests reads like a who's who of the day.

Rückert remained active as a poet and scholar throughout his life. In the first five years after his children's deaths, he published three important works: *The Metamorphoses of Abou-Seyd of Serudj* (2 vols., 1837); *Rosem and Suhrab* (1838); and *Wisdom of the Brahmin* (6 vols., 1836–39).[33] Over time his translations and last poems grew increasingly spiritual.[34] These works reflect significant changes to the grieving father's perceptions. "This mystical experience in our deepest souls," as poet Ludwig Uhland described the Romantic impulse. "This incarnation of the divine, in a word: this foreshadowing of the infinite."[35]

Friedrich sensed that the vastness of the spiritual world may have been beyond his grasp. Instead, it was the endless variety of small experiences, individual and personal, that fascinated him.[36] Lyricist and critic Gustav Pfizer praised his insightful spirit, strength and freedom of thought. "Rückert is a philosopher," Pfizer wrote in 1837, "giving us snippets of the doubts and problems on his mind."[37] Professor of German and linguistics Henry Nordmeyer of the University of Michigan saw in Friedrich's poetry a synthesis of his inner and outer words: "Rückert was a man of lived experience, having seen the hardships, shame and tribulations of his times, yet this same experience gave him a deep desire to help others; he tried to unify both inner impulses in verse."[38]

Friedrich recognized that though he could be ill-tempered, prosaic delights took the sting out of each day in those first few months without Luise and Ernst:

Holly-tree

So I am myself, and so my poem,
like the holly, is prickly and rough below
where the cattle graze and gnaw;
from above the leaves have no sting,
swaying in heaven's breeze, in spring light,
or to birdsong.

Rückert's awareness of eternity contributed to one of his most important works, the sprawling, exquisite *Wisdom of the Brahmin*. One well-known passage warrants attention:

Occasional poetry deserves no comment
when it speaks to meaning and moment.

Sufficient to the day, worthy of praise,
present poems do not eternally raise.

Only when eternity imbues each word
is it enough today, and tomorrow heard.[39]

In his series of lectures at Cambridge, the philologist and Orientalist Friedrich Max Müller made special mention of this work: "One of the most beautiful poems in the German language is the *Weisheit des Brahmanen*, the 'Wisdom of the Brahmans,' by Rückert, to my mind more rich in thought and more perfect in form than even Goethe's *West–östlicher Divan*."[40] Others also admired Friedrich's work.

Rabbinical scholar and founding president of the World Union for Progressive Judaism Claude Goldsmid Montefiore compared Rückert's final stanza in the passage above to Hebrew psalms. "Particular events were regarded in a universal light, and thus a poem for the occasion was capable of becoming a poem for eternity," he noted. "The Psalmists, true poets as so many of them were, followed unconsciously the maxim of Rückert."[41]

After his children died, Friedrich found this kind of praise a bit much. "Had I not made the verse which is nothing to you," Rückert once quipped, "I should not have also conceived those that you hold dear."[42] The poet was aware of his failings and limitations, though at times he did not seem to recognize his own unique gifts. He often felt that his poetry suffered from a lack of what he called "grand personal adventures."[43] Friedrich also feared that the joy he found in creation—original work and translation—could at times stilt his focus in one direction or the other:

My spirit and feelings are equal to 100 separate songs
that I scatter like scent on a breeze, or pearls in the grass.
Were I capable of unifying them, I would be a whole poet, rather than a fragmented one.[44]

Rückert's detractors say that he could be too clever for his own good, that he hid his feelings behind wit and complicated forms of expression. Poet, critic and pastor Gotthold August Neeff disagreed. Neeff asserted that it was the sheer volume of Friedrich's work that gave critics their meager samplings of failures: "They gleefully point to the fact that Rückert has a few thousand impure rhymes in his 200,000 verses, but it is precisely by this remark that they demonstrate how little they understand this articulate artist's mastery of his forms."[45]

Biographer Annemarie Schimmel insisted that even Friedrich underestimated himself. It was not his considerable abilities, she wrote, but his vast output that led 20th- and 21st-century critics to skim his work, if they read it at all, and dismiss it too quickly. "His dual talent as a poet and as a linguist," Schimmel maintained, "has failed to give him the fame he deserves in either of these two fields."[46]

It may be that lasting fame did not interest Friedrich. In grief and loss, his natural modesty was matched by self-confidence and a practical awareness of his strengths and weaknesses. Friends commented on his humility, tenderness, simplicity, gentle wit and total lack of guile.[47] Self-effacing humor came naturally to Friedrich as early as 1826, when he wrote these words in introduction to his translation of al-Hariri of Basra:

Philologist and poet, neither entirely,
for lack of better, a translator I must be....
"Philologically unsound?" Poetic liberty.
"Poor poetry?" Blame it on philology![48]

Rückert's joke is not unlike the old chestnut among computer professionals: system analysts blame the software; programmers blame the hardware; both affix blame that seldom fixes the problem. Friedrich is making light of a similar frustration in Germany, where the science of philology and disciplines of literature had long been separated institutionally. Philology as a school of thought, founded around 1800, was placed under the imperatives of science, rather than the rationale of literature. Rückert saw as a little silly such divisions between the study of language and its practical uses. The tension remains to this day. "The proximity of poetry and philology thus reveals a paradoxical compulsion," observed Christoph König with Osnabrück University, "that simultaneously enables understanding and engenders alienation."[49] Friedrich was artist and scientist, poet and philologist. Whimsical ditties aside, he was to learn that very little in life is entirely one thing or another.

Romantic Poet

Rückert's work prior to the deaths of Ernst and Luise is usually associated with the post–Romantic generation known as Biedermeier poets (c. 1815–50). The so-called Biedermeier period is usually placed at the first half of the 19th century, after the Congress of Vienna (1814–5). Romantics, on the other hand, were born during what is thought of as the Age of Goethe (c. 1770–c. 1830).

There was no Romantic School, per se, merely brilliant, like-minded and highly creative individuals who indelibly influenced German 19th-century culture.[50] They were a cantankerous lot. Most did not consider themselves part of the fraternity and sought to distance themselves from such epithets. Indeed, to be called a *Romantiker,* or romantic writer, was an insult, not a compliment. The word *Romantische* was usually spoken with a sneer by those we now describe as, well, Romantics.[51]

Romantics see reconciliation between self, nature and the invisible world as possible and desirable while Biedermeier poets tend to dourly insist there can be no such union. This is one reason that it is difficult to label Rückert's approach. Before the deaths of Ernst and Luise, his awareness of life's transience seems both hopeful and pessimistic. For example, in one of his most popular poems, Friedrich writes in the voice of al-Khidr, the eternally-youthful wanderer of Islamic tradition first alluded to in the Qur'an.[52]

In Rückert's song, Khidr visits the same location every five hundred years. At first, it is a city. *How long has this been here?* Khidr asks. "It's always been this way," a man tells him, "as it will forever and a day." Five centuries later, Khidr finds a vast grassy knoll in the same spot. A shepherd is tending his flock as he plays a fife. *How long has the city been gone?* Khidr asks. "Things come and go their way," the shepherd replies, "this has been my pasture forever and a day."

Another five hundred years, and on the same road is a sea. A fisherman gives Khidr an identical answer, as does a woodsman—yet another five centuries later—who insists that his ancestors had always lived in the forest that now thrives there. In the final stanza, the wandering Khidr returns:

> 500 years went by and then
> I passed that way again.
> I came upon a city: the hue, the cry,
> the bustle of people rushing by.
> I asked, *How long has this city been here?*
> *Where is the wood, the sea, the fife?*
> They yelled back at me in their strife:
> "It's always been this way,
> as it will forever and a day."
> I'll wait 500 years and then
> I will pass this way again.[53]

***

Rückert came of age during the social and political upheaval of the Restoration of 1815, which ultimately lead to a loose national confederation that lasted most of his adult life. He was certainly and stridently Biedermeier in his early poems, a proponent of the style that would dominate German poetry in the 1870s.[54] Had he remained so, his poems may have been lost to history.

English author and physician Thomas Lovell Beddoes observed that German poets of Rückert's day were victims of fickle celebrity, little more than disposable trash after their deaths, fodder for the next generation. "Alive they are golden heavenly fellows," Boddoes wrote a friend in 1825, "they die a weeping willow & an elegy stick over their graves ... a younger rival sets the roots of his fame in their literary remains, and flourishes as fast as these latter rot."[55]

Certainly many cultures can be guilty of exploiting talent, replacing early adoration with obscurity in death. For every Johann Wolfgang von Goethe or Rainer Maria Rilke there are hundreds of others deserving of cultural memory that have been forgotten by all but a handful of scholars or enthusiasts. Yet if their physical remains rot and decay, their "literary remains" continue on, informing new generations. Their genius and spirit passes into books, waiting to be rediscovered.[56] This is not always for the best.

Rückert's early work was steeped in the arrogance and absolutes of youth. His *Armored Sonnets*, written during the rise of the anti–Napoleonic Wars in late autumn of 1813, is justly admired for its eloquence and energy.[57] Friedrich composed it when he was twenty-five years old. This stirring exhortation to Prussians to join in the Wars of Liberation was also informed by the strident nationalistic fervor of a troubled age.

> What do you smith, smithee? "We smith shackles, shackles!"
> Ah, by the shackles you forge you are shackled.
> ....
> Poet, what do you write? "Words flush with the shame of my people and me, that we think so little of liberty."[58]

Germany as we know it today is relatively new: it was not formed until 1871. Prior to that, the area was made up of precariously allied states. When Rückert wrote his *Armored Sonnets*, the Bavarian state thought of itself as a kingdom. The populace was dominated by what historian Ute Planert called a sense of *federative nationalism* that displayed itself in a "Bavarian politics of memory."[59] Philosopher Johann Gottfried Herder suggested that *Volkskultur*—folk, popular and alternative culture—could organically link these states in a sense of shared, natural belonging and spiritual unity.[60] It was not an easy task.

These politics of memory and nationalism held a special appeal for the National Socialist German Workers' Party. By the 1930s, seventy years after Friedrich's death, the Nazis had co-opted Rückert's *Armored Sonnets* and other of the poet's immature works. German textbook editors of the day dubbed Rückert "one of the greatest lyric poets of all time," claiming his work reflected contemporary Zeitgeist, the defining spirit of the age.[61] The Nazi regime perceived in Friedrich's youthful verse the type of ethnocentric and militaristic undertones they could use. "Even more macabre," observed German philologist Rolf Selbmann, "is the way in which Rückert was cannibalized in the service of Nazi jargon."[62]

This appropriation had its roots in the First World War. The University of Erlangen, where Friedrich taught, was a significant leader of theological thought in the 19th and early 20th centuries. Following the so-called Luther Renaissance of 1917—which marked four centuries since the posting of the 95 Theses—Erlangen's academic community quickly devolved into a bastion of the Christian Far Right. Influential theologians and intellectuals, such as Karl Holl and Werner Elert, were driving forces behind the movement to remove the Old Testament from the Christian Bible. They argued that Jesus was an Aryan, not a Jew.[63] The ideas soon spread to such well-known thinkers as Erich Vogelsang, Reinhold Seeberg and even Adolf von Harnack, who wrote that retaining the Old Testament "as one of the canonical documents of Protestantism is the result of religious and ecclesiastical paralysis."[64]

When Adolf Hitler seized power, respected Erlangen theologian Paul Althaus wrote with ecstatic joy: "Our Protestant churches have greeted the turning point of 1933 as a gift and a miracle of God," adding, "We Christians know ourselves bound by God's will to the promotion of National Socialism."[65]

Little wonder, then, that in this milieu academics and party leaders co-opted the university's famed professor emeritus, Friedrich Rückert. Nazi ideology so infused Erlangen that by 1938 literary history professor Benno von Wiese was misrepresenting Rückert as the "conqueror of Aryan-Eastern culture."[66] However, even in the religious and militaristic fervor of the 1930s, some people of faith saw more in Friedrich's poems.

German theologian Martin Niemöller had also succumbed to the follies of youth. As a young man Niemöller, like Rückert, was prone to nationalistic views. This led Martin to support Hitler. Later, the Lutheran pastor saw his mistake. Soon his sermons contained criticism of the Nazi regime and what he considered to be its anti–Christian actions, particularly the attempt to exclude non–Aryan believers from churches.[67]

Niemöller's unpopular stance led to multiple arrests until he was finally sent to Sachsenhausen concentration camp in 1938 for "abuse of the pulpit." He admitted to his Jewish cellmate, Leo Stein, that at first he had "pinned his hopes" on Hitler. "I am paying for my mistake now," he said, "and not me alone, but thousands of other persons like me."[68]

Martin was transferred to Dachau in 1941, where he remained until the end of the war, barely escaping execution. While Nazi leaders were glibly quoting Rückert for their own ends, Niemöller reached deeper into the poet's mature work, frequently closing his sermons with the fifth verse from one of Friedrich's most beloved Advent hymns, "In lowly guise thy King appeareth"[69]:

> O Lord of grace and faith,
> return to us in our time of
> dire distress.
> We need you, you alone:
> come, renew your peace,
> peace the world despises.[70]

Others also saw Rückert's poems as more than grist for the Nazi propaganda mill. In the summer of 1940, historian and essayist Golo Mann was living in occupied France. He had volunteered with the Red Cross as an ambulance driver. After France fell, Golo was interned at Nîmes and may well have been extradited to Germany had not his famous father, Thomas, arranged for his release from the camp. Golo and his brother Heinrich promptly embarked on a night-time trek across the Pyrenees. They travelled through Franco's Spain to Portugal, where in October 1940 they boarded a Greek ship for New York.

Throughout his ordeal, Golo often recited Rückert's songs during the long sleepless nights, finding solace in poetry. Little wonder, then, that after visiting his parents, Mann soon settled in the attic of the Brooklyn Heights home of W.H. Auden.[71] In 1988, Mann related his experiences in a powerful speech, "About Rückert: one of the most endearing of German poets."[72]

In the 21st century, the University of Erlangen and Friedrich's hometown of Schweinfurt have publicly expressed regret for so grossly distorting the poet's work during a time of immense political pressure.[73]

Grief and poetic wanderings led Rückert out of the narrow confines of a Biedermeier poet's life.[74] Whatever the quirks of his younger days, Friedrich's poems in *Songs on the Death of Children* are most emphatically Romantic pieces. He came to see the separation of the material and spiritual as a false construct: the two are combined into wholly spiritual expressions of poetry.[75] Because of this, modern scholars insist that Rückert's image be reconsidered in the context of his life's work.[76] Thomas Immoos dubbed him "an uncrowned king, who through great effort and concentration subjugated new spiritual provinces each year."[77]

Texts from different cultures and eras affected Friedrich's view of the spiritual and physical realities of the world.[78] His goal in translation, he wrote, was "that humanity might grow in understanding through cultivation."[79] This could easily be said of his personal life as well.

***

Rückert's background and approach to living were a classic example of the German term *Bildung*, which combines formal education with a broader perspective that creates a cultured, well-rounded and refined individual. *Bildung* as yet has no serviceable translation, though many have tried, often at the sacrifice of one aspect of the term in emphasis of another. *Education, development, self-cultivation* and *self-formation* are popular solutions. One scholar prefers "ethical formation" as a working description of the term in German and how it is used in English.[80] Others use "aesthetic education" to indicate a harmonious development and integration of all one's powers.[81] The term for the subsequent literary genre, *bildungsroman*, has grown so vague as to be nearly useless as a descriptor.[82]

Meister Eckhart, a German Dominican mystic of the early 14th century, viewed *Bildung* as the process through which the soul comes closest to the divine.[83] "He who lives in the goodness of his nature lives in God's love," he wrote.[84] Eckhart and the Rhineland mystics, and later Pietists, used the term to describe divine influence in forming the individual; that is, God's formation of humans in his image.[85] The mundane details of daily life were, to Eckhart, the most accurate measure of spiritual and personal enlightenment. His circulation of these ideas to what Pope John XXII called "the uneducated crowd" ultimately brought negative attention from the church, which took exception to many of Eckhart's theological ruminations. But his ideas persisted.[86]

Bildung was seen as a point of contact between the sensory and invisible worlds, since its aim is to promote the spirit's unity with physical reality.[87] This created a mature person, at peace with himself and all that surrounds him.[88] However, the term can also refer to internal development that is seemingly governed by personal motivations. Karl Barth's critique of the idea was that it was perceived as self-involved. This misapprehension had led to an egocentric practice of gratification in theology and Christian culture. However, the *Bildung* tradition was more subtle, focusing on the best of self in connection with others.[89] Romantics insisted that a free expression of imagination fostered the power of "mutually forming into unity," as philosopher Friedrich Schelling put it.[90] In this light, the *Bildung* ideal is an identity based not on a particular religion, nation or culture, but rather on a sense of shared humanity.[91]

Different writers approached the concept with their own ends in mind. Some envisioned *Bildung* as a successor to Christian theology; others saw it as furthering the idea of God's formation of man by tending to oneself with the goal of serving others and thereby serving the divine.[92] Henry David Thoreau perfectly captured the essence of this view of *Bildung*. He was involved in the same determined search for *who* and *where* we are in relation to others and the vast cosmos.[93] "The poet says the proper study of mankind is man," Thoreau wrote in 1852. "I say, study to forget all that; take wider views of the universe."[94] Rückert commented on this apparent contradiction in his own short poem, titled "Bildung":

> "Enlighten the world," easy to say,
> and to achieve, when we get away
> from struggling with "the world"
> and back to enlightening ourselves.[95]

The concept of self-realization was an essential part of late 18th- and

19th-century German thought. It called for a path free from the interference of others, particularly rote learning, in an effort to educate oneself. The idea does not dismiss formal education *per se*. However, it insists that those lessons learned must be taken further. In this it is not unlike modern jazz. Musicians first achieve technical expertise before embarking on an arduous and lifelong path of deconstruction, reconstruction, variation, extrapolation and discovery—precisely the type of poetic exploration Rückert demonstrates in *Songs on the Death of Children*.

"The House Is Empty"

American poet, translator and diplomat Bayard Taylor was a friend of the Rückert family and frequently corresponded with their youngest daughter, Marie. After her mother died in 1857, Marie wrote to Taylor of her father's grief and loneliness, enclosing a number of the poems that would later be included in *Songs on the Death of Children*.

"These poems are exceedingly sweet and touching," Taylor wrote in *The Atlantic Monthly*, "yet they are all marked by the same flexile use of difficult rhythms and unprecedented rhymes."[96] Even in deepest anguish, Rückert's songs are raw, honest, witty and frequently brilliant. His deep set, bluish-gray eyes, Taylor observed, burned with "a deep, lustrous fire" and a "mystic, rapt expression."[97] Yet there was something peaceful and serene about him. The spirituality of Friedrich's later years was not affectation; perhaps he simply saw the world that way.

Marie was born in 1835, a year after the deaths of Ernst and Luise. As an adult, she noticed that in the latter part of his life her father had a surprising connection with nature. He was not himself on overcast days but generally cheerful when the sun was out. "As if all nature would come into harmony with him," Marie wrote.[98] Many of the songs in this collection reflect that harmony, such as this piece written shortly after Luise and Ernst died:

> The house is empty,
> its air heavy in rooms
> of sickness and death.
> Who is cursed among men?
> A father, hapless, when
> his children cry for help.
>
> Out, out, away
> from this horror,
> out into the storm and snow!
> Nature is endless, its face
> is bitter, yet somehow
> I feel free.
>
> Does it help, the uprooting
> of oak and spruce
> to the east and west?
> Does outer devastation
> ease the misery within?
> Never, oh never never!
>
> But still it rages,
> God be praised,
> spring must have showers.
> It leaves winter behind,
> as sunshine follows tears,
> if we survive them.

The sun was also shining on the day that Friedrich and Marie discussed Friedrich Schiller's famous ballad, "Lament for a Sioux Chief." The elegy had so moved Rückert that he committed it to memory.

Schiller wrote the piece in 1797

when he and Goethe were enjoying a "ballad year" of exchanged views and works that were more collaboration than competition.[99] The two friends had been impressed by Jonathan Carver's 1778 book, *Travels Through the Interior Parts of North America*,[100] which had freely adapted a Sioux funeral ritual from an account in Louis Armand, Baron de Lahontan's *New Voyages to North-America*.[101] Schiller's famous lament was the result.

Rückert and his daughter were discussing the piece and its history on the afternoon of 31 January 1866. Friedrich paused over a line that held great meaning to him:

> It is well, he is gone
> to where there is no snow.[102]

While Rückert was reciting the poem, the sun had crept across the room. Marie went to draw the curtain but he stopped her. "Let him shine full upon me," the seventy-seven-year-old man said, "perhaps he may yet make me well."[103] These were the last words he spoke. Friedrich died later that day.

Songs on the Death of Children

Six years after Rückert's death, in 1872, his son Heinrich compiled 418 of Friedrich's laments in the book *Songs on the Death of Children*. It was something of a bestseller. Heinrich organized the poems thematically, which can seem a tad arbitrary when the songs are read from start to finish. However, his approach is useful for the occasional reader who, when opening to a page, will find similarly themed pieces placed together.

Marie Rückert thought the songs should be organized differently. In 1881, after her brother Heinrich died, she published a smaller collection taken from *Songs on the Death of Children*, titled *Sorrow and Song*.[104] Her selections were just over half in number, re-arranged according to clues from her father's diaries. Marie excised those songs that she felt were too painful or personal—precisely the poems that speak most powerfully to 21st-century readers. Although I stand with the many Rückert scholars that prefer Heinrich's anthology, I am careful to note that Marie's love for her father informed her editorial choices.

Michael Neumann, professor emeritus of German literature at Catholic University of Eichstaett–Ingolstadt, observed that Rückert uses a plethora of lyrical genres in *Songs on the Death of Children*, varying and adapting them, and even developing completely new poetic structures.[105] "Whichever form he uses, he is consistent in its use, leaving no doubt that each is a new, separate form,"[106] Neumann wrote. "If one looks at the meters and stanzas used, it turns out to be an enormous treasure trove of the most diverse lyrical forms."[107]

Renowned German scholar Annemarie Schimmel found something more within these poems. "This is no wild outburst of desperation," she wrote. "It is a sigh, a question about the meaning of life."[108] To illustrate her point, Schimmel cited this piece from *Songs on the Death of Children*:

> The death and life of a person
> is a mystery;

what whims the fates weave
are a mystery.

That you were given to me
is a wonder;
that I must give you back
is a mystery.

That you are with me in death
is a marvel;
and at your death my life
is a mystery.

Throughout these songs, Rückert embraces the mystery of sorrow and death through storytelling, remembering and honest lament—a process that counselors have identified as helpful in healthy mourning.[109] In contrast, other specialists urge acceptance of loss and its inevitable mourning with "a less Romantic view of grief."[110] However, Rückert was a Romantic era poet, a translator and clear-headed author. His view as reflected in these songs is more in keeping with philosopher Thomas Attig, who observed that grieving is a "mystery that pervades our human condition."[111]

Some 500 of Rückert's poems have been set to music in more than 2,000 compositions. The popular poem "From Days of Youth" has at least 60 separate musical settings from as many composers. "I Love You" was equally inspiring to musicians: yet another 60 settings were created for that poem as well.[112] Yet Friedrich was all but forgotten after World War II, aside from liner notes for audio recordings of his *lieder* as composed by Schubert, Brahms, Mahler, Strauss, Robert and Clara Schumann, Bartók and many others. Literary scholar Mark Sandy commented on the appeal: "Romantic poetry about grief acts as a defense against, and encounter with, the final silence of death that challenges poetry's eloquent capacity for meaning."[113]

Johannes Brahms admired Rückert's gift for evocative words and moving, memorable imagery. He described Friedrich as a "great stylistic virtuoso."[114] Brahms set Friedrich's poems to solo and mixed choral works as well as canons for female voices. Rückert's collected works had pride of place on the composer's shelf, particularly the third volume, which was heavily marked in pencil. He kept other volumes, as well: *Wisdom of the Brahmin* and *Hariri's Maqam* among them. When Brahms died, his poetry notebook had eight more Rückert pieces that he intended to set to music. One of these untouched songs has a humorous tone that seems tailor-made for the composer's inventive touch:

Good Times, Bad Times

Things were different then,
I wish she would come again;
I had no heartbreak, true,
not many songs, too.
All I needed were her kisses,
and if my songs were misses,
now that my bliss has gone
at least I can sing about it.[115]

Brahms and Friedrich's daughter, Marie, had a curious friendship. When they first met on 12 April 1861, Marie wrote to her father that "he is eminently gifted and even just his playing is compelling, everything about him exudes such vast power." But on a personal level, she continued, the young artist "displeases me greatly and I cannot hide it." The feeling was mutual. Brahms confided to Clara Schumann that he thought Marie was something of a nag.[116]

They renewed contact in 1875 and again in the summer of 1880 and 1887, when Marie hoped to convince the composer to set selections from *Songs on the Death of Children* to music. This led to a tentative agreement that Brahms might create a piece for the unveiling of a Rückert monument in Schweinfurt in 1890. However, the composer's letter reached the mayor too late: they had already commissioned Carl von der Tann.[117] This did not dampen Brahms and Marie's correspondence. One picturesque postcard to Marie, for example, has a bit of descriptive whimsy scrawled in Brahms's own hand: "Grain market!"[118]

When they met in Vienna in 1891, Brahms gave Marie his personal copies of opus 91 and 94 to demonstrate that he had already set many of her father's pieces to music.[119] Five years earlier, in 1886, Marie Rückert had given Brahms a copy of *Sorrow and Songs*, her collection of Friedrich's laments for Luise and Ernst. Brahms kept Marie's book in his personal library till he died.[120]

Brahms's affinity with Friedrich ran deeper than poetry, extending even to instrumental pieces. The composer repeatedly referred to the three Intermezzi of his lonely, impressionistic Op. 117, written in 1892, as "Lullabies of My Sorrows."[121] He was quoting directly from a Rückert poem:

> Lullabies of my sorrows.
> All torments wake anew,
> tear my heart asunder.
> You sang yesterday, Song,
> what of today? This day,
> pierced with pain anew,
> I beg new consolations.[122]

The *lied* as an art song is a compound genre in which poetry and music interact: a preexisting text is often the stimulus from which a composer derives inspiration and ideas for a musical setting. The difference is telling: a *lied* is as much literary work as musical structure. This may explain why so many geniuses set Rückert's poems to music.

In the 21st century scholars are returning to Friedrich's *Songs on the Death of Children* with fresh eyes, admiring his smoothness of meter and rhyme.[123] Mathias Wirth, University of Bern, described the collection as "consolation for the inconsolable,"[124] while scholars A. Aurnhammer and T. Fitzon agreed with Hans Wollschläger that it is "the finest lament in world literature."[125]

This Book

Rückert's life resonates with me. He was a translator, author, poet and professor. We both taught college for years; both published on Asia extensively; both translated from Asian and European languages. Austrian poet and author Barbara Frischmuth considered Friedrich to be one of the greatest translators that ever lived, writing that one must be "as madly devoted as Rückert" to give an entire life to the study of Asian languages and literature.[126] Nobel laureate Octavio Paz called such extravagance "a moral urge" to translate, adding, "You must *love* the text."[127] I may not possess Friedrich's devotion, but I know the impulse to translate poems that I have come to love as companions in my sorrow.

Friedrich and I are bereaved fathers. We both lost children on the same day and month: his son died on 16 January 1834; my daughter died on 16 January 2015. Jessica's death led me to *Songs on the Death of Children* and the meditations that Rückert's poetry inspires.

I began translating this book the summer after my daughter died. The task was one of communion and solace. Like Friedrich, I never intended to publish—did not, in fact, think of it one way or the other. Three years later, ten of Rückert's laments seemed ideal for inclusion in my first book on grief, *Wounded in Spirit*. I persisted in translating these songs more from a sense of shared sorrow than with any definable goal. What I have found astonished me.

Friedrich's laments broke new ground in surprising ways. They seem at times raw and desperate as the poet invites us into his journey of sorrow. Each speaks to us of honest pain, anguish and hope. It is a classic on grief that approaches grief from the inside. With prescient insight, Rückert casts light on aspects of mourning that are recognized as important and relevant to modern death studies.

Structure

From the complete *Songs on the Death of Children*, I have chosen what seem to me to be the most meaningful poems. My primary goal has been to arrange the pieces in a way that is useful to mourners. I followed this general pattern when selecting and organizing the songs: those that are particularly fine and speak with compassion and shared sorrow; insights that are relevant to modern death studies; verse recognized as important by Rückert scholars; and pieces that resonate with me personally. Fortunately, the four criteria have considerable overlap, as the first selections in this book demonstrate.

I start this collection with eleven poems to introduce us to Rückert's laments: pieces that are famous and well-loved in Germany ("In the sacred silence of the wood I see my children," "The maid brings news of their," "Now the sun will rise as bright," "You are a shadow in the day"); admired for their eloquence ("Encircled by mountain," "Over all graves grass must grow," "All our laments do not"); and speak to timeless aspects of grief ("If our dead are not with us," "As the poor hen," "He who finds rest as I do"). I end these prefatory songs with the piece Heinrich Rückert chose to begin his anthology, aptly titled "Preface." Combined, these eleven poems give us a peek into what is to come.

Friedrich's songs have a certain internal chronology, but this can be deceptive. For example, although a piece may seem to have been penned when Luise lay dying, or during her funeral, this could represent an artistic choice of remembered pain. The grieving father may have isolated those moments as settings for verse that he wrote days or months after the events. Even these tend to blur the lines between past, present and future—a perception that is a familiar aspect of grief and many of Rückert's songs throughout his lifetime.[128] "The Future comes unbidden, and hastens all too fast," he wrote in one of his early fragments. "For every Now when present at once becomes a Past." Friedrich observed that the limits of time and space "endeth there in God" and that any boundary of the infinite is mere display:

This show 'tween me and God fades in my Vision fair,
And Space and Time all vanished, my Here is ever There.[129]

Following the introductory selections, I have gathered a number of poems that have these chronological settings. We will read of the children's illness and their deaths; the parents' and siblings' reactions; that first New Year's Eve and the funerals.

Internal clues aside, a number of experts have despaired that there is nothing to indicate the exact dates that the poems were written. Respected Rückert scholar Hans Wollschläger threw up his hands at the hopelessness of a chronological ordering.[130] Psychologist Johannes Wilkes, president of the Erlangen Rückert Circle in Bavaria, writes that it is "simply impossible" to know the order they were composed, adding, "as much as we might want to track the flow of his grief through the songs."[131]

With this in mind, beginning with "When your heart dwells," my arrangement is thematic rather than chronological. I made what I believe is a helpful *pairing* of themes, taking the psalter as an example. One third of the psalms are songs of lament. However, each lament is usually followed by a hymn of praise or gratitude. The idea, well supported by modern grief research, seems to have been that in sorrow and mourning we are not all one thing or another. Our emotions are varied. By their placement, the psalms assure us that *all* of our feelings are expected and accepted.[132]

In a similar fashion, I did not group Friedrich's songs of, say, guilt or anger, into one miserable clump. Rather, when I found a piece on the natural remorse felt by the bereaved, I sought to follow it with a song of memory or hope of future reunion. For example, the aforementioned "When your heart dwells" and "It's too hard, what I've got" are steeped in a sense of regret that may resonate with many of us. These are immediately followed by "When I prayed over my child," a song of sorrow and praise. Likewise, the poignant "From our happy moments you are missing" is paired with a calm yet joyous poem, "Never did I see you wake."

When no clear chronological or topical theme presented itself, I relied on Heinrich Rückert's arrangement.

My final selections are listed under the heading "Supplemental Poems." These were not included in the first 1872 publication of *Songs on the Death of Children*. They are directly related to the deaths of Luise and Ernst and appeared in later editions or separate collections. I chose those pieces that deal with memorial days—that is, the annual observance of the date our loved one died—as well as the continuing grief present on other special occasions. The final poem, "Tender Burial," is known as one of Rückert's finest laments.

Commentary

Friedrich's grief-stricken poems speak eloquently. They require no explanation. At the same time, a word of context or background may be helpful. We might be curious about certain references or what aspect of sorrow led to a given song. On return visits with personal favorites, perhaps we will be interested in learning more about a poem that speaks to us in a new way.[133]

To assist in this, Rückert's poems serve as a framework to explore the spiritual and emotional impact of loss. Each lament is accompanied by a meditation on the nature of grief. Some have personal anecdotes from Friedrich, his wife, and my experience. Most touch on relevant grief research that offers practical insight for the bereaved. Other comments supply historical and cultural information or discussions of the poet's literary and biblical allusions.

In the commentary we come across familiar names: Vincent van Gogh, John Muir, Goethe, Emily Dickinson, John Updike, and many others. We meet bereaved parents, such as Abraham Lincoln, Robert Frost, William Shakespeare, Ralph Waldo Emerson, Isabel Allende, William James and Barbara Eden. Spiritual leaders who have also known suffering and loss speak to grief and the invisible world, including Viktor Frankl, Frederick Buechner, Thomas Merton, Philip Yancey, Mother Teresa, Abraham Heschel, Henri Nouwen, Thich Nhat Hanh, John O'Donohue, Richard Rohr, Martin Buber, Søren Kierkegaard, Meister Eckhart and Beopjeong. Thoughts from noted grief experts combine with insights from philosophers and authors to expand our understanding of the songs: Byron, Milton, Tennyson, Coleridge, Longfellow, Wordsworth, Donne, George Herbert, Elizabeth Barrett Browning, Sigmund Freud, Erich Maria Remarque, Herder, Schlegel, Schleiermacher, Schiller, Hegel and Thoreau, to name a few. There are also a few surprises, such as the tragic story of Rückert's grandson, Hans Berger, inventor of the electroencephalogram (EEG).

Each entry stands alone. Rather than inflict a chronology or a glossary on the reader, requiring tedious page-flipping, each meditation provides the information needed to appreciate that particular piece. This may lead to some repetition, particularly with dates and certain themes that Friedrich revisits, but the convenience seems worth any minor redundancy.

Rückert used no jargon and neither does this book. No expertise in grief research or the German language is required to appreciate the poems or the comments. However, for those readers who are also living with loss, please do not skip the bibliography and notes at the back of this book. In the meditations I often segue from observations about Rückert to material from experts and how this relates to many of us who mourn. When I write "we often feel this" or "it is natural for us to do that," I am writing as a fellow sufferer, one of millions who knows the pain of grief.

The 1872 German-language edition of *Kindertodtenlieder* is freely available on the Internet in text, e-book and PDF formats. My index of first lines lists each poem in English and German, along with the page number from the

1872 edition. Many of the songs are discussed in my translator notes, for those interested in the nuts and bolts of rendering German poetry into English. All translations in this book are my own unless otherwise indicated.

We need no overarching structure to understand Friedrich's powerful imagery or to recognize themes that resonate with our own lives. We are amply rewarded and perhaps even surprised with random reading. Overall, Friedrich's songs are an unfiltered expression of grief: they can at times be rough and a bit unfinished; at others, they represent some of the finest laments ever produced.

My main focus is Rückert's poetry and how his laments help us in our grief today. His love for his children, spiritual yearning, regret and grief inform each song. They are a gift to the suffering, redolent of the emotions many of us share. Most importantly, for me, these poems and meditations help assure us that we are not alone.

Together we trace the pain and hope of terrible loss. As Rabbi Earl Grollman, a pioneer in emotional reactions to death, wrote: "One touch of sorrow makes the world kin."[134] The kinship of grief transcends cultural and religious boundaries. Poems of lament are found in all of the world's literary traditions.[135] How we *express* sorrow may be dependent on our present culture. Such things change. But our *emotions* remain constant, speaking to us across the centuries.[136] These songs belong to all who mourn.

Songs on the Death of Children

> In the sacred silence of the wood I see my children,
> in the buds of each branch I see my children.
> Mother Nature cradles her children in spring winds:
> in the buds of each branch I see my children.
> In flowers that turn their eyes to the sun and,
> childlike, lean into the wind, I see my children.
> Where dust dances in the light, peeking through
> the green lattice of leaves, I see my children.
> Where doves nestle, where fish hatch, where
> butterflies emerge from flowers, I see my children.
> The young cypress and the pine, slender and strange:
> in each unfamiliar gesture I see my children.
> On the crystal lattice of the brook where I
> should see my reflection, I see my children.
> When I close my eyes I feel them near:
> in my heart's holy silence I see my children.

Rückert sees Luise and Ernst everywhere, but more than this, he feels them, senses their presence. He speaks of the sources of creation that help ease our emptiness in loss. This haunting poem claims home and garden as hallowed memory spaces.[1]

Friedrich's list begins with few surprises. Spring is full of new life: flowers, leaves, fish, butterflies and doves. Seeing his children in the birth of the season is powerful and affecting. Then his tone darkens. The trees and brook seem suddenly strange and unfamiliar. In an alien place where nature is more potent, he discovers the lasting comfort of sensing his children near him, seeing them in his *heart's holy silence*.

Rückert borrowed the Arabic poetry form known as ghazal for this song. The ghazal is especially common in Persian literature, usually expressing the pain of loss and the beauty of a continuing love within that pain.[2] To this Friedrich added the early German Romantic tradition that a poet could transform his perception of the world by looking *inward* while reaching *outward*.[3] "Every hidden cell is throbbing with music and life," wrote John Muir in a passage that could easily have come from Rückert, "every fibre thrilling like harp strings, while incense is ever flowing from the balsam bells and leaves. No wonder the hills and groves were God's first temples...."[4]

Honoring nature as a sacred cathedral was not new: "—these are the music and pictures of the most ancient religion," Ralph Waldo Emerson observed.[5] The affinity with life that gave Rückert such solace in the deep wood was part of his growing sense that something ineffable may be lost in the buildings of men. Nineteenth-century German poets acknowledged a profound debt to nature,[6] without which there could be no artistic creation at all.[7] "The world of poetry is boundless and endless," observed Friedrich Schlegel. "But how can it compare to the unstructured and unconscious poetry that stirs in a plant, that lights a child's smile, that shimmers in the bloom of youth?"[8]

Rückert's pacing is almost litany-like in its repetition of the many wonders that testify to the presence and memory of Ernst and Luise. In merging with nature, Friedrich embraces the invisible world.[9] His refrain reveals a father's soul.[10]

> **The maid brings news of their sister's death to our throng of boys; they cry out as one: "She is not dead, it is not true."**
>
> **They stare at her pale lips, her cheeks white, dark hair; and whisper among themselves: "She is not dead, it is not true."**
>
> **Father weeps, his heart a wound; their mother keens; still they resist the truth: "She is not dead, it is not true."**
>
> **They were there in the hour when she was laid to rest, lowered to the cold ground: "She is not dead, it is not true."**
>
> **She remains, she is here, more beautiful each year, more precious each hour:** *She is not dead, it is not true.*

"Our ancestors look gravely and steadily upon things that we cannot," wrote John Updike of 19th-century funeral customs.[11] In Rückert's day, bodies were not hastily removed by discreet morticians. Open coffins were the norm, usually resting at home until the burial service.

In this poem we share with Friedrich the painful necessity of acknowledging that Luise's corpse no longer holds life. This is the only lament in which he describes her body. The result is one of the most poignant pieces in *Songs on the Death of Children* or in any of his works.[12]

Consider Friedrich's simple, powerful repetition. The boys cry out, they whisper, they resist and ultimately face their sister's death, all the while repeating: *She is not dead, it is not true.* The final stanza's refrain of assurance is almost a sacrament. The religious parallel was no accident.

The song is a "kyrielle by Rückert," as one scholar put it, referring to a French verse form characterized by refrains in the fourth line of each quatrain.[13] Kyrielle is from the Old French *kiriele*, a derivative of the word *Kýrie*: part of many Christian liturgies, in which "Lord, have mercy" is repeated in the fourth line. After a loss, we often rely on certain words that offer solace in times of overwhelming sorrow. These take on meaning through repetition and may include a line from a hymn, a passage of scripture or poetry, a fondly remembered phrase spoken by our dead loved one, or private supplications.[14] They form our liturgies of grief.

David McNeish, a minister with the Church of Scotland, found that this type of personal liturgy could be productive and helpful. He suggested that a constraining one-size-fits-all theology or strictly observed models of grief impose more harm than relief, denying the "complex and often bewildering phenomenon" of sorrow. Instead, McNeish recommends practical care that focuses on personal context, open listening and alternative liturgy.[15]

When my daughter was a child, we played a game called *I love you more....* Usually I started with something simple: "I love you more than chocolate!" She would chime in, "I love you more than Power Rangers!" (High praise indeed.) And off we would go, one *more than* after another, until sooner or later Jess returned to one of our favorites:

"I love you more than a poke in the eye!"

Jess died around eight o'clock on a Friday evening, 16 January 2015. I was working at the time and felt an odd pressure on my right eye, solid and unmistakable. The next morning, Saturday, I woke with my lid completely covered in mucus. I thought I had an unexpected case of pink eye. That afternoon my sight returned to normal.

Jess's mother was unable to reach me on Friday or Saturday. Finally, on Sunday, 18 January 2015, I learned that Jess had overdosed. I was cooking dinner when I heard the news. Unlike Friedrich's boys, I knew she was dead, I knew it was true. Had I Rückert's gift, my kyrielle might end each stanza with a different sacramental refrain:

> She remains, she is here,
> more beautiful each year,
> more precious each hour:
> *I love you more....*

**Now the sun will rise as bright,
as though no sorrow had fallen in the night.**

**This sorrow fell on me alone,
the sun shines on everyone.**

**Do not wrap yourself around the night,
bathe it in eternal light.**

**My tent is dark, the lamp is cold,
bless the light, the Joy of the World.**

Rückert's poem comments on a paradox known to many who grieve the death of a loved one: our world seems to have stopped but for billions of others it is just another day. The first two stanzas seem reasonably obvious: they acknowledge with astonishment that the world is continuing on despite the poet's loss. The third stanza, however, shows Friedrich struggling with what sounds like a personal pep talk that rings a tad hollow.

In the line *Do not wrap yourself around the night* Friedrich uses a verb with unpleasant undertones, meaning to *twist, entangle, enfold*[16] the night inside himself. This sorrow, Rückert's metaphorical darkness and cold, is part of him now; he need not wrap himself round it, slipping into unhealthy brooding. The sun still shines.

Dublin poet Seán Brophy, who battled physical illness most of his life, observed that this song is for those "who are struggling to find a way out of a pit of darkness into the light." Brophy penned exquisite haikus on grief and the compassion of Jesus. He wrote of Rückert's lament:

> There is the growing awareness that attachment is not love; that attachment is temporary whereas love is permanent; that each person's soul has its own terms with God that have nothing to do with us, but invite us to be grateful for the privilege of being a witness to the journey of others on earth, to be able to replace the darkness, the sad feelings at the

awfulness of their death, with the consoling light of gratitude for their life.[17]

In the final line of the poem we discover with Rückert a peace borne of sorrow and cherished belief. The grieving father emphasizes this with a contrast of dark and light. His insight served him well. Modern research confirms that Friedrich's dichotomy of lament—heartbreak and hope—often facilitates an acceptance of our loved one's death as we reconstruct meaning in our lives.[18] Through song we may view our inconsolable grief in an *eternal light* that provides expectation of reunion.

"Grief can remind us not to hold on too tightly," observed experts Crystal Park and Roshi Joan Halifax, "as it teaches us tenderness and patience with our own suffering."[19] Taken this way, the blessing of Friedrich's final line is not false bravado. Rather, it is reminiscent of the Jewish mourning prayer, the Kaddish.

After bereavement counselor Harriet Sarnoff Schiff lost her son, she found that the daily ritual of reciting the Kaddish served a surprising purpose which she had misunderstood before her child's death. Returning to the synagogue each day somehow grounded her grief and helped her come to terms with it.[20] The practice has a therapeutic value. It forces the bereaved to go out in public, to join with others who honor the solemn nature of the observance, which in modern times is recited by women as well as men.[21]

The Kaddish is essentially a prayer of worship: *Magnified and sanctified be His great name.... May there be abundant peace from heaven, and life for us....* The congregational response is telling: *May His great Name be blessed forever and ever.*[22] When sung, the Kaddish is thoughtful and compassionate, as is Gustav Mahler's famous musical setting of "Now the sun will rise as bright."

Mahler, a composer of Jewish heritage, chose this poem as the first of five pieces from *Songs on the Death of Children* that he used in his song cycle, *Kindertotenlieder*. Rückert's song follows a slow progression that was not lost on Mahler. As with the Kaddish, Mahler's somber musical setting belies the piece's deceptively celebratory tone.

Mahler marked the first line to be performed "slowly and dejectedly,"[23] placing the second line over an accompaniment "like a lullaby"[24] that should be sung "with restrained voice." The lullaby motif is slightly deformed with the final line. Mahler has it sung in full then repeated only in part, *the light, the Joy of the World*. His softer mode gives an affective duality to the "quaking emotion" of the piece.[25] Mahler's traditional juxtaposition of tone and words perfectly matches Rückert's bittersweet lament.

This song is an invitation to consider the cyclical nature of grief: each day the sun rises on a world without our loved one; each day we face this reality anew.[26] Years after our loss, there will be moments when we are overwhelmed with a sorrow as acute as those first few weeks of mourning. At other times, the light that we shine on our darkness of grief will not be so blinding. We may discover that both are aspects of our new lives ahead.

Woe to me because of my wound! My injury is incurable!
I used to say, "It's only an illness, and I can bear it."
But now my tent is ruined, all its cords are severed;
my children have left me and are no more.
—Jeremiah 10:19–20 CJB

> You are a shadow in the day
> and a light in the night;
> you live in my sorrow,
> you do not die in my heart.
>
> Here I pitch my tent,
> here you are with me;
> you are my shadow in the day
> and in the night, my light.
>
> Here I ask after you,
> here I find you,
> you live in my sorrow,
> you do not die in my heart.
>
> You are a shadow in the day,
> but at night, a light;
> you live in my sorrow,
> you do not die in my heart.

This piece remains one of the most popular of Rückert's laments. Respected poet and translator Karl Krolow admired the powerful simplicity of the song. He considered it the "most delicate piece of the cycle" and the "most artistic" German poem of the 19th century.[27] Ralf Georg Czapla, an expert in German literary studies, gave special attention to its moving repetitions and refrains. "The poet's wish that his children live on in poetry," Czapla observed, "is realized in the memorable wording."[28]

As recently as 2009, André Moraweck, lead singer of the well-known German metalcore band Maroon, used this poem as the lyric for his song "Schatten" (Shadows) on their final album, listing Rückert as author. Moraweck was following a long line of some 500 composers who have set Friedrich's work to music over the last 150 years. Maroon's record label noted: "'Schatten' is probably the darkest, most captivating and emotional song on *Order* and a great climax to the most ambitious and intense album in the band's career."[29] For genre fans, the band's choice makes perfect sense.

Germany lays claim to nearly one-tenth of the world's metal bands.[30] Ethnologists have found that the majority of fans are predominately in their mid-thirties, educated, employed, Caucasian, middle class, well-adjusted,[31] and come from a variety of backgrounds: "bourgeoisified," as one researcher put it.[32] A surprising number of avid female fans are neither subordinate nor groupies.[33]

My daughter was one such enthusiast in North America. I am not a fan. My tastes run more toward Verdi, Mozart, The Blind Boys of Alabama, Johnny Cash and Dave Brubeck. But I listened with her sometimes anyway, because, well, Dad.

I have played Maroon's interpretation of "Shadows" a number of times. Alas, this song, as with music created by Jessica's other beloved metal bands, does not resonate with me. Still, we swapped her favorite discs when she was alive. The tradition still gives me comfort. "If you find an abundance of people that like that kind of music," observed Ray Charles, "you can be sure it has some kind of meaning for them, it may not be your type of music, but if you really stop and analyze it, really listen to it, you can understand."[34]

Metalcore has a surprising place with Evangelical Christians in Finland.

Since 2006, well over one hundred Metal Masses have been conducted in Lutheran churches. Each Mass presents the conventional liturgy, including communion, with a heavy metal band instead of a cantor at the organ.[35] Robert Walser with Case Western Reserve University insists that the power cords of metal music serve a purpose that runs parallel with the volume and force produced by pipe organs "to display and enact overwhelming power—usually, in that context, for the greater glory of God."[36]

This music has meaning that cannot be denied, whatever our personal tastes. When I think of my daughter's love for the genre, I'm reminded that she was patiently enthusiastic about listening to my latest opera CDs. I recall driving the busy streets of downtown Columbia with Jess while Pavarotti played on my stereo. "Turn it up," she cried with delight. "Luciano-o-o!" On 6 September 2007, the day the tenor died, Jess made a point to call the moment she heard the news: "Oh, Dad, I'm so sorry."

Today I am listening to Rückert presented by the kind of band my daughter enjoyed. The act is conciliatory and consoling, a bridge of sorts. In such brief moments our bond continues. She feels less *absent* somehow.

> Some say the word "pop" is a derogatory word to say "not important"—I do not accept that. If the word "classic" is the word to say "boring," I do not accept. There is good and bad music.—Luciano Pavarotti[37]

Maroon's reading of Rückert is, in one metal fan's words, "loud, dark, violent, meditative, powerful."[38] Metal enthusiasts have a keen interest in the "genealogy" of their preferred genre. Jess certainly did. Influences can range from myth and literature to horror films and graphic novels, but for the most part, listeners are eager to uncover the innumerable musical references from previous bands (Iron Butterfly is a worldwide favorite).[39] In this milieu, it is not surprising that Maroon, one of the most sought-after acts in metalcore, dipped into their country's history for a *lied* that fans would appreciate.

All of which make Friedrich's poem something of a puzzle.

True, the themes seem standard for consolation poetry: "They are in the light," "they are with God," etc. But here Rückert does the unexpected. We anticipate that the comforting light of his evenings will also accompany him during the day. Instead, we find shadow. This has led to a certain amount of debate.

Rückert biographer Annemarie Schimmel held that the song progresses from mourning to remembrance. "This simple poem seems artless," she wrote, "but that impression is deceptive." She suggested that the piece begins with a plaintive tone that soon turns to trust. The shadow in the day comes unbidden at first, a seeming shadowy being or the darkness of grief. As the poem continues, Friedrich realizes that the shadow is his own, linked to him in the blazing sun, a tent protecting him from the heat. The light is a guide at night. "If the final verse seems to repeat the first, the tone has changed," Schimmel concluded. "Lament has become consolation."[40]

Another Rückert scholar, Sascha

Monhoff, notes that this poem breaks free from traditional consolations that use light to represent God as an image of hope. "The fact that 'you' is only addressed as 'shadow' and 'light' emphasizes the absence of a live body—or rather: its non-existence—all the more clearly," Monhoff wrote. "Here there is no body to cast a 'shadow.' In no way does the body emit a 'light.'"

Commenting on the deeply spiritual nature of the *Songs on the Death of Children*, and Rückert's religious beliefs, Monhoff draws a parallel between this poem and the Book of Exodus, in which the disembodied but visible presence of God corresponds to the primal, shadowy memory of Friedrich's children in his heart. "Rückert's poems are interesting," Monhoff concludes, "precisely because they ultimately undermine superficial metaphysical references."[41]

Mourners often seek meaning beyond the glib consolations offered by others. Whether I read this poem in English, listen to a recitation in German, or sung by a metal band, the result is the same. I sense a connection with my daughter. My interpretation of Friedrich's lament takes a direct approach. While we may sense that our children live on—the light of solace—this never completely eases the shadow of grief cast daily in their absence.[42]

> Fidelity truly exists only when it defies absence, when it triumphs over absence, and in particular, over that absence which we hold to be—mistakenly no doubt—absolute, and which we call death.—Gabriel Marcel[43]

Encircled by mountain, engulfed by flood, no path leads from you, world, into me.

No voice sounds and no eye sees in the still bay where my grief is seeking.

No wisp of breeze lifts a whiff of scent, nor do swift glimmers light the meadow.

Close weaving shadows! All is from above, wind and scent and light, all that speaks to me here.

Close weaving shadows! All rises above: shimmer of flowers, and breath, a glance, a sigh.

Our world is silent, broken, closed in, sick. The suffering of Luise and Ernst may be over, but that of their parents is not. To exist in this world, the poet observes, is to suffer. Here Rückert is following a literary tradition that traces its lineage to the Book of Job and gained particular importance in Friedrich's lifetime, from the late 18th century on.[44] The idea was simply that we have a disconnect between what we perceive with our senses—the misery in this world—and what exists beyond them. The book speaks to suffering and the silence of God.

No path leads from you, world, into me, Rückert writes, which was (and is) recognized as one of the most important themes of Job. The titular protagonist, after losing his ten children, his belongings and his health, repeatedly identifies himself with "dust and ashes." According to Ariel Hirschfeld, professor of Hebrew literature at the Hebrew University of Jerusalem, Job's awareness of "dust and ashes" progresses from the outside in: he is *sitting in* dust and ashes; he is *like* dust and ashes; he *is* dust and ashes. This movement crosses the chasm between the physical and invisible worlds, between Job's *skin* and his *soul*.[45]

For Friedrich, this gulf, or bay, could not be crossed using his physical senses alone. With a few stanzas Rückert has identified a challenge faced by all who mourn.[46] The loss of a child deeply affects the perceptions of a parent. This is as much physical and emotional as it is spiritual. "Bereaved parents do not 'recover' in the sense of returning to who they were before the death," wrote Ida Martinson in the professional journal *Death Studies*. "Instead, they appear to change as they integrate the loss into their lives."[47] Parents deal with mourning and long-term stress in different ways, but one common thread seems to be a marked neurological change. This occurs as early as three weeks after the loss with measurable biochemical components persisting throughout the first eight months,[48] around the same length of time Rückert spent writing the poems in *Songs on the Death of Children*.

Over the first five years of grief, bereaved parents show demonstrable differences in basic motor skills and how they fashion sentences.[49] These are not hindered; just different. Grief counselors have noted that bereaved parents are seldom embarrassed about such foibles as mismatched clothes, misspeaking, stuttering or misspelled words. It is not that they are unaware of these human frailties; they merely see them as trivial and a waste of energy that could be put to better use. They report that the shift in their lives has resulted in a concurrent shift in their priorities.[50] These and similar attempts to reaffirm or reconstruct meaning are linked to the central process of healthy grieving.[51] Few bereaved parents make an effort to return to previous behaviors.

This poem speaks to Rückert's growing sense that he feels, sees and hears things differently. I have revisited it many times. I am struck by the poet's silence, what he leaves unsaid. With each reading, I get a deeper sense of Friedrich's insight: what for him is *from* above—wind and scent and light—is precisely what *rises* above in different forms. More, there is immediacy in his tone. The poet wholly and completely inhabits the present, the very essence of what has come to be known in English as mindfulness. In his grief, Friedrich is reaching deeper. Whatever is above is within him as well.

> Those who enter a completely empty room know. There in the emptiness they can discover the true present. Cathedrals, mosques, temples, whatever is sacred within them comes from this empty present. This emptiness of all things. This empty present, within which people can see themselves laid bare.—Beopjeong[52]

"Over all graves grass must grow,"
"time heals all wounds," such is the
   solace,
the worst thing to say, as consolations go;
poor heart, not that, not a healed wound.
It is something, at least, this pain;
we amputate the numb and the dead.

By the 19th century societal constraints regarding what to do and say when faced with death had become particularly vexing. The bereaved were offered centuries-old platitudes: it is God's will; they are at peace; and so on.[53] These well-meant expressions of sympathy do little to ease the devastation of losing a child.[54] Here Rückert spins a few common expressions on their heads,[55] reminiscent of Job's cry to his wrong-headed consolers: "Why offer me such meaningless comfort?"[56]

Silence may be the most helpful, but this is often in short supply. When comforting the grieving, the things we say are often worse than the things we do not. It is difficult to sit, hush and listen. But this is what we must do. "Human beings are grieving animals," wrote Christoph Jedan of the University of Groningen, "and consolation, an experiential assemblage through which grief is ameliorated or assuaged, is an age-old response to loss."[57]

In the Jewish mourning tradition of sitting *shivah*, or sitting seven (days after the burial), visitors to the home of the bereaved are advised to say nothing and answer briefly when spoken to. Mourners sit in low chairs and abstain from wearing jewelry or make-up. Men do not shave. The point is to allow the natural reaction of grief to exist in the home of the bereaved.

German-Jewish theologian and philosopher Franz Rosenzweig observed that liturgy, rites and prayers create a shared silence of redemption: each person becomes part of a still community that transcends the misapprehensions and failed communications of words.[58] Words unite us but in harmony, faced with the sacred, we grow silent.[59]

It is considered a special blessing to visit and comfort the bereaved during *shivah* and, by extension, to pay close attention to the needs of the grieving throughout the coming year.[60] Irwin Kidorf, Chief Psychologist at the Cumberland County Guidance Center for many years, held that "the almost naked expression of feeling" involved in mourning plays an important cathartic role for everyone involved in the observance of *shivah*. It presents an opportunity to weep, to speak of deep emotions, questions and pain.[61]

Such customs and rituals accept that long silences are healthy and expected. Despite this, we may feel uncomfortable. It is difficult to resist filling the quiet with chatter or leaving when conversation dies down. *Stay*. It is our presence that is needed. We may best show our love by letting them grieve.

Between long silences, the bereaved often speak through tears of treasured memories. They feel a connection with the dead that is unlikely to wane. In fact, modern studies have found that the sense of a continuing bond between parents and their dead children is healthy, normal and often lasts a lifetime.[62]

This is one of Rückert's finest laments. As with so many of his poems, reading it aloud provides unanticipated rewards. Yale University classics professor Egbert Bakker observed that poetry is simply written speech, and is in this regard a most natural way of using language. We are struck by the immediacy of each sound and its use within the context of the song. "It is no wonder, indeed," observed philosopher Ludwig Wittgenstein, "that we then feel haunted by meanings we can sense but not articulate."[63] Friedrich's poems are alive and vibrant with the tones, lilts, pauses and sighs of the spoken word and unspoken intent.

A simple example of this idea can be found in Handel's *Messiah*, which sets seemingly dry passages of scripture to sublime music. When talented soloists and a rousing choir inform us "for unto us a child is born" and "I know that my redeemer liveth," the words are transformed to more than ink and paper. Bakker suggests that we might view poetry as "a *flow* through time rather than as a *structure* on the two-dimensional space of the written page."[64] For me, it is the power of this flow through time that seems to overwhelm us when we least expect it, when we need it most, or both.

Friedrich's opening lines, in tone and meter, are not dissimilar to Johann Wolfgang von Goethe's "Over all peaks," often called the most perfect lyric piece in German verse. It was also written in a time of confusion and lament. On 6 September 1780, three years after his beloved sister Cornelia died and a week following the poet's thirty-first birthday, Goethe traveled to Ilmenau. He spent the night in a hunter's hut on the tallest peak of the area, the Kickelhahn. It was still summer but at that altitude, even today, the leaves change nearly overnight in September. That night Goethe penned a masterpiece of world literature, a hushed evocation of the calm found in nature.[65] He wrote it on the wooden wall of the hut:

> Over all peaks
> lies peace,
> in every tree-
> top you sense
> barely a breath;
> birds are still in the wood.
> Only wait, soon
> you too will rest.[66]

Fifty years later, six months before his death, Goethe climbed the Kickelhahn one final time.[67] There he rediscovered "Over all peaks" scratched in the wall. Past and present combined in a poignant arc. Goethe wept.[68]

> **All our laments do not
> serve what joy we've lost:
> we call, but those we call
> do not return from the grave.**
>
> **We call, but those we call
> will not return again:
> all these laments do not
> serve those we mourn.**
>
> **All these laments do not
> serve our joy now lost;
> we may call, but they do
> not return from the grave.**

Songs on the Death of Children is a testament to the value of these poems as expressions of finality, mourning, transformation and connection.[69] Rückert is not dismissing creative expressions of grief. Rather, he is lamenting the uselessness of a *specific form* of lament.

For millennia lamentations sought to restore what was lost. One Sumerian lament, for example, was sung in the rubble of a destroyed temple in hopes that the gods would rebuild the structure. Other songs, more painful for the bereaved, begged for the restoration of lost loved ones.[70]

Friedrich's outbursts of harm and hope are also slightly different from elegies, which usually progress from lament to praise to comfort. Elegy is intended to offer some sort of resolution.[71] Rückert avoids such consolations, offering instead grief in all its many and varied aspects. His poems acquire a therapeutic function for himself and his readers.[72]

In this poem, Rückert suggests that crying for the return of a feeling, a person or a time that is now irrevocably gone is worse than worthless. It has no meaning to the dead and hurts the living. He demonstrates this with a surprisingly trenchant tone. The grieving father observes that no one is listening to these pleas for the return of what was lost.

Rückert's contemporary, literary critic and devout Catholic Joseph von Eichendorff, dismissed Friedrich's raw honesty when writing of the divine. "His piety," Eichendorff observed, "is often paralyzed by a touch of irony."[73] Yet poets through the ages have echoed Rückert's despair and frustration.

Laments were often induced by death, such as in the Book of Job, whose protagonist demanded sixteen separate times to know why his ten children had to die.[74] Three of the psalms of lament start with "why."[75] The Israelites' weeping was ignored by God at one point; then, after being promised that deity would hear their cry, their weeping was again not heard.[76] "Even when I cry out, pleading for help," wrote Jeremiah, "he shuts out my prayer."[77]

Rainer Maria Rilke's first elegy, composed in January 1912 at Duino Castle, pointedly asks the question: "Who, if I cried aloud, would hear me among the angelic hosts?"[78] Angels are beings of eternity, Rilke wrote, whose very existence "acknowledges a higher level of reality in the invisible world."

They exist across an unbridgeable chasm, seeming to have already completed a "transformation from the visible to the invisible."[79] The poet holds that the realm of angels can only be comprehended in death.[80]

Rilke and Rückert were in respectable, anguished company. As with Job, the psalmists, and Jeremiah, Friedrich's cries have no easy answers. No amount of lament will return Ernst and Luise from the grave.

> How may laments be answered at all? How does one respond to a language that resists every answer? And how does one answer in such a way that the lament is not dismissed as a symptom of preventable grief, an abnormality or mere happenstance?—Werner Hamacher[81]

**If our dead are not with us
how will we know peace?
When we are surrounded
by spirits each moment?
Awake, we may resist, but in
dreams we must succumb.
Far more have died than
we few who are alive.
Can we, clinging to the few,
hope to resist the many?
When daily, hourly, deserters
join their numbers?
We who remain, the few,
are weak: we cannot resist.
Should we not forge an
alliance with the strong?
Then those who seemed
terrible will walk beside us.
Then our hearts will open
to the lives of the dead.
Poets, sages, the wisdom of
the ages will rise to meet us.
And those we loved will not
leave our love in the dust.
We will walk this earth in the
company of heaven; and those
who stood nearest in life will
be our closest companions.**

Many bereaved parents sense the presence of their children within the first few weeks of the death. Later, as months or years go by, they come to feel that their children remain with them.[82] Isabel Allende said poignantly that her daughter Paula, who died in 1992, "is a gentle presence that is with her always, like a second skin."[83]

Rückert probably wrote this poem in the late spring of 1834. There is a sense of calm in the piece that reveals itself in his deceptively casual tone. Nor was his suggestion that the dead walk with us entirely new. Physical and spiritual communion was much a part of the Romantic milieu.[84] Nineteenth-century poets, authors, philosophers and composers often sought to communicate the intangible influence of guiding spirits that seemed to inhabit and permeate our tangible world.[85] Yet this is not Friedrich's point.

The grieving father writes as if an old idea is suddenly and finally real to him. He chose phrasing that indicates conflict: *the few, the many, strong, weak, alliance, deserters,* etc. The grieving must stop resisting the presence of their loved one, the poet implies, if they hope to find peace. Our imagined battle is one-sided: we react in fear and anger to the dead who are patiently walking beside us as heavenly guides.[86]

Modern research has drawn a similar conclusion about mourning. We resist grief, insisting it is finite, time-limited and predictable. Yet personal and societal expectations of "moving on" only increase a mourner's suffering. Instead, clinicians have observed that many of the bereaved develop a lifelong, livable relationship with grief, according to Nancy Moules with the University of Calgary, "as much filled with comfort and creativity as it is with sorrow."[87]

In Gregory the Great's *Moralia in Job*, the pope wrote that impassioned lament is evidence of a philosophical fortitude that far exceeds the unrealistic demands of stoicism, damaging denial and forced absence of feeling. True virtue lies in neither a dullness of heart nor irrational displays of mourning.[88] Rather, Gregory wrote, "whoever strives to maintain true philosophy, must go between either extreme." He concluded that the lived experience of sorrow and suffering is essential in realizing true wisdom.[89]

Rückert seems to have done precisely that. By this time in his life he had already translated many classic Asian works: *poets, sages, the wisdom of the ages.* Now his concern—as with much of the mythology, ritual and learning he had studied—was turning to the more intimate needs of harmony and a depth of soul that comes through making peace with our dead.[90]

> The dead are here with us, in the air that we are moving through all the time. The only difference between us and the dead is that they are now in an invisible form. You cannot see them with the human eye. But you can sense the presence of those you love who have died. With the refinement of your soul you can sense them. You feel that they are near.—John O'Donohue[91]

**As the poor hen,
gripped with fear
sees her brood of
ducklings slip away,**

**rushes to the water,
cries after her**

> children as they
> ride the river current,
>
> I know this sense
> of loss: my boys
> were reared to
> go their own way.
>
> I have only the one
> girl to call my own;
> never to slip away
> from under my wing.
>
> Divinity alone could
> part us; so from the
> arch of heaven shot
> the talons of a hawk.
>
> Ah, alpine death
> pierces my soul,
> drains the blood
> from my heart
>
> as my pain erupts
> for my little girl,
> away it has flown,
> away with my own.
>
> A lonely hen clucks
> after her proud
> ducklings as they
> ride the river current.

"When your parent dies you have lost your past," observed psychiatrist Elliot Luby. "When your child dies you have lost your future."[92] Loss is an intensely vulnerable experience. What we imagined to be inviolate has been violated. In the aftermath of death, even simple routines seem fraught with the possibility of catastrophe. This thoughtful poem shows by example the banal terror of daily life after losing a child.

Bereaved parents speak of losing their illusions of control and safety, describing the severity of what has happened with comparisons like *a global shift, the rug was pulled out from under me,* or *my whole world collapsed.* Our expectations of security and a bright future have been destroyed. We are beset with fear, anxiety and a concern that in our acute grief we may be "going crazy."[93]

One researcher found that 86 percent of bereaved parents became more protective of their surviving children after the death.[94] This can display itself in positive ways: practical awareness of vulnerability may lead to greater vigilance and more rapid responses to signs of trouble.[95] Families also establish reasonable boundaries, allowing themselves time to grieve privately.[96] However, these same tendencies can cause damaging overprotectiveness.

Parents may conceal their grief from their children out of a misplaced sense of protection, thus cheating the family of the healthy aspects of shared memory and mourning. They may subordinate personal needs for the children's perceived benefit—more than usual, that is.[97] This can also lead to marital strain, blaming, competitiveness for attention and social isolation.

Overprotectiveness contains its own cruel irony: overreaching leads to parental rigidity and an inability to support and emotionally care for surviving children. Out of fear, our desire to nurture and shield may have the opposite effect, causing our loved ones to live in that same fear.[98] This in turn feels, in the poet's words, as though the blood were drained from our hearts. In another poem, published in 1841, Rückert acknowledges this painful dichotomy:

> *To those who remain*
>
> Children age as is their lot
> and small ones must grow,
> rip free from their parents:
> never again to rest in my lap.

But you—whose lot was taken too
soon, never to grow, forever small,
never to rip free from my heart—
you rest, always, in my lap.[99]

How then to endure the inevitable passage of time as our surviving loved ones *ride the river currents* of their lives? With loneliness and trepidation, Friedrich suggests, and perhaps something else: a surrender to our love for them as they proudly make their own way.

This act of surrender causes a surprising shift in our perspective. Having learned the true nature of vulnerability, we see clearly at last what it means to survive. Researcher Ronald Knapp wrote that bereaved parents experience a curious sense of invulnerability regarding life's other hardships: "These parents came to realize that tomorrow might never come. It never came for their child.... Thus *today* took on a new importance in a way that perhaps can be understood only by those who have experienced the ultimate tragedy."[100]

He who finds rest, as I do,
with himself in nature, will
be touched by all that is,
gently eased, subdued.

Joys will cause less laughter,
but will fade less quickly.
Pain will not be a burden,
nor easily forgotten.

How could an image of heaven,
safe as a mild tide caught in
a landscape, shielded from
storm and wind, disappear?

I have rested in a still bay,
did not seek froth and
foam in happier days;
should I now in sorrow?

Obsessed with the world, we
fail to reflect on what we see,
none of which interests me:
I reflect to never forget.

A silent chorus surrounds,
sings your names to me,
and describes your lives
in a thousand images.

This old chorus, known
to the eye, intimate to
the ear, does not distract
me, it is nothing new.

Behind the green of
spring my pain is as
a rose, not to be ignored,
it eases my heart so.

In the end, there is only one stage of grief: *grief. I reflect to never forget*, Rückert writes. We continue to love them, and so we continue to grieve—and breathe—until we see them again. Over time we may learn to make peace with the reality of their death. "Acceptance" of that fact as a preconceived stage of grief is a false landmark.[101] It is also a little silly. I accepted my daughter's death immediately. How could I do otherwise? It was irrefutable. Inevitably, unconsciously, I am learning to live with this fact, as I live with breathing, inhaling my love for her and exhaling my grief.

Mourners describe instances of intense waves of grief years after a death. These may be repeated many times in the coming years, often at the most unanticipated moments. On other occasions we will have an idea of what is coming. For example, researchers have demonstrated that we have a measurable biochemical change around the birthday and memorial day of our loved one now gone.[102] Our bodies know.

To assume we can prepare for this is nonsense, of course. Do we prepare to love or to breathe? Grief is no more a process than these. Do we have a "loving process"? (Pity the person that dates anyone who answers yes!) Or do we consciously employ a "breathing process"? Understanding that such emotions are coming is helpful, but the pain remains.

Grief is the means by which we make sense of the changed nature of our relationship with our dead.[103] Mourning does not take a specific course or follow a predetermined time-line. Moments of keening come and go unbidden, uninvited. At times these waves of sorrow seem to carry me along, rather than the other way round. As with waves in a vast ocean, they may be unseen but ever-present. When they arrive, they can seem overwhelming. We are foolish to fight them; rather, we are forced to accept sorrow as a reality of our new existence. Such moments are normal and expected.[104] As Nina Jakoby, Center for Death & Society, University of Bath, observed, "Grief is integral to life and not a condition to be treated."[105]

Death cannot be fixed or healed or worked through. There is no process for sorrow, mourning and pain. Grief merely *is*, as much a fact of our lives as death. We continue to love them, and so we continue to grieve—and breathe—until we see them again.

Despite this lived reality of grief, felt by millions across the centuries, the myth of a *grief process* persists in the modern mind. There is no such thing. The best researchers and grief therapists have confirmed that our popular perception of stages of grief is unhelpful and inaccurate, as is the clinical term for this so-called process, *grief work*.

"Does 'grief work' work?" asked three of the world's leading grief researchers, Wolfgang Stroebe, Margaret Stroebe, and Henk Schut. Their answers were surprising and changed the course of 21st-century therapy.

They observed that in the current way of thinking, "we must confront and speak of our feelings and reactions to the death of a loved one. But what evidence do we have that this is so?" Not much, they discovered. The Stroebes and Schut learned that there was *no measurable difference in depression* between those who "worked through" their grief and those who did not. "Grief work," the respected experts concluded, "is not always as essential for adjustment to bereavement as theorists and clinicians have claimed."[106]

The hypothesis that we must *work through* our grief has been repeated for well over a century. Ironically, it was first suggested by a man who changed his views completely after losing a child. In 1917, before his loss, Sigmund Freud wrote his influential *Mourning and Melancholia*, in which he defines the work of mourning as a severing from an object (our loved one) that no longer exists. He defined an inability to detach as pathological grief.

Three years later, in 1920, Freud's daughter Sophie died. She was twenty-six. The grieving father discovered the folly of his clinical pronouncements.

"My daughter who died would have been thirty-six years old today," Freud wrote a friend who had recently lost a son in 1929. "Although we know that after such a loss the acute state of mourning will subside, we also know we shall remain inconsolable and will never find a substitute.... And actually this is how it should be. It is the only way of perpetuating that love which we do not want to relinquish."[107]

As Rückert demonstrates in this poem, grief is not a process, it is a reality: *my pain is as a rose, not to be ignored, it eases my heart so*. We do not work through or get over our loss. We come to terms with it. Grief experts Terry Martin and Kenneth Doka maintain that we as a society are wrong to hold to the traditional view that sharing emotions is the only mark of healthy grieving. "Another, equally sound pattern ... tends to be private," they write, concluding, "We must respect individual needs and differences."[108]

Slowly, stumbling and crawling, we may begin to find meaning again. But this often surprises us. We discover that we are *touched by all that is, gently eased, subdued*. We do not crave purpose, we do not work for it, or seek it or even care much about it—yet it comes to us all the same, in moments we could not imagine or anticipate.

> People's relationships with their loved ones may survive the life—death boundary. People maintain their relationship with dead loved ones and the dead continue to influence the lives of the living.— Dr. Christine Valentine, Association for the Study of Death and Society[109]

Preface

You who filled our home with quiet joy remain in song, free of show, present everywhere in everyday things;

don't leave us to tears that hope for smiles of applause as a stroke of fate shatters the joy of our home like glass.

Shall I put away such thoughts? Refuse to crown them with laurels: songs of lament on my brow?

No, you live on in song, in unfamiliar voices, a spectacle of solace at your death.

Rückert continues to sense that Luise is with him in everyday things. He also feels a bond with her through song, a normal and expected reaction.[110] In this poem, Friedrich wonders if his verse is too ostentatious for so still and quiet a presence. Perhaps, he muses, but he refuses to give it up. This was wise.

Laments and the expressions of grief they represent are quite healthy. Psychologist and bereavement specialist Margaret Stroebe observed that poetry "provides us with the metaphors to experience ongoing attachment, to help us understand and find a place for the loss."[111]

For example, when C.S. Lewis suggests that his grief is an amputation,[112] we know immediately that he is comparing two otherwise vastly different experiences that shock us with their similarity in one specific way. The imagery of poetry communicates this dynamic connection between words. *These ideas may not be equal*, the poet implies, *but in this singular instance they are the same*. The tension between what is (grief is not amputation) and what cannot be (grief is amputation) provides a powerful consolation. We sense that others have also experienced a loss that defies words.[113] In this way, metaphor serves the vital role of communion.

The pacing, cadence and pauses of

poetry speak with silent clarity in our emotional devastation after a death. What better way to explain the inexplicable, account for the unaccountable, describe the indescribable? French Jesuit and scholar Michel de Certeau asked the same questions: "Is mystical discourse possible? The 'ineffable' itself structures language. It is not a hole in language or a source of leakage. It becomes, rather, *something* in relation to which language is redefined."[114] The emptiness between words was a vital part of Rückert's laments. Far from being a *spectacle of solace*, his songs resonate with the sacred quiet of grief.

The setting for this song is the first few weeks after Luise's death. Ernst was still struggling with the scarlet fever that was to kill him. Her death was the stroke of fate that shattered the joy of their home, as Friedrich described it.[115] His perspective on *fate*, and his definition of the word itself, comes from a surprising source: Christian Arabs and the sages of the east.

Rückert learned Persian from Austrian Orientalist and historian Joseph von Hammer-Purgstall, producing translations that surpassed his instructor.[116] Friedrich's rendering of Hafez remains unsurpassed in style and content even today. His small collection of Rumi's verse, published in 1819, planted the poetic form of ghazal in the "German language garden," matching exact interpretation with gentle humor, both deplorably absent in previous translations.[117] As he worked, Friedrich was exposed to perceptions of the visible and invisible worlds that inform many of his *Songs on the Death of Children*.

Westerners tend to think of fate as an immutable force over which there is no control. In this view, fate dismisses the possibility of free will and its resulting individualism. It seems to be a negation of the concept of an all-powerful God.

Christian Arabs and Muslims, however, use the term *fate* to express the *will* of God, who by his own definition is merciful and compassionate.[118] Each event—any event—is an expression of God's intent. Rather than perceiving fate as a blind force, they see true blindness as a refusal to accept the designs of God. Believers show wisdom by acknowledging what *is*.[119] Goethe, who studied the Old Testament and the Qur'an, was quick to grasp this concept. "My God, to whom I have ever remained faithful," he wrote in 1779, "has generously blessed me in secret, for my fate is hidden completely from others, who may neither see nor hear it."[120]

The idea is not necessarily at odds with Western ideology, though we usually prefer the phrase *Act of God* over *fate*.[121] In either case, Rückert's poems are a testament to his perception of reality and the divine as they *are*, not as he wishes they could be or thinks they should be: *Shall I put away such thoughts?* he asks. *Refuse to crown them with laurels?*

When Friedrich's eldest son, Heinrich, compiled the first edition of *Songs on the Death of Children*, he selected this poem as the initial entry, perhaps because it so gracefully expresses how creative arts may facilitate meaningful consolation.

The stillness is full of demands, awaiting
a soul to breathe in the mystery that all

things exhale in their craving for communion.—Abraham Heschel[122]

> **Dark premonitions bludgeon and force themselves upon me before turning to song.**
>
> **Thoughts too palpable for shadow *must* exist: "The sick do not die," be insistent, "she will live."**
>
> **Do I push my way into God's province? No, he gave me these thoughts for my own.**

Rückert is struggling with his daughter's impending death. It is unclear when he wrote this poem, but the setting is definitely as Luise lay ill. There is a terrible desperation in his insistence that if he hopes hard enough, his thoughts will become reality.

In modern parlance, this kind of wishful thinking is known in some churches as "name it and claim it" or simply "claim the victory." The idea is often tied to questions of faith, implying that when such victory is not forthcoming, the fault lies with the parents.

But Friedrich is not involved in theological debates or posturing Sunday school discussions. His daughter is dying. He hopes against all reason that his *thoughts* can somehow save her. Does he presume too much, he asks? No, he assures himself, God gave him these thoughts, after all.

Rückert revisited this poem a number of times, making it somewhat unique among his laments. One early draft of the final stanza gives us a peek into the poet's internal debate with himself and with God:

> Do I force myself into
> the province of God's rule?
> No, he would not give me thoughts
> if I were not to keep them.[123]

Friedrich is expressing feelings that are known to many who have watched a loved one suffer with terminal illness. Researchers have found that spiritual beliefs may facilitate hope, comfort and provide meaning and purpose.[124] At the same time, detrimental aspects include significant bouts of depression among those who relied heavily on religious coping, including a struggle with perceived control and the loss of social support in their faith community during the illness and after the death.[125] In this regard, a relationship with God, and our desperate fearful pleas of hope, may feel like a blessing and a curse.

> Oh, take not, Lord, my babe away—
> Oh, take not to thy songful heaven
> The pretty baby thou hast given,
> Or ere that I have seen him play
> Around his father's knees and known
> That *he* knew how my love has gone
> From all the world to him.
> —Elizabeth Barrett Browning,
> "Isobel's Child"[126]

> **Doctors are ruled by the dictum that no child shall leave this earth without first being sapped of life by grotesque leeches.**
>
> **Never again will I carelessly gaze in a spring; now I shudder at my reflection, at the memory of leeches sucking the lifeblood**
>
> **from my little child, pure soul, so mistreated and now, alas, free. But it is not as if leeches live in clear springs;**
>
> **no, they are collected from the Stygian depths of fetid swamps,**

blood brothers united in their Triumph of Death.

Rückert's reference in the final line, *Triumph of Death*,[127] is not unexpected in light of the scarlet fever pandemic that took his two children. The theme had been well known in art and literature since the Black Death (1347–51). The phrase was as typical a reference to plague as the "Dance of Death."[128]

Images of death capering while millions died were so ubiquitous that most depictions of the day did not bother including a title. One of the finest representations, a mid-fifteenth-century fresco that now hangs in Palermo's regional medieval museum, the Palazzo Abatellis, was not named by its anonymous artist. Yet it was known as *Trionfo Nella Morte, The Triumph of Death*.

Images of dance occupied Rückert for most of his life: the mystical dances described in Rumi's work and the symbolism of dance in sacred music. To Friedrich these represented the continuous turning of life grounded by the unity and love of the divine. He found evidence in the mundane: obituaries, birth and wedding notices.[129] Such were inevitable, as Rückert wrote in this ghazal from 1858:

> The dance turns without ceasing,
> you must join in;
> no one is granted a reprieve;
> you must join in.
> ....
> And if you dance longer than others, if that is
> your allotment, this too will end:
> you must join in.[130]

Between 1820 and 1880 scarlet fever was considered no less deadly than plague. It had become a global pandemic centered mostly in Europe and North America. Outbreaks in 1831 and 1834 (when Friedrich's children died) were extremely fatal and caused more deaths than contemporary outbreaks of cholera or typhus.[131] Children ages two to five were at the highest risk, though everyone in an infected household would likely display symptoms, from rheumatic fever to severe tissue damage.[132] The disease was generally transmitted via hands, books, toys and other items. Droplet transmission also occurred in enclosed spaces.[133]

Samuel Hahnemann, the founder of homoeopathy (modern homeopathy), introduced belladonna as a treatment that was much in vogue throughout 19th-century Germany. Other methods included leeches, bleeding, cold and hot effusions, and a host of drugs of an emetic, purgative, diaphoretic, tonic, or narcotic nature.[134]

Luise suffered from this dread disease for six days. On Sunday, 29 December, the doctor applied leeches to her chest. He came again the next day. Luise died on 31 December: *so mistreated* [by leeching] *and now, alas, free*, as her father wrote. Her brother, Ernst, lasted for two weeks before his death. Leeches were also placed on his arms three different times. Their bites became infected, swollen, and black, adding more pain to the boy's suffering. In another poignant piece from *Songs on the Death of Children*, Friedrich addresses Death directly, pleading for mercy while knowing that there is none to be had:

> You stole them, Death,
> who breaks all bonds,

I had no choice, no defense:
my precious pair is gone.

Their roots run deep in
my heart; this much at
least I can say: you will
not rip their roots away.

Grief is born of love,
both are birthed in hurt:
never lost or forsaken,
not here, nor there.

———

Enough, enough pain!
Judge not by what
I owe: have mercy,
judge with grace.

My strength is spent,
I can bear no more:
In your wisdom then
do not strike me again.

**I loved you so, my little girl!
And now I have buried you.
This is my regret: if only
I had loved you better.**

**I loved you more, so much more,
than I dared to show;
too seldom did you see this love,
too often, you heard stern silence.**

**I loved you, so truly,
even when I scolded you so.
I owed you love alone:
repay me now, twice over.**

**Too often I hid this love
behind a façade of severity;
obsessing on some future fruit,
I failed to see the blossom.**

**Oh, had I but known a wind
would strip the petals bare!
My little girl would have
had every wish granted.**

**Instead you did as I wished,
yes, at my urging, you obeyed,
swallowing the bitter.
How I regret the moment
I told you: "Drink!"**

**Your mouth, cramped and shut tight,
opened at your father's command;**

**Oh! And for what? To drink
and prolong your misery.**

**But you, with death so near,
looked at me with tenderness;
your eyes broken, in tears,
your hands dying, caressing.**

**What did your hands tell me,
when your speech could not?
That you know I tried, you understood,
you forgave these cruel tortures.**

**Now I beg forgiveness for
each harsh word, each cold gesture.
Forget them all where you are,
or at least understand them.**

Luise refused to take the galling medicine prescribed by the Rückert family doctor, Johann Friedrich Kittlinger.[135] She clamped her jaw shut so tightly that her parents had to pry it open and spray the bitter down her throat. This ordeal was repeated every three hours, and likely included an infusion of roses, with an excess of acid, made palatable with an additional quantity of syrup, one of the customary prescriptions of the day.[136]

Mustard or pepper poultices were also applied to Luise's chest and neck, causing terrible blistering. It was customary to subject a suffering child to mild purging with castor oil or citrate of magnesia—all misguided attempts to rid her body of infection.[137] These remedies were worse than useless: they were often cruel.

Rückert came to despise the medical profession's incompetence, which may be one reason that his second son Karl was to become a doctor. In retrospect, remembering Luise's needless suffering, Friedrich blamed himself for failing to comfort her near the end. Such self-recrimination is quite common.[138]

In the first year after a loss, the bereaved often obsessively reconstruct events and replay the death in their minds.[139] This blend of regret and grief may be particularly acute for fathers, who frequently show the highest level of grief for men in every bereavement category except guilt.[140]

In point of fact, Rückert was devoted to Luise and was often indulgent of the child. After her death the smallest slight may have seemed magnified to the grieving father. In this context, Friedrich's poem is as much confession as recrimination.

**Worse than being a patient
is caring for one:
to inflict pain as a cure;
to torment rather than comfort;
to watch these gifts from heaven
vanish, empty and hollow;
relieved at last to bury
their bones in the earth.**

**So it was with my little
girl; so it will be now
with my little boy.**

Rückert learned firsthand the cruel realities of two powerful motifs that were common throughout the 19th century: liberation from suffering and the unjust nature of death from illness or accident, particularly of the young.[141] The comments for "I loved you so, my little girl!" (Luise) and "Go! you cannot stay" (Ernst) detail excruciating torments inflicted by the doctors on the children as they suffered with scarlet fever.

Volker Hesse, a doctor with the German Center for Growth Development and Health Promotion in Childhood and Adolescence (Berlin), wrote that Friedrich was disturbed by the treatments inflicted on his children and their effects, particularly those from emetics, laxatives and mercury. "Rückert's agony," Hesse wrote of this poem, "his compassion, his helplessness and his frustration with the medical procedures are in these verses."[142]

"Worse than being a patient" is set around the time of "Go! you cannot stay," during the fifteen days that Ernst lay dying. Friedrich has shared with us another aspect of grief that is frequently ignored out of shame or guilt.

The child's pain seems endless. Parents struggle to be supportive. Family members feel traumatic distress not only from being near their dying loved one, but also from the current loss of interaction and the anticipated death.[143]

Many bereaved parents, seeing the daily suffering of their child, secretly hope for some type of relief. This may take the form of prayers for healing or, subconsciously, ambivalent emotions and secret, seldom acknowledged desires for the misery to end in any way possible.

It is a lonely vigil filled with sporadic moments of bustle amid long hours of waiting for a miracle that, alas, seldom arrives. "Let loneliness be Thy Presence in my soul," as Oxford professor of Hebrew Edward Bouverie Pusey cried when he too felt abandoned.[144]

The child's death may then be followed by a sense of relief. Rückert confesses as much in this poem. The *grief-relief phenomenon*, as it is known, is often accompanied by guilt over harboring such natural emotions.[145] "Though relief appears soon," researcher Michael Bullock observed, "the period of bereavement may be long and painful."[146]

Friedrich writes with terrible clarity of that pain. The second stanza seems oddly out of place. Rückert scholars agree that it was added later.[147] With each song the grieving father struggles to find images and phrases that express the raw emotions of his loss—relief and remorse included.

> Go! you cannot stay;
> why oh why won't you leave?
> Why do you linger, struggling
> against death and pain?
> Quickly now, follow your sister,
> do not let her travel alone.
> Won't you lie down and
> rest with your sister?
> Why wait? Why avoid the
> spot reserved for you?
> Many other boys are there,
> lying down to rest at last.
> And once one has been put
> to rest next to your little sister
> he will not stand up to
> make room for you.
> Fighting and begging
> will not help you then:
> "Please move! I am her
> brother, after all."
> You must go there in the end.
> It may as well be now.
> And we will take what solace
> we may there at your grave.
> Yes, there in the wind and
> the spring and the rows of
> flowers we will see you lying
> side-by-side as you did in
> your beds, a solace of sorts:
> Death cannot separate
> our two inseparables!

Ernst fell ill with scarlet fever on 1 January 1834, the day after Luise died. Four days later, 4 January, was the young boy's fifth birthday. We know little of Ernst's response to his sister's death but it was certainly devastating. The siblings were particularly close: "inseparables," "knife and fork," the family called them.

At age five children still have difficulty grasping the permanence of death. They think that the deceased may yet return. More troubling, children at Ernst's age believe that their thoughts and feelings may cause or reverse a death.[148] These many complex and deeply felt emotions were combined with the cruelties of the boy's illness and the doctor's remedies. Little wonder, then, that during the two weeks of his illness, Ernst often lapsed into stupors that caused the family to fear he had died.

These reversals were a torture for the child and his parents. The doctors told them that the case was hopeless yet still insisted on plying their trade. Ernst was bled from his arms on three separate occasions: the wounds soon ulcerated. As with Luise, Ernst was blistered around the neck with mustard plasters, resulting in itching and bleeding. The child's teeth chattered when he was forced to endure lying under frozen flannels, part of a practice of the day that also included stripping the patient naked and dousing him with cold water.

Sufferers were frequently given emetic tartar twice a day to induce vomiting.[149] In an extreme case such as Ernst's, he would likely have been forced to gargle a tincture of myrrh or—in a remedy popular across Europe—a slight admixture of nightshade with honey of roses and infusion of roses.[150] A blend of mercury, nitric acid, olive oil, lard, and ointment of mercury[151] was massaged into Ernst's scalp, causing him to wail in protest.

Friedrich had watched his daughter suffer terribly. He felt grief and guilt over failing to help ease her misery from disease and doctors. These feelings were now combined with the terror of watching Ernst endure even longer. It all seemed too much: *Quickly now*, he urged his youngest son, *follow your sister, do not let her travel alone.* Later, Friedrich wrote another poem about this terrible time:

> Astonishing, how the heart endures
> what we thought unendurable!
> Holding hope against the pain:
> breaking him more each day.
>
> We hope and hope, 'til hopelessness
> turns to cherished life,
> hope given too late:
> life had forsaken you.

Ernst's final treatment displays how desperate the doctors had become. Their family doctor, Johann Friedrich Kittlinger, had been attending the boy. In the last five days, they called in an associate professor of surgery from the University of Erlangen, Johann Simon Dietz.[152] "I noticed at once that the doctor had little hope," Luise wrote, "and even if he should recover (unlikely as that was) he feared for his mental health."[153] They applied mercury ointments, or *quecksilber*, an effort so unorthodox that those who used it were often called "quick-silver doctors"—what is known today as a quack.[154] Despite all this, Luise wrote, Ernst "let us proceed and obeyed his father and me until the moment of his death."[155]

By 14 January, Ernst had stopped speaking, other than an occasional violent cry of *Mother!* "in a voice so different from his own," Luise recalled. "I will hear it always."[156] On 16 January, Luise felt herself dragged[157] awake in the early morning hours. She rushed to Ernst. "His eyes were already broken, dying," she wrote. The boy fell asleep, unable to feel even his mother's final kisses. He died at half past three.

Luise felt that grief might burst her heart asunder. "I asked God for a little, just a little, consolation." With an inward cry of desperation, she turned to her Bible, which fell open to this passage from the Gospel of John: *Father, I want those you have given me to be with me where I am.*[158] "These words may have a different meaning for others," she wrote, "but they strengthened me wonderfully. It was to me a promise, a divine promise, of reunion."[159]

Inséparables

Inseparables now, alas, separated by death.
Siblings by birth and by inclination, tender
birds who were made for each other!
And you, brother, clinging to her so.
And you, sister, forever beside him!
There in your bright cage, your room,
sitting on your perches, your chairs,
forever side by side, together.
If he sat on the right, she sat
on the left; if he tilted his head left,
she tilted hers right, till your two
small heads touched, so lightly,
one against the other.
Then again, if he sat on the left
and she on the right, as they
often did, then their heads
tilted in the new direction,
finding each other again.
So you loved each other, and
so this love was reciprocal, never
changing save for where you sat.
What you ate, you ate together.
What you drank, you drank together.
What you played, sang, jumped, joked,
all of your lives you lived together.
And so you died together.

When her chest was crushed, caught
in the vulture's iron claws—
that vulture from which no love,
no gilded cage, no bird is safe;
that was when his head tilted,
not to the left or the right, but down
onto his chest, never to lift again.
And let us bury them together now,
under tears, at the foot of the Tree of Life,
where we weep for them in dark shadow.
They are not there, they have taken wing
to sing in the light, in the treetops,
supping gold fruit, sipping nectar goblets,
perched beside each other, side-by-side
on the branches of life, as one again.
There they never again hang their heads.
They lift them together, gently touching.
You are happy there, you are well,
united in love, not missing those
who miss you here, my little birds,
inseparable, never separated in death.

This poem illustrates the children's genuine and tender love for each other. For his title, he chose a word borrowed from French, Italian and Latin for lovebird parrots, "Inséparables." The double meaning, combined as *inseparable lovebird parrots*, creates a moving portrait of Luise and Ernst, whom Friedrich often referred to as "my two dearest and loveliest children."[160] Even their father's use of the word reciprocal,[161] which seems slightly out of place, was chosen with care. Modern researchers use that precise word to define the type of relationship Friedrich described in his children.

One observational study found that relations between preschool age siblings such as Luise and Ernst are far more *reciprocal* than *complementary*. In early childhood, siblings share a daily life of great intimacy and emotional importance.[162] Their often intense feelings are usually expressed between themselves in a surprisingly layered relationship.[163] Yet sibling bonds are the least understood and most under-studied of all family ties despite their vital role in children's social development.[164] They contribute significantly to interdependence and pro-social behavior.[165]

Even very young children display empathy, nurturance, and a subtle understanding of their elaborate relationship patterns with siblings.[166] Their reciprocal emotional support is established early in life, particularly between preschool aged children.[167] A sense of connection and dependency in a close-knit family, such as the Rückerts, can be a source of great comfort during the early years before the age of five.[168] This reveals itself in camaraderie, intimacy, support and—between brothers and sisters—mutual concern rather than conflict.[169]

Or as Friedrich observed, *siblings by birth and by inclination.*

I repeat as I heard them
words with her mother, though
not out of grief, loathing or
some vague premonition:

"So many lovely things.
Would you like a treat?
A toy?" Wearily, she replied:
"No, nothing more, nothing."

Better still if she had said
good words for bad times—
How I admire the one who
first coined that phrase.

With his little sister gone, her
brother saw our terror that
he would leave us too.
"No!" he said, "I'm staying."

Yes! We took you at your word.
Our gate was locked against
your sister so she would not
take you with her.

> But we knew you were
> inseparable: "knife and fork,"
> we used to call you.
> Away with these fancies!
>
> Our food is tasteless,
> set on a table
> with a broken fork.
> Little knife, stay with us!
>
> You have joined the others.
> Slight and graceful, you have
> a place set in heaven,
> set alongside life itself.

This poem was likely written shortly after Luise's death during the two-week period of Ernst's illness, or is at least intended as representative of Friedrich's feelings during that time. The two children, so close in age, were constant companions.

Sibling relationships between those of preschool and toddler age are notably intense, much more than with older siblings, parents or friends. The children spend far more time interacting with each other and come to know each other extremely well, even at a young age. One observational study found that the complex emotional interaction between siblings at this age is uninhibited, "both positive and hostile emotions are freely expressed."[170] Another study of three- to five-year-old siblings—precisely the ages of Ernst and Luise—discovered that age hierarchy and gender were irrelevant to the intense nature of this sibling bond.[171]

This may be why the family often called Ernst and Luise "knife and fork"[172]—utensils that are most assuredly reciprocal in German table manners. Although the table setting is similar to most Western countries, with forks on the left and knives on the right, in practice many Germans continuously hold their fork in one hand and their knife in the other. The knife is used to cut and guide food onto the fork. The utensils even remain together after the meal, being laid side-by-side along the plate, facing inward in the 5 o'clock position.[173] In other poems, Rückert was to make further reference to the children's inseparable characters, now united in heaven, a knife and fork *set alongside life itself.*

> Sitting on your mother's knee,
> your sweet chatter is interrupted
> by painful screams: your brother
> pushes his way in. This then is
> how it all ends.
> Your mother catches you!
> Her deep grief seeks to
> sink into memory and sorrow,
> yet again your brother cries,
> dying as you died from this
> dreadful disease.
> In death as in life you endure much,
> as a dove among the vultures.
> They at least recover, thank God!
> Now you walk, dear heart, unseen
> in a house of silent dreams.
> How I hoped that you would rule
> these wild young savages, lauded
> and celebrated, the picture of
> grace and tradition.
> Soon they will forget you.
> They do not feel the measure
> of your loss as I do.
> But your breath, a breeze over
> your grave, will help me rule
> this unruly storm of boys.
> Brothers, think! Your sister
> is gone while you yet live.
> If you recover and rouse yourself,
> hush now hush! Young vulture,
> hearty screamer, we bury
> our dove today.

Ernst had also taken ill. Rückert's recollection of Luise's final moments was interrupted by the boy's screams on the day they buried his sister. Friedrich did not resent his other children's lives, despite referring to them as a storm of boys,[174] wild savages[175] and vultures.[176] Quite the opposite: he was a devoted and attentive father to each of his sons. This poem, however, captures the grieving poet's sense of being overwhelmed during those terrible weeks when both his children were dying of scarlet fever.

Past and present combine in a poem of immediacy and pain. This sense of unified time is an expected aspect of mourning, demonstrating that there is no connection between the intensity of the memory of our dead, the acuteness of our grief, and the number of years since the death.[177] Decades later Rückert was able to reconstruct the smallest details of his children's deaths with uncanny immediacy and clarity,[178] a phenomenon that arises throughout the life cycles of many bereaved parents.[179]

> The greatest suffering at the death of a friend does not occur immediately upon the event. It comes when the world has forgotten that you have cause to weep; for when the eyes are dry, the heart is often bleeding. There are hours,—no, they are more concentrated than hours,—there are moments, when the thought of a lost and loved one, who has perished out of your family circle, suspends all interest in everything else; when the memory of the departed floats over you like a wandering perfume, and recollections come in throngs with it, flooding the soul with grief.—Nehemiah Adams[180]

**My angel, my little angel,
come and play but not
with these little devils,
your many brothers.**

**I know you would love to
dance in our halls, to weave
between your brothers. It
costs so little for you to**

**come to us in Neuses, where
I had hoped to bury you.
Still, you come to us from
above, neither near nor far.**

**Here you join in their games
at rest or at play; and if
they do not see you,
I see you, in-between.**

A struggling child puts the lie to any Faustian fantasies of bargaining our souls to gain our desires. Many parents have offered to God or the devil their lives if only their children could survive.[181] Alas, the bargain is not struck.

Rückert relied on similar traditions, desperately putting an old saying to the test: "Those who are *said* to be dead *live* longer."[182] He spoke to his friends of Luise having already passed, even while she lay dying. The overwhelmed father did the same while Ernst was ill, a full eight days before the boy died.[183] The hope was superstitious nonsense, to be sure, but before and after his children's deaths, Friedrich was not himself. He was willing to try anything.

Luise and Ernst were buried in Erlangen, some 46 miles (75km) from the Rückert ancestral home in Neuses.[184] The decision was made in the first days after their deaths, when the bereaved are nearly incapable of rational, long-term thought. An inability to initiate and maintain organized activity is a primary characteristic of acute grief.[185] Friedrich and his wife may have been influenced by public sentiment regarding a relatively new tradition.

In 1527, Martin Luther had expressed a desire for graves to be located away from churches and outside of towns in separate, peaceful locations, where mourners could reflect and commune.[186] Over time, monastic burial places were closed, giving weight to public health arguments that ultimately led to relocations. By the 19th century, Coburg had shifted from church burials to garden cemeteries, marked by orderly rows and individual headstones.[187]

Rückert came to regret his choice, as he wrote in this and other poems. Although they lived in Erlangen at the time, he yearned to have Luise's grave closer to Neuses, where he knew they would ultimately settle. This was but one custom that would haunt the broken father. Yet in time he found a different solace.

Friedrich's declarations prior to his children's deaths were equal parts anguish and the onset of his own timeline of sorrow. One scholar suggests that the moment we start to mourn is highly personal and different for each individual. Douglas Davies, an expert in the history, theology and sociology of death with the University of Durham, coined the phrase "Grief Mean Time" (GMT) to indicate when actual mourning begins. "Experience counts," he wrote. "The question 'when is death?' thus becomes 'when is grief?'"[188]

I learned of my daughter's passing two days after her death. I still refer to that evening as "the day I learned my daughter died" to indicate when my grief began. Author Cara Paiuk's father died of cancer shortly after her fourth birthday. As an adult, she relates that her few memories of him are flimsy, flickering and distorted with time. "What I lost was intangible—an idea, a dream, a whisper of a parent," she writes. "I am mourning a past that never was and a father I will never know."[189] Paiuk's sense of loss may at times seem hazy and undefined.

Journalist Philip Yancey lost his father a month after his first birthday. However, it was not until the author was eighteen that he learned of disturbing events that contributed to the death. "The most important fact of my father's death I learned by chance, from a scrapbook," he said.[190] Philip's father, a twenty-three-year-old husband and parent of two, died of polio after being removed from his "iron lung" in a doomed attempt at faith healing.

The death had cast a pall over Yancey's life long before he learned that his father's treatment had been cut short against medical advice. This was something else entirely. "Once exposed," the author confesses, "the mystery of my father's death acquires a new, compulsive power."[191] Although nearly two decades had passed, Yancey's reaction was typical of the first year after a sudden, unexpected loss. Survivors often seem to obsess over the death, replaying it in their minds, filling in details that they do not know and may never learn.[192] In a very real way, an important aspect of Philip's grief began the shocking moment he read a few newspaper clippings in the family scrapbook.[193]

Another *beginning* of grief may be associated with identity loss, such as occurs with Alzheimer's disease or the slow advancement of dementia, when valued interaction with loved ones declines along with social recognition of the afflicted as a *person*. Survivors relate that they mourned these losses in prelude to grief that began at the end of biological life.

Davies concluded his essay on the timing of sorrow by suggesting that the onset of grief is also a start of something else: "Death can mean the beginning of a sensed presence of the dead, or of an eternal God with whom a sensed affinity seems to guarantee one's own immortality."[194] This seems to have been the case with Rückert.

The grieving father often speaks of experiencing Luise and Ernst, of their places in heaven and with their family on earth. To Friedrich, the invisible and visible worlds were intertwined, as in this poem written that same spring:

> All that is in heaven
> resonates on earth:
> their sister's smile
> among our boys at play.

Rückert takes some comfort in the thought that his daughter is with them in spirit, but he does not stop with sentimental cliché. Luise, the little angel, walks among *these little devils* but none of her brothers senses her presence.[195] Friedrich, however, is absolutely clear: *I see you, in-between.* Reading this as figurative seems presumptuous. It also flies in the face of the lived reality of bereavement.

In 1995, researchers interviewed 1603 bereaved people about sensing of the presence of their dead. Five hundred sixty-one reported experiencing their loved ones in their homes, while driving, in a dream or when ill. Only 23 individuals—barely 1.4 percent—were uncertain if their sensations were real at that moment or merely memories.[196]

Christine Valentine with the University of Bath relates that in the Centre for Death and Society's work with the bereaved there have been numerous occasions when interviewers and interviewees sensed an active and palpable presence of the deceased in the room.[197]

Rückert was a skilled poet: his analogies and metaphors are readily apparent. He also had a gift for plain talk. He communicated the silent words of grief in what German-born Israeli philosopher Gershom Scholem called the "completely unsymbolic language" of lament.[198] "For poets do not share the doubt that most mystics have in regard to language," Scholem observed. "It is their belief in the mystery of language which has become audible."[199]

> Did you ever know, dear, how much you took away with you when you left? You have stripped me even of my past, even of the things we never shared.—C.S. Lewis[200]

**Carry on, go ahead, but
don't expect me to join in.
You rang in the new year with
shots that pierced my heart.**

**I woke to the sound, startled,
but in the next room, her
tiny pale face did not
stir in her bed.**

**It is beyond me now:
that I once took to the
streets at midnight,
roaming, celebrating.**

**Here and there a candle
is burning in a window:
the ties broken within
cannot be seen without.**

**The New Year's revelers arrive,
street performers and musicians,
wishing us a happy new year,
asking a coin for their trouble.**

> **Street performers and musicians,**
> **your good wishes for a new year**
> **have arrived too late,**
> **my happiness died in the old.**
>
> **Musicians, clergy, relations,**
> **come to wish us well, ring the**
> **bells of the new year in a**
> **heavenly church for my little bride.**
>
> **And you, street performers,**
> **Go, off with you, play elsewhere!**
> **She dances at a different wedding**
> **and has no need of fiddles.**
>
> ——
>
> **The raucous cries of sheer joy**
> **that usually rip at my ears**
> **now rip apart the heart in my chest**
> **since you are gone.**

Fireworks were costly in early 19th-century Coburg, so the midnight celebrations for a new year were often accompanied by the sound of gunfire. The following day, revelers would go door-to-door wishing their neighbors happiness. They started when it was still dark, as early as 5 o'clock in the morning. Guns were fired to announce their arrival, but this was often accompanied by the sound of fiddles, drums, horns or any other instrument that was handy.[201]

The raucous celebrations of the night before were replaced with noisy but good-humored traditional greetings, such as "Wishing you a happy New Year, health, peace and harmony in this life and eternal joy in the next."[202] It was customary to give the visitors food and drink as well as a coin or two.[203] The chiming of the bells on New Year's Day was not unexpected, but for Friedrich their celebratory nature rang false, out of sync with the terrible reality of his daughter's body. Luise had died the day before, on New Year's Eve.

> My angel, my little angel,
> you hope to fly away!
> Won't you stay? Say you will!
> You stretch your wings
> with such impatience.
>
> My angel, my little angel,
> you hope to float away!
> You grow in loveliness, a blow
> to my heart each day:
> you are too lovely for life.
>
> My angel, my little angel,
> you hope to slip away.
> You grow lovelier each hour
> as a new fear grips me:
> perhaps I love you too much.

Luise was buried at 9 a.m. on 3 January 1834. The corpse midwife, or "laying-out woman,"[204] had washed the body and clothed it in Luise's favorite white dress.[205] She placed the child in her coffin with a garland of myrtle on the child's forehead and surrounding her with flowers. Coffins had become the rule by the 17th century, particularly in funerals that included a laying-out. Many Protestant coffins were painted with biblical quotes.[206] "Two of the gorgeous red hyacinths I had planted with the children had bloomed that day," Luise's mother wrote. "I placed them on her chest, looking as she did like the bride of an angel."[207]

The bride was the richest and most developed of the female images applied to children in German funeral verse.[208] In another poem, "The New Year's revelers arrive," Friedrich refers to ringing the bells *in a heavenly church for my little bride*, implying that he now thought of Luise as a bride of heaven. The image was heavily influenced by biblical passages and had been commonplace in Germany for two centuries.[209]

On My First Son

Farewell, thou child of my right hand, and joy;
My sin was too much hope of thee, loved boy.
Seven years thou wert lent to me, and I thee pay,
Exacted by thy fate, on the just day.
Oh, could I lose all father now! For why
Will man lament the state he should envy?
To have so soon 'scaped world's and flesh's rage,
And, if no other misery, yet age?
Rest in soft peace, and, asked, say here doth lie
Ben Jonson his best piece of poetry;
For whose sake, henceforth, all his vows be such,
As what he loves may never like too much.
—Ben Jonson[210]

To be dead must be bliss,
dying is no great pain either;
harder by far is watching a loved
one die, though that passes;
if we could be left in peace,
if not for the worst, the burial.
The morbid and the freeloaders arrive
***en masse*, extending our torment,**
the rabble of the funeral procession,
who at the tolling of the redemption bell
carry the dead from this house that
I am also desperate to leave, to be
at last outside, but then there is
the reception, the feasting,
a traditional horror that intrudes
on my soul, when what I need most
is time for memory and prayer.
What, did we have a child,
rear her and lose her, so these
strangers could glut themselves
on Christening cake and funeral cake?
Peace, dear heart, try not to swear!

In late 18th- and early 19th-century Germany, funerals and burial feasts had slowly progressed from communal gatherings to events of socially sanctioned opulence. Contemporary articles condemned the trend as vulgar, an "unnecessary extravagance" that placed emotional and financial burdens on the mourners.[211] These trends had a long tradition.

"Death watch" dances[212] were part of European funerary traditions throughout the Middle Ages. They included drinking, conjurations and loud or even lewd carousing.[213] Singing and laughing during these funeral watches remained an active practice through the 18th century.[214] A century later the traditions were seen as distasteful.

When Tennyson's close friend, Arthur Hallam, died in 1833 at the age of twenty-two, the poet began work on one of the great requiems of the English language. Hallam had been engaged to the poet's sister. Fearing that his masterful lament had grown overlong, Tennyson urged his sister:

> Peace; come away: the song of woe
> Is after all an earthly song:
> Peace; come away: we do him wrong
> To sing so wildly: let us go.[215]

In Rückert's day the festivities were less festive but they could be onerous to the bereaved. Added to this was another financial burden. By the 17th century, there was a surprising volume of consolatory writings printed on the loss of children in Germany, demonstrating private and public awareness of the anguish felt by bereaved parents. While the funeral, burial and wake could take a heavy toll, families often bore the additional cost of funeral booklets, which usually contained a sermon, a biography of the deceased, speeches, and poetry. Print runs usually ran from 100 to 300 copies. Some printers kept old editions for their display catalogues. The tradition was known to bankrupt some mourners. These lavish booklets fell out of favor by the mid–18th century, condemned with other baroque practices as pompous and aggrandizing.[216]

New trends emerged to fill the void, and by the time Rückert buried his children, the bereaved faced other crass customs in the form of lavish funerals and burial feasts. With such a long history supporting these cruelly intrusive traditions, it is little wonder that Friedrich cried out, *Peace, dear heart, try not to swear!*

And why shouldn't I curse the custom of feasting after a funeral?
We go to the house to bake almond cakes because we buried our daughter.
The corpse midwife takes cakes,
hot from the oven, for our ailing boy;
he should have been able to visit
the spot set aside for his sister!
And why shouldn't I curse the custom of feasting after a funeral?

In Rückert's day, a funeral was often followed by a reception held at the bereaved family's home, known as the burial feast.[217] The tradition is not unlike a wake and serves a similar purpose. Where a funeral provides therapeutic and structured ritual, the wake is a time for openness, fond memories and tears. Both play important, though separate, roles in mourning.[218] The procession first gathered at the home for a vigil with the body, following which they carried the remains for burial. The feast following Luise's funeral was particularly difficult for the grieving father.

Death is destructive. A mourner's sense of security is often ripped away, leaving acute feelings of frustration, anger, sadness, helplessness, terror, loneliness, despondency and hurt.[219] The bereaved may focus these volatile reactions toward funeral professionals, family members and friends. One counselor reports that he was often surprised to see mild-mannered people transformed by grief into raging, temperamental and resentful individuals.[220]

Friedrich's mocking reactions are not uncommon. He lashes out at the wake itself, the visitors and the corpse midwife[221] tasked with preparing the body. He even takes exception to the platters of almond cakes, a traditional sweet served at German Christening celebrations and burial feasts. Ernst was already ill at the time and was unable to attend the funeral or visit his sister's grave. He died two weeks later.

Bitter-Sweet

Ah, my dear angry Lord,
Since Thou dost love, yet strike,
Cast down, yet help afford;
Sure I will do the like.

I will complain, yet praise,
I will bewail, approve;
And all my sour-sweet days
I will lament, and love.

—George Herbert[222]

I have covered you with roses,
too many to count,
so many that I am blind
to your death.

Then I fancy that you are still
alive, still mine,
perhaps only a dream,
or so it seems.

> Until the wind rises and lifts
> the roses away.
> I rediscover, to my horror,
> that you lived.

I dread mornings. I wake to a world without my daughter in it. Many bereaved parents know this particular pain. Throughout the day, we may not consciously *think* of our children. There is no need. They inhabit our minds the same way our brains tell us to breathe or blink. They are always here.

Barbara Eden lost her 35-year-old son, Matthew, to a heroin overdose in 2001. Ten years later, she wrote that although she still finds joy in life, part of her will always be missing. "Matthew is never out of my mind," she wrote, "and the pain of losing him and of missing him doesn't get less.... I still think of him every day and dream of him every night."[223]

Naps are slightly different. A short doze may leave me a tad hazy for a few seconds when I wake. That is when the full impact of my loss slams into me. My first reaction, my most frequent lament, is torn out of me in a torrent of pain: "Dear Lord, I want to hold her in my arms again!" Her absence is in my cry. I desperately want her near.

Rückert wrote the poem below, "Once I held the reality of you," in a similar gasp of sudden anguish. It is a rough sketch, unfinished and raw, which may explain why his son, Heinrich, did not include it in the first 1872 edition of *Songs on the Death of Children*.

Friedrich clutches the pastels of Luise and Ernst, realizing their cruel irony: the images are a sweet reminder of when his children were alive, within arm's reach; and a bitter confirmation that he can no longer hold them, save in a pair of two-dimensional portraits.[224]

> Once I held the reality of you,
> young and alive;
> unforgettable, a dream swept
> away too soon.
>
> We need irony to endure the
> dictates of heaven:
> these will have to do for now,
> portraits of you.

Blindness, dreams and absence are frequent themes in *Songs on the Death of Children*. In another poem, probably written in late January or early February of 1834, Friedrich weeps that he cannot see even the pastels of his dead children in the bitter winter air:

> Oh sad wintering tears,
> you eyelash-squeezing tears!
>
> Soon you will thaw in the
> warmth of pain, freezing tears.
>
> Soon the embers in my heart will
> burn you away, chilling tears.
>
> Their portraits are blurry now;
> oh, you cruelly soothing tears!
>
> Oh, my children are gone, save
> in you, newly falling tears.

Portraits (or photographs) may provide much-needed confirmation of the reality of our loved ones' lives. Visiting a grave offers a similar sense of solace and communion in the difficult adjustment to a world where they no longer exist.[225] For this reason, the seemingly morbid sentiment of the song, "I have covered you with roses," is actually quite useful: an occasional sharp reminder of our new future. "Denial and disbelief are initial reactions to the stress you are undergoing," counseled Earl Grollman.[226] Rückert communicates his genuine terror at "rediscovering" the grave by using a shocking word, *horror*[227]—which was intended to be as jarring and out of place as the death of his child.

> **When your heart dwells
> on crowded thoughts—
> "What if this had happened?"—
> when, alas, it did not,
> say, when chance turned one way
> rather than turning another;
> the doubts never end,
> if they do not end your faith:
> happiness in this life
> is not left to chance;
> for chance itself is of necessity
> part of an unending web,
> whose net spans the globe,
> whose fixed strands
> follow an unknowable course;
> straining from the center
> and returning to it.**

The doubts never end, if they do not end your faith. In this poem, Rückert describes an easily overlooked aspect of grief. It is also one of the most persistent. Our doubts continue, relentlessly, it seems, and yet this is expected and a surprising sign of active belief, as Miguel de Unamuno observed in a mirrored echo of Rückert: "A faith that does not doubt is a dead faith."[228]

In 2014, researchers found that among the many mourners who experience a spiritual crisis after a loss, most express resentment and doubt toward God and significant changes in their beliefs.[229] The bereaved are beset with deep questions and crippling fears of future loss. They struggle to find meaning in life. This can lead to a sense of abandonment by our dead loved ones, our faith communities and the divine. Such concerns can cause others to condemn mourners as faithless because they challenge pat answers and glib platitudes, adding to the anxiety and helplessness of the grieving.[230] Death expert Paul Irion decried this approach: "In the religious community we need to be reminded often that faith is not a substitute for grief, but a resource."[231]

There are no easy answers, but in this poem Friedrich expresses a new perspective: *Chance itself is of necessity part of an unending web.* Chance, like doubt and faith, strains from the center and returns to it. The poet's observation is hardly the point. The act of introspection itself is helpful, though often painful. Mourners who find a way to make sense of a loss feel less distress within the first year after the death.[232]

Nineteenth-century poets were not seeking to construct a new self so much as attempting to rediscover their true selves.[233] In this regard, Tennyson's insight, written fifteen years later in 1849, would have come as no surprise to Rückert: "There lives more faith in honest doubt, /Believe me, than in half the creeds."[234]

Friedrich's faith that his children's deaths have meaning, and his hope for a future reunion, eases the sense of solitude in this poem. Ultimately our sorrow is wholly centered within ourselves, straining outward and returning home. One role that grief plays is to force us, unwillingly but inevitably, to come to terms with our loss and all the changes that entails. In this way, change is as much *from* something as *to* something.[235]

> When you come to think of it there can be no such thing as chance from God's point of view. Since He is omniscient His acts have no consequences which He has

not foreseen and taken into account and intended.... This is not Predestination: your will is perfectly free: but all physical events are adapted to fit in as God sees best with the free actions He knows we are going to do.—C.S. Lewis[236]

> "It's too hard, what I've got.
> It's too much, what I fight.
> I thought I could beat it,
> but I've got to give in."
>
> "It's too much, what I've got.
> It takes me with it.
> I tried to resist
> but I've got to go."
>
> "I knew this would happen:
> I can't stand it! I tried for
> so long but no more.
> It's too hard for me now."
>
> I whispered in my daughter's
> ear when I lost her:
> "If you cannot stay with me
> I will go with you."
>
> She took me at my word
> and took my words
> with her, as death has now
> turned them against me.
>
> "And know that you do wrong
> when you dwell on suffering."
> I do not dwell on this pain:
> it breaks my heart on its own.

This poem inspires a number of personal thoughts. Influential German scholar Annemarie Schimmel observed that because of the deaths of Rückert's children "darkness fell over his world that he could not overcome." He wrote this poem, she noted, "because he was unable to follow his daughter as he had promised."[237] I too think of promises I made that I desperately wish to keep, if only Jess were here. Reality would have it otherwise.

During and after the American Civil War, thousands of people wrote they could not quite *realize* the deaths of their loved ones. The term had a slightly different usage at the time. It meant, in essence, that they could not "make it real" in their minds. "With a heart depressed with a dark and bitter grief," wrote one man of a fallen friend in 1864, "I cannot realize that he is gone, that I am to see his gallant figure or hear his cheering voice no more."[238] Abraham Lincoln used this familiar expression in a letter to twenty-two-year-old Mary Frances "Fanny" McCullough, who had lost her father in December of 1862: "You can not now realize that you will ever feel better.... I have had experience enough to know what I say." Lincoln's eleven-year-old son, Willie, had died ten months earlier. But for Fanny to experience life's joys on some distant day, he wrote, she must also realize, or make real, her current sorrow. Then, Lincoln assured her, "the memory of your dear Father, instead of an agony, will yet be a sad sweet feeling in your heart, of a purer, and holier sort than you have known before."[239] In this same sense, I fully realize my daughter's absence: this is all too real. We *realize* grief. It is known to us, a constant companion.

Friedrich recreates how he envisions his three-year-old daughter would have spoken if she could. German lament poetry frequently had the dead speaking from a place of wisdom and comfort, usually with eloquence beyond their years, as in this 1658 poem written in the voice of one-year-old Maria Sophia Mayer:

I finished my race ere I knew how to run it:
I ended my time ere I knew how to tell it.
Now I sit at a Christian's feast—my body

and soul free of oh so many sorrows!—embraced in peace and rest.²⁴⁰

However, Friedrich makes no attempt to give Luise's dialogue either adult profundity or a childish tone. Instead, he writes her "voice" with heartbreaking simplicity. The final stanzas shift the poem to her father's terrible present. Rückert's dark undertone is as much regret as resignation.

I am reminded of a line from Psalm 88 by the priestly choir known as the sons of Korah: "You have taken away my companions and loved ones. Darkness is my closest friend."²⁴¹ Equating grief and darkness is not as far-fetched as it might seem. Scholars generally agree that the original word in Psalm 88 was probably *tzalamut*, meaning deep darkness, almost certainly the same term used in Psalm 23. Like David and Rückert, we are walking through the valley of the shadow of death, a valley dark beyond imagining.

Tradition holds that David wrote Psalm 23 while a young man tending his flock. Picturesque, to be sure, but unlikely. The King James Bible translators took it as two words, *tzal mavet*, the shadow of death. This may have captured the meaning of the original better than a literal translation, which might be rendered as "through the darkest valley."²⁴² Deep darkness, the shadow of death—these are phrases of a mature man acquainted with sorrow; a king who had lost two sons.

Psalm 88 assures me that grief, this darkness, will remain with us. It is liberating, in its cruel way, to accept this reality. Ours is an abiding sorrow; a lifetime of asking and finding answers that seem like they are not answers at all, none that we might expect; yet answers nonetheless, whispered and shouted. In my ignorance before losing Jess, I might have anticipated some healing of my grief—a particularly vicious chimera. Now I know better. Miraculous healing occurs in this world, I believe, but no bereaved parents speak of it. To heal we must have our children back.

Yet as with Friedrich and so many others, there is solace from an unexpected source. I am certain that I will see my daughter again. This assurance may be cold comfort in my pain and sorrow, but it is consolation nonetheless. In silence I feel Jess near. She is somewhere, elsewhere, yet here, as close as a whisper.

Rückert's final stanza demonstrates why *Songs on the Death of Children* is not easily pigeon-holed as a collection of consolation poetry. In an inner voice, Friedrich reproaches himself for dwelling on suffering, and then quickly replies that he is not dwelling on it—grief is beyond his control.²⁴³ Reality exists regardless of his inclinations. Friedrich's insight lead literary critic Stefan Weidner to observe that this poem's "simple, linguistically undemanding verses are finer and more profound" than many similar laments.²⁴⁴

No worst, there is none. Pitched past pitch
  of grief,
More pangs will, schooled at forepangs,
  wilder wring.
Comforter, where, where is your
  comforting?....
O the mind, mind has mountains; cliffs of
  fall
Frightful, sheer, no-man-fathomed. Hold
  them cheap

May who ne'er hung there. Nor does long our small
Durance deal with that steep or deep.
—Gerard Manley Hopkins[245]

> When I prayed over my child:
> "Lord, spare her for me!"
> a gentle voice spoke inside:
> *as is best for her and for you.*
>
> You do as you please with her,
> Lord, not as I asked of you;
> but still this inner voice, gentle:
> *it is best for me and for her.*
>
> It is best for a mother and
> child to be separated? not that
> I can see; still, a gentle voice:
> *as is best, Lord, before you.*

On first reading, this poem may sound cliché-ridden and overly sentimental. But then I think of Holocaust survivor Corrie ten Boom, whose positive, seemingly simplistic books are easy to dismiss until we learn how painfully she earned the right to be heard.[246] Taken out of context, Rückert's refrain, *as is best*, could unwisely be judged as optimistic twaddle; but knowing Friedrich as we do, we may consider the long, dark valley that led him to these words.

Rückert wrote many laments expressing anger, loneliness and pain. He was derisive of platitudes and trite answers. Here his *inner voice* is reassuring in the face of a question that plagues many bereaved parents: Why my child and not me? Job-like, we hold accountable a God who professes to hear us and to care.

Job lost all ten of his children in a single day. His wife, unjustly condemned by history as a shrew, was defiant in her terrible sorrow. She too lost the sons and daughters she carried in her womb, whom she suckled at her breast. "Why do you still hold on to your integrity?" she demanded of her husband. "Curse God, and die!"[247] Pause a moment to consider the faith involved. Job's wife has no doubt whatsoever that God exists. Oh, he lives all right, just look at what he's done. Her children are dead, her life shattered and now God picks on her husband. Unlike Job's visiting friends, she surely knows that they have done nothing to deserve such misery. It is entirely unjustified, unfair, obscene. How could God do this? With a god like this, who needs enemies?[248]

Bereaved parents are at a higher risk of divorce than other couples. This remains a hotly debated topic among researchers. In 1998, Reiko Schwab with Old Dominion University reviewed existing literature and found no evidence that parental bereavement posed a higher risk of divorce.[249] However, in 2013, Torkild Hovde Lyngstad, a sociologist with the University of Oslo, conducted a detailed longitudinal data study of the entire population of Norway. Lyngstad observed that bereaved parents have higher divorce rates than other parents, regardless of family size or the births of other children after the death. Time somewhat increased this risk.[250]

Counselors write of frustrations over patient perceptions of the question, feeling that the sense of an inevitable split is harmful and may even be something of a self-fulfilling prophecy. Judith Bernstein, a practicing psychologist, acknowledged that while the loss of a child caused intense stress on marriages, she did not see a higher divorce rate among her patients.[251]

A split is not inevitable. Rather, this information indicates the extreme stress of grief, the need for attention to our actions and the importance of giving ourselves time. In post-war Britain, for example, with the death toll catastrophically high, physicians frequently used words such as "strain" or "worry" to describe grieving patients, with one doctor commenting in a patient's file, "stress—death of husband."[252] It seems foolish to ignore this painful aspect of mourning. At the same time, it may be equally foolish to assume that divorce is a foregone conclusion for bereaved parents. Perhaps, being aware of the stress that a child's death places on any relationship, couples may be in a better position to be gentle, calm and understanding.[253]

Whatever the many complex reasons for divorce among bereaved parents, one common thread is precisely what happens in the Book of Job. They are hurting so they quarrel.

In the first terror of losing his children, Job tears his robe, shaves his head and repeats almost by rote: "The Lord gave and the Lord has taken away; may the name of the Lord be praised."[254] This was not his only response.

Job did not curse God, as his wife in her anguish demanded, but he would come to curse the day he was born. For the next thirty-seven chapters, he rails, cajoles, pleads and demands an accounting of God. He says God has denied him justice and brought his soul to bitterness. "For sighing has become my daily food; my groans pour out like water," Job cried. "I have no peace, no quietness; I have no rest, but only turmoil." And later: "If ever my grief were measured or my sorrow put on a scale, it would outweigh the sands of the ocean: that is why I am desperate."[255]

Job refused to relent; he demanded answers. He seeks justice from God. He persists in asking *why* only to hear a voice in the whirlwind explaining, well, nothing. At the end of the book, God stands with Job, declaring that the bereaved father spoke correctly about him in all his anguished questions. Later God would list three men of great righteousness: Noah, Daniel and Job.[256]

The wisdom of the book is not in theodicy, examining the cause and effect of evil or Job's suffering, but in God's presence. He commended Job's honesty and acknowledged his pain. Job was not forgotten.[257] "People are prepared for everything," wrote author and theologian Frederick Buechner, "except for the fact that beyond the darkness of their blindness there is a great light."[258]

From our happy moments you are missing,
from our joyous throng you are missing.
Swallows announce the summer;
from their glad tidings you are missing.
Flowers bloom in the meadow;
from this flowering soil you are missing.
Roses laugh gaily as they open;
from their laughter you are missing.
The world has found joy and delight;
from its happy find you are missing.
Your brothers form a circle and dance;
why are you missing from the round?
Mother tells a fairy tale so well;
why are you missing it?
You are missing, I don't know why,
for no reason at all, you are missing.
We miss you each moment,
each second you are missing,
from every place, save as a wound in
my heart, where you are never missing.
What ails my heart? the lack of you,
never again whole, for you are missing.

This is what it feels like when someone dies—some part of us that cannot be measured has been taken away, we are not ourselves, we are not whole, we face each day soul-crippled. In this poem, Rückert uses repetition to telling effect, reminding us that his daughter's death, her absence, the lack of her, is a wound and a paradox: she will never be missing from his heart, which will never be whole again, *for you are missing.*

My daughter and I used to watch foreign films. Jess could be quite adept at picking up languages. I chose her middle name, Autumn, for two reasons: it is lovely in itself and the same pronunciation (*Ah-reum*) means beautiful in Korean. For breakfast one morning, after having watched a family-friendly Samurai film the night before, my sweet four-year-old girl announced in perfect burly-man Japanese, "Time for chow." Later, a few years before she died in 2015, Jess scolded me for not teaching her other languages. Now that she is gone, our roles are reversed. Jess is teaching me a new perspective.

The French phrase for "I miss you" illustrates how my world has changed. *Tu me manques* literally means "you are missing from me." The usage is the same as in English, but the emphasis is reversed. To miss someone is to know the lack of them in our lives.

Mourning is never about us, not really. In grief we may seem self-absorbed, but this is because we are now missing something in ourselves. Our sorrow is focused on the ones we have lost. I miss my daughter, yes, yet when I think of her, I realize that she is missing from me. Each morning there is a brief millisecond when, in a dream state, I am unaware that Jess no longer exists in this world. All too soon, the knowledge returns, settling on my shoulders, an old companion. She is missing.

Friedrich expanded on this theme in another poem that appeared in *Songs on the Death of Children*. Here he again lists the many times and seasons when, hoping for their return, his children remain absent:

> The sun sets each evening,
> as does the moon at midnight;
> still, the sun rises at dawn,
> the moon at twilight.
> For you, the sun of my days,
> my nights' moon,
> there is no dawn, no twilight,
> when you will return to me.
>
> Swallows migrate in September,
> in October, nightingales;
> still, the swallow returns in March,
> the nightingale in May.
> For you, nightingale of our house,
> swallow of our hall,
> there is no home or hearth
> where you will return to me.
>
> Violets die each spring, as do
> roses before autumn;
> roses and violets return the breath
> of summer to our garden.
> Summer's breath, in the frost,
> in the garden of my heart,
> my violet and my rose died,
> nor will you return them to me.

This pain does not go away. Fighting it is useless. "Keeping busy" is a chimera and a rather callous way to treat ourselves. There is nothing we *can* do, nothing we *should* do or *must* do, but if we are lucky, we may find something, however small, that we *want* to do.

This pain will now be part of our lives, even in the *happy moments* that Friedrich describes, which do come and will come. These small pleasures may help us in the tiniest way to face each day without them, to come to terms with our new reality.

Because, after all, *tu nous manques*—they are missing from us.

> The autumn leaves can dazzle us with their magnificent colors: deep red, purple, yellow, gold, bronze, in countless variations and combinations. Then, shortly after having shown their unspeakable beauty, they fall to the ground and die.... As we look at the barren trees and remember our dead, let us be grateful for the beauty we saw in them and wait hopefully for a new spring.—Henri Nouwen, "The Autumn of Life"[259]

**Never did I see you wake
with other than a joyous laugh;
as if in a dream you picked blossoms
from the Tree of Life.**

**And so I hope, with a joyous laugh
you will now wake
from this brief dream of life
under the tree of Paradise.**

By the late Romantic period, trees and springs were often associated with slumber. In fact, most natural forces were seen as more purely sublime than human constructs.[260] For Rückert, dreams were often tied closely to Paradise, where death and life are closely attuned, as in one of his most touching ghazals[261]:

I saw her once, a little while, and then no more:
'T was Paradise on earth awhile, and then no more.
O, might I see but once again, as once before,
Through chance or wile, that shape awhile, and then no more!
Death soon would heal my grief: this heart, now sad and sore,
Would beat anew, a little while, and then no more![262]

The Paradise Tree, or Tree of Life, was also part of medieval Christmas celebrations, a precursor to the modern Christmas tree. Decorating a tree was an important part of German holiday traditions. The custom sprang from an interesting source.

In the 14th and 15th centuries, mystery plays were a popular way to reenact biblical scenes. Paradise plays were performed in front of cathedrals on Christmas Eve, which was also the feast day of Adam and Eve. An evergreen was decorated with apples to represent the Tree of Life in the Garden of Eden; it would also represent Christ himself as the tree of Paradise.

After the plays were banned and the decorating of public trees became a nuisance, many German believers continued the tradition in their homes, placing wafers to represent the Eucharist on pines. Later the wafers were replaced with candies, cookies and cakes in the shape of the Nativity, set among fruit and candles. Later still, these changed to the decorations enjoyed on Christmas trees today.[263]

In this poem, Friedrich suggests that Luise used to wake with buoyant spirits because she had dreamed of the Tree of Life, just as she now wakes from the dream of life in Paradise. The poet's association seems natural: Luise fell ill on Christmas Day.

> The passing joys of human life do not have to disappear forever. This Child will show us how to see them all in the mystery of endless day. Most precious of all joys are those that come from love. More than all else we do not want to be separated forever from those we love. He came that we may be forever with Him—and with them.—Benedict Groeschel[264]

O Christmas tree,
O Christmas dream.
How dark is your brilliance,
how broken is the dance
that, cut short, scattered
your garland.

O Christmas tree,
O Christmas dream.
The candles on each branch
burned but halfway before,
mid-celebration, we
snuffed them out.

O Christmas tree,
O Christmas dream.
The candies on each twig
are uneaten, untouched.
Ah, that you survived the
ravages of revelry.

O Christmas tree,
O Christmas dream.
With your virgin fruit,
your unburnt candles,
stand until Christmas returns,
until their memorial day.

O Christmas tree,
O Christmas dream.
When we light you again
we need buy no angel:
our pair will be here
celebrating with us.

The popular carol "O Tannenbaum" (O Fir Tree) came to be part of the holiday in Rückert's lifetime. The tune was based on a 16th-century folk song. Although it was mentioned in David Sammenhaber's lute book as late as 1590, it was the court music director of Coburg, composer Melchior Franck, who first set the tune down. The modern composition was finalized in 1819 by August Zarnack, director of education at the Royal Military Orphanage in Potsdam.

It wasn't until three years later that the connection to Christmas grew more pronounced. In 1824, Leipzig teacher Ernst Anschütz, borrowing heavily from the moody tones of Biedermeier poets, edited the lyric and added the second and third stanzas.[265] By the mid–20th century, "O Tannenbaum" was second only to "Silent Night" in popularity among German carolers.[266]

Rückert wrote his own version of "O Tannenbaum" after the deaths of Luise and Ernst. He retained the rhythm and cadence associated with the popular tune, but any similarities end there. Friedrich renamed it "O Weihnachtsbaum"—"O Christmas Tree."

Trees were a part of holiday celebrations across Europe. "I have been looking on, this evening," wrote Charles Dickens in 1850, "at a merry company of children assembled round that pretty German toy, a Christmas Tree." Dickens also described the many small, tapered candles on the tree, lighting a myriad of bright decorations and candies, much as Rückert did. Dickens meditated on the pathos of the trees:

> A moment's pause, O vanishing tree, of which the lower boughs are dark to me as yet, and let me look once more! I know there are blank spaces on thy branches, where eyes that I have loved have shone and smiled; from which they are departed.[267]

As Rückert describes, the tears and memories invoked by a Christmas tree are painful. They are also sacred. "Be those remembrances admitted with tender encouragement," wrote Dickens of his Christmas observance in 1851. "They are of the time and all its comforting and peaceful reassurances;

and of the history that re-united even upon earth the living and the dead."[268] In the final stanza of this poem, Friedrich expresses a similar thought. When Christmas returns, he writes, they need buy no angel for the tree: Ernst and Luise will be there with them.

Clinicians have observed that significant dates, such as holidays and birthdays, cause a marked increase in psychological distress for mourners.[269] Days that include family gatherings may be especially difficult. In another poem in this collection, "Now for the dark days," Friedrich speaks to the grueling nature of their first Christmas without their two youngest: *And in the midst of this dark there was a star, bright with solace: the children's joy in holy Christmas.*

My daughter's birthday is 29 November 1988, forever associating Thanksgiving weekend with memories of her. Christmas was an important part of her childhood, as it is for so many families. Jess died on 16 January 2015. These dates combine to make the entire season a time of sorrow and quiet memory, from Halloween (her favorite holiday) through New Year's Eve to Jessica's memorial day.

I treasure my holiday memories with Jess. They are precious to me, as difficult as they may be at times. Each year I remind myself that I would gladly choose twenty-six years with her— twenty-six Christmases—over none at all. She is worth this wound.

> Lost friend, lost child, lost parent, sister, brother, husband, wife, we will not so discard you! You shall hold your cherished places in our Christmas hearts, and by our Christmas fires; and in the season of immortal hope, and on the birthday of immortal mercy, we will shut out Nothing!—Charles Dickens[270]

We abolish many manners of death, end torture chambers, flattered, enlightened. Alas, the innocent sick lie in futile struggle against torturous lingering death. Yes, we grow humane; Mother Nature remains ancient, hallowed, barbaric.

Self-recrimination is all too easy in bereavement. It often leads to a sense of failure, shame and guilt.[271] Over and over we may revisit the death in our minds and the roles we played in helping, or failing to help, our loved ones.[272] I still feel this way with my daughter's addiction. *I didn't do enough*, I berate myself, or *I did too much* or *Nothing I did would have mattered.* Such unhelpful thoughts may be expressed in aggressive behavior, lashing out at the dead, at those around us, at nature and at God.[273]

Rückert holds the failings of medical care and the barbarism of nature jointly responsible for the prolonged deaths of his children.[274] Frustrated and feeling betrayed, he condemns the glorification of their humane, enlightened age while grimly acknowledging nature's barbaric rule over humanity. He had good reason.

The curatives inflicted on Luise and Ernst were little more than torture in a father's eyes. He could see the treatments were worthless even as he assisted the doctor in their application. (Other poems in this collection offer painful details.) Friedrich's sense of reproach was directed as much at himself as at physicians and the advancements of the times, whatever manners of death they may have abolished.

Breaking the cycle requires patience, reason and compassion, as Rückert knew well. In other songs the poet displays hope, peace, resolve and calm. But on this day, he gave us a peek at another side of grief, reminding us that in *all* our emotions, we are not alone.

My daughter is three months into her "very
    aggressive
treatment protocol." The clinic and hospital
    define
our world.
... I know what's important.
There is no baseline assessment for a
    mother's fear
of cancer. Therapy won't eradicate traits of
    my daughter
that truly matter.
—Kimberlyn Blum-Hyclak, *in the Garden of Life and Death*[275]

> **Perhaps it was desecration.**
> **I fear that I profaned our**
> **family life when I dedicated**
> **a collection to an uncaring**
> **world. Most of the poems**
> **had been written for another**
> **world, that of my children,**
> **now collapsed, dreams broken.**
>
> **And yet in mockery, it seems,**
> **just as their world collapsed,**
> **this latest almanac arrives**
> **with my fee, my wage of sin.**
> **So I have enough—**
> **generous fee—**
> **to pay for the graves of**
> **my children now dead.**
>
> **And was it sin, I wonder?**
> **This harp that strums the**
> **tune of my heart rather than**
> **keeping time with yours?**
> **I wasn't boastful but I was**
> **happy to flower the path**
> **before me: a path now**
> **offering only thorns.**
>
> **It is a commonplace sin:**
> **a poet seeks to unearth**
> **his inner nature. And now**
> **my songs well up from**
> **deep within this pain.**
> **To sing them is a sin**
> **perhaps, but if so,**
> **leave me to my lament.**

This latest almanac arrives, Rückert writes, referring to forty-nine new poems that were published in December 1833 as part of the *German Muses Almanac of 1834*.[276] This type of collection was a popular venue for poets. Each issue usually featured short lyric pieces from various contributors.[277]

Draftsman Carl Barth, who in the autumn of 1833 had created the engraving of Friedrich that decorates the frontispiece of the almanac,[278] published a number of his own poems in the same issue.[279] Barth was such a frequent guest in Erlangen that the Rückerts referred to him as "friend and engraver," in that order, and very nearly saw him as a part of the household.[280] Friedrich wrote a prefatory song as an introduction to Carl's poems.[281]

Rückert's likeness opposite the title page was enough to ensure a second glance by potential book owners. Despite disclaimers to the contrary, publishers are seen by readers as guarantors of the authors they present, just as authors are the guarantors of their words. In the 19th century, as today, there was a social dimension to the title page, which combines customer assurance with advertisement.[282]

Friedrich's poems in the almanac were well received. They were reprinted later that year in the first of six volumes of his collected works. Volume One included Friedrich's famous "Spring of Love,"[283] written in 1821 when he was courting his future wife, Luise Wiethaus-Fischer. The book also included an addendum, added in 1833, in which the poet asks, "Can't a father love his own daughter?"[284] This sentiment would be echoed by another bereaved father, Robert Frost, whose firstborn son Elliot died of Cholera in 1900: "Can't a man speak of his own child he's lost?"[285]

In the same volume, Friedrich had added a second addendum in early 1834. This poem is the first published lament for his children. In it, he writes that Luise is "free of grief," singing now with her brother Ernst:

> With harp and flute they
> give life to each word. There
> in the red of the coming night
> my little angels are singing,
> singing their father's songs.
> Let each note ring down
> to an unknowing world:
> sing courage to my heart,
> consolation to your mother,
> and be patient with your brothers![286]

The first volume of Rückert's collected works was hailed for its vibrant, epic verse. One venerable literary journal compared his glittering poetry to a palace from *Tales from the Thousand and One Nights*, but this was not what struck the reviewer. Noting pieces like those about Friedrich's wife and daughter, the critic concluded, "There is a cottage attached to the palace, where Rückert lives, next to a garden, serene and green, beside a gently murmuring spring. If you wish to visit Rückert, he will show you through all those magnificent rooms, and in the end you will likely prefer to rest with him a while in his modest little house."[287]

Rückert is hard on himself in this song. Phrases like *desecration, profaned, mockery*, and the bitter *my wage of sin* seem particularly hurtful at a time when he is most vulnerable. Barth's engraving may provide a clue to this onslaught of self-recrimination.

Around the same time that Rückert sat for Barth, the artist also painted two pastel portraits of Ernst and Luise.[288] They both died a few months later. It would be natural for Friedrich to have been reminded of these events when he saw the frontispiece. In the convoluted blend of blame and self-loathing that so many mourners experience, he may have viewed the illustration, and his poems, as somehow tied to the deaths of his children.

In Friedrich's time as today, many believers have an idea implanted in childhood: sin has consequences; we must pay; if not us, then our loved ones. A number of bereaved parents have reported feeling that their transgressions led in some terrible way to the deaths of their children. Their guilt is usually tied to the seven deadly sins or one of the Ten Commandments, most frequently adultery, theft, deceit and greed.[289]

These feelings of self-recrimination are nearly universal after losing a child. Bereavement experts Margaret Miles and Alice Demi identified five common sources of guilt: cultural role guilt; death causation guilt; moral guilt, survivor guilt and recovery guilt.[290] Rückert will write of each in his songs. Here he gives full sway to a perceived moral guilt, choosing vanity as his poison.

The arrival of royalties may have eased financial burdens but it also added to his sense of wrong-doing. He draws a tenuous connection between his children's deaths and what he now sees as a vainglorious dedication. This is damaging nonsense, of course, as Rückert acknowledges in other songs.

I did much the same when my daughter died. Every book I have written was dedicated to Jessica: computer and translation texts; histories; and after she died, a book on grief. Jess was tickled with all of them except one that led to my conviction for criminal impersonation. Her disappointment and sense of betrayal were excruciating, as are my sorrow and guilt.

In the first year after Jess died, I found myself certain that it was my fault, that she paid for what I did or what I failed to do. I even convinced myself that I was to blame for her addiction and death. Consider how insulting this is. Jess was twenty-six years old, a grown woman with her own attitudes and experiences, her own choices. I was dismissing her as a person, treating her as if she were an extension of myself. As time passed I could see the absurdity of this thinking, but it took some doing. Others have faced the same challenge.

Decades after Sigmund Freud's adult daughter died, he wrote to a friend of the lasting impact of his loss: "Quite deep down I can trace the feelings of a deep narcissistic hurt that is not to be healed."[291] By this he meant an irremediable wound to his self-interested self.[292] Perhaps Freud was right. Part of healthy grieving includes a stark realization of the false perceptions we hold of our loved ones and ourselves.[293]

In Rückert's pain we may recognize some of our own foolish but deeply felt shame. Such feelings often do considerable harm. "Things can no longer be undone," observed grief counselor and bereaved parent Harriet Sarnoff Schiff. "Reviewing mistakes is of less than no value when reliving the time spent with your now dead child."[294] As Friedrich demonstrates in *Songs on the Death of Children*, any damage to the false self may lead to a clearing of the detritus of delusion. Ultimately, grief allowed him to see his children as they were, not as he imagined them to be.

Ernst and Luise were free of the petty concerns of family funds or vanity. Friedrich understood the folly of such thoughts while simultaneously accepting his need to express them: *To sing them is a sin perhaps, but if so, leave me to my lament.*

> My own experience and my work with clients have led me to accept that feelings such as anxiety, guilt, and grief are not destructive or pathological but provide the traumatically bereaved individual with opportunities for growth and creativity.—Albert Zandvoort, bereaved parent and psychotherapist at the University of Witten/Herdecke[295]

Fifty Fables for Children,
**with endearing illustrations
drawn by Speckter,
intended for young readers;
you, dear friend, suggested it
and had a copy sent round.**

**Alas, it arrived too late!
They are gone now,
the two who would have
loved the fables best;
their eyes are dark, shut
to these illustrations.**

**And my surviving children,
their schooling well apace,**

must chew on the Latin
fables of Phaedrus,
leaving them scant time
to study German.

And so it is,
and what can I do?
My old hands shall
treasure these stories
of childhood for my
pair of children.

Come in silence in the night,
see these bright illustrations,
hear me read the rhymes aloud!
There in your eyes I spy
your secret joy and know
the worth of each line.

Here you shake your head:
the rhyme doesn't suit you.
Here you nod up and down:
this one pleases you.
And so we share in each line
your delight and mine.

Fifty Fables for Children was written by Protestant pastor and teacher Johann Wilhelm Hey.[296] In 1832, Hey was appointed superintendent of Ichtershausen, near Erfurt, in Thuringia, and had recently married for the second time. Both circumstances led him to publish the book anonymously. Otto Speckter's lithographs illustrated each fable and since his was the only name on the title page, readers assumed he was the author as well. Later editions listed both contributors. A sequel followed, as did many printings.[297] The book was a popular alternative to the fables of Phaedrus that were part of most schools' Latin curriculum. The first edition of *Fifty Fables for Children* appeared in 1833, a year before Rückert's poem was written.

As with many bereaved parents, Friedrich is careful in his phrasing about reading the book to Ernst and Luise: it is unclear if he feels he experienced his children in a tangible way or in his imagination. The scene Friedrich describes is indicative of *acute grief*—the overwhelming burden of sorrow that is often accompanied by a sense that a lost loved one is present. This is not without precedent.

Reports of similar visions were commonplace among Christians in the early first century, as they were during Friedrich's lifetime and so continue today. "In 1988, when my husband of twenty years died in a hiking accident," wrote historian Elaine Pagels, "I became aware that, like many people who grieve, I was living in the presence of an invisible being—living, that is, with a vivid sense of someone who had died."[298]

This type of "external dialogue," as grief experts call it, is an ordinary experience that is rarely discussed. It consists of literal interactions with the deceased, whether as a sense of presence or a visual or auditory expression. Researchers note that a vast majority of the bereaved—particularly those who have lost a child or a spouse—report such subtle but meaningful exchanges nearly in a whisper, as though fearful that they will be perceived as irrational or deluded. "It may seem the stuff of a suspense novel," observed respected psychotherapist and grief counselor Ashley Davis Bush, "but the stories are so consistent and so typical that they cannot be easily dismissed."[299] The bereaved come to have a new relationship with them, *loving in separation*, as the philosopher Thomas Attig put it.[300] These continuing bonds provide a hope for presence and reunion.[301]

"The American Psychiatric Association, author of *The Diagnostic and Statistical Manual of Mental Disorders-IV*, considers these phenomena (when 'one hears the voice of, or transiently sees the image of, the deceased person') as non-pathological," observed researcher Stacy David. "They are viewed as common characteristics of uncomplicated grief, and not attributable to a mental disorder."[302] The bereaved rarely *expect* to experience their lost loved ones. They know they are dead. Even so, when they report hearing, seeing or sensing a presence, it is usually comforting and almost never associated with a belief that the dead have come back to life in any physical way.[303] Rather, their dead loved ones seem to inhabit and inform the mourners' lives.[304]

Rückert's poem is reminiscent of Henry Wadsworth Longfellow's "Footsteps of Angels," in which the American poet writes of an experience with his wife Mary, who died during a miscarriage in 1835:

> With a slow and noiseless footstep
> Comes the messenger divine,
> Takes the vacant chair beside me,
> Lays her gentle hand in mine.
> Uttered not, yet comprehended,
> Is the spirit's voiceless prayer.[305]

**There are your beds,
as empty as my
heart is heavy;
you are resting now,
never to move again.**

**Oh my winged cupids,
you have eclosed
from your beds, slipped
free of the loose chains
that bind you to us.**

**There were two chrysalides
on our fence post: dark,
brown and empty, it's true,
and two sylphic butterflies
flew over the fence.**

Many bereaved parents feel that they have an active interaction with their dead.[306] They relate stories of sensing their children in a fallen leaf, a bird, a presence, a knick-knack, a random word, an unexpected wind or scent.[307] These events are often highly personal and difficult to explain.

Rückert uses evocative imagery to help guide us to just such an experience. The beds are empty and, like his children's new resting places,[308] are lifeless. Friedrich suggests that his winged cupids have *eclosed*[309] from their beds, an oddly specific verb that refers to an adult insect's emergence from the pupa or a larva hatching from an egg. The images seem cumbersome. But suppose the poet did in fact see two butterflies flying over a pair of empty chrysalides? He is sharing just how meaningful the simple moment was for him. He describes the butterflies as sylphs,[310] free from chains that were too loose to hold them. Such experiences can easily be rationalized by onlookers, but as Rückert demonstrates, to the grieving only one explanation matters.

> I feel very strongly (and I am not alone in this) that some great good comes from the dead to the living in the months or weeks after the death. I think I was much helped by my own father after his death: as if our Lord welcomed the newly dead with the gift of some power to bless those they have left behind.... Certainly, they often seem just at that time, to be very near us.—C.S. Lewis[311]

**Spring buds would
wilt on their stems**

> if they knew what
> gives them luster:
> air of the grave,
> putrifaction purified
> in aromas that flavor
> the air of spring.
>
> Well, if long life is
> to be our lot, let
> us forget what
> is loved, is lost.
> Abandon and bury
> and forget? no!
> let us love, tho'
> not in torment.
>
> Rather, as flowers
> love thru divine
> colors, drawn from
> the land of death,
> let us breathe in
> from a wisp of air,
> from darkened
> eyes, gentle grief.

A eulogy for Abraham Lincoln was among the last poems that Rückert wrote.[312] It was published after Friedrich's death in 1866.[313] Titled simply, "America," the piece speaks in reverent awe of Lincoln and a democratic people that mourns a man from such humble beginnings. "What monarch fell to his grave so adored," Rückert asks, "so genuinely loved, so truly respected by his own land and by all?" Near the end of the piece, Friedrich calls on three decades of grief to address the importance of finding solace and meaning in the death of the beloved president:

> He sought for nothing,
> his own needs to fill;
> asking only this—
> be my people's will.
>
> What was asked of him
> has been paid in full;
> in the face of this
> our laments fall still.[314]

Rückert kept abreast of international events. In reading about the War Between the States, he would likely have seen the heartbreaking news, three years earlier, of Lincoln's personal loss.

Abraham Lincoln's eleven-year-old son, Willie, died on Thursday, 20 February 1862. Shortly afterward Lincoln burst into the office of his secretary, John Nicolay. "My boy is gone," he sobbed. "He is actually gone!" The sight of Willie's washed and dressed body in the Green Room stayed with Lincoln for years. The next Thursday, and many Thursdays after, the president sought seclusion in the room where his son had lain. "The blow overwhelmed me," he told a visitor, "it showed me my weakness as I had never felt it before."

Lincoln spent a good deal of time in the stables with Willie's horse, which the boy had been riding shortly before he fell ill. He also sought insight and communion in reading, notably William Shakespeare and the Holy Bible.

During a visit to Fort Monroe in May of 1862, Lincoln borrowed a copy of Shakespeare's works from General John Wool. After reading for a few hours, the president asked Colonel Le Grand B. Cannon if he might share a few selections with him. Lincoln then recited from *Macbeth*, *King Lear*, and *King John*. Cannon noticed that the president's voice trembled. Lincoln reached the end of the passage and set the book aside. "Did you ever dream of some lost friend, and feel that you were having a sweet communion with him, and yet have a consciousness that it was not a reality?" he asked. "That is the way I dream of my lost boy Willie." Lincoln then broke down into convulsive weeping, as did Cannon.

After Willie's passing, spiritual concerns came to dominate Lincoln's life. Though never formally associated with a church, he was impressed with Francis Vinton's sermons on death and asked for a collection. By July of 1862 Lincoln was speaking of emancipation.

The president shocked his cabinet after the Confederate retreat at Antietam. "He had made a vow, a covenant," wrote Secretary of the Navy Gideon Welles on 22 September 1862, "that if God gave us the victory in the approaching battle, he would consider it an indication of Divine Will, and that it was his duty to move forward in the cause of emancipation." The Emancipation Proclamation was issued less than a year after Willie's death: 1 January 1863. That same day the White House held its first public reception since the boy's passing.

Lincoln's famous address at Gettysburg, delivered on 19 November 1863, was not unexpected. As with his views on emancipation, the president's thoughts on American national purpose had for years been leading up to this point. Still, we are stunned by his compassion and resolve. Lincoln's search for meaning had raised him to new heights of eloquence.[315]

Abandon and bury and forget? asks Rückert; and in answer, *let us breathe in from a wisp of air, from darkened eyes, gentle grief.* The death of a child extracts a heavy toll. The pain plays no favorites, whether president or poet. Parental bereavement is as profound as the lifelong changes that accompany it.

Oh! memory—thou mid-way world
'Twixt earth and Paradise,
Where things decayed, and loved ones lost,
In dreamy shadows rise.
—Abraham Lincoln[316]

**The spear that struck my wound
will heal my wound.
Where death took my life,
bear me there without delay,
bear me in the cortège this day
and without respite lay
me to rest in the ground!
The spear that struck my wound
will heal my wound.**

**"The spear that struck your wound
will heal your wound.
His hand is heavy upon you; who
but He may do so with ease?
Who but He may console?
Gently now, let God above
do the waiting with you!
The spear that struck your wound
will heal your wound."**

"Our souls have taken harm," I wrote in December 2017, nearly three years after Jess's death. "I will be healed the moment I hold my daughter in my arms again."[317] In the first stanza, Rückert mourns his children and wishes to join them. The spear that strikes and heals is death itself. Friedrich implies that true healing will only occur when he, too, is laid to rest and joins his children. This speaks to me and perhaps to many bereaved parents.

Michael Cholbi, Chair in Philosophy at the University of Edinburgh and founder of the International Association for the Philosophy of Death and Dying, resists the idea of "closure," "healing," and "journeys," etc., in favor of the pursuit of understanding our sorrow. He argues that grief is not a medical problem. "Some of the challenges grief presents are 'problems in living,'" he notes, "problems arising not because our lives have gone wrong somehow but because human life has certain predicaments baked into it." Many of the questions we confront after a loss, and the overwhelming aspects of mourning, are about lived experience. Life after all, is not a condition to be treated. We grieve those we love and how much our practical identities, as Cholbi calls them, are intertwined with our assumption that the relationship was going to continue into the future. The greater our investment, the greater our sorrow.[318] "Grief occurs because of our ties to other people as well as our ties to our own past and future selves," Cholbi writes. "Grief is thus about *how our minds relate to the wider world*."[319]

This is precisely what Rückert is doing in this poem. In talking with himself, he focuses on the world around him. His second stanza replies to the first. Friedrich turns to deity with accusation and expectation. The symbolic spear now holds despair in death and hope for reunion. God's hand alone allowed this wound, the poet suggests. God alone can help. *If only God will wait with him.* Friedrich is combining a Greek metaphor and Hebrew tradition to present his case to the divine.

The spear that wounds and heals is taken from a tale in Euripides's fragments: the tragedy of Telephus (438 BCE).[320] It is a story of suffering and redemption. King Telephus was stabbed in the thigh by Achilles. The wound suppurated for nine painful years. Finally, the king consulted an oracle, who told him, "Only your attacker may heal you."[321] In 1882, Richard Wagner used this scene in *Parsifal*, changing the famous line a little: "One weapon alone will do:—only the spear that struck you closes your wound."[322]

Telephus went to Achilles, dressed in rags, and begged for help. After some haggling, Achilles agreed, and healed the king by scraping some rust off of the same Pelian spear that had caused the wound.[323] Rust is far from efficacious, but it hardly matters, as anthropologist James George Frazer observed, "It is clearly a folklore remedy based on the principle of *sympathetic* magic."[324]

Rückert is not invoking folklore or magic. But he appears to have felt some sympathy with Hebrew tradition. One psalm, for example, is presented as a dialogue between God and David, who uses phrasing similar to Friedrich's, "because of my groaning all day long; day and night your hand was heavy on me."[325] In the Book of Job, the speeches were *also* presented as dialogue between Job and his friends. After God allowed the slaughter of his ten children, Job *also* insisted that God's hand is heavy.[326] He *also* sought refuge, justice and solace: "Then I would feel consoled," Job said in an expression that informed Friedrich's song. "Have I enough strength to go on waiting?"[327]

Rückert is asking the same question.

"Watchman, how much longer is it night?"
The watchman answers:
"Morning is coming, but also the night."
—Isaiah 21:11–12 CJB

> My homespun tunes,
> my journal of joys:
> I penned only delights;
> these were my muse;
> never of loss in
> my homespun tunes.

> My homespun tunes
> are of your loss alone—
> your bill came due
> so soon!—of joys
> never again, if ever, in
> my homespun tunes.

Rückert was known to have a practical understanding of his limitations. Of the thousands of poems he wrote in his lifetime, many focused on the joys of love, family and nature. He eschewed epic themes in favor of the lyrical that he found in everyday life. This contributed to a certain wry, self-effacing humor, as in one quatrain written before his children died:

> Much I make as make the others;
> Better much another man
> Makes than I; but much, moreover,
> Make I which no other can.[328]

Now grief was upon him. As Horace observed in *The Art of Poetry*: "If you would have me weep, you must first feel grief yourself."[329] Friedrich was faced with a new task: expressing the depth and breadth of his sorrow. To do so, he turned to verse, an important part of how he experienced the world.

In this poem, Rückert uses a somewhat folksy descriptor; *My Homespun Tunes* was also how he referred to his daily journal of occasional poems. From 1838 on, he would refer to similar diaries as *House Songs* and *Annual Tunes*; then from 1846, simply *Song Journal*.[330]

Bayard Taylor, writing of Rückert for *The Atlantic Monthly*, struggled to describe the poet's mystical expression as though his words "were actually visible in his brain."[331] Perhaps they were. Reading the poets laments, we are struck by his insights into the spiritual aspect of sorrow. If grief is more than an emotional response, if it is in fact a wound to our souls, then Friedrich's tunes are far from homey or homely—they speak of *home* in the most powerful sense of the word.

> Is it only now at her
> death that I see what
> was precious to me?
> No, I always knew.
>
> I dared not say it,
> trembling before
> Fate, for you are
> jealous of all joy.
>
> Disaster has struck,
> our virtue gone. I
> no longer fear your
> cunning, serpent.
>
> And our songs will
> speak of beauty that
> lived, and lives on
> in the singing.

Rückert inhabited what he read. Unconscious references often seeped into his work. Later, subjecting a poem to edits, he might remove or at least clarify seemingly vague allusion. These laments, however, were raw drafts of pain. They show a fine mind struggling with grief.

This song of remorse and resolve alludes to the Garden of Eden and is simultaneously informed by an Indian perspective that Friedrich knew well. Respected expert in Indo-Iranian studies, Hans-Peter Schmidt, suggested that one important theme of the Hebrew Bible holds a shocking revelation that is often seen in Indian mythology: our sense of guilt delivers us from the uncaring whims of fate.[332] In the garden, Schmidt observed, Eve, pure and innocent, dared to express her happiness to the serpent. The snake, jealous of all joy, used cunning to harm her virtue. This in turn brought guilt into the world, forcing humanity to turn to God, and thereby freeing them from the power of fate.

Though a century and a half apart, Schmidt and Rückert seem to have read the same books, as the saying goes, and it shows in this poem. Friedrich feels remorse for his perceived failure to lavish love on Luise, a sentiment he echoes in "I loved you so, my little girl!" Part of the reason, he confesses, was his fear that fate would punish him for such unfettered joy. Now his young daughter, virtue itself, is gone. He no longer trembles at what the serpent may do. Instead, he will sing of a beauty that lives on in the singing. With the loss of his daughter, guilt and fear are replaced by love.

All suffering has an element of the divine.—Johann Wolfgang von Goethe[333]

Your life was so short there is little to report in histories of nations or eras or the world. Still, you must be remembered. Your tombstone and eulogy are not enough. Only one thing will make your poems timeless: the stuff of love.

Rituals such as funeral sermons, burial services and obituaries serve the vital role of transition. These and other commemorations are also vehicles for transformation and connection.[334] Participating in rituals serves many roles: it helps us mourn; gives others a time and place to grieve to with us; acknowledges the reality of the death; provides opportunities for comfort; facilitates the sharing of memories; and increases a sense of control at a time when the bereaved feel none.[335]

Rituals take many forms. They are not one size fits all, as O. Duane Weeks observed, "To be helpful, a death ritual must have some value to the survivors. To have value, the ritual must also have meaning. And to have meaning, the ritual must be personal."[336]

In this poem, Rückert despairs that the usual memorials are woefully inadequate. This sentiment was not unheard of in his day. The individual nature of mourning was already firmly established in 19th-century Germany, which had clear cultural guidelines for public ritual and private grief.[337] Friedrich seeks commemoration over biography, preferring to capture moments of his children's lives and of his grief in songs of hope, memory and anguish.[338]

Rückert alludes to the 17th-century topos of his children living on through his poems in other pieces, but here he addresses a pressing need. His children were too young to list their accomplishments. Friedrich has a more enduring measure in mind: love, of which poetry is made.

He revisits this theme with "In loss it is difficult to begin."

In loss it is difficult to begin anything, much less hold our own, other than perhaps with love and Poetry.

Love allows for no escape, nothing gets out, only in; and yet from nothing, despite herself, love creates Poetry.

What departs does not pass away: it remains in essence, if not in the senses; intertwined for eternity, love and Poetry.

Friedrich comments on an important truth: "to grieve is to love." The song suggests that in loss love has nowhere to go; it cannot be felt or touched yet its essence remains. One scholar maintains that the last two verses of the second stanza (*and yet from nothing, despite herself, love creates Poetry*) summarize the point of Rückert's *Songs on the Death of Children*.[339]

In Japan, government-funded support groups for suicide survivors have identified three liberating perspectives that help mourners find meaning: *We live with grief; Grief is ours;* and *Grief is love.*[340] Rückert's songs of lament, written 172 years earlier, speak to each of these affirmations.

Friedrich's poems will not return Ernst and Luise to him. Nor are his songs biographical sketches of highly-detailed memories. The children are the subjects of his laments, to be sure, but the poet is writing primarily of grief, of missing them, of their absence. It is precisely in this *nothing* that love continues on.

Love may be worth the wound but it extracts a heavy toll, as Leo Tolstoy observed, "Only people capable of loving deeply can experience profound grief."[341] The struggle to continue a relationship with our dead in their physical absence can be sustained in healthy ways through memory, ritual and emotional and spiritual bonds.[342] Friedrich has found just such a ritual. His poetry gives the ineffable expression. It provides meaning to a love that is part of all sorrow, *intertwined for eternity*.

**Muses, my old friends, you
often came in times of trouble
to console us in our grief.
Not now, not when the
plague took our children,
not when its spark of death
is so cruelly contagious.
We once relied on the ladies
of the village and other friends
for comfort and tender care.
But no more. They dare not
step into our house out of fear
for their own children, out of
justified terror that they bring
this poison back to their homes.
No one came to ask after our
deaths or lives: not one word of
consolation from friendly lips;
no shared lament when my
child's corpse was laid out.
Only you, my old friends,
do not fall prey to fear for
you know, there up above,
how to put fear to rout.
Contagion poses no danger,
so I ask of you: lament with
me, nurse me, help me,
come don the kitchen apron.
As long as you remain I will
not fall into despair; with
your help I may yet shoulder
the burden of any plague.
So before all my friends—
while blaming none for each
is mortal, after all—I say to you,
dear immortals, thank you.**

The Rückerts were left alone during their children's illness. In an age of pandemic, visits to help with household needs were in short supply. Friends attended the funeral, but even then, the customary consolations were cut short out of *justified terror*.

Neighbors did their best, Friedrich wrote, but they had their own children to think about. After Ernst and Luise died, one "deaf, willing but long-winded" friend stayed with them for two whole days before retiring.[343] The Rückerts were forced to rely on each other.

"God spare us more suffering!" Friedrich wrote to his father-in-law, Albrecht Fischer. "Luise has been unwell for many weeks, forcing herself to go on out of worry for the children. She was bedridden after young Luise's death, but is now able to move about and has regained a sense of composure." In April of 1834, Friedrich asked his mother-in-law to visit them, assuring her that it would be "a real consolation."[344]

Bereaved parents often complain that people seem to distance themselves after learning of their child's death. Bad news is contagious and best avoided, the thinking goes.[345] In Rückert's day the fear of losing a child to scarlet fever was not figurative or based on superstition. This led to understandable caution among parents and a distancing that, while nearly unbearable for the bereaved, was necessary for public health. Friedrich turns to his muses instead.

In this song the poet does not speak of healing or recovery, merely relief. Writing provides simple but powerful solace.[346] For those so inclined, creative arts allow us to acknowledge and express the complex images and impressions that are a real part of mourning. Poetic responses, rather than interpretations or analyses of feelings, allow sorrow to be shared in fresh and unanticipated ways.[347] For Rückert, writing offers the comfort of *old friends* while simultaneously providing a productive outlet for his grief. In verse he finds a brief liberation from despair.

> When all without is dark,
> And former friends misprise;
> From them I turn to Thee,
> And find love in Thine eyes.
>
> When all within is dark,
> And I my soul despise;
> From me I turn to Thee,
> And find love in Thine eyes.
>
> When all Thy face is dark,
> And Thy just angers rise;
> From Thee I turn to Thee,
> And find love in Thine eyes.
> —Solomon ibn Gebirol,
> "The Royal Crown"[348]

Still in my words I obey their whims, as they do mine.
Still in my soul they ease such pain, when they appear.
Now they come to weep with me, a pair of shadows:
can we not have this at least?

We gave you life only for you to leave us too soon.
Did your mother deliver you for no more than this?
No, I swear you will live on in these words:
free of death, free of decay.

For many years, a silver birch stood over the graves of Ernst and Luise.[349] The tree supported a plaque inscribed with the second stanza of this poem, a living reminder of Friedrich's plea, *can we not have this at least?*

Rückert had the sapling planted by the graves in 1841, when he left Erlangen. There it grew for some 170 years until time and weather took their toll. The tree reached a considerable size and the trunk was no longer deemed completely sound. The cemetery ordered it felled in 2016.[350]

Author, psychiatrist and chair of the Erlangen Rückert Circle, Johannes Wilkes, relates that their group prevailed on the administration to leave a stump, a few yards high, now completely covered in ivy. The Rückert friends, as they are known, also secured some of the wood. Children at the local Friedrich Rückert Elementary School used the branches to make candlesticks.[351]

Each January, the school children join Circle members for a small memorial observance at the graves. The occasion includes musical numbers and readings from *Songs on the Death of Children*. Friedrich's lament, "Still in my words," is recited in full.[352]

The silver birch at the graves had rising branches. Another piece Friedrich wrote in 1834, "One Hundred Tercets," uses 137 haiku-like triplets to address the plants, animals and insects that the grieving father saw around him. In the eightieth stanza he compares the whizzing sound of a birch rod, often associated with parental discipline, to the softly sighing, dangling branches of a weeping birch:

> Sprigs of birch!
> Switches that whistled and roared now whisper and rustle on a weeping birch.

Friedrich's songs demonstrate one way that he dealt with grief, keeping the memories of his children close not only in his heart, but also in his words.[353] The concept of poetry as an immortal memorial dates back to Horace and was especially popular during the Renaissance. Stone may decay, the idea suggests, but songs will live on in the hearts of listeners, poems in the hearts of readers.[354] Friedrich dares to contradict the inevitability of death. His poetry challenges the biological end of life with a new beginning in the medium of art.[355]

Rückert and other proponents of this thought, such as Robert Herrick and William Shakespeare, may have had a point. Their words are cherished to this day. However, the funeral verse, elegies and laments of a thousand others have disappeared.[356]

Friedrich understood all too well the transience of life. He was calling upon a long history of reaching out from isolation to share with fellow sufferers. German theologian and philosopher Friedrich Schleiermacher suggested that the meaning of a poem is not limited to the text alone, but achieves its true purpose when a stranger—many miles and years later—is involved with the author's words. The act of reading is a direct communication in which time and distance have no meaning. It creates something new: a unity and communion between poet and reader, or, as with Rückert, between one mourner and another.[357]

> *What is dying? What is dead?*
> So he asked, my son, so full of life.
> How should I answer?
> "Without color, no longer red."
>
> *What is dying? What is dead?*
> Oh, so he asked of me!
> As does my heart, weak, weeping!
> "Decay, its threat and dread?"
>
> Was it a message, an ill breath?
> Yes, a premonition, perhaps.
> And so no longer asking, you died:
> "What is dying? What is death?"
>
> *What is dying? What is death?*
> And so I ask, as you asked me;
> and you answer, as if to say:
> "To leave this earth, to be free."

The image of a Romantic poet strolling through the lonely mountains was more aspiration than reality. Even in Rückert's time, most authors of the period worked for a living. They could not afford to do otherwise.[358] Romantic writers were part of an often fractious social, political and ideological community in which they exchanged and argued over their positions in public and private. Collective independence of thought was every bit as vital as individual expression.[359] That Friedrich had time to mourn, reflect and write after his children died is as much a testament to the largesse of his university colleagues as the grieving father's desperate need for communion with nature. I know this grace well.

I was working for a television network when my daughter died. An executive and the producer immediately granted me an indefinite period away from the rigors of broadcast deadlines. I was able to return to work after two months. Even then, the crew members were patient with flubs and generous with their understanding. They did not shy away from my sorrow or fail to acknowledge that such feelings are inevitable and cannot be dismissed or controlled.

A stoic response to emotion and grief is often mistaken as a rejection of feeling. In fact, Romantic Stoicism, such as expressed by Rückert, has an inescapable pull *toward* emotion.[360] Life is transient. In the newly awakened awareness of death's finality, which cannot be denied however much one may try, Friedrich saw that the only way to manage sorrow is to stop trying to do so. Put another way, the only way to live with grief is to live with it.

We may be surprised to experience moments that help us in what seems a daily struggle of survival. To our astonishment, suffering and tenderness often go hand in hand. After William Wordsworth's seafaring brother died, and around the time of Lord Nelson's passing in 1806, the poet refused to ignore his feelings of loss. Rather, he embraced the new awareness that he had gained at such terrible cost:

More skilful in self-knowledge, even more pure,
As tempted more; more able to endure,
As more expos'd to suffering and distress;
Thence, also, more alive to tenderness.[361]

In loss we understand perfectly that life is finite. We grasp logically and emotionally that death is permanent. Then we pause. Somehow these simple, factual words ring false. Why is that? Dead is dead, after all. Nothing is more unalterably human. Yet one of the aims of Rückert's generation was to overcome the gap between mind and matter, reason and emotion, the compartmentalized thinking that ignored unity within all life.[362] German philosopher Friedrich Schlegel believed in just such a unifying principle, not as an ethereal hope or an intellectual puzzle, but as a practical reality of living in the world that surrounds us.[363]

> Through all the tones and
> colors of this earthly dream,
> one faint tone resonates
> with he who listens within.[364]

Rückert was doing just that, listening to his grief, his hopes, and in many of these poems, to the quiet resonance of his dead children. Suddenly his concerns with the relation between mind and nature, between oneself and others, between the finite and the infinite, seemed more than a Romantic dream.[365] They were imperative. He now saw the world as one of active participation, both reflecting what is around us and by action or inaction, transforming it.³⁶⁶ What he once knew as a metaphysical exercise was suddenly, painfully real: we are part of this world, visible and invisible, whatever we may do.

Such thoughts were not limited to poets and philosophers. Composer Gustav Mahler also thought and experienced the world as a Romantic.³⁶⁷ His musical setting of *Kindertotenlieder* premiered in 1905. It is powerful work, but his most personal work was still to come. In 1907 Gustav's four-year-old daughter, Putzi, died of diphtheria and scarlet fever. His next song cycle, *Das Lied von der Erde* (Song of the Earth), speaks of life, death, parting, and redemption.³⁶⁸ It was Mahler's masterpiece. "My need to express myself musically and symphonically starts only where the dark emotions begin," he wrote to a friend, "at the door leading to the 'other world,' the world in which things are not any more separated by time and place."³⁶⁹

Mahler and Rückert strove to break free of the separation of place in our time-enslaved world. Despite their earlier efforts to compartmentalize the facets of song (and life) in their minds, they learned in sorrow that all of life must be experienced as one.³⁷⁰ What may have once been a clever metaphor was in their new lives of grief a painful reality.

Consider the syllables of a poem. They are inextricably part of the sounds they create, just as spaces and words are part of each line, and the reader or listener is also part of the whole. When we note how a person phrases something, we refer as much to the pauses and inflections as the sentences.³⁷¹ We speak, we listen; we imply, we infer; the acts are separate yet inseparable. The tiniest change in tone and sense contributes to our experience.

For example, music can be just as fun to sing alone, sing along, or hear in performance, yet no one way of listening is quite like the other. Similarly, a poem takes on new shades of meaning when we read it in our minds, speak it aloud, or enjoy a skillful recitation. Each is a way of knowing: unique, mysterious and redemptive.³⁷² This is especially true with lament, when the bereaved are insensate while simultaneously hypersensitive to everything around them.³⁷³ The silences between each word, each syllable, resonate on a level deeper than thought.

Ultimately, our perception of the finality of death does not jibe with our secret selves, more certain and powerful than the physical world. If there is such a thing as a soul, it rebels. We seem certain that there is more in this universe than what we see each day. Despite all evidence to the contrary, we know our loved ones continue on; we sense that we are not alone.

Rückert's lament addresses this undeniable reality of grief. In the end, it may be the only consolation that lasts.

> The Brain is just the weight of God—
> For—Heft them—Pound for Pound—
> And they will differ—if they do—
> As syllable from Sound—
> —Emily Dickinson³⁷⁴

At first I accompanied poetry, cultivated it, tended to its forms. I accompanied it but as an observer, from a distance.

Over time my poems have drawn nearer, closer. They

> **have won me over: our forms
> are no longer two but one.**
>
> **My children have died and
> in pain I sing for them, pain
> tinged with gratitude for lines
> that ease the sting of death.**

Bereaved parents often note that they now measure their lives *before* and *after* the death of their child. Immediately following the loss they entered "a new state of being" that has no end point.[375] This displays itself in many ways, a common thread being a dramatic shift in perspective, compassion and meaning-making.[376] Rückert's new perspective is evident throughout *Songs on the Death of Children*. His changing poetic style was accompanied by a shift in his view of the world.

After Luise and Ernst died, Friedrich no longer saw the gap between nature and self, the physical and the invisible, as insuperable. In fact, throughout his laments, he stresses the opposite. Friedrich wrote of spiritual unity, nature as God's creation and the very real possibility of resolving the disharmony of the world.[377] He sought harmony underneath the seeming contradictions and opposites of existence. Rückert's views grew more and more inclusive, hopeful and expansive. His work eschewed passive observation in favor of an active part in a world of perpetual creation.[378]

This shift in attitude—from the cynicism of his youth to communion after he lost his children—would stay with him for the rest of his life. Friedrich embraces poetry and creative expression as a type of therapy, liberating him from the rigid confines of his past expectations as he faces a new reality without his children. The final stanza of this song demonstrates just how much the act of writing these lines meant to him.[379]

> Between the language of the universe and the universe of language, there is a bridge, a link: poetry. The poet is the translator.—Octavio Paz[380]

I

> **In prose and poetry
> what seemed the loveliest
> was lovelier still in you;
> and to my astonishment
> I saw in your eyes what
> I thought only lived
> in poetry and prose.**
>
> **From poetry and prose,
> as though in a picture,
> you stepped out of the
> frame, alive, astonishing,
> though less so now:
> your eyes slowly dim,
> you are fading, returning
> to prose and poetry.**

II

> **In a milder, softer climate—
> as under the Italian
> sun or perhaps in
> paintings by Raphael—
> buds of your beauty
> thrive and grow free
> of withering deformity.
> But how could you
> thrive, I worried, here
> in this wild, rough climate?**
>
> **In this wild, rough climate
> the looking glass of grace
> is clouded too soon:
> clusters of buds break
> forth stunted, dull,
> shrunken and lifeless!
> So I say—my heart breaks!—
> heal, be on your way, and
> flower now in heaven
> and bloom in my song;
> flower here and there
> in a milder, softer climate.**

Rückert employs many metaphors in this collection. This is not poetic conceit. He understood their utility in living with grief. Metaphors provide graphic, non-judgmental symbols that enable us to freely express sorrow, loss, anger and guilt.[381] "Through the imagination," wrote poet and priest John O'Donohue, "the soul creates and constructs your depth experience. Imagination is the most reverent mirror of the inner world."[382] In this song, Friedrich memorializes his dead children's eyes, a well-known metaphor to depict the experience of loss.[383]

In struggling with the deaths of Luise and Ernst, their father accepts the cold reality that, though their eyes were lovelier (literally)than any poem or prose, they will live on (figuratively) only dimly, fading, in words that can never compare. In one of Friedrich's best known *lied*, "Now I know why," he writes that their eyes are now as stars in the sky—but even so they remain distant. This may be why, in the second poem, he shifts his metaphor to the closer, earthier wish that his children will *flower now in heaven and bloom in my song*.

**Surrounded by old extravagance of joy,
I scooped it out; still an excess remained.**

**Why not? Could exuberance run dry?
It filled, extended, overflowed each cranny.**

**Where did the water run in the night?
Passed away, unprepared, exhausted.**

Such opulence rushes off, roars:

just the once, distant, then gone.

**Shall I shed tears in her stead?
So weep!
This grey river my companion in life ahead.**

**Where to hear a river of sorrow on an evening breeze?
When chords of gold greet from a distant shore.**

**Whiffs of my dark songs, planted on the bank,
waft to where I must go on wings of my own.**

Rückert wrestles with outward displays of mourning and inner grief throughout his many laments. At times he veers into melancholy; at others he expresses the acute pain of loss: *So weep!* he cries. *Where to hear a river of sorrow on an evening breeze?* Friedrich is echoing a stanza from philosopher Johann Gottfried Herder who, despite feelings of sorrow, was seldom prone to melodrama, making his verse similarly poignant[384]:

> Let us weep!....
> More soulful and heavenly
> a river of sorrow
> the lips never speak than when they tremble,
> inexpressibly tremble in a sigh![385]

Rückert was not merely revisiting a familiar passage. His poem is steeped in the philosopher's perception of sound. An important influence on Goethe and, later, on most German thinkers, Herder insisted that humans do not merely hear and react to sounds, as animals do, but also engage in discourse, or "reflexivity."[386] We listen and respond. This is precisely what Friedrich hopes to do, seeking to hear the river of sorrow, the chords of gold from across the water, and to reply with his own dark songs, planted on the bank in waiting. Rückert revisited this theme in another song that spring, pleading with God to help him empty his heart and mind to the world around him:

> Colors float before my eyes
> though none with beauty,
> and sounds ring in my ears
> though none rings truly.
>
> God, lift this gauze of misery
> from my eyes, from my ears;
> clear my senses, let me drink
> in the world as I did before.
>
> When eyes and ears give birth
> to their own sights and sounds,
> there is no chorus of color,
> there is no dance of joy.

**I would have an ancient
Egyptian embalmer, expert
in cheating death by the
art of his decoration,
all our torments
purify,
transform to song.**

**I would have an ancient
Greek mourner gather
your ashes, tender and
hesitant, as my requiem;
all combine to
testify
of a father's yearning.**

"Not flesh and blood," wrote Friedrich Schiller in 1781, "the *heart* makes us fathers and sons."[387] The lineage of Rückert's brief poem can be traced back through 4,700 years of Egyptian lament. In these ancient expressions of grief, the dead, it was thought, retained their ability to create.

The litanies of Isis and Nephthys, for example, were aimed at reviving the deceased by resuscitating this precise creative power.[388] One poem from a Theban tomb, dating to the last centuries of Egyptian civilization, as moving as any lament written today, refutes any comfort for a weeping heart. The bereaved, the anonymous poet cried, has lost everything in an instant. He is like a calf lost in the night.[389]

Rückert was familiar with such texts, which may have influenced his frequent references to a link with the dead via his songs of sorrow. Death was seen as a spiritual process of ascension, first as a metaphor, then by visualizing the return of the dead to the lives of the living.[390] They present an important narrative of loss. "Laments are more than discourse," observed anthropologist Jim Wilce, who identified them as a link with the dead that resonates in our modern world, adding: "The similarity of these ... memorializations to traditional lament's memorializations is essential, not trivial."[391]

**I thought to pick a bud
in the morning,
to decorate a wreath,
a breath of spring.**

**Then I heard the bud
speaking softly:
"And would you pluck me
in the morning dew?"**

**"For the sake of your child,
taken so soon:
Give me another day
in the winds of spring!"**

In our new calendar of grief, we measure days and years differently. Three months after our loved one died, we feel as though only a day has passed. After a year, it seems no more than a week; five years, and the pain is as fresh as last month. Time seems to shrink. Conversely, it also seems endless. Our new perception gives weight and meaning to the briefest moments, as if we might slip sideways and disappear into them. Time has an aspect of slowness for those in mourning.

German literature scholar Helmut Koopmann noted that 19th-century artists broke free of the shackles of convention, poetically and chronologically. They faced life with raw honesty and allowed their verse to reflect what they saw. "Rückert's poetry is a particularly good example," Koopmann observed, citing Friedrich's exploration of pain as lyric raw material, not as a conceit, but in an expression of his lived reality.[392] Rückert often and skillfully weaves past, present and future in a single song.[393] This is due as much to Friedrich's poetic gifts as the timeless nature of grief.

The poet's pause over a flower is not mere affectation. Mourners often feel a renewed appreciation of their surroundings. While a fear of their own deaths may be greatly diminished, they also come to value the experiences of others and the continued existence of life. From such changes comes a shift in their personal philosophies.[394] Friedrich's intense focus on a single moment is reminiscent of the final stanza from one of his most famous poems, in which he speaks not as a grieving father but as a dying flower:

> Heart of the world, you continue
> to burn as I fade away in blue:
> your sky surrounds me, while
> my colors wither and die.
> Goodbye, glow of spring!
> Morning, your weeping dew!
> I let myself drift away, free of
> sorrow, free of hope, free of you.[395]

**Nature is unsettled,
as is my heart;
outdoors, it is merely the spring,
in me, there is other harm.**

**Spring knows its pain:
the outdoors born anew;
but for me, o broken heart,
what was born is lost.**

After the deaths of Ernst and Luise, and for many years to come, Rückert sought daily solace in the outdoors: in their garden, at the children's graves in Erlangen, strolling in the meadows along the Itz River or in the wooded hills that surround Callenberg Castle.

The castle was the summer residence of Ernst I, the first sovereign duke of Saxe-Coburg and Gotha, who had begun a restoration project in 1827 that included an exhibit farm and a vast landscape garden. Heir and future duke Ernst II made Callenberg his permanent summer residence in 1842. Local residents were invited to wander the hills. The castle was about two miles (3.3km) from Friedrich's home in Neuses, a short jaunt for the long-legged, experienced walker.

The aloneness of grief invites openness to the world around us. "Most wanderers have lost something," observed David Brown Morris, Emeritus Professor of English at the University of Virginia. "Solitude comes to embrace emotional experiences ranging from social isolation to cosmic interconnection."[396] Samuel Taylor Coleridge and William Wordsworth, while working together on *Lyrical Ballads*, suggested that while wandering alone "accidents of light and shade" may transform the known and familiar into places of unforeseen discovery.[397] Wordsworth, who walked some 175,000 miles in his lifetime, spoke of "the bliss of solitude" that combines specific locations with reality and memory.[398] Our wanderings ground us in ways we may miss otherwise: unhurried accidents of brilliant clarity that assure us we are not alone.

I too spend more and more time in the wood since my daughter died. Is this helpful? Yes and no. Many people feel their dead loved ones with them in nature, whether in parks or trails, joining them as surely as the birds and deer and otters. I certainly do.

I walk the creek for miles, resting on the large rocks in the center of the stream for up to an hour at a time. The longer I sit, the more visitors come to the water: birds, of course, and plenty of deer, often in small herds. Now and then I've seen an otter float by, sometimes quite close, unaware of my presence or uninterested. Beavers, though nocturnal, may rear their heads to see what I'm up to.

Then there is the occasional black bear or bobcat. Bears are terrifying but relatively congenial, so long as we both understand who runs the wood. (It isn't me.) Our local bobcat is intriguingly bold. I've spotted him around dawn. He will slowly approach the water, pause and look my way, then drink, stealing glances now and then. Bobcats rarely stalk large mammals, thankfully, and this one seems to have little interest in me other than as a potential threat.

The deep wood is a dangerous place. I make plenty of noise before sitting down on whichever rock I find that day, splashing through the creek, coughing or even daring a poor Pavarotti impersonation. This scares away the snakes and small critters. Even lumbering skunks and porcupines slowly saunter off if I alert them to my presence well in advance.

My noise, though, is nothing compared to the chatter of my companions. Once the birds and frogs have grown accustomed to me, there is no shutting them up. This is useful. When they fall silent, I know to keep an eye out for predators. As Rückert observed, nature is indeed *unsettled*.

Hawks float overhead, circling, sometimes hunting, but often as not seeming to catch the winds simply because they love it so. One memorable week, a male broad-wing joined me for breakfast each morning. It was early spring. I walked to the creek, about a mile into the wood, and settled onto a large boulder beside the stream. There I ate fruit and nuts. Within minutes, a young hawk gracefully landed on a branch no more than ten feet overhead. He often stayed there as long as I did.

Time spent in nature carries great risks and unforeseen rewards. In mourning, we are not as alert as we should be, and so may miss the dangers around us. At the same time, surrounded by so much life, I feel my daughter near and the concern of an attentive God. Nature may not be safe, but it is *communal*. In the deep wood, I know I am not alone.

> Everybody needs beauty as well as bread, places to play in and pray in, where nature may heal and give strength to body and soul alike.—John Muir[399]

**Deep in the wood
and the rocky valley
my heart and voice cry**

a thousand times:
Children, are you there?
"Here!"
Where is here? "Here! Here!"

Dark wooded brush
stands between us,
I do not see you;
tell me, are you
far? near?
"Near!"
How near? "Near, near!"

Do you want to draw near
from where you are?
Always mine, the one
joy in this pain?
Mine? No? Yes?
"Yes!"
Always yes? "Yes, yes!"

Rückert wrote this song as an echo poem. The form usually has a disembodied voice repeating a single syllable word in answer to a question. The voice may originate from an inanimate object, a muse or a spirit.

Echo poems originated in Greek and Byzantine traditions and enjoyed resurgence in the Renaissance and Baroque periods.[400] The Baroque literary society, the Nuremberg Pegnitzschäfer (Pegnitz shepherds), was particularly fond of them. Seventeenth-century German funeral poetry occasionally employed the form to little affect.[401] The reason is simple: echoes are most effective as a confirmation in poems of whimsy, devotion or debate.[402] They offer little solace in lament, as Friedrich's poem demonstrates. Although the echo may declare itself "a timelessly authoritative answer to the time-bound uncertain and anxious questioner,"[403] as one scholar put it, the form is limited to monosyllables. Luise and Ernst's answers are poignant but painfully short.

Dialogue poetry better serves the needs of the bereaved. It offers a unique form of expression for the poet—somewhere between the narrative focus of prose and the imagery of verse. Friedrich seemed aware of this when he wrote this poem after Luise and Ernst died:

"Good night and good morning,"
so I said each day,
and you, without a care
laughed at our play.

"Good night and good morning,"
so your smile seems to say,
though it is in grief and sorrow
that I now greet the day.

Yes, I'm not kidding myself:
I understand, I can see, my
"good night and good morning"
is not for you, but for me.

Consolatory dialogue in particular has a long literary tradition dating back to the Book of Job. Most early examples were concerned with the mysteries of suffering and existence. By the 14th century, dialogue poems served as representative conversations between the living and the dead.[404] Three hundred years later, in the 17th century, German dialogues were structured to provide solace, alleviation and an outlet for grief.[405] The dead may then speak peace and counsel from beyond.

This poem also demonstrates Rückert's affinity for the deep wood. One study of forty participants found that strong emotional responses to grief in nature often provide a means for the bereaved to feel that their loved ones are near. Any sense of dissonance dissipates in what the researcher called a "psycho-spiritual transformation"; that is, a sense that the emotional

In the Churchyard

Your spirits are not here
where the dead bury their dead.
Nor do I sense your bodies
in this burial ground.
I cannot persuade myself that
you lie under this mound.
Were you physically near,
my heart would say.
Body and spirit know you
are lifted to the light.

Rückert often writes of sensing the presence of Luise and Ernst. Here he observes that he does not have this feeling at their graves. What may seem to be a contradiction is actually quite common. One counselor observed that a number of mourners experience the presence of their loved ones while *simultaneously* feeling with certainty that they have moved on.[407] Friedrich provides a clue to this apparent paradox.

In the second line, the poet references a well-known and enigmatic saying of Jesus: "Let the dead bury their dead."[408] This passage is so famous that it is nearly a parable.[409] Rückert was well read, even by academic standards. He and his wife kept a copy of the Luther Bible in their home. There is little doubt that he knew the biblical source of the phrase and its full implications.

Many other Bible verses had entered into colloquial speech in Rückert's day. Their popularity depended in large part on their translation. For example, one proverb that was cumbersome in King James English, "out of the abundance of the heart the mouth speaketh,"[410] was translated in the Luther Bible with a decidedly *folksy* tone: "What fills your heart, flows out your mouth."[411] Today this expression has become so integrated into the language that many native German speakers are unaware of its biblical origins. In a similar way, "the dead bury their dead" had long since achieved proverbial status when Friedrich wrote his poem.[412]

The phrase comes from the gospels of Matthew and Luke. At the time of Jesus, who said these words to a grieving son, burial was a private affair. The remains were interred in a family tomb, usually a cave carved out of limestone rock, with shelves for their dead. A full year later, the family would return to collect the bones[413] and place them in an ossuary.[414] This had a pragmatic purpose: the shelves could be used again and again for the dead, allowing a family to remain together in a single tomb, literally gathered to their ancestors.[415]

Eric Meyers, professor emeritus and founder of the Center for Jewish Studies at Duke University, described this later *second burial* in the ossuary as both an internment and a symbolic expiation of death: when "the dead bury their dead," redeeming body and spirit from its decomposed state. The reference seems to have been to this traditional Palestinian practice; in other words, let the atonement of death in the *second burial* tend to itself.[416] Or as respected historian and New Testament scholar John Dominic Crossan translated the passage, "A follower to Jesus 'I must stay to rebury my father. Jesus to follower 'Let the dead rebury their dead.'"[417]

While it may be a bit much to ask

that Friedrich's poem take the whole load of this biblical meaning, his allusion leaves recognizable traces and unmistakable signs of sentiments a grieving father could well understand—their bodies are gone; their spirits are free.[418]

> **Little May Bells
> ring in the air:
> deer and antelope
> hear their sound.**
>
> **Deer and antelope
> run their race:
> branches and twigs
> do not bother them.**
>
> **Over branches
> they leap:
> no snowflake
> bars their way.**
>
> **No snowflake,
> not in May:
> free of frocks
> they leap away.**
>
> **Free of frocks
> so, too,
> my tiny dolls
> leap in the air.**
>
> **My tiny dolls
> leap about,
> in their tiny socks
> slipping and sliding.**
>
> **In their tiny socks
> they jump,
> their curls
> bouncing free.**
>
> **My tiny dolls,
> red in the dawn:
> your curls now
> cut by death.**
>
> **Your curls now
> cut and trimmed,
> your frocks
> in ruin.**
>
> **My tiny dolls
> disguised and covered:
> Little May Bells,
> hush, now, hush!**

Rückert is indulging in a bit of whimsy. Lilies of the valley usually bloom in May. The flower's name, *little May Bells*, describes perfectly the fragrant white bell-shaped blossoms of this hardy woodland plant.

In the Coburg area, May Bells usually bloom in late April or early May and last about one to three weeks. However, the spring of 1834 was unseasonably rainy, windy and cold. The flowers would likely have bloomed around mid–May and lasted little more than a week, adding poignancy to the grieving father's observations on the transience of life.

Friedrich gives new life to an overused poetic conceit that May Bells are ringing or calling, as in August Heinrich Hoffmann von Fallersleben's famous *lied*, later set to music by Felix Mendelssohn in 1843:

> The May Bells ring in the valley,
> their peeling is bright and clear:
> Come, little flowers, come,
> join in the dance!
> ....
> The May Bells are calling, calling:
> the little flowers join in the dance.
> I hear them, I must go![419]

Rückert and his wife were keen gardeners. He was doubtless aware that May Bells are one of the few spring-blooming bulb plants that deer avoid. Here Friedrich envisions that the bells call to the deer and the royal or dwarf antelope,[420] comparing the animals to his "tiny dolls," Ernst and Luise.

He replicates this chiming of the bells through meter and, with slight variations, repetition of the third line of each stanza in the first of the next. The final stanza is purposefully out of step with the previous refrains. Friedrich's dead children, unrecognizable in their graves, are now deaf to the figurative ringing and literal beauty of the flowers.

May Bells often appear in wedding, communion and confirmation bouquets as symbols of purity and hope. Little wonder, then, that the grieving father urges the blossoms to hush. Throughout these poems, Rückert is frequently reminded of a future that his children will no longer have. His wistful resentment toward spring may seem morbid or counter-productive. However, researchers and counselors have identified a positive link between healthy mourning and what they call "ritual leave-taking."[421] These small poetic rituals of acknowledging his children's graves help reinforce Friedrich's awareness that the loss has in fact occurred.[422]

Primula Veris

**Earliest, tiny golden bowls,
open your blooms of heaven.
Spread this table of spring
with your bowls of dew.**

**This table of spring is spread
with your bowls of dew:
your fragrant dishes laid
out for the feast of bees.**

**My heart, like the bees,
feasts on your bouquet;
earliest, tiny golden bowls,
join me on the grave of love.**

Rückert's poem is as endearingly unobtrusive as its titular flower. Primula veris, known as cowslip primrose, is common in Coburg. It grows in meadows, along paths and under trees. It is marked by lance-shaped leaves and small, yellow blossoms that have a lush fragrance. Their drooping, bowl-like shapes led to their genus name, *primula*, which is a feminine diminutive meaning "earliest tiny one," flowering in spring. These are the *earliest, tiny golden bowls* of Friedrich's poem, a fitting name for a flower blooming over the graves of Luise and Ernst.

This poem hints that these golden *blooms of heaven* may have been on or near their resting place. In the modern world, we relegate such visits to weekends, holidays and memorial days. We sometimes mistake lingering over graves as a failure to heal or move on. In fact, the opposite is true. Nearly 70 percent of bereaved parents report that it took three to four years to put their child's death into perspective and continue with their own lives.[423] They were forever changed by the loss.

"Grief is not an illness," observed Paul Irion, grief expert and a champion of Hospice care, "but a response to a new situation."[424] Tending the graves of our loved ones is an important ritual that offers solace and a sense of a healthy, ongoing relationship. It also reinforces the finality of death while simultaneously helping us adjust to our new identities without their physical presence.[425] This identity is in part social: we face the reality of our loss in the context of our evolving interactions with family and friends, with all that such a future entails.[426] Friedrich's gentle invitation to join him over the grave was as much for his children as it was the tiny flowers.

**In the first leaf of spring
I found a strange cipher
that my heart did not tire
of attempting to decipher.**

> It was a love note, written
> by a hand that, accustomed
> to pens made my men,
> was not overly practiced
>
> And then, *touched!*,
> I hit upon the key.
> An angel had guided
> my child's hand for me.
>
> He sits still at last, though
> he felt school was grim;
> in my hand I now hold
> my first letter from him.
>
> Such a short time—but
> these letters, *look here!*,
> calligraphy so fine that
> I hope he writes all year.

Rückert's songs often seek to *restore* meaning in his world by *reading* meaning in the world around him. His description of a letter from Ernst, written in a secret cipher on a leaf, reflects a deep need among the bereaved to discover signs from their dead. This sense of a loved one's presence, both literal and in the mind's eye, is significant and complex.[427] Friedrich writes of such experiences in other poems in ways that suggest they were very real to him.

This song, however, feels more like fancy. He imagines young Ernst, who hated his studies, as writing on a leaf, and continuing to work on his newfound calligraphy in the future! Such whims are not unheard of in the Romantic verse tradition. In 1829, American poet William Gilmore Simms wrote that the deep wood seemed to speak to him in the voice of his late father. "I hear the sacred words," Simms observed in one of his most poignant poems. "My heart receives the music, not mine ear.

> His grave is in the forest, and he sleeps
> Far from the groves he loved—his voice no more
> Is in mine ear; yet through my memory creeps
> Its echo....
> I feel
> As if I were a listener to the spell
> Of one whose voice is power! My senses reel!
> It is his language,—I should know it well,—
> He speaks through these sweet waters which he loved[428]

There is another aspect of Rückert's poem that is easy to miss. Sometimes I joke with other bereaved parents that if an angel appeared to me today—say Michael or Gabriel—my first response would be "Mike, Gabe, glad to know you. Where's Jess?" Friedrich has written something similar here: the angel may be helping his son write, but for the grieving father, it is Ernst who now bridges the gap between the physical and invisible worlds. This is the key that deciphers the strange cipher on the leaf. "Clearly," observed Rückert scholar Sascha Monhoff, "his child is the only interpreter that has meaning to the mourner."[429]

> God has granted you a task
> that should have been ours:
> we had hoped to teach you
> but now you do the teaching.
>
> O children, you are rearing
> your parents on sorrow;
> guiding us, guiding us until
> you bring us to you at last.

"Grief includes depressed mood, yearning, loneliness," observed psychiatrist Karl Goodkin, "searching for the deceased, the sense of the deceased being present, and the sense of being in ongoing communication with that person."[430] This poem communicates each of these distinct states: desperation, longing, sorrow and a sense that Ernst and Luise still have an effect on their parents' lives. Rückert infuses these brief lines with undertones of regret and self-recrimination that lead to an unexpected sense of hope for future reunion. This hope does not come easily, however, as he writes in another poem for Luise:

> Your hurts, small as a child,
> you brought to me, mother-like,
> for consolation and care.
>
> Now my hurt, not so small,
> I bring to you:
> Oh my child, console me!
>
> So we exchange love for loss:
> a heart full of care;
> a hurt inconsolable.

It is difficult to know just how literal to take Rückert; this, too, is experienced by many who have lost loved ones. I still feel my daughter with me: her kindness, love, spirited enthusiasm and gentle encouragement on my darkest days. I believe she is with me in a way that is beyond words or signs. Perhaps Friedrich expressed it best: she is guiding me, consoling me, bringing me to her at last.

> Is it not at least conceivable, therefore, that around us now in this mysterious universe are those we have loved and lost for a while, but that between us is a barrier through which we can see only in rare moments when for some reason the frequency in them corresponds with some higher frequency in ourselves? I think so.—Norman Vincent Peale[431]

**Here rests in this chest
much that was yours;
sacred and silent:
like you, undisturbed.**

**Your dress in this chest,
camisole in your coffin.
Your little shoes
never to remove.**

**Each day from this chest
I lift dress after dress;
seeking sorrow, perhaps:
or solace or mercy.**

——

**Because you were the smallest
your clothes will not be handed down;
your finest, saved for best,
will never be soiled.**

**Saved for best, your smallness,
preserved now as she,
in her pureness,
also lies preserved.**

**The smallest, dearly loved;
shining now and gone,
but radiant still, when I
catch a glimpse of you.**

These two poems speak of mementos. Keepsakes are natural. There is no time limit to how long such items remain in the home: months, years or for the rest of the survivors' lives. The vital difference seems to be in the emotions invested in these inanimate items.

A *transitional object*, for example, is a comfort as we adjust to life without our loved one, such as a favorite stuffed toy, a blanket or as in these poems, treasured clothing. A *linking object*, on the other hand, may veer dangerously close to imagining that our dead loved one is the object itself—with resulting anxiety and emotional breakdown when the object is removed. Healthy mementos may be put away when the time is right, which might in fact be never.[432]

Such small memorials may seem odd to casual observers. "Not getting over it," they may sniff. "Complicated grief," they intone knowingly. This is nonsense, of course. Memorials and memorabilia may be surprisingly helpful.

While my daughter was alive, our home was festooned with Jess things: her artwork, certificates, newspapers and magazines with her model shoots, handwritten notes, doodles, knick-knacks, and photos, photos, photos. There is no reason for this to change now that our relationship is one of loving in separation. In fact, to take reminders of Jess down from my shelves would be odd—as though with her death I would somehow sponge away her life as well.

Removing our treasured memorabilia can also be damaging. It is easy to dwell too much on negative or unpleasant memories that we wish we could change. Such ruminations may lead to brooding, self-recrimination and remorse. However, guilt offers no solutions and no hope.

Photos, treasures, creative expressions such as art or poetry, may be helpful and productive. They allow free expression of many damaging emotions that, if not faced, may fester and canker. This is in itself liberating. They also remind us of those many happy moments that are all the more precious in our loved one's absence.[433] They speak to us of hope for a continuing bond in this life and a future reunion in the next.

> You never *want* to forget. You never *will* forget. Because all you have are your memories. It should be your task to make them good and give them substance so that others too will never forget.—Ronald Knapp[434]

Ah, if only a child fell free of pain, as a petal falls to the ground.

Free of suffering, as rose petals are free, sinking, passing into dust.

A mother lifted her dying child, carrying the pain of her death in her heart.

The painful pace of oncoming death is inescapable and frequently overwhelming for all who know loss. This may be compounded by sudden, traumatic loss, but for bereaved parents such as Friedrich and his wife Luise, no time is acceptable. "Whatever the age, the death of the child is seen as untimely by his parents," observed pioneering bereavement expert Beverly Raphael. "Even when mourned, the child is not forgotten. He is always counted as one of the children."[435]

Friedrich had not resorted to hyperbole: parents *do* carry the pain of the death in their hearts for the rest of their lives. There may be joy-filled days ahead, moments of calm and gentle humor, but our grief stays with us. We carry it as we once carried our children. "You will not awaken one morning miraculously filled with a joy of life," wrote grief therapist and bereaved parent, Harriet Sarnoff Schiff. "You will not leave your sadness behind; to be told you could is neither realistic nor truthful. But, instead, your sadness will no longer pull you down. You will now carry it with you, inside you. Remember this: you will carry it. It will not carry you!"[436]

The Death-bed

We watch'd her breathing thro' the night,
Her breathing soft and low,

As in her breast the wave of life
Kept heaving to and fro!

So silently we seem'd to speak—
So slowly moved about!
As we had lent her half our powers
To eke her living out!

Our very hopes belied our fears
Our fears our hopes belied—
We thought her dying when she slept,
And sleeping when she died!

For when the morn came dim and sad—
And chill with early showers,
Her quiet eyelids closed—she had
Another morn than ours!

—Thomas Hood[437]

**You five rose thorns,
you five knight's spurs,
you five devil's helmets,
into the dragon's mouth!**

**You five rose thorns,
where was your wrath
when your rose was
weak and undefended?**

**You spurred knights
made no move when
the reaper stole
your damsel away.**

**Oh you bedeviled helmets
did not lift your heads
as the reaper cast
his grim spell!**

**Alas, you mouths of lions,
gaped like cubs staring
into the throat
of a terrible dragon.**

**The youngest dared
to fight for her, only
to be caught,
only to be killed.**

**Stay, I cannot lose
you four as well!
Stay with me in the
rain, in the tears.**

Friedrich spent countless hours in his garden. Before his children died, it had been the inspiration for some of his most endearingly folksy quatrains:

> You need no market quote
> for the cabbage you've grown;
> it is seasoned with sweat,
> irreplaceable dew, your own.[438]

An enthusiastic gardener, Rückert was familiar with the many appellations given to flowers. In this poem he uses common names in a flight of fancy. *Knight's spur* fits his poetic conceit nicely, though for *wolf's bane* he chose a lesser-known term, *devil's helmet* or *iron cap*. *Foxglove* is also known as *lion's mouth* or *dragon's mouth*, two names that he adapts with aplomb.

Now the grieving father returns to his old passion with a mix of whimsy, regret and foreboding. He provides a romantic image of Ernst, gallantly fighting for Luise, only to be caught in the clutches of the same disease that took her life.

Rückert reserves his deepest fear for the final stanza. He may fuss at his boisterous boys, comparing them to failed knights, but if they are indeed like the flowers he lists, they too may wilt and die. Such fears of abandonment are part of grief. With our loved ones gone, apparently left undefended by God, we worry that those who remain may also soon leave us.[439]

This would be too much for Friedrich. *Stay with me in the rain*, he implores, *in the tears*.

**A tree would buckle under the weight
if every flower ended in fruit.
Why does God allow more flowers
than its boughs can bear?**

**To garland our hope and when spring
winds gather their flowers,**

to leave untouched, God willing, those that ripen into fruit.

The spring of 1834 was particularly windy, lending pathos to Rückert's lament. Friedrich was likely aware of proverbial wisdom associated with this poem: *Every fruit starts with a flower, but not every flower ends in a fruit.* Pollinating insects and weather conditions are outside the control of any gardener. The tree is trapped in two contradictory conditions: if every flower resulted in fruit, its branches would buckle under the weight. Because of this, blossoms are not merely steeped in transitory beauty; they are also rich with sorrow. Inevitably, as Friedrich laments, the spring winds must gather precious blossoms, leaving those, by God's will, that will ripen into fruit.

Rückert's poem is equally contradictory. Why would God offer hope of a future, he asks, only to take these two children? To preserve those who remain? His questions have no answer, yet in asking them, the poet speaks to the cold realities of mourning.

Mary O'Neill, whose research focuses on contemporary art and bereavement, suggests that creative expressions such as these offer permanence to "our death denying cultural worldview." They provide means for understanding shared grief. "When a culture no longer provides adequate forms of mourning," O'Neill observed, "these works can act as a means of engaging with bereavement, disenfranchised grief and ambiguous loss."[440]

To leave untouched, God willing, Rückert writes, *those that ripen into fruit.* The metaphor of his remaining children is difficult to miss. Friedrich communicates the desperation, fear and hope that so often mingle with love and grief. Others who have known suffering also wrote of similar mixed emotions.

Erich Paul Remarque was drafted into the German army in November 1916. The following year, in July 1917, he served in Flanders during some of the most brutal fighting of World War I. Erich was wounded by shrapnel in the neck, wrist and knee. He was evacuated and sent to hospital. A little over a month later, his mother, Maria, died of cancer on 9 September 1917.

After the war, Remarque struggled with returning to civilian life: he taught school and published as a journalist and a poet. In 1926, over the course of six months, he wrote *All Quiet on the Western Front* under his preferred name, Erich *Maria* Remarque, in memory of his mother. He submitted the manuscript to the most prestigious literary house of the day, S. Fisher. The editors tersely dismissed the work out of hand.

Remarque received more callous rejections from other houses before Ullstein, an established liberal German Jewish publisher, printed the novel in serial form between November and December of 1928. *All Quiet on the Western Front* was an instant success, hailed as a modern classic by the Berlin literary establishment. Ullstein quickly published it in book form, which was then translated into French and English editions. Within six months the volume sold well over half a million copies—the first German title to do so in so short a time.

Fame earned Remarque an interesting place in history. Sales continued at a remarkable pace for five years. Then the author and his book caught the attention of the Nazi party. Joseph Goebbels condemned the book as "a literary betrayal of the soldiers of the world war." *All Quiet on the Western Front* joined the works of Sigmund Freud, Thomas Mann, Ernest Hemingway, James Joyce and Albert Einstein in the infamous book burning before the Berlin Opera House on 10 May 1933.

Grief is a difficult subject. Descriptors fail us. I have noticed that authors familiar with real sorrow tend to avoid unnecessary flourishes or purple prose. Like Rückert, Remarque speaks calmly and plainly of mourning and unexpected hope:

> I felt the dull grief, that had sunk in me like a stone, awash again and again with wild hope, changing and strangely blending, one becoming the other: grief, hope, the wind, the evening ... yes, for a moment I had the uncanny sense that in a real and profound way this is life and maybe even happiness: love with so much sorrow, dread and silent knowledge.[441]

How your five brothers doted
on you, a sister to die for.
Each sought your favor:
eager to please, to do without,
to perish if they must.

You showed no favorites.
Each kindness was welcome
until you left and took the youngest
of your brothers with you:
a favorite after all.

Luise was the youngest child and the only girl among five boys. In this poem, Rückert chose a cumbersome descriptor for Luise's position with her brothers, *a sister to die for*. Friedrich uses this as part of his slightly exaggerated phrasing in the first stanza, hinting playfully at the gallant attentions of his daughter's young knights. But there is also an undertone of foreboding. The boys' chivalry was well-received until, alas, death "chose" a favorite among them. Rückert's fanciful poem ends on a morbid downbeat.

This type of dark humor is not uncommon among the bereaved, though it is often gently ironic.[442] Humorous asides serve as a coping mechanism. They may arise spontaneously, providing catharsis and objectivity.[443] In fact, quiet humor is an important aspect of mourning that is easily overlooked or misunderstood by a society eager to "heal" or "get over it."[444] Grief expert Earl Grollman insisted that expressing pain in all its aspects is helpful and necessary. "Talk things out," he advised. "Sorrow, like the river, must be given vent lest it erode its bank."[445] In these songs a grieving father is doing precisely that.

"I ask only a hint
of light in the dark;
if you know, tell me:
where are they now?"

"Do they wander from
star to star in the black;
skipping ahead of where
we search for our child?"

"Teach me that I may learn:
does space divide us?
We must know lest
we be blind in the light."

"Praise the Lord of light!"
But here in the dust believe:
no time, no space, may
rob a mother of her child.

Nothing near, nothing far:
barriers broken, in thought

    and in deed, those we love are close, they are here.

We are obsessed with the *why* of things. Why did my loved one pass? Why do mass shootings continue? Why is there suffering in the world? Why evil? The study of why is called theodicy—a paltry term for such an important topic. To me, *why* is the wrong question. *How*, the close cousin of *why*, interests me even less.

    I know how my mother died: cancer. I know how my father and uncle died. Age and disease, alas, are the way of the world. There is little mystery to how my niece and my wife's younger brother died. How my daughter died is written on the death certificate: a fentanyl-laced heroin overdose. These details are crass, uninteresting, morbid. After all, *how* they died is not nearly as important as *who* they were to us.

    Now words like "eternal" and "afterlife" have new meaning. *Is my daughter happy and safe?* I ask. *Is she near, as close as a falling leaf or the taste of an apple or a distant hawk's cry? Does she continue on?* In our grief, we have only one question. Tell us this that we may endure the rest.

    Where are they now?

    Rückert acknowledges the yearning and need to praise the Lord of light. At the same time, the cold realities of loss are part of his daily existence. *We must know*, he writes, *but here in the dust they must merely believe.* These and other expressions in this poem seem to have been influenced by Psalm 119, which by German tradition encompasses all other psalms and is an important part of mourning.[446] The connection was well entrenched by Friedrich's day.

    In 1671, Heinrich Schütz had set Psalm 119 to music. The composer died a year later. Per his request, his setting and a separate motet using the same psalm composed by his former student, Christoph Bernhard, were performed at the funeral. It was also the text of the sermon.[447]

    After a sudden traumatic death, undertones of rituals linger in our minds, often just below the surface. Without them, we feel adrift.[448] Rückert may well have felt something similar when he echoed the psalmist's cry, "give me understanding, so I can learn."[449]

> I lie in the dust;
> revive me by your word.
> I weep with sorrow;
> encourage me by your word.
> —Psalm 119:25, 28 NLT

    The Book of Job and Goethe's *Faust* address similar concerns of dust and eternity, approaching them from different perspectives. Where the misery of Job is universally known across the centuries, *Faust's* Mephistopheles feels especially modern. Both stories feature a bet with God over a man's soul; each speaks to our struggle to embrace the spiritual when faced with a daunting physical world.

    In the Book of Job, Satan slaughters Job's children, destroys his belongings and ruins his health. In *Faust*, Mephistopheles overwhelms Faust with transient worldly joys. "Dust he shall eat," chortles Mephistopheles. "And he'll like it."[450] Both tales have a similar goal: Job and Faust must betray the transcendent and focus entirely on the tangible.[451]

    For Job, his immediate condition has little to offer. Misery seems to consume his world. He is unable to see beyond his pain, as Emily Dickinson wrote in 1862:

> Pain—has an Element of Blank—
> It cannot recollect
> When it begun—or if there were
> A time when it was not—[452]

God appears at the end of the book. Job declares: "I have spoken of the unspeakable and tried to grasp the infinite ... but now my eyes have seen you. Therefore I will be quiet, comforted that I am dust."[453] Theologians have wrestled with this enigmatic ending for millennia, but I see this passage in practical terms. God showed up, eternity and the spiritual are real after all, and therefore Job's children live on. As answers go, it is better than most. For Job, this may be the only comfort with meaning.

Goethe's *Faust* is an unsettling mirror of Job and yet the play holds a fond place in my heart. On 30 October 2009, I saw Hector Berlioz's *La Damnation de Faust* at the Metropolitan Opera in New York City. The next day I called my daughter for Halloween, one of her favorite holidays. I was in Manhattan to present at the American Translators Associations 50th annual conference. That was my big news, but Jess didn't care. "You saw *Faust* on Devil's Night?" she interrupted my crowing. "How cool is that?"

By 1932 there were forty-four English translations of *Faust*. Nearly a century later, the number is over one hundred—though I know of no one that has managed to count them all. The quintessentially modern drama took Goethe a lifetime to complete.[454]

Faust falls prey to an entirely human quirk: when things go well, the spiritual world can seem uninteresting if not unimportant. Mephistopheles provides shallow copies of all that was taken away from Job: Faust has companionship; wealth; health and the renewed vigor of youth. Fame, fortune and excess are all his. These may prove to be temporary and insubstantial, but this seldom stops us from hungrily consuming them as treasures of value.

Mephistopheles gloated to God that he would have Faust wallowing in the muck "like my famed relation, the snake," and so he does.[455] Faust discovers that the largesse of the world is dust. Near the end of the play, he can tell little difference between the eternity of his soul and his gluttony of dirt.

My father was a professional photographer. From him I learned that "forced perspective" is a photographic trick in which objects appear smaller than they actually are. Death, alas, forces an entirely different perspective. What we imagined was important recedes from our view. What matters most looms larger than before. We are desperate for any word of our loved ones. "Adonai has compassion," sang the psalmist, "for he understands how we are made, he remembers that we are dust."[456] In grief, perhaps we see clearly for the first time.

When she left, my little girl,
I had hopes that the songs
of angels would lift her,
teach her to soar,
gliding on the wind.

But that was the night
of a storm so fierce
that even the old tower
yearned to be alive,
gliding on the wind.

> **This wind is perfect
> for eagle's wings,
> no doubt, but what
> of a solitary butterfly
> gliding on the wind?**
>
> **Rough winds, winter winds,
> beautiful, merciless!
> You scattered the scent:
> would you send the rose itself
> gliding on the wind?**
>
> **The storm crashes down
> like lightning, as quickly
> returning to its seat in the sky.
> It leaves a single spark
> gliding on the wind.**
>
> **I would love to fly
> and in this weather
> a man might soar
> like a dry leaf
> gliding on the wind.**
>
> **Sand and dust, yes,
> and gravel and stone;
> not just old leaves
> but entire groves
> gliding on the wind.**
>
> **But I have no wings
> and soaring aloft I am
> like an ostrich trying to
> escape myself,
> gliding on the wind.**
>
> **For by longing alone
> I cannot ascend to where
> you soar in the light.
> And so I must live
> gliding on the wind.**

This poem is steeped in fear, assurance and loneliness. *Is Luise lifted up by angels,* Friedrich asks. *Is the storm too much for her? Is she in the light?* His concerns are as ancient as humanity. The death of a loved one shatters our world. Grief surrounds us. Our expectations and hopes have disappeared. We are adrift and bereft. We felt this emptiness the moment they died and may feel it for the rest of our lives. Our pain and doubts cannot be wished away.

Researchers have discovered that mourners give priority to finding meaning in their lives. This is a response to the natural questions caused by death, especially sudden unexpected loss.[457] We demand answers. *Why did our loved one have to die?* we may ask. *Where was God when we needed him? Where is the justice? The grace? The mercy?* Rabbi Earl Grollman said that these doubts are a healthy part of the life of faith. Asking *why*, he wrote, is a cry of anguish and a natural reaction to pain: "The statement: 'Dear God, why me? Why us?' may be not only a question but your own normal cry of distress, a plea for help."[458]

These questions can make others uncomfortable.

After someone dies, our friends may seek to fill our silence with chatter. Churches can be especially guilty of false bonhomie that sounds less like honest compassion than a desire for us to hush up and stop bringing everyone down. Unhelpful congregations can make us feel abandoned or shamed as faithless for daring to challenge the faith community with deep questions.

We shouldn't be surprised. I doubt many of us were much better before we lost a loved one. Human nature may be inherently compassionate, but we are also and often self-interested. Seeing another person's grief goes against our desire for a good life and our cheerful delusions that all is well. We ignore millennia of lament and understanding in favor of our own needs of the moment. What use, we asked in our trite assurance, is the self-pitying twaddle of old Lao Tzu?

Forlorn, alas: I am homeless.
All have plenty; I alone have none.
I have lost everything.
Broken and a fool!
Chaos, chaos.
Others shine so bright.
I am dark, I am alone.
—Tao Te Ching[459]

Once I may have dismissed the honest questions of mourners as being naïve or self-involved. Now I learned that I was the one who had been both. After Jess died, I knew what I had never understood: the pain, guilt, frustration, desperation and doubts of grief. To feel dark and alone while others seem to shine so brightly, as Lao Tzu wrote, is not hyperbole: it is an accurate expression of deep and abiding loss. In "Now the sun will rise as bright," Rückert wrote of this shocking sense of solitude: *This sorrow fell on me alone, the sun shines on everyone.*

Ultimately grief is a solitary journey, but not one that we must travel alone. We may find family members and trusted friends that patiently walk with us. Many healthy churches are filled with others that know pain and suffering. They too have felt the burden of doubt and understand our desperate hopes for a future reunion. These faith communities may encourage our questions and commiserate with us as together we explore the mysteries of sorrow and belief. "Perhaps there are no answers," they assure us as much in silence as in words, "but we will listen to you."

When I read this song, I am reminded of an elegy that may have been known to Rückert—he was a student of ancient Egypt. Entitled "His Journey to the Sky," the poem was preserved in two pyramids from the end of the Old Kingdom (c. 2613–2181 BCE):

He that flies, flies! He flies away from us, all of us.
He is no longer on earth, he is in heaven.
You, his God, have his soul in your arms.
He rushes the sky as a heron, kissed the sky as a falcon, leapt through the sky as a grasshopper.[460]

Those who did no harm on earth must still suffer harm; you found her tolerable and so, apparently, she must die.

Suppose life wins and she blooms, fresh and young; she will forget the memory of this pain—as will you.

But if she succumbs to agony and death; that, too, will be forgotten in her flight as an angel.

The first stanza is so poignant we want to weep. Who among us has not felt cheated and abandoned by deity as our loved one suffers? After the death of his beloved sister, Cornelia, Goethe felt wholly changed. He spoke of her as a sturdy, reliable root that had now been chopped away, leaving the branches she once nourished to wither and die. He had no other choice than to surrender himself to nature, he wrote, "which allows us to feel terrible pain for a brief time, but lets us mourn for much longer."[461] A month later, Goethe composed this poem about Cornelia:

> The gods, endless, give all
> to those they love, entire:
> all our joys, endless; all
> our pains, endless, entire.[462]

Goethe is hinting that the gods' largesse may be too extravagant. In giving all, entirely and without reserve, perhaps they give too much. Like Goethe, Rückert is also heartbroken and feeling a tad snide. This is not unexpected.

Anger, vindictiveness and hostility are acknowledged aspects of grief.[463] Many bereaved parents express bitterness, disillusionment and a sense of betrayal by the divine.[464] They may blame God and, as in Friedrich's poem, even mock deity's apparent lack of concern: *you found her tolerable and so, apparently, she must die*, or if Luise survives, *she will forget the memory of this pain—as will you.*

Rückert's prayer is set during the brief week while Luise lay ill. However, this does not signify the actual period when it was written. Friedrich frequently set his poems in the past, the future or the present, depending on the specific requirements of a given piece. Some in the collection were written in the voices of his wife and children. The timing doesn't matter. Whether writing from current frustration or recalled emotion, the poet hinged his song not on *when* but on *how* he was feeling as his daughter lay dying. And they are powerful emotions indeed.

In comparison the final stanza seems weak, more plaintive hope than calm assurance. Yet this, too, offers insight. Rückert's prayer echoes many psalms of lament. As with those hymns, an upbeat ending provides poor solace.[465] It is in the poet's pain that we find true communion.

> Dark is the world to me, for all its cities and stars. If not for my faith that God in His silence still listens to a cry, who could stand such agony?—Abraham Heschel[466]

**Blight has fallen
on my garden.
You, loveliest rose,
wilted with the rest.**

**Wilted flowers, too
many to count:
listless, since you
died, on wilted stems.**

Rückert's home in Neuses had a garden behind the house, bordered by a small clear brook. They kept ivy, plum trees, gooseberry bushes, hyacinths, asters (among many other flowers) and a large bed of roses. Friedrich and his wife tended the garden together, separately and with their children.[467]

Many counselors and bereaved parents speak of the consolations of spending time in nature[468] yet here the poet addresses a different aspect of horticulture. "Rückert's poetry is filled with his own dual vision," observed German philosopher Karl Fortlage. Friedrich saw the external realities of physical phenomena while simultaneously piercing their deeper meaning with his "poetic vision." Rückert reminds us, Fortlage concluded, that although much is dying in nature, nothing is truly dead: "All the world is alive, all the world talks to us, all the world shares with us, all the world speaks to us of joys and sorrows. We become the confidants of all things."[469]

Friedrich was fond of symbolism, but not as a poetic conceit. The clarity of his vision came from viewing the world sideways, perceiving connections in ways that sometimes surprise us. The wilted flowers in his garden, hanging listless on their stems since death had taken his loveliest rose, Luise, reminded the grieving father of so many other blossoms that had died. Death seemed to permeate the air itself. This parallel with the scarlet fever pandemic is understated, precise and poignant.

"*Every* lament can be expressed as poetry," suggested German-born Israeli philosopher Gershom Scholem. The language of lament sits on the border between the known physical world and what is unknown and silenced. It is an expression of the infinite, the symbolic, the implied. Lament is steeped in mystery, Scholem wrote; its opposite is revelation.[470]

> If the very air we breathe might kill us, how can we ever be safe? To be killed by hailstones or by gunshot is one thing—but by breathing in air from another person? I realize I'm flirting with heresy by questioning God's design in nature, but shouldn't air nourish us, not destroy us? ... But to die from breathing in common air! What foul air that I may encounter in the street, or in a slaughterhouse, or a garbage heap or sewer, can do as much harm as what I have somehow inbreathed in my own home?—John Donne, after contracting the plague[471]

> **Sighs, as you float,**
> **tears, flowing so free,**
> **I would go with you**
> **and so be free of grief.**
>
> **Sighs, as you float,**
> **hear my plea: Bring**
> **my joy back to me!**
> **Yet you return empty.**
>
> **Tears, as you flow,**
> **do not be so quick:**
> **stay awhile, be still,**
> **linger in these eyes.**
>
> **Sighs, as you float,**
> **tears, dried and gone,**
> **I too would disappear**
> **into love and lament.**

Rückert makes frequent reference to sighs, a common aspect of grief that can be easily overlooked or misunderstood. Sighs underscore the constant presence of grief. They express the desire for things to return to how they were before, the hopelessness of that desire and the resulting need to cry out in sorrow.[472] Friedrich's repetition of the phrase *Sighs, as you float*, sounds itself like an expulsion of breath.

In 1985 clinicians and therapists at Massachusetts General Hospital identified sighing among bereaved parents as a correlate to the physical sensation of breathlessness. The patients' oxygen and carbon dioxide levels bore striking similarities to those of depression sufferers.[473] These symptoms of grief are considered transient and require no professional attention, the key difference being the long-term loss of self-esteem associated with depression.[474] There is a strong psychological and physiological basis for sighs and weeping. Our life experiences, social environment and cultural mores each affect how we mourn, but there is also a biological imperative.[475]

Sighs are a coping mechanism as vital as more overt displays of mourning. An expulsion of breath is often unconscious and can be therapeutic: a brief respite from pent-up sorrow. But the sensation may be illusory, as Friedrich reveals in this poem's complex web of emotions. He envies the freedom of sighs and tears as they escape into nothingness while simultaneously begrudging their departure; he would *be free of this grief* only to *disappear into love and lament*.

In other poems, Friedrich refers to

Ernst and Luise as *inseparable* in life and death: they were known as "knife and fork" in the Rückert family. He also often makes allusions to Luise *floating* over her grave or up to heaven. In this light, "Sighs, you float away" is as much about Luise and Ernst as it is sighs and tears.

This *stay/leave* dichotomy is a poignant echo of emotions known to many bereaved parents. German theologian and priest Martin Luther lost his thirteen-year-old daughter in 1542. She died in his arms. "I would gladly have kept my daughter," he said later, "for I love her very much, if God had wanted to leave her with me.... The separation vexes one way beyond all measure. It is a marvelous thing to know that she is certainly in peace and that all is well with her and yet to be so sad!"[476]

How long, Adonai? Will you forget me forever?
How long must I keep asking myself what to do,
with sorrow in my heart every day?
—Psalm 13: 1–2 CJB

I
When in the door
your mother steps
and the candle shimmers,
I catch a glimmer
of you beside her,
slipping in too
as you used to do.
Am I awake, asleep?
Have my eyes grown weak,
a trick of the light?
No, you are a shadow
following your mother
as always, alas,
your mother's shadow.

II
When your mother
steps in the door
and I turn
to see her there,
I glance not on her face
but in the place
there in the door
where you should be,
your face
alive with joy,
slipping in the room
as ever, my little girl.
Oh you, light of my heart
too soon
gone out too soon.

Rückert introduces a well-known metaphor that suddenly seems painfully real. Young Luise, whom her father called *Luischen*, was constantly next to Friedrich's wife, her *mother's shadow*, as the saying goes.[477] In the gloom of the evening, he senses his daughter's presence, a figurative shadow now made literal in the darkness of her absence; the light of his heart gone out.

Modern experts call this pattern *shadow grief*. It is not overt nor is it debilitating. The bereaved continue in a more or less normal life. But their sorrow is never completely resolved nor can it be.[478] For example, after Sarah Spratt Polk Rayner lost her eldest son, twelve-year-old Henry, in 1859, the formerly bright, prosperous mother carried her grief for the rest of her days. "Susan does not give one the idea of a happy woman," a friend observed. "What it is one cannot define, but there is a shadow there."[479]

William Shakespeare's eleven-year-old son Hamnet died in 1596. The playwright eloquently described long-term grief in *Richard II*: "Say that again. / 'The shadow of my sorrow'—ha, let's see. / 'Tis very true: my grief lies all within; / And these external manner of laments / Are merely shadows to the unseen grief / That swells with silence in the tortured soul."[480] Shadow grief cannot be avoided. It demands that we who have known loss find a way to adjust. We are faced with a new direction and a new identity, whether we would have it so or not.

Loss often opens paths to transformation and growth, including: a new appreciation of life; a quest for meaning; recognition of life's transience and frailty; closer relationships; appreciation of others; personal strength; humility; a feeling of being fully present; compassion and commiseration with the suffering of others; a marked spirituality; attention to kindness; and a feeling of transcendence or transfiguration.[481] These many ways of coping do not alleviate our loss. Bereavement is a permanent state, as is the love we feel for our dead. The shadow caused by their absence remains.

This poem was the third of the five pieces from Rückert's *Songs on the Death of Children* that Gustav Mahler set to his song cycle, *Kindertotenlieder*. The composer transposed parts I and II. Mahler's musical progression begins with the first line of Rückert's part II, *When your mother*. The poet looks for little Luise only to find she is no longer there. The remaining *lied* is an overwhelming lament, returning as the song ends with the last line of part I, *your mother's shadow*.

**That I should drink and eat,
eat and drink,
forgetting all the while
that you are lost to me!**

**Yet this chair, your chair
stands empty on my left.**

**Eat—how you ate!—
my mouth to yours no more.**

**Your place is set,
your napkin, your plate;
and fresh from the cellar
stands your glass of wine.**

**I look to see your
hands lifting, emptying it
but there it remains
full to the brim.**

**Full, yes, I must face what
should be emptier at least.
Full my heart, full of pain,
and in my eyes a flood.**

This poem could have been written at any time during the first six months after Luise's death. Rückert may be describing a period when the family kept her chair beside him and set a place for her at the table, though it is just as likely that his thoughts are figurative. He may simply see her place setting in his mind.

These small rituals, such as keeping a place at table, are normal and expected. Over time the tradition may be isolated to special occasions as a gesture of remembrance. They can facilitate adjustment and be genuinely positive.[482] Many bereaved parents are surprised by the power of these customs. Noted German philosopher and psychologist Erich Fromm observed that a calm, thoughtful ritual "*expresses* strivings recognized as valuable by the individual."[483]

William James learned this firsthand in the summer of 1885. At the time, the American philosopher and professor of psychiatry at Harvard University had three sons: Harry (six), Billy (three) and the apple of his father's eye, one-year-old Herman. The toddler was slightly chubby and irresistibly jovial. William took to calling him "Humster."

In July of that year, William's wife, Alice, fell ill with scarlet fever. Despite his mother's quarantine, Humster also caught the infection—perhaps after returning to her side too soon. The boy died on 9 July 1885. Two days later, the grieving family buried him in their family plot. They wrapped his tiny casket in a white flannel blanket, lowered it in the grave and surrounded him with flowers and leaves. Prior to losing Humster, William had dismissed such rituals as sentimental. Later, he confessed to an aunt that the ceremony meant a great deal to them: "There is usefully a human need embodied in any old human custom and we both felt this."

A month later, in late August, William returned to the Cambridge home where his young family had once lived. He stood in the street under a "clouded moon," he wrote, staring up at one window on the second-floor. Behind its shutters lay the room where Humster had been born. "It *must* be now," William wrote a cousin the next day, "that he is reserved for some still better chance," some life beyond this one.[484]

James's interest in the invisible world increased. "Immortality is one of the great spiritual needs of man," he wrote.[485] "The surest warrant for immortality is the yearning of our bowels for our dear ones."[486] Interactions with the hereafter came to dominate his research, but not in a spurious or sensational way. The heartbroken father sought confirmation and assurance, leading him to declare in 1897, twelve years after Humster's death: "Religion is the great interest of my life."[487]

Now I know why the flame in your eyes
was dark and flashing at me,
o eyes, as if they could be
all that you are, all that you see.

I did not know, in the pall,
blinded by fog and fate,
your light must go, the hour was late,
returning home to the light of all.

Your light might speak and so you tried:
"We would stay if we could,
but fate will not have it, we are denied."

"Look, look now! for soon we will be gone.
Look in our eyes, today is the day,
ere we go, ere you have stars alone."

The grieving often reflect deeply on their dead loved ones' motives and actions that were easily misunderstood in life—and are now painfully clear in their absence. Rückert hints at regret and self-recrimination but then he surprises us. Rather than brood on his failure to grasp Luise and Ernst's intent, Friedrich writes of what they would have said if they could: *Now I know why*, he writes with a new understanding that draws him closer to his dead children, turning potential blame to compassion.

There are many pieces in this collection that feel rough, written in a deceptively off-hand style that is still rich with Friedrich's natural lyricism. This poem's Petrarchan sonnet structure lent itself well to a musical setting, which may be why this was the second of the five pieces from Rückert's *Songs on the Death of Children* that Gustav Mahler set to his song cycle, *Kindertotenlieder*.

The composer may have noticed that Friedrich seemed to be laboring with this *lied*. Mahler infused a volatile cadence in his adaptation that lacks linear closure. Cold chords strive without success to hints of warmth, only to relapse into sonorous longing. Mahler's subtle approach echoes the complex imagery of Rückert's regrets and the poet's bittersweet hope that his children are looking at him via the stars, *dark and flashing*.

Friedrich remembers his children's eyes with love and anguish. He thinks of them frequently. Although I am fond of Mahler's selection, Rückert wrote another song in the spring of 1834 that resonates with me in a different way. *As long as your dark eyes burn...*, Friedrich asserts, *I cannot call you dead*. Here the grieving father describes why he cherishes the memory of Luise's eyes:

> They forgot to
> close your eyes,
> which no longer
> reflect my light.
>
> Their mistake was
> a boon, perhaps,
> for with my spirit
> I see a glimmer of yours.
>
> As when a man sees
> his beloved in a window:
> her expression remains
> on the glass.
>
> She is long gone,
> of course, but still
> he imagines he sees
> her in her room.
>
> Your life is gone,
> emptied from head to toe;
> I imagine I see you, or
> that my spirit sees yours.
>
> Perhaps you are not yet
> ready to leave our old house.
> Perhaps you linger
> in your own room;
>
> looking about you,
> taking in this earthly life,
> before taking flight
> to your new one.

> And your spirit does
> not shine from within;
> the light must be mine
> reflected from without.
>
> Yet as long as your
> dark eyes burn in
> pain and fire, I cannot
> call you dead.
>
> As long as this pain
> burning in your dark eyes
> remains in mine, how could
> I call you dead?

> **I casually listened—**
> **O such a loss—**
> **my ears lost track of what**
> **flowed from your mouth.**
>
> **Words flowed and swelled**
> **and rolled so clear and light;**
> **I never dreamed the spring**
> **could ever run dry.**
>
> **I heard without hearing,**
> **spoke without speaking,**
> **worked without interruption,**
> **as you chattered on.**
>
> **There were times when**
> **I really was too oblivious:**
> **"Oh Mother, I asked a question.**
> **You aren't paying attention."**
>
> **And did you require**
> **my full attention?**
> **My chatterbox, my life,**
> **now silent to me.**
>
> **Now I would set in gold**
> **the tiniest word that**
> **fell from your lips:**
> **my treasure, my memory.**

Rückert wrote this song in the voice of the children's mother, Luise. Although he penned each poem alone, some may have been suggested by inference or observation of his wife. Friedrich spent a great deal of time walking in the nearby hills after his children died, but he did not ignore his family.

Clinicians that worked with forty-six married parents (twenty-three couples) learned that sorrow as a couple and individually was eased through what is known as dyadic coping; that is, the sharing of emotions with each other while maintaining healthy bonds with the dead child.[488] Grief is solitary and intimate. We have no choice but to travel this dark path. Yet if we pause to look around, we may discover to our astonishment that we are not walking it alone.

After my daughter died in January 2015, the television network that had for twelve years used my subtitle translations granted me a two-month sabbatical, as they graciously called it. I spent most of my days in the deep wood. In the forest, we are never truly alone.

Our cat, Yeti, came to us three months after Jess's death, nearly to the day: 14 April 2015. I work at home. For six years, Yeti was a close companion. He sat with me in my anguished keening, my inconsolable grief and my moments of quiet memory. He was a patient, unfaltering source of solace. A rescue animal, Yeti always seemed to know when a wave of grief for Jess was about to overwhelm me and would come to me in advance, stand with me, rarely leaving my side until my renewed mourning had passed. His participation in our lives was real and deeply felt.

Yeti's unassuming presence helped ease those six long years after Jess died. The old saying among animal shelter volunteers, "Who saved whom?," was never more true.

My wife, Jess's step-mother, was also deeply distraught. She returned to work sooner than I did, but still we relied on our evenings together on the hardest days. Martin Buber referred to this kind of communion as "healing through meeting." At the Erano Conference in 1934, Buber spoke on the theme of "to heal the 'between,'" suggesting that it is only in the shared space between us that we find true understanding and the will to continue.[489] Later in his 1951 introduction to Hans M. Trüb's *Healing Through Encounter*, Buber explained, "A soul never hurts alone, it is always gripped between, existing between itself and others."[490]

Rückert did not return to his duties as a professor until later that year. Luise was bedridden after Ernst's death. For a brief period, she left much of the daily household maintenance untended.[491] In June 1834 Friedrich presented Luise with the hundreds of laments he had composed since their children died. It is not unreasonable to suggest that the grieving mother may have recognized occasional snippets from their previous conversations. Her feelings of remorse in this poem are understandable.

Evidence suggests that there is a temporal pattern to self-recrimination. Actions and errors of commission lead to immediate short-term regret; but long-term regret is often the result of inactions or errors of omission.[492] Such treacheries of time were a familiar theme in Sefardi poetry, with which Rückert was familiar. For example, on the Istanbul tombstone of Reina Roman, who died in 1675, her grieving mother inscribed that time "set a trap for my tongue and my lips."[493] Or, as Luise sighs, *I heard without hearing, spoke without speaking, worked without interruption, as you chattered on.*

This psychological trick of time, as Yale literature professor R. Clifton Spargo put it, feeds a damaging fiction of recapturing or altering what is now gone forever.[494] Such anger and frustration with time is known to many bereaved parents. They may brood over words spoken (or unspoken) and futilely yearn to return to precious moments lost.[495] German psychoanalyst Erich Fromm wrote that in our religious and personal rituals, it is often the things we did *not* do that burden us with anxiety and guilt. "Nonperformance may be regretted but it is not feared," Fromm wrote. "In fact, one can always recognize the *irrational* ritual by the degree of fear produced by its violation in any manner."[496]

The grieving may feel intense remorse for what they have *done* but it is the *should-haves* and *if-onlys* linked to what they did *not* do that cause persistent torment: fear that we did not do enough; guilt over what we wish we had said. Luise's perceived failure to act—to listen—is what now plagues and mars her otherwise joy-filled memories.

> The joys of parents are secret, and so are their griefs and fears; they cannot utter the one, nor they will not utter the other.—Francis Bacon[497]

I found a wondrous plant, loveliest in the crown of spring: I do not know how or where, only that I found her there.

She had roots, it seemed, I planted her in a sacred spot: in the garden she would grow, or so I thought.

Then a frost from the North, and she grew ill; and with it a fire from the South, and she lost her will.

Now I hear she is in a fresh grave planted near the church: a dream or so it seems.

I shall water her with tears, she will sprout and grow. Heaven is where she wears a crown of her own.

There she wears a crown, here her roots beat time with the pain in my chest, the pain I love best.

As early as the 16th century, funeral wreaths or crowns were buried with children to signify the blameless and innocent nature of the young.[498] Luise had been buried with a garland of myrtle placed on her forehead for precisely this reason.[499] Friedrich's references to the crown of spring, a crown of flowers and ultimately the crown that his daughter now wears in heaven lead to a startling revelation: the pain he feels keeps time with Luise's heavenly crown and earthly roots. He would rather have this harm than none at all.

There is a tremendous amount of pain associated with healthy grief.[500] This may fade and ebb over the years, but for most bereaved parents, the pain lasts a lifetime, returning at expected moments, such as holidays or memorial days. Just as often, it arises unbidden, seemingly for no reason at all. One phrase is repeated almost universally by bereaved parents and those who know them: *they never get over it.*[501] The ordeal is so monumental that most bereaved parents turn to spirituality to cope with a seemingly irrational world, even those who previously were not so inclined.[502]

Yet not all memories associated with grief are unpleasant. There are occasions of gentle joy amid the many tears. This kind of "healing pain," as two grief counselors called it, fosters permanent change in the bereaved.[503] To deny such anguish would be unhealthy; to deny our memories, impossible.

> The love which survives the tomb is one of the noblest attributes of the soul. If it has its woes, it has likewise its delights; and when the overwhelming burst of grief is calmed into the gentle tear of recollection; when the sudden anguish and the convulsive agony over the present ruins of all that we most loved, is softened away in pensive meditation on all that it was in the days of its loveliness—who would root out such a sorrow from the heart?—Washington Irving[504]

> **By all appearances, today I may have hope; but this curse of ours gives me pause. Illusion stole all joy from me: the most I can hope for is what I dread.**

After a sudden loss, mourners may feel betrayed and abandoned. There is a period of shock as the death slowly, inevitably sinks in. Yet over time, what philosopher Thomas Attig calls the "the constructive labors of hope and love at the heart of grieving"[505] may emerge, slipping in unexpectedly.

Mental health counselor and poet Miriam Greenspan insists that these dark emotions hold within them the kernels of emotional well-being. "Aborted grief, fear, and despair are at the root of the characteristic psychological 'disorders' of our time," she writes.[506] Such emotions are not negative in themselves, but we may deal with them in negative ways. Greenspan suggests that these emotions have within them wisdom that is essential to healthy mourning. "We need to honor three basic emotions that are an inevitable part of every life: grief, fear, and despair."[507]

Ignoring these natural inclinations, often out of guilt for appearing too happy or too distraught, cheats us of our lived emotions and reinforces an already pessimistic view.[508] This in turn can lead to mental and physical health problems. Soft laughter and memory are as much a part of grief as fear and anguish. Each has its place. In this poem, Rückert candidly acknowledges both his constructive glimmers of hope and the destructive pull of despair.

> When man falls silent in torment, a god helped me to say how I suffer.
> —Johann Wolfgang von Goethe[509]

> **Life and death are the miseries of this world! You are not free to procure this or that as you like.**
>
> **As Abraham buried his dead near Mamre's grove, so you should be buried near me, but in this I am denied.**
>
> **So the ravens overhead, sensing that we have a corpse in the house, are circling, eager for their feast.**
>
> **Oh that your little body had flown off with your soul, then neither man nor woman could trouble your remains.**
>
> **I cannot stand to look at your dead face, once life to me, now that you are in the hands of ghoulish corpse midwives.**

Rückert worked and lived in Erlangen when his children died, but he knew even then that they would ultimately reside in Neuses. He despaired that Luise had not been buried there. In later years, Friedrich frequently made the 45-mile (75km) trip to her grave in Erlangen, but still, her final resting place seemed too distant. This is why the reference to Abraham's burial of his wife near Mamre's grove held great meaning for the grieving father.

The story takes up the entirety of Genesis 23. When Sarah died Abraham was living in an oak grove on land that belonged to a man named Mamre. Nearby was a tract of land known as "The Makhpela," something of a catch-all term that had the same intent as "the fells" or "the downs." The Makhpela contained a field and a cave, both owned by Ephron. Adding to the confusion, Mamre was also a term for Hebron. As tombs and caves were nearly always in the side of a hill, it seems likely that Abraham wanted the cave to be "facing Mamre" so that Sarah's resting place would be within sight of the oak grove on the opposite side of the valley.[510] In a prelude that seems ideally suited to Abraham's eulogy in the next chapter, the widower is consoled by neighbors who are eager for him to procure the cave and *bury his dead*—a refrain that is repeated six times in twenty verses.[511]

Friedrich, in contrast, feels helpless in the face of death: he could not save Luise nor can he now bury her at a time or in a place of his choosing. Corpse midwives, or "laying-out women," had prepared the body and were participating in the reception after the funeral.[512] The men and women in attendance seem to be ravens circling over the house, *troubling*[513] his daughter's remains. Rückert's reaction is not unexpected.

While funeral rituals serve a vital role in providing a time and place for the acknowledgment of death, not all traditions are welcome. One study found that of those mourners who participated in funeral customs, 43 percent experienced "adverse events" that detracted from the consoling intent of the rituals.[514] This may have been partly the case for Friedrich, who in this and other songs yearns for the funeral to be over.

> **I carry this grief each day
> with resignation
> so, in sleep, I may pray
> with exaltation.**
>
> **My angels smile in dreams
> through the gloom:
> how hard waking seems
> to empty rooms.**

Rückert writes of dreams in a number of other poems but this song, haiku-like, captures a moment known to many bereaved parents. Reality returns when we wake each day to a world without our children. Yet even these distressing experiences may serve a purpose.

Dreams of our dead reflect a deep need for spiritual union after a loss. They facilitate adjustment to the death by helping us process trauma and understand the many complex emotions of mourning.[515] These "grief dreams," as researchers refer to them, have a connection to our spiritual awareness of self in relation to others. They often awaken a growing sense of compassion while also serving as a coping mechanism.[516]

We are naturally confused about dreams of our lost loved ones. *A message*, we wonder? *Deep yearning? Or both?* Rabbi Adin Steinsaltz, a renowned Torah scholar and translator, observed that Joseph's reactions to his dreams in the Book of Genesis were not so different from ours today. "The great dreamers have often been in profound conflict about the authenticity of their visions," he wrote. It was only in retrospect, years later, after all was said and done, that Joseph understood his dreams to have been visionary. "The intricate interplay of forces was no longer entirely dependent on him; the drama was not his to direct," Steinsaltz concluded. "Some other fact was involved."[517]

Such dreams are not easily dismissed as hallucinations nor are they readily accepted as spiritual visitations. In either case, it is clear that they provide insight into the emotional impact of death and the mystical union it inspires.[518]

Not all dreams are positive. Nightmares are also a part of grief. They may be normal and expected, but their occurrence is no less traumatic, as Friedrich wrote in another lament:

> I asked God
> to send my children
> to me in dreams
> "shining and bright."
>
> Now I have my answer,
> oh dread reply!
> They are here:
> faces of the dead.
>
> And so I pray again:
> "Not like this, not
> without life and light,
> never again, not ever!"

David Aberbach, a professor of comparative literatures and Hebrew, observed that many aspects of grief have striking parallels with the mystical process: withdrawal, searching, keening, despair, communion and the realization of a new identity. Mysticism and grief are not equal but grief may lead to transformation, transcendence and a previously undiscovered communion with the spiritual.[519] "Mystical union may at times be linked to the yearning for union which a bereaved person often feels toward the dead," Aberbach notes, adding that by envisioning the "harmony which underpins existence, it may act as a stay against anger and the horrifying apprehension of the random, chaotic nature of existence."[520]

> **Spare me these delights!**
> **They cannot fool my heart,**
> **adding grief to grief.**
>
> **Leave me to my mourning!**
> **My eyes are accustomed to it now.**
> **Do not say, "See the spring**
> **coming to the meadows!"**
> **Spare my eyes the weaning**
> **of such joys!**
> **Spare me these delights!**
>
> **Do not invite me to the garden,**
> **where the blooms hold sway!**
> **What is there for me,**
> **what can I now expect?**
> **Each bloom on its wilting stalk**
> **will eagerly tell its lies,**
> **but it cannot fool my heart.**
>
> **It feeds on itself,**
> **leaving only decay,**
> **drawing out my solace**
> **leaving only my sorrow.**
> **Each ray of eastern light**
> **will darken my soul,**
> **adding grief to grief.**

Rückert found great solace in nature. In this lament, however, he despairs of its deceptions. Spring may be filled with new hope, but it can be cruel, offering promises that are too often cut short.

Friedrich's poem expresses a complex grief reaction that is made up of self-recrimination, guilt, a sense of betrayal, abandonment and misplaced trust. Such feelings are normal.[521] *Leave me to my mourning!* he cries. *My eyes are accustomed to it now.*

I am reminded of an old Etta James tune. "I would rather go blind than to see you walk away," she sang.[522] The first time I heard it I was attracted by the power of her emotions. *Yep, that's how it feels during a break-up*, I thought, *though we might not* actually *trade our eyesight!*

After my daughter died, I realized that this song is not just bluesy hyperbole. Many bereaved parents have pleaded with God to take them instead of their child. Alas, it was not to be. "I'd rather be blind," Etta sings in refrain—and she's right.

I cannot exchange my sight to have my daughter back, but in a very real way, my expressions and perceptions have changed. If eyes are windows to the soul, then in grief our eyes reveal souls that have taken harm. Look in the eyes of other mourners. You may see yourself.

In 2018, *Time Magazine* photographer Adam Ferguson was assigned seven bereaved parents whose children had died in a school shooting twenty years before. "Photographing each parent was complex and hard," Ferguson wrote. "No photograph I made seemed able to capture the grief of losing a child."[523] He needn't have worried. The diverse people featured on his cover of *Time* come from many walks of life, yet their eyes tell a shared story that transcends words.[524]

This realization is surprisingly helpful. Looking at photographs of fellow sufferers, I am moved by an ineffable yet wholly palpable quality of grief: a sense of communion. We are not alone. Emily Dickinson may have understood this when she wrote of her grief that she is "still fascinated to presume that some are like my own."

> I measure every Grief I meet
> With narrow, probing, eyes—
> I wonder if It weighs like Mine—
> Or has an Easier size.
>
> I note that Some—gone patient long—
> At length, renew their smile—
> An imitation of a Light
> That has so little Oil—[525]

Rückert may also be denying himself the joys of nature as a form of punishment.[526] In his acute grief, he likely suffers from survivor's guilt and is reprimanding himself for a perceived failure to protect his children from harm.[527] There are days of joy ahead, to be sure, of new life, but each moment must be traveled at its own pace. "Asking when mourning is finished is a little like asking how high is up?" observed Harvard psychologist and grief expert J. William Worden. "There is no ready answer."[528]

> This is my sole consolation:
> I am inconsolable.
>
> Oh, you speak of consolation
> yet offer no solace.
> I am resigned: in my
> pain there is none.
> This is my sole consolation:
> I am inconsolable.
>
> Oh, you speak of consolation
> to ease my suffering.
> Will it pass? No,
> it will rise above.
> This is my sole consolation:
> I am inconsolable.

> Oh, bring this consolation
> to light the night in me.
> The dark will deepen
> with each glimmer.
> This is my sole consolation:
> I am inconsolable.
>
> Yes, gently console me
> with tales of solace.
> Where they contradict,
> I have the solution.
> This is my sole consolation:
> I am inconsolable.
>
> Help, return me to myself,
> solace large and small.
> I seek your pain, solace,
> to put an end to you.
> This is my sole consolation:
> I am inconsolable.

Many of Rückert's songs follow a tradition that wrestles with the conundrum in this poem. We hear tales of spiritual consolation in an invisible world while facing the permanent nature of loss in our painful present.[529] *Where they contradict,* Friedrich writes, *I have the solution.*

Sorrow can be both unconsoling and inconsolable. However, millennia of experience and current research assure us that lament and mourning provide a means to honor our dead and the abiding love that continues without them.[530] When others speak of healing from our loss, they seem to miss the point of mourning. Grief is an aspect of love. We will never stop loving them. We will never stop feeling the absence of them in our lives.

The suggestion seems slightly off-kilter. Loving my daughter is not something I might possibly move past or work through. Nor could I stop missing her now that she is gone. I love her today as much as I did the day she was born. In mourning her, I am expressing that love. Sociologist and death studies pioneer Geoffrey Gorer characterized parental bereavement as "the most distressing and long-lasting of all griefs," adding that "it seems to be literally true, and not a figure of speech, that the parents never get over it."[531]

Like Rückert, Ralph Waldo Emerson also lost a five-year-old son to scarlet fever one terrible winter. Waldo, or "Wallie" as he was called, died on 27 January 1842. The day after Wallie died, Emerson wrote to a close friend, "Shall I ever dare to love any thing again. Farewell and Farewell, O my Boy!"[532] Two months later he lamented the coming harvest, its attendant duties, and the new fields of thought that called to him. "An eye fastened on the past unsuns nature," he wrote, "bereaves me of hope, and ruins me with a squalid indigence which nothing but death can adequately symbolize."[533] Emerson spent the spring composing a memorial poem for his son, entitled "Threnody":

> Not mine—I never called thee mine,
> But Nature's heir,—if I repine,
> And seeing rashly torn and moved
> Not what I made, but what I loved,
> Grow early old with grief that thou
> Must to the wastes of Nature go,—
> ....
> The eager fate which carried thee
> Took the largest part of me:
> For this losing is true dying[534]

Four lines taken from the second stanza of Emerson's lament are on Wallie's gravestone, where the boy rests in Sleepy Hollow Cemetery, Concord, Massachusetts:

> The hyacinthine boy, for whom
> Morn well might break and April bloom,—
> The gracious boy, who did adorn
> The world whereinto he was born[535]

Two years later, Emerson wrote an essay that detailed his inability to find meaning in Wallie's death. "Souls never touch their objects," he wrote. "Something which I fancied was a part of me, which could not be torn away without tearing me nor enlarged without enriching me, falls off from me and leaves no scar.... I grieve that grief can teach me nothing, nor carry me one step into real nature."[536]

I am struck by the determination and resolve in this last sentence. Emerson scholars have long wrestled with it. One suggests it indicates indifference. Another posits that Emerson is acknowledging his own limitations. Others maintain that he is expressing an awareness of the uselessness of grieving.[537] Harvard philosopher Stanley Cavell spotted the desperation in Emerson's tone, interpreting the passage "to mean the ground of the world falling away, the bottom of things dropping out, ourselves foundered, sunk on a stair."[538]

Poet Linda Pastan also compared grief to a circular staircase. In her 1977 poem, "The Five Stages of Grief," she relates that after completing the false construct and victoriously reaching the goal of ACCEPTANCE (her capitalization), she realized she had achieved nothing. "But something is wrong," she concludes. "I have lost you."[539]

The following year, 1978, Pastan used this piece as the title poem for her third collection of poetry. The poem has since been anthologized in grief books and medical textbooks. "If I remember correctly," Pastan wrote in 1996, "the poem seemed to write itself."[540] Neither Pastan nor Rückert, for all their hard-bitten fatalism, is dismissing songs of sorrow or the role they play in healthy grieving.[541]

For Emerson, it had been two years since Waldo's death—no time at all in the calendar of grief. Common knowledge among support groups and therapists holds that the second year is one of the most difficult. With each birthday, anniversary, special occasion or holiday, the finality of the death is brought home with ever increasing force.

This finality is a devastating aspect of loss. As the years continue, we may learn to live with waves of sorrow, occasional moments of regret or self-recrimination, even the unending loneliness. But death and its accompanying grief remain the one constant of our lives.

Emerson wrote that grieving can do nothing for him at this point in his life. This is not a denial. He is not decrying mourning for its lack of utility. The finality of Wallie's death presses upon him. "I grieve that grief can teach me nothing" means just that. Grief and death are forever part of life, inextricably linked. They do not benefit us; they do not bother with us at all: they simply *are*.

Jody Bottum suggests that grieving well demands acknowledgment of "the always present absence of the beloved dead person whom we mourn." To ignore our sorrow is to hinder our mental health, he writes: "Short of the immediate opening of the graves—short of resurrection now—there is no consolation."[542]

Emerson and Rückert reveal a frustration of grief: finding comfort can feel like a betrayal. Friedrich resists consolations while forcibly illustrating in verse that his wishes are not taken into account either way. He need not fight against solace, he observes. There is none to be found. The grieving father's desires have nothing to do with it, however much he might tell himself otherwise.

> Grief is the price you pay for love, but how you grieve is not necessarily a measure of that love.—Kenneth Doka[543]

My role, I think, is done,
paid in full, this pound of flesh:
exhausted, expelled, expunged,
excluded, expired, lamented.
For in grief all joy must cease;
lead me, I am sated, away from the feast!
My reason for living is gone.
Or my grief would be too much.
For my heart, I feel, since it took
this harm, breathes through sighs alone.

Rückert is ruminating on his exhaustion, a recognized aspect of grief.[544] He also questions his reason for living. Bereaved parents occasionally think of ending their lives, even years after the death, and yet the incidents of suicide are strikingly low. "People get very scared about suicidal talk," said Delia Battin, chief social worker at Montefiore Hospital's bereavement project in the 1970s, "but I find now that these are really normal feelings and it is important to help the bereaved to express them."[545]

The expression of such thoughts seems to be an important factor. Mourners who talk of suicide are less interested in ending their own lives than in finding understanding, love and compassion. Another difference lies in frequency. Those who intend to end their lives may at first speak of it obsessively before falling into a disturbing silence—the most dangerous period.

There are no hard and fast rules but certain behaviors are suggestive. For example, complicated grief (also called persistent complex bereavement disorder) is typified by an inability to function in society, develop relationships, accept the reality of a loss or make allowance for feelings of mourning and pain. Among patients who were diagnosed with a high instance of unhealthy or complicated grief, some 13 percent attempted suicide at least once in their lifetimes, suffered from depression, had functional impairment and poor social support.[546]

However, Friedrich does not brood. Instead, he is giving a healthy vent to his normal thoughts via a bit of word play through repetition that sounds almost like a sigh: *ex*hausted, *ex*pelled, *ex*punged, *ex*cluded, *ex*pired, lamented.

A Mother Speaks

I did not want to grieve,
or say what I might say,
the ground of my heart broken:
so, "healthy grieving," then.

Other mothers grieve,
when hearts take wounds,
but this I cannot do,
it dies in my mouth.

Will my grief for the dead
afflict he who remains?
How may I mourn
when I am so afraid?

"No one ever told me that grief felt so like fear," wrote C.S. Lewis shortly after the death of his wife.[547] In this poem Rückert speaks in his wife's voice, recording his impressions of her struggle to put on a brave face while Ernst lay ill. This is a snapshot in time which could have been written months later.

Friedrich gives Luise's dialogue an undertone of disorganization that typifies *acute grief*.[548] It is typified by fear, denial, disruption and a desperate desire to hold on to a normalcy that is now forever changed.[549] She may have suffered from what modern grief counselors call *prolonged grief*.

One study of sixty-one Germans found that women with high levels of religious belief, combined with low levels of satisfaction in those beliefs after a death, were the most likely to battle with the depression and feelings of helplessness that are symptomatic of prolonged grief. Luise was solidly in both categories. The same researchers found that closeness to the deceased and unanticipated deaths are also important contributing factors.[550]

Another five-year study of 239 bereaved adults revealed that those people who had a high frequency of religious practice felt the greatest terror at the thought of their own demise. Such fears were considerably relieved among those who found meaning in the death of their loved ones and in their subsequent lives without them.[551]

In other poems both Friedrich and Luise embrace and challenge their beliefs. Neither expected such a catastrophic loss. Their love for their children underscores every song. This lament speaks to a mother's heartbreak and her self-sacrificing courage.

**Lift me above
this dull cloud cover,
up to where it is clear,
to waxing stars,
the waning moon,
and the sun in its splendor.**

**For in the sun- and moonshine,
in the quiet wreath of stars
smiling upon me;
I do not hear
as they ask:
"Is the Eternal Light in our light?"**

The idea that Luise and Ernst do *not* continue on seemed too much for Rückert. In this he was not alone. Grief experts have found that the bereaved cannot sustain a certainty that there is *no* afterlife.[552] One ten-year study found that almost all bereaved parents feel they will see their children in heaven.[553] This has proven true even with parents who do not believe such a place exists.[554] Most major religions speak of a reunion with loved ones after death.[555]

Rückert clearly embraced his Christian faith in these laments: whether in anger, pleading, questions, demands or gratitude. Researchers have concluded that belief in a soul provides the bereaved with a hope that they may somehow sense the deceased.[556] For those who lose a child, this sense of "knowing" is nearly universal.[557] It is felt immediately in the initial shock and disbelief of mourning. It comes as no surprise, then, that Friedrich wants to rise above the dull cloud cover to experience Luise and Ernst more clearly, to see in their light an eternal light.

When we grieve, we are desperate for any sign from the invisible world: a crazy little peek behind the curtain, as Frederick Buechner put it.[558] We yearn to feel the presence of our dead loved ones, to know they are still with us.

I believe that this desperation may be counter-productive. We naturally focus so much on the object of our heartbroken desire that we can miss what would otherwise be obvious to us. Swiss physician Paul Tournier observed that interactions with the divine are convincing precisely because they are unforeseen and defy any psychological explanation. "God's intervention is also seen in sudden experiences," wrote Tournier, "like an unexpected signpost upon an uncertain road."[559]

There is no formula. I hold suspect anyone who offers a glib step-by-step program to legitimate spiritual experience. Our grief is unique, as is our love—as is whatever way we may experience, by God's grace, our loved ones now gone.

My personal litmus tests regarding spiritual experiences are *mystery, the unexpected* and *grace*. These moments do not fit easily into neat categories. They often seem surprising. Poet and priest John O'Donohue had much the same thought: "As with all great arrivals in the soul, it comes from a direction that we often could neither predict nor anticipate."[560]

My wife is a librarian. Usually I take her to work, though we rarely lunch together—perhaps two to three times a year. One day, out of the blue, I felt compelled to go to the library a good hour before her lunch break. I use the word *compelled* with care.

When I arrived in the library parking lot, a man was struggling to get his walker out of the back of his pick-up truck. His name was Thomas, 84 years old, though he looked no more than 70. I helped and that was that. Or so I thought.

I went inside. Then in comes Thomas, hobbling on his walker. "I spent two hours on the phone trying to get my vaccine appointment," he said in an accent that my wife barely understood. I've lived in South Carolina longer. This is where my daughter grew up and where she died.

"Then I drove to the hospital," Thomas continued. "They said I had to make the appointment on the computer. I don't know nothing about computers."

With COVID-19 rampant in our state, the library staff was no longer permitted to assist patrons with the computers. They have a sign posted: NO COMPUTER HELP. At times like this, with people like Thomas, the staff is stymied and heartsick. They would help if they could.

Of course, I was under no such restriction.

Thomas did not know it, but he needed an email address (which he lacked) and an account on the hospital system (which, again, he lacked). Then he needed to sign in so he could simply make two appointments for his vaccination.

I taught college computer classes at one time. For me, it took no more than 30 minutes from start to finish. I suspect for Thomas, it would have been nearly impossible. "It's nothing once you get the hang of it," I assured him. "Like working on your old pick-up out there."

While we sat at the computer, Thomas spoke up out of nowhere: "My son drowned." We talked it over. His son, Derrick, was 37 when he died in 1997. I told him about Jess.

Non-bereaved parents might think

my selection for the account password was insensitive—*derrick1997*. However, Thomas, 84 years old and still alert, merely nodded his head. "I don't mind. Yep, I won't ever forget that."

That day I made a rare appearance at the library in the precise moment that I could be of use to a fellow bereaved parent. Thomas and I spoke together, shared our stories and communed as only mourners may. I believe that our children, Jess and Derrick, helped us both when we needed them. The events of that day remain a mystery. And a grace: unexpected, unearned, undeserved.

> People who've had any genuine spiritual experience always know they don't know. They are utterly humbled before mystery. They are in awe before the abyss of it all, in wonder at eternity and depth, and a Love, which is incomprehensible to the mind.—Richard Rohr[561]

**You did not see what you had:
happiness beyond all knowing.
God has taken a piece of you:
now you know, now you see.
Still, a part remains, left behind:
may you prove worthy of it.**

God has taken a piece of you, Rückert laments in a near-perfect expression of bereavement. This is what it feels like to lose a child: some part of us that cannot be measured has been taken away; we are not ourselves; we are not whole.[562]

The poet's happiness was *beyond all knowing*, he writes, but now he knows, now he sees—what he had and what he has left. "The purest faith has to be tested by silence," observed Thomas Merton, "in which we listen for the unexpected, in which we are open to what we do not yet know...."[563] The same might be said of the lifelong trial of grief.

Rückert's grandson, psychiatrist Hans Berger, invented the electroencephalogram (EEG). Born in 1873 in Neuses near Coburg, Berger never met Friedrich (who died in 1866) but his grandfather was an important influence in his life. Hans also felt an impulse to be of use to others, and a surprising connection with the invisible world.[564] He revered Friedrich and recited his poetry all of his days.[565]

In 1892, while serving in the German army, Hans was thrown from a horse. The incident placed him in mortal danger. He recovered, but that same day, Hans received a telegram from his father, physician Paul Berger, and his mother, Anna Berger (née Rückert; Friedrich's daughter, born in 1839). It was the first cable his parents had ever sent to him. The message related that Hans's older sister had an ominous premonition and they were checking up on him.[566]

The telegram astounded Hans. *Do our brains somehow interact with the external world?* he wondered. He referred to the incident as a case of *spontaneous telepathy*. Berger had always been particularly close to his sister. He felt that when his life had been in jeopardy, his sister had acted as a type of psychic receiver. This led to his life's work: investigating the electrical activity of the brain.[567]

Hans studied at the University of Jena, in the German state of Thuringia. He later took a position at the university hospital and stayed there as its director until 1938.[568] In 1924, Hans became the first to record electrical pulses generated by the human brain. Berger published his findings in 1929.[569] Twenty-three more papers on the subject would follow over the years.[570]

The idea was startling. Berger's research drew mockery from the scientific community. His instruments were dismissed as quackery. His hook-up (the electroencephalograph) was too complicated, they sniffed; the record produced on tape or film, the electroencephalogram or EEG, was simple gibberish. Despite this initial resistance from his peers, Hans persisted. By 1934, his discoveries were recognized as established fact.[571] "The Berger rhythm is a reality," declared *Scientific American* in 1938, "and immensely important."[572] One hundred years later, modern physicians use Berger's EEG to save lives every day.

In October 1938 Berger was obliged to retire. He was informed via telephone that he would not be reappointed as director of the hospital.[573] Although there was talk that he had run afoul of the Nazi party, Hans was by nature a social conformist: obedient, reliable and conservative in his politics. The human brain was his main concern.[574]

Devastated, Hans accepted a position as head of a private sanatorium near Jena, in Bad Blankenburg. There he continued his work on what he considered to be the central problem of psychiatry: the physical basis of psychic function. In 1940 he was nominated for the Nobel Prize but due to the war, awards were suspended. Of sixty-five total nominations submitted to the selection committee that year, three named Berger.[575] Ulf Svante von Euler wrote a favorable opinion of Berger and the widespread international acknowledgment of his EEG.[576]

Hans had no idea that his name was being considered. The following spring, he was misdiagnosed with an incurable heart condition. He ended his own life by hanging on 1 June 1941.[577]

Berger felt keenly the gap between his inner vision and the realities of life. His commitment to research alienated colleagues even while they admired him.[578] His rich private life of introspection, poetry and impassioned journal entries were entirely separate from the driven professor seen in public.[579] A compulsion to perfect and establish the EEG dominated his existence. Yet despite many successes, he never felt good enough. For decades, Hans kept a copy of one of his grandfather Friedrich's early quatrains on the wall in his study:

> We each face an image:
> who we are meant to be.
> True peace eludes us
> until it is reality.[580]

Rückert wrote this poem in his youth. The four verses may be read as reprimand or comfort: a choice between *I'll never measure up*; or as the teacher of Ecclesiastes saw it, *God has given human beings an awareness of eternity; but in such a way that they can't fully comprehend*.[581] Commenting on this passage, Søren Kierkegaard observed that this sense of the eternal assures us immortality is not a future change occurring at the moment of death. "On the contrary," he wrote, "it is a changelessness that is not altered by the passage of the years."[582] Peace is not found in pursuit of an image of ourselves as we think we *ought* to be, but in an awareness of the eternal present that is within us each moment.[583]

Older and more experienced, Friedrich seemed to have taken an eternal view after the deaths of Luise and Ernst. God took a piece of him, yes, but *still, a part remains, left behind*, the poet muses, *may you prove worthy of it*.

While there are many familiar aspects of sorrow, others are very different indeed. "Be aware of the general picture of grief," psychiatrist M. Katherine Shear and her colleagues advised care providers, "but try not to have preconceived expectations about the specific constellation of symptoms or their time course."[584] The expectations that we place on ourselves, like our griefs, are our own.

> **Oft I think, they're out and about,**
> **they'll be home soon no doubt.**
> **The day is soft, not to worry,**
> **they are strolling, in no hurry.**
>
> **Yes, they're out and about,**
> **coming home now no doubt,**
> **not to worry, the day is still,**
> **they stroll up ahead to the hills.**
>
> **They are only out and about,**
> **and will not be looking to come home,**
> **we will catch them up on the hills**
> **in the sun, where the day is still.**

Rückert is wistful in this piece, to be sure, but not glib or trite. The emotions he describes are painful and mixed. The poem as a whole illustrates what philosopher Thomas Attig identified as the difference between grief and the coping process of grieving. "It is misleading and dangerous to mistake grief for the whole of the experience of the bereaved," Attig noted. "The experience is far more complex, entailing diverse emotional, physical, intellectual, spiritual, and social impacts."[585] Each day the bereaved must choose to go on, to find meaning *in* and giving meaning *to* the hours ahead. "This fundamental choice," continued Attig, "may require a kind of hope or a faith rooted in convictions that support and sustain the very capacity to affirm life and its meaningfulness."[586]

This poem was the fourth of the five pieces from Rückert's *Songs on the Death of Children* that Gustav Mahler set to his song cycle, *Kindertotenlieder*. The shortest of the Mahler *lieder*, under four minutes in most recordings, the music begins with an undertone of hope in bright warm tones. The final stanza is all the more poignant for Friedrich's acceptance of his children's absence and his anticipation of reunion. Mahler echoes these sentiments: the singer's climactic reading of the last line, *where the day is still*, seems assured and unexpectedly peaceful. The composer's musical refrains add dimension to this already moving *lied*.[587]

As with many of Friedrich's poems, it is difficult to know if he expects to sense that Ernst and Luise are with him in the hills—a common experience among bereaved parents[588]—or if he is speaking of a reunion in the afterlife, or both. Either way, the hills seem less foreboding and more welcoming for the poet's confidence that his children wait for him there.

This poem is reminiscent of a passage from Augustine that was frequently used in German funeral consolation literature: "We have not lost those who have left this life, we have merely sent them on ahead. They do not die, but they go away."[589]

> It wasn't just you that died.
> The joy woven into my world
> died with you. The light of day
> that hid from me the depths
> of death is gone. Its cover
> has been lifted at last,
> its glitter now scattered.
>
> Now I see grief far and near.
> Once I saw nothing but happiness
> in others, or so I thought.
> I did not look closely.
> Now I pause in recognition
> of the pain in each face.
> They, too, have lost something.
>
> The tolling of mourning bells
> never bothered me before.
> It was so much hollow noise.
> Now I cannot pick up a paper
> without scanning the death notices.
> Once I saw them as filler;
> now I read each one.
>
> The tolling of the bells
> has new meaning to me.
> I ask, "Why do they ring?"
> I know the pain of these bells.
> *Who are they for today?*
> There was a time I thought that they
> pealed only at baptisms or weddings.
>
> I grow ivy in my garden, enough
> to share with visitors from town.
> I never once bothered to ask,
> "Why do you need it?"
> Now I must step outside: "I see you
> gathering ivy. May I ask on whose
> head your dark wreath will rest?"

"Everyone knew the Code, the language of the bells," observed author and theologian Wolfgang Vögele. The bell tower was the hub of community life in 19th-century Germany. People generally wanted to live as close to the tower as possible: its tolling structured daily life, from striking the hour to church services to important social events.[590]

Rückert was surrounded by bells. From 1826 to 1841, Friedrich taught in Erlangen, where Ernst and Luise are buried. Erlangen takes pride in its bells, particularly those of the Huguenot Church, which was erected 1686–93. Its bell tower dates from 1732–6.

The poet lived most of his life in the small village of Neuses, a suburb of Coburg covering no more than 677 acres (2.74 km^2). A leisurely stroll from Neuses to Coburg along the meadows of the Itz River was not much more than 1.5 miles (2.4km) and took about twenty minutes. On a calm day the sound of Coburg church bells would echo along the Itz, faintly joining the chiming bells of Neuses' single parish church. The village was incorporated into Coburg in 1934; its church was officially named St. Matthäus in 1970.

In this poem, Rückert's previous deafness to the bells is now compared to his acute awareness of each note. The juxtaposition of *light / once* and *dark / now* in this poem is particularly telling. The light of day hid from view the depths of death; and yet in that darkness Friedrich sees most clearly the suffering of others. His awareness echoes a similar insight from German theologian Meister Eckhart: "In the dark, in suffering, we see the light most clearly."[591] This compassion is characteristic of those who have grieved many losses. Studies show that the bereaved often feel a sense of transcendence or transfiguration: in their search for meaning they turn outward, commiserating with pain and loss.[592]

The ivy Friedrich describes has long been associated with death and immortality. Garlands of ivy or myrtle were often placed on the heads of the deceased for burial. The evergreen nature of the leaves symbolized attachment and eternal life, a meaning that was no longer lost on the poet.[593]

> A thought of compassion and forgiveness has a healing effect on your body and your mind. It also has an immediate healing effect on the world.—Thich Nhat Hanh[594]

> **A letter from a friend arrives at the right moment; in fairness, any timing is bad timing these days. I am abandoned by others who are free to abandon me.**
>
> **I have abandoned myself; abandoned by the breath of God's grace. Your consolation gave me this solace: if such as you still loves me, God does, too.**

Feelings of abandonment are often associated with long-term grief. After the funeral and the initial outburst of support, the visits and letters soon disappear. In 19th-century Germany, as in America today, there was a certain pressure to move on or get over a loss.

Mourning is a solitary act, even when surrounded by supportive friends and family. The bereaved often feel alone and abandoned.[595] Progressive social isolation can follow.[596] This is particularly true in the first six months after a death—precisely the time Rückert spent writing these poems. Add to this Friedrich's particular sorrow.

Parental bereavement is a persistent grief that often lasts a lifetime. "We know little about what triggers attachment to children," wrote researcher Robert Weiss. "Nor do we understand fully why parental grieving so regularly persists indefinitely."[597] Rückert's acute sense of feeling *abandoned by the breath of God's grace* is also expected with sudden, traumatic loss. The bereaved frequently feel betrayed by the divine, left alone physically, emotionally and spiritually to struggle with their sorrow.[598]

Another poet shared this same sense of the mystical in mourning and verse. When his son Hamnet died, William Shakespeare had been working on *King John*. What started as a desultory historical epic, filled with the same jingoism as *Richard II*, was after Hamnet's death transformed by some of the poet's most poignant verse. "I'll go with thee," declared a character that echoed William's grief, "and find the inheritance of this poor child, his little kingdom of a forced grave."[599]

In *King John*, Cardinal Pandolf reprimands Constance for her displays of mourning over her dead son. "You hold too heinous a respect of grief." Constance lashes out at his pious statement: "He talks to me that never had a son." King Philippe chimes in on the same note, "You are as fond of grief, as of your child." Constance replies:

> Grief fills the room up of my absent child,
> Lies in his bed, walks up and down with me,
> Puts on his pretty looks, repeats his words,
> Remembers me of all his gracious parts,
> Stuffs out his vacant garments with his form.
> Then have I reason to be fond of grief.[600]

Sadly, exchanges like those in *King John* continue even today. One study of 184 grieving families found that many believers stopped going to church because they felt ostracized for not celebrating a death or for failing to recover after a desirable period. Those who had been active churchgoers before the loss found little solace in their faith community.

Mourners listed three detrimental behaviors among clergy and congregations: a lack of support in general; pressure to celebrate; and a tendency to ignore feelings of anger, resentment or grief. The bereaved that "fell apart" at church were often told such a response displayed a lack of trust in God.[601] "The faith community can sometimes be a source of re-victimization," observed Janice Harris Lord, an advocate for victims and survivors of crime and traumatic loss, "even though they do not intend to be."[602] This in turn leads to a fear that grieving openly might set a poor example.[603]

This trend is not universal. Many churches host grief groups, encouraging the bereaved to attend for as many months or years as they feel necessary. Others recognize the long-term impact of loss with such important annual rituals as "Blue Christmas" services, held on Christmas Eve, designed specifically for those whose sorrow makes the holidays a difficult time.

Within a month of my daughter's death, family members and well-meaning people from work and church encouraged me to cheer up. "She'd want you to be happy," they said. This may be true, but the phrase is laden with subtle recrimination. If we are not happy, it is implied, we fail to honor our dead. They will be disappointed. This is nonsense, of course. I suspect that my daughter would prefer that I be true to myself and mourn at my own pace.[604]

It is unclear when Rückert received the letter he describes, but from his tone it was probably a few months after the deaths of Luise and Ernst. He is keenly aware of the anomaly he portrays: the timing may have been bad (or belated), but expressions of love often seem to arrive at just the right moment.

> Grief is an honorable emotion. It is the expression of the feeling we have about the value of life. It recognizes the relationships that are now broken in loneliness. It recognizes the love now moved beyond the physical object to its spiritual meaning. These feelings have their important place in life.—Edgar Jackson[605]

**Once I was out of town for
a month and oh, how you
had grown in my absence,
much to my delight!**

**And now, oddly enough,
it has not been a month
since you left, and yet
oh, how you have grown.**

**Thank you. I know what this
means to you: how you would
grow for me now as you did
in life, ever older, never to age!**

**Taken together—growing
and learning, remaining
forever young—your fate
seems beautiful indeed.**

**And if one day—gracefully,
shyly—you welcome me,
I will know you as old and
new, not estranged, not frozen.**

"We haven't talked in three weeks," I once messaged my daughter. "You know how long that is in DAD YEARS???" Jess promptly replied: "Hahahaha! Geez. Well, your little lady loves her dad! I'll give you a call." Which she did. In this poem, Rückert recalls how he missed his children while traveling—a feeling all parents know well. I used to joke that when Jess was with her mother each week, I would feel relief and freedom on the first night she was away, and then spend the rest of the time waiting for her to get back.

Friedrich is anticipating a reunion after death that will not wait until a future physical resurrection. As with most believers of his day, he felt the soul was immediately accepted by God after leaving the body.[606] While all humanity may be estranged in life and seemingly frozen in death, at least to those left behind, Ernst and Luise are free of such miseries. Cold comfort, perhaps, but in grief the thought that our loved ones continue on, whole and happy, provides a deep and meaningful solace.[607] In another lament, also included in *Songs on the Death of Children*, the grieving father describes Luise as sleeping:

I thought to teach my little girl weaving;
a spinstress from an early age.
I bought a spinning wheel;
and only silk for spinning.
Oh my hope, poor little thread!
Never to see that first thread spun.
Now she sleeps, my little spinstress,
while over her grave women weave in the light.

Philosopher Hermann Lotze admired Rückert's "genuinely Christian and pure ideas" while simultaneously chiding him for the "paradoxical rigor and Hellenistic treatment" in his poems.[608] The observation was not unjust, but Friedrich's classical bent changed after Luise and Ernst died. His laments speak to the infinite.

This new style appealed to Lotze. An undaunted champion of the unity of traditionalist religion with natural science, he asserted that the finite minds of humanity will only find "perfect Personality" when they are united with God. "The finiteness of the finite is not a producing condition of this Personality," Lotze wrote, "but a limit and a hindrance of its development."[609]

Which was no surprise to Rückert.

> **My little ones could not contain themselves when the sheepdog guided his flock to the fields. They leapt and ran in the evening with the lambs, drifted home at twilight with the flock.**
>
> **Look now, the shepherd is gathering his sheep; you still sleep, missing it, you who never lie in! But there in the red of dusk I see you bright, clear, resting with your lambs, the cotton clouds.**

Vincent van Gogh was moved by the unity of nature, nostalgia and hope in Rückert's songs, particularly those set at twilight.[610] These so impressed van Gogh that in 1876 he laboriously inscribed four of them in the visitors book of Anne Slade-Jones, the wife of Pastor Thomas Slade-Jones, when he was staying with the family in Isleworth.[611]

Van Gogh held many German writers in high esteem,[612] Rückert in particular.[613] This is not surprising. Word, nature and image were closely connected in Vincent's mind,[614] an affinity with Friedrich that is most apparent in this song about sheep, clouds and grief.[615]

Van Gogh also copied a number of Friedrich's verses in the poetry albums that he began compiling in 1875 for his brother Theo and artist Matthijs Maris.[616] His enthusiasm was not one-sided. Vincent and Theo frequently corresponded about Rückert's poetry, writing them out in full or in part, adding personal asides and comments in their letters.[617] When Theo sent him Rückert's "At Midnight," Vincent was moved by the "poignantly beautiful" verse.[618] The poem is an early example of what was known as "world-pain" or the weary burden of suffering,[619] which in Rückert and van Gogh's belief could only be relieved by God:

> At midnight
> I woke and
> looked to the sky;
> no star smiled on me
> in that vast expanse
> at midnight.
>
> At midnight
> my thoughts stretched
> deep in the black;
> no hint of light
> offered me solace
> at midnight.
>
> At midnight
> I paused at each
> beat of my heart;
> a pulse of pain
> roused my heart
> at midnight.
>
> At midnight
> I waged your war,
> Man, of suffering;
> but victory was
> beyond my strength
> at midnight.
>
> At midnight
> what strength I have
> is in your hands;
> Lord! keep watch
> over death and life
> at midnight.[620]

Rückert wrote "At Midnight" in the autumn of 1833, around the time that Luise and Ernst posed for the small pastel portraits that Friedrich was to carry with him for the rest of his life. The children fell ill shortly thereafter.[621] He described this piece as a shepherd's song.[622]

In January 1835, exactly one year after their deaths, Friedrich included it in a collection for Nicolaus Lenau's spring almanac. Lenau was certain these contributions would make the new issue a success. "Rückert promised a submission of four sheets," he wrote to a friend that month, "with which fact I am very pleased. For some time now I've wanted to contact this poet, who is probably one of our finest."[623]

Rückert was well-known, yet he decided to contact an editor with whom he had never worked, submitting to a periodical in which he had never published. Friedrich did not indicate to Lenau why he approached him, but this behavior highlights an important aspect of grief, known as meaning-making or meaning reconstruction.[624] The bereaved frequently seek out new interests and new means of expression in what researchers call their "gradual discovery of new meaning and identity" after a traumatic loss.[625] Rückert granted Lenau permission to reserve half of the songs for a future issue. The editor was struck by Friedrich's generous and easy-going manner. "He must be an exceptionally nice person," he confided in a letter, "and we have already become friends."[626]

The Gogh brothers were not alone in their appreciation of the poem.

Almost immediately after it was published, "At Midnight" was translated into English by Nathaniel Frothingham of Boston. The reverend's rendering was published in a number of transcendentalist journals across the United States.[627] Much of Ralph Waldo Emerson's poetry and prose from the period is clearly influenced by Rückert's song. This comes as no surprise: Friedrich had a huge following in the United States. Even today, 19th-century American anthologies consistently lump together three great contemporary German poets: Goethe, Schiller and Rückert.[628]

Gustav Mahler recognized something of himself in Rückert's poems.[629] He set "At Midnight" to music in the summer of 1901.[630] Having recently recovered from a life-threatening hemorrhage that had interrupted his work in February and March of that year,[631] Mahler was concerned with questions of death. He began exploring thoughts of another world, looking beyond the here and now in a "profound and grave peace"[632] that found resonance with *Songs on the Death of Children* and his *Rückert-Lieder*, including "At Midnight."

That summer, he played three of his settings from Rückert's *Songs on the Death of Children* for his friend Natalie Bauer-Lechner.[633] "It hurt me to write them," he told her, "and I grieve for the world which will one day have to hear them, they are so sad."[634] For the next four years he would also work on his fifth, sixth and seventh symphonies. Each has perceptible influences and echoes of his settings to Friedrich's *lieder*, which is why to this day they are called the Rückert symphonies.[635]

Mahler, van Gogh and Rückert each perceived death as a transition to another, more palpably real life in an invisible world. "At Midnight" provides a peek into the poet's thoughts that were fully realized after the deaths of Ernst and Luise.

My little ones could not contain themselves, Friedrich writes in memory and hope, demonstrating with their presence among the clouds that he believes they still exist, that they will someday be reunited.[636] Rückert saw death "as a kernel inherent in each being that eventually becomes the fruit of that life," as musicologist and Mahler expert Stephen Hefling put it. "The afterlife that follows is the realm of eternal light."[637]

**In this weather, in this gale,
I'd never have sent the children out;
they were taken, carried away
with no respite, I had no say.**

**In this weather, in this storm,
I'd never have left the children out;
their health—*they might fall ill*—
a fear, alas, now vain and shrill.**

**In this weather, this horror,
had I left the children out—
tomorrow they might die!—
a fear, alas, now realized.**

**In this weather, in this gale,
they rest as in their mother's house,
the storm carries no fear,
God's Hand holds them near.**

The winter of 1833–34 had been relatively mild but the spring, when Rückert wrote "In this weather," was unseasonably cold, wet and windy. The weather was more than a muse for poetic fancy. In this tumultuous song of remorse, Friedrich writes of the loneliness known to all who mourn.

The bereaved often mention loneliness as *the* biggest challenge of daily life, a feeling closely aligned with a sense of emptiness and disconnection.[638] The emotion is powerful and devastating, but few mourners talk about it. Society frequently judges loneliness as a matter of choice or personal weakness. It often remains hidden. One study of fifty-two parents who had lost a child to an unexpected death by illness, accident or suicide found that grief and loneliness tend to *rise* over time, though accident survivors report coming to terms with the loss in ways that ease such feelings.[639]

Maïté Snauwaert, an expert on sorrow and literature at the University of Alberta, relates that many grief memoirs, such as *Songs on the Death of Children*, have "a very modest programme: that of finding ways to get through the day." Snauwaert discovered some incongruities that frequently appear in such journals of lament: poets and authors name loneliness as their cruelest battle, yet at the same time they relish their solitude and the resulting communion with their lost loved ones in presence and in dialogue. "Ultimately, their own writing allows the bereaved to spend time with the dead and with the loss itself," Snauwaert concluded. "Acting as a ritual, it is able to capture the ever-shifting moments of grief, and to connect the writers to their inner life."[640] They also find solace in the time alone for walks in nature and reading the works of other mourners. This was certainly true for me after my daughter died.

These findings may help to explain why Mahler chose "In this weather" to conclude his musical setting of five pieces from *Songs on the Death of Children*. Many translations are available. To this day it speaks to the bereaved across the world in times of sudden, terrible loss. Two recent examples:

> On the morning of Sunday, 12 July 1998, one month before the infamous Omagh bombing of Northern Ireland, loyalists threw explosives into the home of 29-year-old Christine Quinn in Ballymoney, some thirty miles north of Belfast. Her three children—aged 9, 10 and 11—burned to death. The next day, *The Irish News* published on its front page photos of the three Quinn children with the entire text of "In this weather" underneath.[641]
>
> After the Sandy Hook Elementary School shooting on 14 December 2012 in Newtown Connecticut, journalist, essayist and popular Christian author Philip Yancey was asked to speak to the heartbroken community. His remarks included a reading of "In this weather." Writing of the experience later, Yancey observed that the poem, "hauntingly reminiscent of Sandy Hook, ends with the same hope that brought comfort to a grieving mother."[642]

Friedrich's wife, Luise, did indeed find solace in the poet's raw expression of grief, with its poignant line, *they rest as in their mother's house, the storm holds no fear, God's Hand holds them near.* However, after Friedrich presented hundreds of laments to Luise in June of 1834, both parents agreed that the poems should not be published in their lifetimes, a wish honored by their surviving children. The feelings were too raw, the loneliness too acute.[643]

> Lord, I ask you not to separate me when I am dead from those who were so dear to me while I lived. Lord, I beg you that where I am, they too may be with me. As I have not been able to see much of

them here, let me enjoy their company in heaven for ever. I beseech you, God most high, to grant a speedy resurrection to these children whom I love so much. As the span of their life on earth was cut short, make it up to them by calling them the sooner to eternal life.—Ambrose of Milan[644]

> Let me join them in sleep
> among the flowers,
> if your breeze, May,
> will not wake them.
>
> If they will not wake,
> they who sleep,
> let me join them
> cradled in your wind.
>
> Let me join them in sleep
> under the fragrant meadow.
> If they will not, why
> must I be awake, alone?

——

> If only I slept
> with you in the dark,
> as you cannot join
> me in the light.
>
> If only I could take
> your place in the dark,
> and you mine
> in the light.
>
> Your dreams have faded.
> How much more would
> you revel in the spring,
> its greens and blues.
>
> My dear boy playing at
> peace near Father's grave;
> tears flowing, bittersweet,
> in the joy of life.
>
> My little girl, my boy,
> I would sooner see you
> happy at play near my grave
> than be standing over yours.

In these two poems, Rückert's response to the deaths of his children is closely related to what is known as "survivor syndrome." This is a typical reaction to sudden, unexpected death, such as the disease that took Luise and Ernst. The heart of the problem lies in discovering a reason that he survived and his children did not. Friedrich feels guilty and abandoned. He surely would exchange places with them if he could. Failing that, he would join them *in sleep among the flowers*.

Nearly all parents that lose a child contemplate their own deaths, if not suicide than a wish that somehow life would end. As with Friedrich, this is a desperate, vulnerable and revealing experience. This is usually short-lived—it was for Rückert and it was for me—but according to one researcher who interviewed some 300 parents, the thoughts often extend over many years.[645]

Such thoughts are hardly new to the world. One of the most memorably heartbreaking passages in the Holy Bible expresses this same desire. "O my son Absalom, my son, my son Absalom!" cried King David when he learned of his adult child's death. "Would I had died instead of you, O Absalom, my son, my son!"[646] Many of David's laments—nearly one third of the Psalter—give words to the worst experiences of suffering. In doing so, we step outside ourselves, entrusting our grief with a God who understands.[647] Such feelings often seem too large for expression, but with poets such as David and Rückert, we may find voices that echo our own yearnings.

> This terrible sense of loss—this untold darkness—this loneliness—this continual longing for God—which gives me that pain deep down in my heart.—Darkness is such that I really do not see—neither with my mind nor with my reason.—The

place of God in my soul is blank.—There is no God in me.—When the pain of longing is so great—... Where is the soul in my very being?—Mother Teresa[648]

> I weigh this
> poem thoughtfully,
> and it is incomprehensible:
> you are lost to me.
>
> Did I not see the bier
> and the dark wreaths
> in your hair, my pair
> of beautiful children?
> Yet still this poem is inconceivable;
> the thought is incomprehensible:
> you are lost to me.
>
> So I replace the obvious with
> the oblivious: what is true
> is untrue! Yet still the jewel
> around my neck is missing;
> this pain, however, is
> impossible to remove:
> you are lost to me.
>
> Years come and go.
> Nature's course cannot alter,
> changing one outfit for another,
> from the wedding altar to the bier.
> It is indelible:
> you are lost to me.

Written after both Luise and Ernst had died, this poem shows a grieving father allowing himself, of all things, to play as he weeps. Rückert was known for his clever word use and for using jarring terms to suit his purpose. This song would surely have been reworded or excised had Friedrich returned to it. As it stands, his word salad shows an important aspect of the grieving father's mourning. He has granted himself permission to return to something that gives him pleasure: teasing out multiple meanings from words of similar sound or form; in this poem, *incomprehensible/inconceivable/impossible/indelible, hair/pair*, etc.

Clinicians have found that the initial response to death is often shock and disbelief: the loss seems truly "incomprehensible."[649] At first the idea of play and allowing ourselves simple, childlike pleasures seems unthinkable. The mere suggestion is often avoided. Yet studies demonstrate that these small gestures are an essential part of adjusting to life without our loved ones. Such play may clarify feelings, remove confusion and facilitate healthy mourning.[650]

Thomas Bauer, professor of Arabic and Islamic Studies at the University of Münster and a specialist in grief-related poetry, observes that there is an "artistic and playful element" in verse that is helpful in mourning. The act of creation expresses pain and provides a means of coping while simultaneously reaffirming the poet's existence. This in turn offers relief from the sense of passive suffering that can occur with grief.

Creative expression is also an act of love. We feel helpless in the face of death: creation in honor of our loved ones allows us to give voice to that love through sorrow and memory. "A poem (or any other work of art)," Bauer concludes, "is a means to break the speechlessness of death."[651]

> A light shines on me
> in the dark night;
> calm and bright
> expression of delight.
>
> Calm and bright
> expression of delight;
> in a picture, it seems,
> painted in heaven.
>
> In heaven this light,
> it seems, is transfigured;
> a scent that makes me
> hunger as a bee hungers.

> Hungering as a bee
> hungers, lost in delight;
> heaven's gifts of
> early morning dew.
>
> Heaven's gifts of
> solace and comfort,
> expressions of delight
> caress and console.
>
> In their expressions of
> delight I am renewed;
> a light still shines on
> me, never to go out.

Death disrupts our lives in the most fundamental way. We feel a strong need to come to terms with our loss, to grasp the sudden abyss that the death has created.[652] Poetry and all creative arts express, as grief expert and psychology professor at the University of Memphis Robert Neimeyer put it, "the subtle ways in which language and narrative configure our experience and the extent to which our most intimate sense of self is rooted (and uprooted) in our shifting relationships with others."[653] This normal reaction is known as *meaning reconstruction*, which includes putting the death in perspective as well as finding some purpose to our lives ahead. In this way, Rückert's songs serve the dual role of lament and coping.[654]

Friedrich saw unity in the simplest and the most complex aspects of existence. He embraced scientific inquiry while simultaneously maintaining his belief in a deeper, essential reality that is just outside human perception. "He listened to all of nature with a lively imagination and profound compassion, as he did to life," wrote German literary historian Franz Muncker in his 1890 biography of Rückert, "so too in the histories and legends of all peoples he heard a thousand-thousand-voiced song of poetry, which for him encompassed the aspirations of every artistic, religious, scientific and spiritual endeavor."[655]

Read alone, this poem may seem to be filled with nonsense platitudes. But as so often happens with Rückert, there is more going on. His voice is all the more heartening when compared to another piece, also written for *Songs on the Death of Children*:

> What good, then, is sunshine
> when I can't see it for the
> the night that clouds my eyes?
>
> Sunshine flees to where love
> cannot be seen by these eyes,
> accustomed now to the night.
>
> I cannot see my child.
> Ask not which is blind:
> the sun or my eyes.

Many of the Romantics were involved in a passionate search to understand the world of spirit. They believed that reality held more than what we see and know—that beyond the physical lay mysteries of life and meaning. Significantly, they saw the visible world as a means for embracing the essence of a sustaining, invisible reality.[656]

Rückert's poetic expressions of these views significantly influenced philosopher Gustav Theodor Fechner, whom Gustav Mahler read with enthusiasm.[657] This in turn influenced the composer's surprising grasp of psychology that so impressed Sigmund Freud when Mahler consulted him in late August 1910.[658] But for Rückert, suggestions of an invisible world were not fodder for philosophical debate or psychoanalytical discussion. The question was more immediate. *In heaven this light, it seems, is transfigured*, he wrote. Friedrich experienced heaven's gifts as intrinsic parts of daily existence: they inhabited and influenced his mundane physical world.

> Looking up at the night sky, we are reminded of the immense mystery in which we are immersed.... When we truly encounter the night in all its beauty and terror, we have no assurance whatsoever that we are going to come out unscathed.—David Steindl-Rast[659]

> **Ah, tell me this, and this alone:**
> **do they still know us there?**
> **Or does it escape them:**
> **how sorely we miss them,**
> **how our hearts were torn**
> **when they were ripped from us?**
>
> **No, spare them this harm,**
> **this pain that we feel.**
> **Let them in our hearts**
> **rest, and know only their**
> **father's and mother's smiles,**
> **the quiet joys of dream.**

I would trade places with my daughter in a heartbeat. *If one of us had to die*, I think, *surely it should have been me*. Alas, it was not to be. Faced with the reality of this overwhelming grief, I pause over a different thought. If one of us has to face a world without the other, then, as Rückert wrote, I would spare her this harm. Friedrich's sentiment calls to mind Mother Teresa's hope that she be named a saint of darkness: "I will continually be absent from Heaven—to light the light of those in darkness on earth."[660]

Rückert seems to sense that his children miss him. At the same time, he believes that they are happy. They do not suffer. If they are aware of their parents at all, their father would wish for them only the *quiet joys* found in love, not loss. If one must suffer, Friedrich suggests, let it be him.

> You will find sorrow moving through you, like a dark mist over a landscape. This sorrow is dark enough to paralyze you. It is a mistake to interfere with this movement of feeling. It is more appropriate to recognize that this emotion belongs more to your clay than to your mind. It is wise to let this weather of feeling pass; it is on its way elsewhere.—John O'Donohue[661]

Misfortunes are cowards,
for they always arrive in mobs.—Calderón

> **Consider a man alone,**
> **standing at peace, defenseless.**
> **To attack him is dishonorable.**
> **Yet this is the way of misfortunes.**
> **They fall upon me,**
> **I cannot fend them off, not one,**
> **never mind the lot of them,**
> **for they always come in mobs.**
>
> **Courage! They are cowards,**
> **they cannot equal one man;**
> **if ever you were a man,**
> **today is the day to show it!**
> **Keep on! When they strike,**
> **pick yourself up yet again.**
> **They will flee at the sight,**
> **for misfortunes are cowards.**

Rückert begins this song by quoting a passage from Pedro Calderón de la Barca's *Life Is a Dream*, written prior to 1630. The play was first performed in 1635 and published a year later.[662] The famous drama was a meditation on the illusions and transience of existence:

> I today,
> Guided by a wiser will,
> Have here come to cure my ill,
> Here consoled my grief to see,
> If a wretch consoled can be
> Seeing one more wretched still.[663]

German Romantics saw Calderón's theological and philosophical work as the ideal of *Poesie*, loosely translated as literature, envisioning the physical world as something of a divine pageant. This was particularly true with an earlier drama, *The Constant Prince* (1628/1629).[664] After reading August Schlegel's translation of *The Constant Prince*, Goethe sang its praises to Friedrich Schiller: "Yes, I would suggest that, should literature disappear completely from this world, it could be restored from this play."[665]

Rückert was an accomplished translator: his German rendering adapts the Castilian playwright's intent while slightly altering the phrasing. The original Spanish reads, "Misfortunes are cowards for it seems they never work alone," or as translated by Irish poet Denis Florence MacCarthy,

> Once a wise man called them cowards,
> Seeing that misfortunes never
> Have been seen to come alone.[666]

In this poem, Friedrich feels beset by a mob of misfortune. People of faith often feel a sense of helplessness in the face of sudden and traumatic death. This may challenge their previously held beliefs in divine protection. Paradoxically, those who find meaning in the catastrophe and in their future lives are the most likely to experience a renewal of redemptive faith: a powerful combination of fatalism and ultimate trust.[667] Perhaps the poet's pep talk has the hollow ring of false bravado, but this may have been all he could muster.

Experts assure us that bereaved parents have a particular form of depression that is normal and expected: it is not necessarily chronic, manic or pathological. Rather, mourners often relate a surprisingly healthy acceptance of the loss of their child and the permanence of the pain that will persist indefinitely.[668] In this light, it is remarkable that Friedrich wrote anything at all.

> A messenger comes to the mourner's house. "Come," says the messenger, "you are needed." "I cannot come," says the mourner, "my spirit is broken." "That is why you are needed," says the messenger.—Leon Wieseltier[669]

**Flowers exposed, dead,
reborn lovelier still.
So have I lost you
that I may find you.**

**And your beauty at last
flows over me, unveiled
smiles from a distant
lovelier place.
So have I lost you
that I may find you.**

**Weak when awake, my
eyes did not see as
I see you now come
to grace my dreams.
So have I lost you
that I may find you.**

**A wall, it seemed, parted
you from me; now it is
transparent sapphire
clear and blue.
So have I lost you
that I may find you.**

**Now your gentle lips say
more words in an hour
than I heard from you
four years together.
So have I lost you
that I may find you.**

**Garden flower exposed,
dead, rest in my heart,
blossom forever, never
to freeze again.
So have I lost you
that I may find you.**

At first Rückert's reference to a transparent sapphire, clear and blue, seems a bit overwrought.⁶⁷⁰ Perhaps it was: the poet was not himself, after all. But his choice of descriptor may have been something more. Friedrich was calling on imagery that dated back to Medieval German epitaphs. In *Parzival*, for example, Wolfram von Eschenbach writes of a transparent and eternal presence of the titular protagonist's dead father. His body, entombed in ruby, emits its own light⁶⁷¹:

> He shines through the ruby slab
> of his grave, of his tomb.⁶⁷²

In the Middle Ages, death was frequently represented as a metamorphosis from red, the color of life, to green and blue, associated with a continued existence.⁶⁷³ Even today mourners who report sensing the presence of their loved ones frequently speak of just such clear and simultaneously colored visions.

Modern clinicians categorize such experiences as non-pathological and at times quite helpful. The grieving commonly report hearing and seeing their beloved dead, though smell and touch also occur, particularly among bereaved parents like Friedrich. They also report that their continuing bond with the dead has a "spiritual" quality.⁶⁷⁴

Professor of spiritual care at the University of Zurich, Simon Peng-Keller, describes the "hyperreal" nature of these visionary experiences. Unlike dreams, they have an intense grounding in reality and a high level of clarity. The visions are not fleeting; rather, they are powerfully imprinted in our memory.⁶⁷⁵

Whether or not Friedrich actually interacted with Luise in a spiritual form is hardly the point. In this song, he has recorded the sensations of experiencing her. In losing her, he writes, he has found her true self, unveiled at last—a chatterbox of beauty and grace beyond his imaginings.

> The great secret of death, and perhaps its deepest connection with us, is this: that, in taking from us a being we have loved and venerated, death does not wound us without, at the same time, lifting us toward a more perfect understanding of this being and of ourselves.—Rainer Maria Rilke⁶⁷⁶

Lyric

With the eyes of my mind
I see you as brightly as before.
But these eyes that saw you
once, see you now nevermore.
—Spanish Romance

Ah, my physical eyes are
weak: they cannot pierce
the dark haze of death,
or the lighted joy of heaven.
You shone so brightly in
life. Now you have drifted
and I remain, weeping,
for I have lost you.

I see your graves thru
a long, dark tunnel—
as astronomers see the sun
thru a long dark funnel—
I see you above with
a choir of angels, not
bright as in life; brighter,
brighter than before.

Rückert has spun a rather desultory musical trope on its head. He cannot see his dead children with his physical eyes, nor can he quite see them in heaven. Instead, he perceives something that is neither mystical nor physical, observing them *as astronomers see the sun thru a long dark funnel*. This provides a clue to Friedrich's struggle to grasp a deeply felt sense of presence and the mystery of God.

In the second stanza, Rückert is alluding to the famous passage from Paul's letter to the believers in Corinth, "For now we see through a glass, darkly."[677] Ironically, Greek linguists and Bible scholars find the *glass, darkly* reference as puzzling as the mystery it represents. Paul may be writing of peering into a shadowy riddle, as some specialists suggest, but even that fails to capture the nuances that Martin Luther and Rückert seem to have understood. The Luther Bible that Friedrich read translated Paul's letter a bit more literally: "we see through a glass in a dark Word."[678]

The Greek term in question, *ainigma*, also means "an underlying truth" or "a truth clothed in imagery," or perhaps as Luther's translators suggested, the Word. "As the context shows," explained linguist David Gill, "*ainigma* clearly does not refer to a riddle in the sense of something that is utterly baffling, but … to an 'indistinct divine revelation'—or perhaps better, 'the problem of the divine.'"[679]

To further muddy the reflection, scholar D.J. Behm saw the Greek term *di' esoptrou* not as a simple mirror of glass, but a reflection of the divine through the creatures of God's world.[680] By the time we're done with Paul, the passage reads, in effect: "Now we see God through the mirror of his creation in a way that makes us reflect on His true nature."[681]

Although Rückert was a skilled linguist, his interest in Paul's passage may have been more pragmatic than revelatory. In this poem, he peers down a dark tunnel to discover Ernst and Luise reflected brightly with an angelic choir—a true and beautiful mystery of the divine.

**Angels hover round us
wherever we go.
Angels surround us,
where we don't know.**

**But in the light, we
cannot grasp who
they are or by what
names to call them.**

**They shine too
bright: blinded,
we turn away—
in whole or in part.**

**Now we have our
pair of angels;
these, at least,
we have named.**

**Nor do we forget:
after all, once we
held their light
in our arms.**

**Shall we turn away,
are they too bright?
Are we too blinded—
in whole or in part?**

**No, we see your
joy in the light:
you are known; we
call your names.**

**Smiling, you help us
to see and to know:
you hover round us,
wherever we go.**

Grief has an immediate effect on internal perceptions of our bodily experience, that is, our *lived* world.[682] Grief experts label the type of inner vision that Rückert describes as Extraordinary Experiences (EEs). They have found that EEs help maintain a continuing bond with the deceased and facilitate acknowledgment of the death. As such, the question of whether the grieving father actually sees his dead children in a mystical vision or as part of a "personal mythology" is beside the point. Such experiences often contribute to a spiritual or religious belief system that fosters healthy grieving as the bereaved adapt to life without a loved one.[683]

Friedrich suggests that we seldom notice angels around us—until they are our own. Other poems in this collection tackle spiritual frustrations: doubt about God; dissatisfaction with faith community support; moments of frustration or resentment with his religious beliefs prior to and after the deaths of his children.[684] Yet Rückert did not succumb to bitterness. Instead, as the years went by without Luise and Ernst, his last poems grew more mystic in nature.[685] In sharing his experiences, Friedrich explored a new awareness of the physical and invisible worlds that helped him cope with loneliness and loss.

Modern sciences have maintained since the 17th century that the search for truth belongs with poets and philosophers, while science strives not for beauty but fact.[686] To clarify the difference between fact, beauty and truth, we need look no further than the Bible. The parable of the Good Samaritan is recognized the world over as a story of meaningful truth. However, it does not represent facts: there was no specific Samaritan nor could we identify an inn on the road from Jerusalem to Jericho to provide documentary evidence of events that Jesus clearly intended as illustrative fiction. What is *true* need not be *factual*.[687]

German theoretical physicist Werner Heisenberg saw things differently. A key pioneer in quantum mechanics, Heisenberg thought truth and beauty were inextricably linked to fact. He described beauty as the proper alignment of disparate parts with one another and the whole. In his lecture "The Meaning of Beauty in the Exact Natural Sciences," Heisenberg cited the philosophical view of Plotinus, who described the *One* or *Ground of Being* as ineffable but absolute. The One can only be known indirectly by deducing what it is *not*: the One remains unnamable because it cannot be described.[688] "Without any reference to parts," Heisenberg suggested, "beauty is the eternal splendor of the 'One' that shines through tangible exteriors."[689] The same concept had a powerful impact on young Augustine after his conversion to Christianity.[690]

This blend of philosophy and religion is not as idiosyncratic as it seems. "Why should not we keep truth, and keep it whole?" asked renowned scholar Étienne Gilson. "It can be done. But only those can do it who realize that He Who is the God of philosophers is HE WHO IS, the God of Abraham, of Isaac, and of Jacob."[691] In this light, awareness of a statement does not make it accurate. The statement may still be false. Such awareness fails as true knowledge. The popular assumption that knowledge is by its nature accurate carries with it a responsibility of discernment.[692]

Lutheran Protestant theologian Paul Tillich was also influenced by Plotinus's concept of the One.[693] The meaning that so many mourners seek, in Tillich's view, is reflected *through* and *part of* truth, beauty and goodness. Each is dependent on the other, leading to our ultimate, unconditional concern with God. "Religion," Tillich concluded, "is the state of being grasped by the power of Being itself."[694]

These perceptions of an intrinsic connection between the tangible and intangible—between fact, beauty and truth—are surprisingly similar to Rückert's views. The professor and linguist knew of Plotinus's famous One, of course, but most often his work seems informed by the teachings of Friedrich Schleiermacher. By the early 19th century, particularly in the lively theological milieu of Erlangen, theologians tended to agree with Schleiermacher's assertion that creeds and church doctrines were subordinate to an individual's experience of God.[695] In his grief, Rückert did not see being overwhelmed by the divine as a topic for philosophical introspection. It was his reality.

> We align thirty spokes: a wheel
> whose use depends on empty space.
> We turn the clay: a vessel
> whose use depends on empty space.
> We cut doors and windows: a house
> whose use depends on empty space.
>
> We use what is and know
> the use of what is not.
> —Tao Te Ching[696]

**You need something to love,
if only a single face,
and more faces remain
than death has taken.
Think, what part of love
was taken with that face?
From each, from what remains,
death has taken nothing.**

This poem was Rückert's answer to the platitude "At least you have other children." He had lost two; four remained. The poet is speaking to himself, a familiar feature of Romantic lyric poetry and a particularly effective way for the grieving to deal with loss. Advice from others may be irksome, but spoken to ourselves, such gentle reminders can be potent and helpful in the first months of grief. Just two years earlier, in April–May of 1832, Friedrich had written a similar, prescient song:

> A heart needs something to desire,
> to fear that it will move on,
> to wish and hope and require,
> and grieve when it is gone.[697]

Grief is a universal, biological imperative found in all human cultures. It is expressed by weeping and withdrawal as well as reaching out to others in service and communion.[698] In this respect, the myth of "letting go and moving on" is revealed as typically ineffective, uninformed and perhaps even deleterious.[699] Daily reminders of joy and loss remain, as does the love that inspires them.

"Suddenly he is here again," wrote philosopher Nicholas Wolterstorff of his son, Eric, who died in a mountain-climbing accident at age twenty-five. "The chain of suggestion can begin almost anywhere: a phrase heard in a lecture, an unpainted board on a house, a lamp-pole, a stone. From such innocuous things my imagination winds its sure way to my wound. Everything is charged with the potential of a reminder. There's no forgetting."[700]

Margarethe Susanna von Kuntsch lost thirteen of her fourteen children. Ten had already passed when her nine-year-old daughter, Dorothea, died on 31 January 1690. Margarethe

Susanna was devastated. Shortly afterward, she wrote a poem in response to the kind but empty platitudes of family and friends:

> Spare me your attempts at consolation:
> little wonder that they seem to shatter
> the bond between my body and my soul[701]

> **As the lower branches of a
> banyan tree sink in the soil
> and take root and flourish;
> I lowered my youngest
> in the earth, hoping they
> are kept no less safe.**
>
> **I would not lower the tops
> in grief, but find memory in
> absence, solace in example:
> as the lower branches of a
> banyan tree sink in the soil,
> its upper limbs sway in the sun.**

Rückert knew the powerful imagery of the plants and flowers we associate with our dead. My daughter's middle name was Autumn. I still think of her each time I see a falling leaf. She had a maple leaf tattoo on her chest and often told friends, "I put this here because my dad is next to my heart." I also think of her when I see ferns: these same plants cover her grave in the nature preserve where she rests. In another song, "Primula Veris," Friedrich wrote of the cowslip primroses that grow over Luise and Ernst.

In this piece, the poet is likening his children's graves to a tree that, while not indigenous to Coburg, has a long literary tradition. Early Europeans referred to the banyan as an Indian fig tree. John Milton's imagery of the tree as a mother and her children was not lost on Rückert:

> The fig tree, not that kind for fruit
>   renowned;
> But such as at this day, to *Indians* known,
> In Malabar or Deccan spreads her arms
> Branching so broad and long, that in the
>   ground
> The bended twigs take root, and daughters
>   grow
> About the mother tree, a pillared shade
> High over-arched, and echoing walks
>   between.
> —John Milton[702]

Banyans are associated with death in India, where it is the national tree. They are often planted outside villages near crematoriums. There is little doubt that Rückert was aware of the cultural, historical and spiritual significance of the tree. Being conversant in Sanskrit, it is likely he knew that the tree's name, *Bahupāda* ("many-footed"),[703] refers to its branches that droop low to the ground.

A banyan's numerous prop-roots touch the earth, sink into the soil and come to resemble new trunks.[704] A single tree can grow multiple trunks; old banyans may form an entire wood.[705] One famous tree, over 250 years old, covers 1,347 square meters, with branches that grow as high as 24 meters. The oldest banyan is much larger, covering an area of 22,000 square meters. It is 570 years old with prop-roots so large they are described as pillars.[706]

This image provides a clue to the solace that Friedrich finds in the banyan's example. He would not see the tops of the banyan (himself, his wife, his remaining children) droop or touch the earth; at the same time he hopes that Ernst and Luise are no less safe than the living roots of this massive, sprawling and ancient tree.

Rückert's allusions to eastern

traditions informed much of Rainier Maria Rilke's work.[707] In a passage from *The Book of Hours*, Rilke explores his personal relationship with a banyan tree (or a genus quite like it) and the dark, silent, invisible world. His final lines read like an introspective response to the second stanza of Rückert's song. The similarities in content and phrasing are striking.[708] Both speak of living roots, branches that hang low, and limbs that sway in the sun or barely stir in the wind. "The holy is below us, not above," observed Robert Bly in his comments on Rilke's poem, "and a line moves to descend, to dip down, to touch water that lies so near we are astonished our hands haven't dipped into it before. The lines suggest holy depth, always distant, always close."[709]

> Yet as much as I lean into myself:
> my God is dark, like a web of
> a hundred roots drinking in silence.
> From this warmth I arise, I know
> only this, for my branches reach
> low, stirred by wind and little else.
> —Rainer Maria Rilke[710]

**I did not want so many
but when they came, I said,
"Dear Lord in heaven!
If you're here, you're here to stay."**

**And when it happened
that some left us, I said:
"Dear Lord in heaven!
If you must leave, you must."**

**The storms have passed
that took them from us:
"Dear Lord in heaven!
God left me these, thank God."**

Rückert is indulging in a sense of play. When his wife told him that she was pregnant with Ernst, followed by Luise two years later, he may well have cried, "Dear Lord in heaven!" Remembering this, or something like it, the poet demonstrates how a common expression may turn to supplication.

In the coming years both parents were faced with the complicated task of relinquishing their parental role with the deceased children while simultaneously continuing in this role for the survivors. Some researchers call this *bereaved parenting*.[711]

Rückert was a supportive, kind and loving father to his remaining children as they also came to terms with the loss of the two youngest. The parents were then forced to revisit the loss as their children matured and grew in understanding of death. This was painful yet Friedrich seems to have kept in mind his own self-revelation: *God left me these, thank God.*

**From the silver bloom of morning
emerges the gold of the sun,
smiling upon a world that
looks up, smiling in return.**

**The flowers open to its warmth,
the choir of birdsong rises to greet it.
The prayer of all creation
calls to the Creator's ear.**

**All life hopes anew
and forgets what was lost;
and the day's steady gaze warms
what was frozen in the night.**

**Prayers are heard, the golden
gate is thrown open. Unlock your
heart, embrace life and the
joy you may find in it!**

Rückert was a believer. He wrote many hymns, some that he translated into German from various languages, others that were original to him. "In lowly guise thy King appeareth" may be his best known.[712] The poet was not shy about invoking God in his grief, though it could be in questions or anger as often as pleading and gratitude. At the same time, Friedrich was not fond of the pastoral predilection in 19th-century Germany of teasing out a message or wrapping up a lament with an easy answer. This may be why his songs resonate with us so deeply. There is little sentimentality or false bonhomie when Friedrich finds brief solace in nature. After all, to grieve is to love and, on good days, to find gratitude for the time we had with our dead.

One researcher based in Montana concluded that experiences of weeping and other deep emotions in response to nature provide transformation and a unity of the mind and body.[713] Francis Bacon prescribed "contemplations of nature" for sadness,[714] which led English poet Joseph Addison to observe that delightful scenes in nature "are able to disperse grief and melancholy."[715] Put another way, in nature our grief may not be easier but it may at times be eased. Life suddenly seems precious, as eloquently expressed by Korean Zen master Beopjeong: "I am careful when walking on leaves. They are scattered, it's true, yet each exists, each has meaning. All things that exist are part of the world. So, too, with leaves."[716]

> You ask, "Where is God's hand, the god you trusted to save?"
> And here I am shackled by chains of pain.
>
> "Where," you ask, "is God's hand, the god who breaks the chains?"
> And here I lie in flames of pain.
>
> God's hand is here when, wounded by grief, my soul finds the strength to go on.
>
> Yes, God's hand is here when, in days of suffering, my heart is not paralyzed with despair.

"Where are the exits," cried one bereaved mother whose eleven-year-old son was killed riding his bike home from school. "How do I find my way out of this?"[717] Rückert's poem of endurance and despair reflects the feelings of bereaved parents the world over.

Grief expert Ronald Knapp interviewed over three hundred parents who survived the deaths of their children. He observed that the pain is long-lasting, acute and requires an act of courage to face each day, even years after the loss. Few experiences compare to losing a child. There is only one way to ease the suffering, Knapp concluded. "Coping means allowing ourselves to mourn a loss actively."[718]

Rückert was one of the early German voices that offered grief in all its raw honesty. His poems represent an important shift in lament literature.

A number of psalms, the books of Jeremiah, Lamentations and most specifically Job have a long tradition of anguished cries and protests *against* God. However, by the 18th-century German believers were expected to express grief and pain *to* God while accepting their suffering.[719] Explosive rage toward God over the loss of a loved one was seen as a spiritual and psychological threat. In fact, early Protestant theology had insisted that human transgressions led to God's wrath which in turn was the source of suffering and grief.[720] The idea was to accept pain meekly.[721]

Friedrich was a heartbroken supplicant, to be sure, but he was far from meek. He alternately finds solace in the assurance of a future reunion with his children while also crying out against a God who would take them away.

The question of *belief* in God is irrelevant; rather, Friedrich asks whether God can be *trusted*, echoing Job's frustrated lament, "If I summoned him, and he answered me, I still can't believe he would listen to my plea."[722] Many mourners face this chasm between the world as we want it to be and the loss before us.[723]

In this poem, Rückert presents a dialogue between himself and the children's mother. Luise asks pointed questions; Friedrich has no ready answers.[724] Together they challenge deity. The poet acknowledges their pain, and sees some small evidence that God has not abandoned them.

> [W]e must never forget that we may also find meaning in life even when confronted with a hopeless situation as its helpless victim, when facing a fate that cannot be changed.—Viktor Frankl, psychiatrist and Holocaust survivor[725]

Do not speak to me of this earthly vale of tears!
Torment not yourself, and feel no torment.
Let me rejoice in this earth and the joys heaven pours upon it each day.
Shall I grieve that two heavenly pictures stole away from my morning dream?
I prefer to think of them as shining on in my soul; where they now,
on other paths, follow the Leader of all, or make their own way.
But here below I confidently trudge on, between reality and ideals,
rejoicing where I find blossoms, and planting flowers where I do not;
increasing the treasures entrusted to me, returning them with gratitude.

After the deaths of Luise and Ernst, Rückert became an inveterate walker, often hiking for hours and miles each day. I too found solace in such daily walks in the woods of the Carolinas where I live in the United States of America. I know how random passages from books can come unexpectedly to mind, or how flights of fancy may reveal a deeper meaning. This poem has both.

Friedrich's son, Heinrich, who collected and edited *Songs on the Death of Children*, selected this as the final poem for the first edition in 1872. Perhaps he was thinking of his father's daily jaunts or, just as likely, he saw this song as a fitting end to his laments.

In this song Rückert quotes Psalm 84, which speaks of the valley of tears, or more famously in English, our vale of tears.[726] Friedrich's final line refers directly to the Parable of the Talents in the Gospel of Matthew,[727] in which the servant, having multiplied his two measures of gold, was blessed to share in his master's happiness.

The poem also contains a bit of whimsy that takes a moment to explain. In the fifth line, he plays on a popular 19th-century pastime, *living pictures*. The term originated in France, known there as *tableaux vivant*, in which an amateur cast of characters enacted a famous literary, historical or artistic scene. Goethe was especially fond of the game and used his knack for creating unabashedly "high culture" out of trivial practices to elevate *living pictures* to upper- and middle-class salons. Rückert's contemporary, translator and fellow poet August Schlegel, was also an enthusiast.[728] Friedrich may have been alluding to such "living pictures" when he refers to his dead children as *two heavenly pictures that came to life and stole away from his early morning dream.*

"God is a poet, say, searching for the right word," suggested American poet and author Frederick Buechner. "Word after word God tries ... to get it all into one final Word what he is and what human is and why the suffering of love is precious and how the peace of God is a tiger in the blood."[729] Like Rückert, the theologian was not resorting to hyperbole. Both men knew pain.

Buechner was ten years old when his father ended his own life in 1936. The family did not keep the details a secret; however, Buechner chose to do so. When asked how his father died, he spoke of it as heart trouble.

"The word suicide seemed somehow shameful and better left unsaid," he wrote. Years later Buechner would admit that the grief did not fade, because he never allowed himself to experience it fully. His secret took its toll in the form of repressed emotions, anxiety, and guilt.

After a friend compassionately listened to the truth about his father, Buechner finally began to grasp the impact of the death. "Only in my middle age," he wrote, "did it become real enough for me to weep real tears."[730]

It is easy to dismiss Rückert's gentle humor and his obvious celebration of nature as a form of denial, but recent studies have found the opposite is true. Quiet laughter and appreciation of the moments we had with our dead loved ones promotes a balanced outlook.[731] This in turn may serve as a catharsis that facilitates healthy enjoyment of life, a pragmatic view of grief, and hope for a future reunion[732]—helping us, as Friedrich wrote, to *confidently trudge on between reality and ideals.*

Supplemental Poems

***The children's birthday wish
for their mother
—17 November 1834***

Four come to you
to wish you joy on
the day of your birth.
Last year they were six;
now two are missing. No!
These two come as well
from heaven like a breath
to wish you joy and
happiness for their part:

"We too, whom you gave
birth, are not lost to you.
We are your children,
grateful to have had life:
not long nor shining, perhaps.
We each of us exist:
they for this time,
we for eternity;
they vital and alive,
we silent and waiting
as we rest in peace
and bless all that you are."

Luise roused herself as best she could for the sake of her surviving children.[733] It wasn't easy. Along with the lifelong grief of losing young Luise and Ernst, she had a busy household to run. Luise's letters to her parents, Albrecht and Luise Fischer, detailed the many challenges of everyday life with a home full of children, unreliable servants and an occasionally eccentric and solitary scholar for a husband.[734]

Friedrich wrote this piece for his wife's thirty-seventh birthday, ten months after Ernst's death.[735] The poet speaks with an undertone of love and gentle thankfulness. Many bereaved parents are surprised at their gratitude for even the smallest kindnesses, especially from family members or friends who knew and loved their dead children.[736] At the same time, parents also relate moments of emotional connection and disconnection with their surviving children, made more acute by the often competing and potentially incompatible tasks of "parenting" and "grieving."[737]

One study of ninety boys and girls, ages four to sixteen years, conducted in the two years after the death of a sibling, found that some 50 percent displayed signs of aggression in their attempt to gain parental attention. The hostility and anger was not isolated to a specific gender or seen as instinctual. Rather, the behavior problems were a direct result of failing to include the surviving children in the type of observance that Rückert records in this poem.[738]

Involving children in commemorative moments such as birthdays helps alleviate fears of death and abandonment and reminds the survivors that their celebrations are normal and healthy.[739] This also helps the family as a whole acknowledge love for their dead in a helpful and productive way.[740] Nigel Field, a pioneer in the area of continuing bonds, saw such ongoing attachments as multidimensional. He asserted that the point of grief is not detachment, but rather identifying which bonds may be continued and which need to be relinquished in a "reconstruction of the relationship with the deceased."[741]

We were and are—I am, even as thou art—
Beings who ne'er each other can resign;
It is the same, together or apart,
From life's commencement to its slow decline
We are entwin'd—let Death come slow or fast,
The tie which bound the first endures the last!
—Lord Byron[742]

> **Now for the dark days, a time of sorrow, already for me a joyless time, long before they wounded me so.**
>
> **A time to lament light's loss, to pine for an earth bedecked; this time when my precious pair was taken, like sun and flowers.**
>
> **And in the midst of this dark there was a star, bright with solace: the children's joy in holy Christmas;**
>
> **o blessing dearly missed, buried in your grave, clutched in your hand, your gifts from that day.**

The bitter cold brought a flood of memories for Rückert. The winter of 1834/5 was particularly hard on him, the first year without Ernst and Luise.[743] In the modern age we stave off the darkness of winter until January at least. We launch our celebrations with the garishness of Halloween, followed by the warmth of Thanksgiving, then a flurry of shopping, Christmas and—coming full circle in a way—we finish the season with another frequently gaudy holiday, New Year's Eve. There are religious observations, to be sure, but for many in the 21st century, the time is more busy than solemn.

Friedrich's holidays were different. The winter dark was descending, a joyless period for Friedrich, lit all too briefly with Christmas celebrations: the tree, a few gifts, carols and a generous feast. Winter was bad enough, according to this poem, made that much worse when death stole even that *star, bright with solace*.

Rückert relates that they placed Luise's Christmas gift in her hand when she was buried. The joy of Christmas was replaced with memories of gifts now buried, clutched in dead hands, candles half-burnt on the tree, and a darkness no longer lit by his children's joy.[744]

This poem was likely written sometime during the family's first holiday season after the deaths of Ernst and Luise, in the winter of 1834/5, though it certainly could have been written later.

Such laments may seem to be destructive. The opposite is often true. Psychologist Elizabeth Lewis Hall found that lament, particularly as a spiritual discipline, constructively helps the sufferer deal with grief and pain. Lament helps us to move "from disorientation to new orientation,"[745] and so find meaning in a life that suddenly seems meaningless.

A year is now gone as you were gone a year ago, as this deadline reminds me like two dark hours.

And had you lived, sweetie, this day in this year would memorialize nothing: just another two happy hours.

Alas, it was not to be, and having buried you, my child, I think how precious are the few years we are given.

Years, like hours, dark or bright, slow or fast, must soon pass, vanished, gone.

Once I yearned for long life, to see you bloom over the years. Now you are gone. I cannot vanish soon enough.

The first memorial day, or death anniversary, is particularly difficult since it carries with it a sense of finality that will continue throughout the second year as each holiday or special anniversary is faced alone. Friedrich's use of the familiar term *sweetie*[746] provides a clue to the date of this poem. He probably wrote it close to 31 December 1834 in observance of Luise's first memorial day. All around them, people were busily celebrating the *two happy hours* of New Year's Eve: the last hour of the old year and the first hour of the new. But for the grieving father, the midnight deadline reminds him of loss, *like two dark hours*. His final thought, *Now you are gone. I cannot vanish soon enough*, is redolent with equal parts yearning and despair. It is also a normal and expected part of grief.

Experienced counselor and psychotherapist Ashley Davis Bush compares certain aspects of grief with a surprising source. The Alcoholics

Anonymous model insists that addicts never fully recover, even if they have not had a drink for decades. The alcoholic is still affected by the disease: they are recovering but never recovered, according to AA wisdom and the experience of millions.

My father, Dennis, was an alcoholic. Dad was forty years sober when he died in 2019. But rather than sit in smug satisfaction at four decades of temperance, he reached out to fellow sufferers.

Dad returned to the twelve-step recovery program with church-sponsored addiction groups. Losing my mother in 2013 was a terrible blow that left him heartbroken and at times desperately lonely, yet still he did not take a drink. Instead, he went through each difficult step, participating with those who may have slipped the week before or the day before, reminding them that a journey of a month or forty years could only be traveled one day at a time.

A younger member of the group summed up my father's influence. "I don't care much about Sunday school," he said. "But when the old guy talks, I listen." Dad, in his usual lively way, replied: "Well, for that I'll be the 'old guy.'"

My father was in fact sober until his death, though he would have been the first to say that he had never recovered or healed. "In much the same way," observed Davis Bush of the AA model, "a griever is recovering and healing, but is never fully recovered.... [T]he grieving process is life-long in that the griever will be forever touched and affected by his loss."[747]

Summer flowers were a comfort, scattered over their graves: each bud struggles, as I struggle, to be born anew.

Spring children, fragile and frozen in the fury of winter: their gentle illusion now gone, only poetry eases my loss.

My children, my joys, my sorrows, rest not in hard earth, but in this soft heart;

this hearth of roses, from which songs, not lilies—flickers of sacred candles—are plucked.

As grueling as the first memorial day may be, most bereaved parents report that *all* death observances and holidays are difficult, though different each year.[748] For me, one of the best bits of advice I received after my daughter's death addressed this very topic.

On the Saturday when we launched Jess's memorial film collection at the local library, a man who had lost his child some twenty-five years earlier told me, "It never gets any easier." His words may seem insensitive but in reality were (and are) surprisingly helpful. "Each individual's grief process is unique," observed grief experts Paul Boelen and Geert Smid. "The concept of stages of grief occurring in a specific order is a popular, yet inadequate representation of what grieving people go through."[749] Knowing what to expect, and what *not* to expect, offers a peculiar assurance.

Friedrich is finding his own sources of comfort and practical help, as he describes in this poem. Such times of remembrance have a definable impact on the health of the bereaved.[750] Creative expressions may take the form of personal, unobtrusive rituals that provide a means to grieve openly.[751] The nature of such ritual is unimportant: only that it resonate with the mourner, offering meaning and memory. For Friedrich, writing poems, like *flickers of sacred candles*, offers some measure of solace, which he plucks from his hearth of roses, from a heart that remains soft and welcoming for his children.

A precious life gone too soon.
It sprouts and blooms in a single night.
It wakes in the early hours,
earlier than you expect.
This child, leaping
through flower bushes,
arms swinging, filled
with life, with life.
Come evening
this child is dead.
Never to lie down again,
never to rise again,
never to wake.
Good night, good night.
Your race is run,
your grave is dug,
good night, good night.

Romantic era poets often wrote of mythical, magical childhood, "a time of endless dreams, when innocence and divinity exist in harmony," as German literature expert Ortrud Gutjahr observed.[752] Rückert's songs have the same undertones and Biblical flourishes, but with an important difference: the grieving father was not working from fanciful nostalgia but powerful memory.[753]

Memory may be triggered by many things: a song, a laugh, a smile or smell or fleeting wisp of the past so real that it seems to be fully present. It tears into us in a way that is at once emotional and spiritual. "Remembrance has a Rear and Front," wrote Emily Dickinson. "Leave me not ever there alone / Oh thou Almighty God!"[754] It is all too easy to focus on the unpleasant occasions of the past: a harsh word, an opportunity missed. This type of selective memory, coupled with guilt and remorse, is common among the bereaved.[755]

We cannot always control our thoughts—this seems nearly impossible—but over time we might stop fighting them. Instead, we may slowly be able to choose which thoughts have meaning to us, which are helpful and kind. In the same way, our welcoming embrace may ease the power of memory to wound. Special occasions need no longer be crippling.[756] In consciously combining thought and memory, we may suddenly find ourselves remembering at our own pace, at times of our own choosing.

Rituals associated with special days give us a time and space to remember and to mourn.[757] They are our allies along this dark road of sorrow. Seen in this light, Friedrich's lament is steeped in peace and calm. He may in fact have been recalling a specific moment: *This child, leaping through flower bushes, arms swinging, filled with life, with life.*

As we return to some semblance of living, we gain a new appreciation of the seeming seconds that we had with our loved ones—and the years we must now endure without them. In remembering, we experience the truth of who they were.

> The holiest of all holidays are those
> Kept by ourselves in silence and apart;
> The secret anniversaries of the heart.
> —Henry Wadsworth Longfellow[758]

---

*As the years pass
since my children died*

**On days like today
I still want to mourn
that you left us around
this time last year.
Your faces are still clear,
I see them with a calm
and precious peace.
Rather than despair,
I feel a sense of solace that
has nothing to do with me
but is a peace from above
where my two darlings
have now and forever
made their home, free
of all hurt or harm,
there among the blessed.**

Memorial days hold emotional and religious significance for family members. They have a very real physical effect on the bereaved even years after a death, whether they are acknowledged or not.[759] This *anniversary reaction*, as it is called, usually occurs near a date that is emotionally important to the bereaved.[760] The second memorial day is often marked by anxiety and distress. In this poem, Rückert makes an important observation that has been confirmed by modern research: the time passed since a death is not nearly as important as finding meaning in the years ahead.[761]

On my daughter's seventh memorial day, 16 January 2022, our neighborhood was struck by freezing rain and high winds. We lost power that day. Fortunately, living in the country, we had a natural gas fireplace. Spending that evening with nothing but candlelight and firelight seemed fitting somehow. The slower pace gave me time to remember.

"You're the best thing that ever happened to me," I told Jess from the time she could walk. After I remarried, Jess noticed that I said pretty much the same thing to her step-mother. As a teenager, she didn't understand how they could *both* be the *best* thing that ever happened to me. Years later, as an adult with a fiancé of her own, Jess confided in me, "Now I get it, Dad. You're the best thing. So is he."

> Important reality operates on a different level of things—it is not in the overt subject, but in the little brush strokes, all the little, everyday events and *things* that make up our lives. They may be past in a historical sense, but they are nonetheless present, each one of them, on the canvas, and it is they, taken together, that make up our painting ... each of us gets to paint one, and when it is done it is ours forever—it is all that *is* ours, on into howling eternity.—James Kugel[762]

Tender Burial

**Shepherdess, oh how tenderly
they have laid you to rest.
The air groaned, May Bells
tolled, a glow-worm meant
to bear your torch but a
star would not have it.
Night wore mourning black;
dark shadows made the choir.
Dawn sheds tears of dew, and
the sun? It shines in blessing,
shepherdess, on how tenderly
you have been laid to rest.**

Rückert seldom dated his poems. The pieces in *Songs on the Death of Children* were written between January and June of 1834, for the most part, though in no discernable order.

"Tender Burial" was published after this period and certainly has the same tone and style of Friedrich's poems of lament. However, it is more polished. Whatever its origins, there is little doubt that Friedrich returned to it with his customary exacting edits. This may be why so many composers set this *lied* to music, most notably Carl Loewe. A gifted tenor, Loewe created settings for twenty-five Rückert *lieder*. He composed "Tender Burial" in October 1837.

The 19th-century *lied*, or art song, was part of a general desire to merge the various arts, particularly poetry, in music.[763] Loewe succeeds admirably. The tempo is steady and serene. The piano stops double the voice at the final words, seeming to finish in a form of duet.[764] Friedrich's subtle but moving variation on the first and eleventh lines is echoed in the music. "A sweet creature has died," Loewe said of the song, "and the beautiful things of Nature have come together to beautify her burial."[765]

Friedrich writes of Luise that the sun shines in blessing *on how tenderly you have been laid to rest*. This thought resonates with me. Our loved one is gone. We may find that there are moments when we spare the smallest hint of gentle grace for ourselves, as well.

Researchers and therapists agree that it usually takes three to four years to put a death into perspective.[766]

Therapists suggest that we make no major changes in the first year. Mourners relate that the second year is the hardest. The idea is that the first round of anniversaries bring reminders of the finality of our loss.[767] Perhaps so, though I found the third year and each year after have held their own unique moments of crippling grief and challenges for living.

We are not ourselves and, as with someone in a drunken stupor, we may *think* we are behaving rationally when in fact we are *not*. Nor should we be. We are bereft, bereaved, broken and need tending to. Waves of sorrow will come and go for the rest of our lives. It never gets *easier*, but there are days, in the years ahead, when with kindness and compassion toward ourselves, we may find our pain is slowly *eased*.

It took me six years to reach a point where I felt even a remote semblance of normalcy. This is not to say I'm "myself" again—there is no such thing. I have changed in the most profound way we may experience. I'm attempting to face my new life ahead with whatever meaning I may find in each day.

We need time. More than we may know.

Coda

Songs on the Death of Children was a consolation after the death of my daughter. I immersed myself in Rückert's overwhelming grief, sharing with him the acute pain known to bereaved parents the world over. I came to understand in some small way the "living soul" of Friedrich's words, coupled with what Germans call *Sprachgefühl*: a sense—innate and instinctive—of his language.[1] David Magarshack wrote that a "translator has to feel rather than apprehend intellectually" this undercurrent of meaning, to which he added, "a translation ought to produce [the] same effect as the original work."[2] My task of rendering Friedrich's laments into English was not daunting; it was solace.

Rückert published a great deal of work prior to his children's deaths, which enabled me to assess his particular approach to poetry and how it changed over the course of writing the pieces in *Songs on the Death of Children*. I then considered context, tone, style, voice, and historical and cultural background as they relate to his laments. This required a detailed knowledge of the Rückert family, their home life and the deaths of Ernst and Luise.

Rückert sometimes speaks in the voice of the children or of their mother; at times he is whimsical or playful (not uncommon in grief); he may keen, weep, rage or berate himself and others; he often changes time and place in each poem—and with it tone and style. In two simple examples: Friedrich's anger at German burial feast customs required familiarity with the funeral practices in Coburg in the 1830s that produced surprising results; Friedrich's guilt over his children's suffering demanded an understanding of medical practices of the day and the cruel symptoms of the scarlet fever pandemic. These revealed aspects of grief that relate directly to what modern death researchers have confirmed as relevant, important and useful to the bereaved, as are the poems themselves.

Finally, I let each poem sit a while and returned to it for an aggressive edit, to view the piece with a fresh perspective and to remove the cumbersome phrasing of *translation-ese* that plagues my profession. At this stage there is a temptation to "fix" the lesser poems (there are only a few) but this betrays the original's intent and the author's honest sorrow. Most of these pieces were scribbled notes that Rückert never intended for publication, though the resulting posthumous book has never gone out of print in Germany. My translations attempt to replicate Friedrich's raw emotions, whether eloquent or jarring, sentimental or profound.

Wordplay and Humor

Rückert was given to alliteration and wordplay. Derek Attridge, professor of English at the University of York, noted that translation requires a critical eye for whatever is most important in a work, always allowing that certain formal elements cannot be reproduced. Translation inevitably involves trade-offs between one feature of the original over another. This is "especially acute in poetry," Attridge observed, "whether to sacrifice aspects of meaning in order to keep the same length as the original, or to sacrifice the ideal of quantitative faithfulness in order to corral more of the meaning."[3]

Each poem in this collection has been approached with this same critical eye, acknowledging that no single poem is like another, especially for a grieving father. In choosing which allusions and rhymes to include, as with all wordplay, a translator is left with three choices: literal rendering (which can sound like nonsense or lose the original intent); adaptation for the target audience (which may replicate the original audience's experience with equivalents); or skipping the word play, what specialists call "neutralizing" (which removes the problem of allusions and humor that falls flat with the target language).[4] The task of translating word play and rhyme is not an impossible one, but it requires negotiations with the text and calculated choices. Combining both is desirable to communicate the full power and scope of a poem.[5] When a decision must be made, however, we are forced to choose between the *intent* of the content, its lyrical *beauty*, or its *cleverness*.

Anything may be translated into any language. However, this does not mean that the kaleidoscope of nuances in a source word may be represented with a perfectly equivalent term in the target language.[6] That type of communication is rare between two people as it is, even in our native tongue! The reason is simple.

Linguists hold that no word is wholly transparent.[7] Each carries multiple meanings and a variety of far-ranging social contexts.[8] How we understand a word is unique for each person. The meaning is in *us*, not in the word itself.[9] Terms are bound to phrases, implied by the speaker and inferred by the listener, so that translating such connections is not "either-or" but "more or less."[10] A specific word does not seem to be the problem. Context is far more complex.

Suggesting that a word cannot be translated contradicts centuries of factual and textual evidence. However, the question of understanding looms large when rendering these terms.[11] Phrases that are deemed "untranslatable" are often tied to concepts that are fiercely defended as unique and important to a given culture.[12] The translator must go beyond definition and meaning to convey the text's significance.[13] In this light, translation is not a question of *if*, but *how*.

Formal fidelity to the source text

prioritizes transfer of *information*. More often than not, any humorous quality is decreased or lost entirely. Many translations veer away from this structured literalism, sometimes interpreting the original to preserve as much of the comic value as possible. This carries certain dangers, including negative reactions from those who deem any divergence from the source as indicating a "wrong" or inaccurate translation. Successful comedy, however, is often received with appreciation for the innovation required to communicate the humorous intent and effect of the original, if not its precise literal meaning.[14]

One of the great English translators of German poetry, Michael Hamburger, quipped: "All translation is impossible and *that* is the reason why one does it."[15] Each translator may be brave or foolhardy, I suppose, a Don Quixote in his or her own way. And yet the pursuit is noble. We create a bridge where none existed before: a shaky bridge at times, perhaps even rickety, but a bridge nonetheless, the first of its kind for others to use and build upon.

Rhyme and Reason

Rückert had a great gift for rhyme. However, at times he could sacrifice clarity in service to his rhyming scheme. In *Songs on the Death of Children* his rhymes are occasionally desultory, seeming to be produced more out of habit than with a particular purpose in mind.

When rhyme seems essential to the poem—or at least to the poet—I have included it in the translation. When Friedrich's keen and compassionate insight into his experience of grief seems to be the poet's main concern, my translation replicates his intent with phrasing that is freed from meter or form constraints. Many translators, Rückert chief among them, have not adhered strictly to replicating formal structure. And for good reason.

"The literal is not a translation," Octavio Paz said. "Poetry is what gets transformed…. An art of shadows and echoes."[16] We seek to produce an analogous effect comparable to the original.[17] In doing so, we are replicating its intent while simultaneously creating something new. Poet and translator Edwin Honig suggested that a good rendering brings "what was irreplaceable in the original together with what was missing from it."[18] It provides something that had not previously existed: a translated poem.

Most literary translators, myself included, focus on intercultural and interlingual communication, an intricate exchange that transforms the original into a new language. We give precedence to the meaning, feel and style of a piece in the hope that readers will have an emotional and artistic experience similar to that of the poem's original audience.[19]

In mid–18th-century Germany, translators confidently held that the worthy products of other cultures should be rendered understandable so that they easily and harmoniously enhanced literary and cultural life.[20] Then as now, most working translators aimed to stay close to the source text while making it clear, even enjoyable, for a new audience. Ideally, translation offers the best of the original culture, its differences and similarities.

Rückert kept the Luther Bible in his home. He and his wife, Luise, reference it frequently in poetry and prose. As a scholar and translator of Hebrew, Friedrich's choice is suggestive. Martin Luther was one of the earliest outspoken supporters of ensuring that a translation be accessible to general readers. "We must inquire … of the mother in the home, the children on the street, the common man in the marketplace," he instructed his Bible translators. "We must be guided by their language, the way they speak, and do our translating accordingly."[21]

Rückert understood this. In his translation of al-Hariri of Basra, *Die Makamen des Hariri*, Friedrich was faced with obscure cultural and historical allusions that were entirely alien to German readers. To avoid endless annotations and pedantic quibbling, he wrote that he focused on the original's "incessant word- and sound-play, the rhymed prose, the over-the-top images, and the hairsplitting, overwrought expressions."[22] He often resorted to equivalent verbal salad in German. For example, he translated palindromes with *Doppelreim*, in which the last two syllables of each line rhyme with similarly placed syllables in the next line. (The rhyme extends over several syllables.) Even then, Friedrich was often as not forced to forego equivalents altogether, choosing intent over stylistic niceties. The result is recognized today as a masterpiece of translation.[23] Ultimately, Rückert's approach was practical, as he wrote in the introduction to al-Hariri:

Meine Arbeit giebt sich für keine Übersetzung, sondern für eine Nachbildung.[24]
My work is not translation, but replication.

I'm fond of Rückert's word here, *Nachbildung*. It could just as easily be rendered as recasting, simulation, reproduction or imitation. However, in the task of translation, *replication* was Rückert's, and my, practice and intent.

Abbreviations

KTL	*Kindertodtenlieder* (Sauerländer, 1872)
KTL-W	*Kindertodtenlieder und andere Texte des Jahres 1834* (Wallstein, 2007)
LEB	*"...euer Leben fort zu dichten.": Friedrich Rückerts "Kindertodtenlieder" im literatur- und kulturgeschichtlichen Kontext*
RW-1	*Rückerts Werke*, v1 (Bibliographisches Institut, 1897)

The first edition of Friedrich Rückert's *Kindertodtenlieder* (Sauerländer, 1872), edited by Friedrich's eldest son Heinrich, is freely available on the Internet in PDF and other formats. The abbreviation KTL indicates the page number in the 1872 edition. Later Rückert collections included additional pieces written around the same time or directly related to the deaths of Ernst and Luise. For these, I use KTL-W to indicate *Kindertodtenlieder und andere Texte des Jahres 1834* (Wallstein, 2007) and RW-1 to represent *Rückerts Werke*, v1 (Bibliographisches Institut, 1897). Poems not in these texts are cited accordingly. Rückert pieces that were not part of *Kindertodtenlieder* are referenced in the endnotes.

Translator Notes

Encircled by mountain / *Von Gebirg umschlossen*, KTL, 242–3. I frequently pause over Rückert's subtle gifts. This piece is free of jargon, steeped in rich concepts expressed in vivid sensory images. The poet's half-recalled past blends into palpable, present reality only to dissolve again into shadow. He achieves this with his usual penchant for repetition, precise language and a certain knack for *Präteritum* and *das Perfekt*, the present perfect tense.

In many modern German dialects, the *Präteritum* (corresponding structurally to the English simple past) is for the most part extinct.[1] The Perfekt has assumed the same function as the *Präteritum* in what the Finnish linguist Kaj Lindgren dubbed *oberdeutscher Präteritumschwund*; that is, Upper German Preterite Loss in the verbal system of southern dialects of German.[2] *Präteritum* is relegated, again most notably with the southern dialects, to when people are speaking Standard German.[3] In modern Standard German, the Perfekt corresponds for the most part to the simple or progressive past tense.

Absolutists and literalists hold a much caressed view of a mythic unchanging (and unchangeable) German language. Even today, they see as linguistic decline the replacement of a synchronic subjunctive *Präteritum* with present tense. By the late 19th and early 20th centuries, complaints were rife in German magazines that a present tense usage was destroying the purity of the language. These essays were usually couched in vague language and subjective criteria.

These detractors attempted to stigmatize and deride innovative poets and writers such as Rückert and his contemporaries, but their assumptions were inaccurate. *Präteritum* as present tense in usage and intent can be traced back to the Early New High German period (1350–1650), where there is abundant documentation showing that synthetic use of subjunctive *Präteritum*—based entirely on syntactic relations expressed with *inflection*—was a substitute for present and even future tense. This latter usage was in common currency with both protasis (the clause expressing the condition in a conditional sentence) and apodosis (the main or consequent clause of a conditional sentence).[4]

Today conversational German is dominated almost exclusively with the present perfect. However, German speakers are not particularly careful in usage: they often indiscriminately mix the two tenses.[5] Remnants of the many idiosyncratic uses of *Präteritum* and *das Perfekt* persist and were far more common in Rückert's day. In the line "Schatten dicht gewoben!" there is a "characteristic combination of presentness and pastness," as linguist Wolfgang Klein put it, that corresponds to the English present perfect. A literal translation, say "Shadows thickly woven!," fails to communicate that the present situation is the result of a past event, or, put another way, that the past events have present implications. Our intuitive sense is one of immediacy, of the here and now; simultaneously what *was* and *continues to be*.[6] To communicate Rückert's phrasing and intent, this translation uses the same emphatic present tense throughout, including those "Close weaving shadows!."

Sascha Monhoff observed of this poem: "'No path' leads from the outside world into the poet.... There is no comforting revelation arising from a moment of transcendence.... It is pure *memento mori*, a reminder of the transitory nature of the world, offering the poet no better alternative to the 'here and now.'"[7]

Rückert's repetition in the third stanza, *fremden/fremde/fremden*, subtly shifts the intent with each usage of a relatively pedestrian word for something foreign, alien or strange. The German is replicated in this translation with *wisp/whiff/swift*, communicating the poet's sense of the transitory in the overall piece, highlighted by the aforementioned use of the Perfekt, while retaining his tonal quality.

Over all graves grass must grow / *Über alle Gräber*, KTL, 153. There is an unwritten rule in translation: the shortest lines require the longest explanations. (I suppose the same could be said for any exegesis.) In "Over all graves," Rückert combines irony, frustration and resignation to create one of his finest poems. There is more going on than is readily apparent on first reading. Beneath his sardonic stance rests an acceptance of the inevitability of death and the new life ahead without his children. As this discussion is a bit longer than most, I will first provide the original German song:

Über alle Gräber wächst zuletzt das Gras,
Alle Wunden heilt die Zeit, ein Trost ist das,
Wohl der schlechteste, den man dir kann ertheilen;
Armes Herz, du willst nicht daß die Wunden heilen.
Etwas hast du noch, solang es schmerzlich brennt;
Das verschmerzte nur ist todt und abgetrennt.

Below is an *early draft translation* of "Over all graves" that may please the literalist or the novice, but it fails to satisfy in many important ways, as I will explain:

Over all graves grows grass at last in the end,
Time heals all wounds, this is a solace,
indeed the worst thing which one could confer to you;
poor heart, you do not desire that wounds are healed.
You retain something still, as long as it burns painfully;
The one who gets over it is left dead and detached.

Oh, this is terrible translation. It fails to sound like a bereaved father in nearly every line. It also misses the point of the piece. However, it provides a number of interesting clues to how we might turn a simplistic literal rendering into lyric expression. Take the first line, for example. The original poem uses the word *zuletzt*, meaning "finally." The word also communicates a sense of the *inevitable*, something that *must* occur, that "at last" misses entirely.

The next line is equally amateurish: *ein Trost ist das* refers directly to the previous platitude, "Time heals all wounds." Rückert's pattern of poetry and speech is giving us a mental shrug, "Yes, we've all heard it; such is the solace they dish out." In context, "This is *a* solace" is nonsense. It is nothing of the sort. It is *the* solace that is offered, yes, but it is also a platitude that offers no consolation

The third line begins with *Wohl*, meaning indeed or arguably. There are other terms that stand out: *man*, meaning one, the subject; *dir*, a dative "to you"; and *erteilen*, meaning to confer upon. However, they are all subtle in the original and should, in better English phrasing, be implied with equal nuance. After all, a consolation is, by my inference, conferred upon me, just as the descriptor "worst" communicates that it is indeed worst without hammering it home to the long-suffering reader. That this consolation is directed to the poet is not only obvious, it is also somewhat tedious to say so.

The third line ended in a semicolon, implying a sense of "because" that would have been inferred by 19th-century German readers. *du willst nicht* provides the subject and verb, "you do not want," which are unnecessary after the meaningful "Poor heart." The subordinate conjunction *dass* connects the subsequent qualifying phrase, making *heilen* the verb, literally "that the wounds are healed." The line as rendered, "you do not desire that wounds are healed," reads great on paper but sounds awful to the ear. A change is required. By making the word healed an adjective, it retains the power and intent of the original that is far more contextually accurate than a literal approach provides.

Etwas hast du noch might seem to be saying "still" but here it mixes possibility and necessity. *Noch* is a common term that also serves a role of anguish and demand in this poem, fully equivalent to the yearning of the English phrase, "at least."[8] The subject of *du* is implied and unnecessary, as is the conjunction *solang*, or "as long as." Rückert uses an adverb, *schmerzlich* (painfully), which when combined with the verb *brennt* (burns), is cumbersome no matter how it is rendered:

- There is something you still possess, as long as the pain sears
- You still have something, so long as it painfully burns
- As long as it burns painfully, you still possess at least something

The phrase *es schmerzlich brennt* uses *es* to refer to the pain of his wounds. Here I pause. Does pain do anything other than burn? In this poem, at least, simply using the word "pain" communicates Friedrich's poignant intent. This may be a bit of poetic license, to be sure, but one that shares the poet's grief more effectively than the jarring twaddle of "burns painfully," an expression that sounds like angst-ridden teen poetry, which Rückert's song most emphatically is not.

The poem's final line asserts that if we tell ourselves that we have gotten over or recovered from a loss, then we must be dead or unfeeling. Rückert insists that the heart does not seek closure or healing, as is so popular in grief therapy. To do so would seem a betrayal of the bereaved, a forgetting of their loved one, leaving the mourner dead inside. It is also impossible.

This is presented as a "but" or "however," meanings that are implicit in the use of a semicolon at the end of the fifth line. As was customary with Romantic era poetry in general, and Rückert in particular, his use of *du/dir* is addressed to himself, to his own poor heart. The idea of "merely" (*nur*) is relatively obvious. While *abgetrennt* may refer to being detached or separated, in combination with *Verschmerzte* it takes on a much more emphatic and jarring meaning. It is particularly powerful in Friedrich's song, but in literal translation it sounds like gobbledy-gook:

- that gotten-over only is dead and removed.
- only that which hurts no longer is dead and chopped off.
- only what is forgotten is dead and left behind.

None of these translations capture the intent or beauty of the original. My solution hinges on Rückert's problematic use of one word: *Verschmerzte*. This takes a bit of explaining.

The vexing and nuanced nature of *verschmerz* is not new for those attempting to render it in English. Translators have wrestled with it for centuries; some have deemed it "untranslatable." German scholar Carl Adolph Buchheim made an admirably brief note on the word, which deserves to be reproduced in full:

> *Verschmerzen*, say: *overcome*.—This verb is without an equivalent in English: it literally means, "to cease to feel grief or pain," or, as is commonly said, "to live down," "to get over grief." Those who understand the function of the inseparable particle "*ver*," which chiefly denotes the ceasing of a condition, will be able to form a correct notion of this and similar verbs.[9]

Buchheim had a point. The particle *ver* can be helpful in arriving at a suitable translation of *verschmerzen*. Whether there is an English equivalent or not, as Buchheim suggested, the word must be translated. The many interpretations of a passage from Friedrich Schiller's *Wallensteins Tod*, which uses the term twice, may help to demonstrate the challenges involved:

Verschmerzen werd ich diesen Schlag, das weiß ich,
Denn was verschmerzte nicht der Mensch![10]

When Samuel Taylor Coleridge translated *Wallenstein*, he was initially excited about the project, looking back on the time as "the happiest attempt, during the prime manhood of his intellect."[11] But his variation on *verschmerzen* plagued him. At first, in 1800, Coleridge translated a passage with the troublesome word as follows:

This anguish will be wearied down, I know;
What pang is permanent with man?

He quickly added that this was "a very inadequate translation of the original," noting that it could be literally rendered as:

I shall *grieve down* this blow, of that I'm conscious:
What does not man grieve down?[12]

Addressing the *Wallenstein* project later, Coleridge wrote: "In the translation I endeavored to render my Author literally wherever I was not prevented by absolute differences of idiom; but I am conscious, that in two or three short passages I have been guilty of dilating the original; and, from anxiety to give the full meaning, have weakened the force."[13] Coleridge may also have been thinking of *verschmerzen* in his *Lectures of European Literature of 1818*, when he observed "the infallible test of a blameless style; namely, its untranslatableness in words of the same language without injury to meaning."[14] However, many scholars agree that the merit of Coleridge's translation is that he is not strictly bound to the original.[15]

Abraham Hayward took rather rude exception to Coleridge's choice, despite his admiration for the translator. "I really see no earthly reason for excluding the literal translation from the text," he wrote of *Wallenstein* in 1834.[16] That same year, and likely after reading Hayward, Coleridge changed his mind about his translation. Shortly before his death, he had the more literal translation ("I shall *grieve down*") substituted in current and all future editions. (The footnote was subsequently omitted.)[17]

The challenges presented by *verschmerzen* did not lessen over time. In 1826, George Moir translated the same *Wallenstein* passage that vexed Coleridge with a deft touch that displayed even greater poetic license:

I know I shall forget the blow at last;
What will not man forget?[18]

Forgetting and *forgiving*, or at least *forbearing*, are interesting aspects of *verschmerzen*, though even then they are more often than not used with tongue firmly in cheek. *Ameliorating* or *overcoming* were part of Francis Lamport's solution, one hundred and fifty years after Moir's rendering of Schiller, in a modern translation of *Wallenstein*.[19]

Pause with me for a moment to enjoy the plethora of solutions these skilled translators have come up with: *wearied down/pang; grieve down; forget; sorrow/overcome*. Even Buchheim's suggestions—"to cease to feel grief or pain," "to live down," "to get over grief"—fail to satisfy completely, particularly when these variations are applied to Rückert's poem. None quite captures the irony of his song.

As often as *verschmerzte* may be used in the vernacular, it frequently appears among people of letters with a slightly sardonic, if not flat-out sarcastic, tone. For example, after Friedrich Gottlieb Klopstock's 1774 work on the regeneration of German letters, *Die Gelehrtenrepublik*, failed miserably, Goethe teased him despite having previously admired the work. This was intended to suggest that Klopstock failed to speak to ordinary readers.[20]

> Die Bestürzung war allgemein, die Achtung gegen den Mann aber so groß, daß kein Murren, kaum ein leises Murmeln entstand. Die junge schöne Welt verschmerzte den Verlust und verschenkte nun scherzend die teuer erworbenen Exemplare. Ich erhielt selbst mehrere *von guten Freundinnen*, deren keines aber mir geblieben ist.[21]

John Oxenford's literalist translation captures this humorous, albeit slightly snarky passage, giving even the most common translation of *verschmerzte* ("got over their loss") a certain ironic twist:

> The astonishment was general, but the esteem for the man was so great, that no grumbling, scarcely a murmur, arose. The young and beautiful part of the world got over their loss, and now freely gave away the copies they had so dearly purchased. I received several from *kind female friends*, but none of them has remained with me.[22]

Verschmerzte is not written solely for irony, but this usage occurs enough that we must consider carefully the ironic aspects of Rückert's poem. The other lines are most emphatically written in pain and dismissive anger over the insensitivity of others. In this context, translating *verschmerzte* demands subtlety, balancing literalism and intent. This is where the art of translation comes in.

Author Karl Philipp Moritz was an important influence on early German Romanticism. He held that in German poetry, sensation or sentiment[23] rolls the individual syllables and words back into themselves, so that all ideas—secondary and primary—blend together with equal significance. A literal translation may capture the formal structure of a poem and still miss the overall sentiment.[24]

After months of consideration, I decided on a solution that most accurately reflects Rückert's poignant final line. He uses *tot* (dead) as an adjective. By making it the indirect object and adding the original's implied sense of *damage* or *numbness*, I was able to communicate the straightforward power of the poet's phrasing. As I have discussed, a literal translation of *das verschmerzte*, "the *gotten-over / pained-out* is dead and removed," is cumbersome and fails to capture Rückert's lyricism and economy of words. There is a certain jarring aspect to *das verschmerzte* that is effectively replicated by the verb *amputate*.

Betrayal and abandonment are plain in this poem. Rückert insists that to forget or "heal" from grief is a paradoxical, if not impossible, task. We would no longer grieve or love. To "get over it" would excise our dead from our hearts, implying that the loss no longer hurts, in much the same way that we might amputate an infected, unusable or malignant body part. We only "get over" or remove what is damaged, unfeeling or dead. In this respect, my final translation honors the cadence and structure of the original in ways that the earlier draft did not, as well as the poignant and affecting tone of Rückert's memorable lament.

All our laments do not / *Alles Klagen frommt nicht*, KTL, 154. "All our laments do not serve" (*Alles Klagen frommt nicht*) uses an interesting term, *frommt*, hinting at devotional or pious service. In this poem, Rückert's use of repetition is replaced by variations. As Michael Neumann, professor emeritus of modern German literary studies from the Catholic University of Eichstaett–Ingolstadt, observed, while the nominal verb *Alles Klagen* in verse 1 is replaced by the noun *Alle Klage* in verse 7, "the sound and position in the verse are so similar that the ear perceives an almost identical repetition." To replicate this, my translation makes a similar, subtle variation, from "All our" (1) to "all these" (7). In Neumann's informative breakdown of this poem, he also noted that verse 10 (*Das verlone Glück*) "finds a completely different continuation than the identical verse in the second stanza [verses 7–8]," returning it directly back to verse 2 (*Um verlornes Glück*), with only a slight variation. This translation combines both these insights: verses 1–2, "All *our* laments do not/serve *what joy we've* lost"; and verses 9–10, "All *these* laments do not/serve *our joy now* lost."[25]

If our dead are not with us / Wenn dir nicht deine Todten leben, KTL, 392–3. The poet addresses this consolation to himself: "*You* this, *you* that," he writes. However, his style and intent are inclusive. By *you* he means *me, you, all of us*, as this translation makes clear.

As the poor hen / Wie's der armen Henne, KTL, 171–2. Rückert uses the word *Entenbrut* for the hen's brood of ducklings, a term that indicates a group on dry land; as they slip away into the water and begin to swim, they would be called a raft of ducks (*EntenFloß*), a less common term notable for its absence. This may indicate that the ducklings were slipping into the water and floating away when their mother spotted them.

Another interesting allusion comes from Ovid's elegies: the terrifying talons of a hawk. Johann Heinrich Kirchhof's popular translation into German from Latin, published in 1777, uses the specific term, "des Habichts Wuth," the exact phrasing used by Rückert. This is Kirchhof's translation from Ovid's first elegy: *Ein Täubchen , das vorhin des Habichts Wuth geschmeckt , Wird durch den mindsten Schall der Vögel leicht erschreckt.*[26] An English translation from the Latin illustrates why this hawk imagery resonated with Friedrich: "The least rustle of a feather brings dread upon the dove that thy talons, O hawk, have wounded."[27] "The talons of a hawk" seemed an effective translation into English, in light of Friedrich's overt literary allusion and his reference in the previous stanza to his *Flügel Hut*, from under which Luise would never slip away as the ducklings have done. The *Hut* (hat) in question is idiomatic and most effectively translated as simply the father's protective wings. Rückert does not stop there.

The next stanza startles us: *Ach, des Todes Senne*. The *Senne* in question refers, more often than not, to an alpine pasture. While an English rendering of "pasture of death" has a certain morbid appeal, that phrase does not quite capture the poet's intent, living as he did in the foothills of the Thuringian Forest. With the images of the arch of heaven (*Himmelsbogen*) and the hawk, the poem is stressing dreadful height over the pastoral. "Alpine death" matches this terse, frigid tone.

Finally, this poem demonstrates a common foible in translation. "Was uns Beide trenne," Friedrich writes, "Müßt' ein Wunder seyn." "It would take a miracle to separate us," is a reasonable translation that is entirely wrong in tone, style and intent. It would certainly not be a *Wunder* to have a child taken away. In this context, the poet is clearly saying that only a divine hand (or hawk) could accomplish this terrible act, as this translation demonstrates.

He who finds rest, as I do / *Wer gewohnt ist wie ich zu thun*, KTL, 255–7. "All that is": *Was immer* is a surprising choice for the poet but one that has pedigree in German verse. Rückert used the same form in an earlier poem, "Wünsch." Often the German *was* has the force of *etwas*, to be sure, but not in this poem. Rückert was careful with words: he did not write *immer etwas* precisely because he did not mean *immer etwas*. Similarly, common German usage would be *immer [an] was*, if that was the poet's intent. The metrical requirements of the line would not be disturbed had Friedrich used *An was immer ihn mag berühren* instead of his preferred line, *Was immer ihn mag berühren*. He could have simply used *immer was* as the colloquial of *immer etwas*. But he did not.

Here Friedrich's form *was immer* is intentional and may be rendered as "no matter what it is" or, conversely as in this translation, "all that is." This has nothing to do with the common expression "always something" (*immer [et] was*). Rückert's usage is equivalent to *was es immer sei* (whatever it is). This use of *immer* is certainly well known in German, as this example from Goethe's *Hermann und Dorothea* demonstrates: "Ich tadle nicht gerne, was immer dem Menschen / Für unschädliche Triebe die gute Mutter Natur gab." ("I do not like to cast blame on whatever it is in our harmless instincts that good Mother Nature has given us.")[28] Ibershoff presented these arguments and quoted many other examples in his discussion of *was immer* in Rückert's "Wünsch."[29]

Another term in this poem demonstrates the poet's penchant for using cliché to take us in new directions. *Braus* is easily translated as bluster, as in the common idiomatic expression *in Saus und Braus* (in swish and bluster), an equivalent of the English expression, *in the lap of luxury*. However, neither the literal nor idiomatic expression quite captures Rückert's intent in contrast to the still bay (*stillen Bucht*) in which he has rested, or in conjunction with the storm of the previous stanza. In this context, while being at rest in nature, the poet suggests that he has not stirred up the waters (rather than sought luxury), or as with this translation, not sought froth and foam.

This is a rare occasion when I do not follow the stanza placement of the first edition. There was an error in the 1872 edition that led to some of the stanzas being swapped. For this translation, I follow the preferred placement of later editions.[30]

I loved you so, my little girl! / *Ich hatte dich lieb, mein Töchterlein!*, KTL, 47–8. Here the poet's intent outweighs literalism. *Mach "ich mir Vorwürf"* might be literally translated as "I reproach myself," but that fails to suggest the subtlety of Rückert's phrasing. The entire line is so steeped in self-reproach that to use the dative noun, *mir*, in English comes off as whining and ineffective. The attention in this phrase is shifted to the present by use of the subjunctive verb phrase "hätte fein / Noch lieber dich können haben." It is tempting to combine this with *fein* (subtly) and *lieber* (rather) into a nonsense line, such as "I reproach myself: I could/should have been capable of loving you even more finely still." However, this rendering lacks Friedrich's lyricism and the nuances of his phrasing. The current translation, "This is my regret: if only / I had loved you better," combines the poet's rebuke within his present regret in a way that honors the grieving father's overwhelming sense of guilt.

Inseparables now, alas, separated by death (Inséparables) / *Unzertrennliches, ach vom Tod getrenntes (Inseparables)*, KTL, 157–9. Rückert used an interesting bit of word play. In another song, the poet called Luise and Ernst "you two inseparables!" using the German word for inseparable, *unzertrennlichen*. He uses the same word in the first line of this poem. However, the poet and linguist did not title this piece "Unzertrennlichen." Instead, he used a French word for lovebird parrots, "Inséparables."

Sitting on your mother's knee / *Wenn du an das Knie dich setztest*, KTL, 45–6. This poem is marked with a pervasive use of *das Präteritum*, or "simple past," overt or implied, with words such as *"setztest, ersetztest, waren, stürzten, wollt,"* ward, starbest, solltest, etc. As so often happens with *das Präteritum*, particularly in Rückert's songs, there is a "characteristic combination of presentness and pastness," as linguist Wolfgang Klein put it, that corresponds to the English present perfect. Exclusive use of the past tense would disregard the narrative impact of the piece, confuse its temporal trajectory and fail to communicate that the present situation is a direct *result* of that past event.[31] See the detailed discussion on the *Präteritum* in the translator note for "Encircled by mountain."

It's too hard, what I've got / *Es ist zu schwer, was ich erlitt*, KTL, 156–7. This translation replicates Rückert's plain words for the voice of Luise with contractions and equivalent idiomatic expressions.

When I prayed over my child / *Wenn ich betet' über meinem Kinde*, KTL, 407. As is best, *Daß es gut*, or "that it is good." The poet's inner voice, or "voice inside me" (*Stimme spricht in mir*), does not clarify the author of the voice, which is very much Rückert's way. *Fass' ich nicht* is a catch-all idiomatic expression, meaning more or less, "I'll be damned," though how that intent expresses itself changes considerably in usage. For this poem, "not that I can see" communicates in equal parts Friedrich's frustration and resistance.

From our happy moments you are missing / *Zur heiteren Stunde fehlet ihr*, KTL, 161–2. Rückert uses repetition to telling effect. Again and again he returns to the refrain, "you are missing" (*fehlet ihr*). He spins this in the final question, "What ails my heart?," replacing *fehlet* with *fehlt*, commonly used in the colloquialism, "What ails you?" (*Was fehlt Ihnen?*).

Never did I see you wake / Niemals anders sah ich dich erwachen, KTL, 74. Rückert was fond of repetition and double meaning. Here he used *Paradiesesbaume* twice. This word is alternately translated as *Tree of Life* to match the cadence of the original (Tree of Life/dream of life) and as *tree of Paradise* to communicate the poet's intent.

We abolish many manners / Abzuschaffen geschärfte Todesarten, KTL, 88. The term *Todesarten* has long been a topic of discussion among translators. Literally meaning "ways of death," some early renderings preferred the phrase "death styles." But in this poem, "to abolish many *ways/types/styles* of death" is cumbersome and does not express the full intent of the term. *Todesarten* carries a subtle allusion to *ways to kill* as well as *ways of death or dying*. In this regard, as Lilian (Friedberg) Banks suggests, "manners of death" is a much closer equivalent. It has the added benefit of being more suggestive of multiple meanings, as well as being pleasing to the eye and ear in a way that replicates the cadence and tonal quality of Rückert's poem.[32]

The spear that struck my wound / Der Speer, der meine Wunde schlug, KTL, 373. In other poems, Friedrich offers "conversations" with his wife and his children: each has a unique voice that is easily recognizable. Here the poet's emphatic, muscular tone is evident in both question and response, indicating a dialogue with himself.

My homespun tunes / In meine häuslichen Lieder, KTL, 5. Häuslichen, referring to a domestic household, can imply homey or homely, familial or frumpy. A literal translation, such as "household songs," is cumbersome and slightly misleading. This translation honors Rückert's somewhat folksy and self-effacing air with a more apt "homespun tunes."

Is it only now at her / Hab' ich jetzt erst eingesehn, KTL, 7–8. Rückert used a word, *zierde*, that can be interpreted as a decorative ornament or as virtue. This was the usage in the title of a 1771 book by Munich Jesuit priest Matthias von Schönberg, *Die Zierde der Jugend* [The Virtue of Youth], which Mozart kept in his library.[33] The dual meaning was not lost on Rückert. Here he refers to purity in relation to the infamous decorative apple, used by the serpent to tempt Eve. Both are gone with the loss of his daughter: her parent's innocence and young Luise, who was virtue itself.

In loss it is difficult to begin / Im Verluste zu gewinnen, KTL, 10. Capitalization of German words can be problematic in translation. While important to specialists, the placement of uppercase letters may to the English reader seem random. They seldom help to communicate a poem's meaning and are often cumbersome. However, in this song, Rückert uses an expression that deserves an uppercase letter: "love and Poetry" (*Lieb' und Poesie*).

The term *Poesie* has fallen out of fashion. It is archaic. It refers to poetry, to be sure, but also includes serious drama and fiction, what is known today as literature (*Literatur*). In this poem, translating *Lieb' und Poesie* as "love and literature" may have been pleasingly alliterative but it would fail to capture the particular tone of Friedrich's original. "Poetry" with an uppercase "p" retains the poet's intent while communicating that he also means much more.

German philosopher Friedrich Schelling used "Poesie" to refer to the creative power that exists in all life. His friend, Friedrich Schlegel, wrote of "the unconscious poetry (*Poesie*)" that "moves in the plant, that streams forth in light, that laughs out in the child...."[34] Early German Romanticism, or *Frühromantik*, is often defined by a narrow literary view, taking *romantische Poesie* as nothing more than literary concept that rebelled against classicism. American philosopher Frederick Beiser thinks that this interpretation has been a disaster. For him, Poesie and Romanticism encompassed all that is moral, aesthetic, natural, practical, ethical and spiritual.[35] There is no doubt that Poesie was of vital importance to Romantics, Rückert among them.

Still in my words I obey their / *Immer that ich ihren Willen*, KTL, 13–4. The final line of the first stanza, *Sollten wir's uns nicht gestatten?*, literally "shouldn't we allow ourselves this?," is an emphatic phrase that mixes both possibility (*gestatten*) and necessity (*Sollten*). *Sollten wir nicht ...?* (Shouldn't we ...?) is a common expression that also serves the role of anguish and demand in this poem, fully equivalent to the type of yearning expressed in the English phrase, "at least."[36] Rückert has turned a colloquialism into a poignant cry of pain. In this case, "can we not have this at least?" captures his intent.

Sprigs of birch (from One Hundred Tercets) / *O Birkenreiser (from Dreizeilen-Hundert)*, KTL-W, 288. Rückert uses the term, *Trauerbirken*, or weeping birch. This can be problematic, as many 19th-century writers were inexact in their phrasing, using the same term for the European white birch (*Betula pendula*). However, Friedrich was an enthusiastic gardener. His poems are usually quite specific. In this triplet, he refers to the dangling branches of a weeping birch, a tree that is indigenous to the Coburg area. The poet likely saw just such a tree on his many walks. This is the eightieth triplet from the 137 stanzas in "Dreizeilen-Hundert" ("One Hundred Tercets").

Surrounded by old extravagance / *Von Freuden floß um mich vorzeiten*, KTL, 17–8. Sorrow: *Wehmuth*, the archaic spelling of *wehmut*, is used in both original manuscripts. The term may refer to melancholy or wistful nostalgia, depending on context, but in Rückert's and Herder's poems, the intent is clearly the uncontrollable sorrow of mourning.

Deep in the wood / *Tief im Waldesgrund*, KTL, 206–7. *Waldesgrund*: literally translated as forest ground or floor, the term is seldom used for a glade or park. In this poem, Rückert is clearly alone in the deep wood.

Little May Bells / *Maienglöckchen*, KTL, 209–11. The image of *Maiglöckchen* (May Bells) ringing, tolling, chiming or calling was something of a trope in German *lieder*. Many English liner notes for audio recordings translate *Maiglöckchen* as "lilies-of-the-valley," which misses the point of the symbolism. This seems odd since "May Bells" is an equally common English name for the flower.

In the first leaf of spring / *Das erste Frühlingsblatt*, KTL, 239. The translation of this poem uses a rhyming scheme that matches Friedrich's playful tone. Often a translator must decide between meaning, tone, style and context or slavish adherence to meter and rhyme. Usually my translations veer toward the former, but this was clearly an occasion when for Rückert "the sounds of words mattered as much, and sometimes even more, than their meaning," as Henry-Louis de La Grange put it.[37]

Here rests in this chest / *Hier lieg' in der Truhe*, KTL, 279. For this poem regarding their keepsakes of Luise, Friedrich chose a double entendre: *truhe*, chest or trunk, which may also be used to describe a coffin. To emphasize this, he uses the apt descriptors, *Heilig, ruhe* and *ungestört*. The small chest, like the small coffin, is sacred, silent, and undisturbed.

Because you were the smallest / *Weil ihr wart die Kleinsten*, KTL, 279–80. Rückert uses an old-fashioned term, *staat*, which has a similarly old-fashioned equivalent in English: "for best."

You five rose thorns / *Ihr fünf Rosendorne*, KTL, 33–4. Knight's spur (*rittersporne*); iron cap (*eisenhütchen*); lion's mouth (*löwenrachenblütchen*): Friedrich was fond of spinning common expressions to suit his ends. In the sixth stanza, he gives a new meaning to the well-worn chestnut "Cling together, swing together" (*Mitgefangen, mitgehangen*). He changes the second verb to *mitgegangen*, meaning "end up together." The poet's intent is rather grisly. His five knights failed their damsel, save the one who joined her in death. To replicate Friedrich's grim and slightly morbid (though alliterative) intent, this translation uses a variation on the well-known English phrase, "caught and killed."

How your five brothers doted / *Von fünf Brüdern, o beneidenswerthe*, KTL, 79. *Beneidenswerthe* represents an enviable position or "enviable sister," to be sure, but it is also frequently used in the common colloquialism "to die for." For example, *mit äußerst beneidenswerten Wangenknochen*, "with cheekbones to die for."

That I should drink and eat / *Daß ich trinken soll und essen*, KTL, 59–60. Friedrich captures the calm, inevitable flux of emotions that are part of every bereaved parent's life. He does this through repetition and juxtaposition: *empty, emptying, emptier* (*leer, leeren, leerer*) is developed in direct contrast to the steady beat of *full, full, full* (*voll, voll, voll*) until we are faced with a flood (*flut*).

By all appearances / *Wie den Anschein es gewann*, KTL, 89. Rückert uses an idiosyncratic term. "...ich sicher hoffen kann Das nur," he writes, or "I can only hope with certainty." However, in this poem, the particle *sicher* is fully equivalent to *meiste* "the most." The phrase is perfectly colloquial, meaning "the most I can hope for."[38]

This is my sole consolation / *Das sei mein Trost allein*, KTL, 131–2. The refrain of this piece, *Das sei mein Trost allein: Untröstlich will ich seyn*, communicates a sense of permanence. Although a literal translation of the final line might veer toward "I choose to be inconsolable" or "I will be inconsolable," both phrases seem a tad redundant. "I am inconsolable" is a permanent state, both present and future.

My role, I think, is done / *Meine Rolle, denk' ich, ist nun ausgespielt*, KTL, 153. Rückert's repetition in this poem uses a familiar preposition and prefix, *aus* (*out* or as a prefix, *ex-*), which when spoken sounds akin to a sigh. This is something of a multi-purpose word that may mean "outside," "to exit," "from somewhere," "out of," "made out of," "due to" or any number of variations. In the poet's day, the archaic use "going up" was still common currency. The quick succession of *aus*-words (aus*gerungen*, aus*gestritten*, aus*gewagt*, aus*gesungen*, aus*gelitten*, aus*geklagt*) is meant to sound like the sighs his heart needs to breathe. This is translated with equivalent *ex*-words, save one, matching the repetition and intent of the original: *ex*hausted, *ex*pelled, *ex*punged, *ex*cluded, *ex*pired, lamented.

Once I was out of town for / *Als ich einen Monat einst*, KTL, 334. The last line, "I will know you as old and / new, not estranged, not frozen," may seem out of place to modern readers. *Unentfremdet* or "unalienated" refers to a concept that was much a part of the world view of German Romantics and proto-Romantics. "Alienation" represented an estrangement from society and, significantly, from oneself. Many of creative artists (Friedrich Schiller, Rückert, etc.) sought "non-estranged" ways of life that would ease the spiritual strain of 19th-century society.[39]

My little ones could not / *Es waren meine Kindchen*, KTL, 335. Rückert's perception of death in "My little ones could not" provides insights on the failings of literalism in translation. *Kindchen* serves double duty as either plural or singular. (*Kinderchen* is strictly plural in use.) Here Friedrich uses *kindchen* to refer to both Ernst and Luise. In another piece, "A year is now gone as you," he uses *kindchen* as an expression of endearment for Luise, equivalent to the singular "sweetie" in English.

His opening line, "My little ones could not contain themselves when the sheepdog guided his flock to the fields." (*Es waren meine Kindchen/Zu halten nicht im Haus,/Wann mit dem Schäferhündchen/Die Schafe zogen aus.*), is rich with the implicit presence of a sheepdog guiding the flock and the shepherd himself. The line focuses on animals. A more literal translation might read, "When the sheep set forth (*zogen aus*, the past participle of *ausziehen*) with the sheepdog." However, this fails to communicate to modern readers an aspect of shepherding that would have been understood by a 19th-century audience.

Many people in Coburg and its surrounding states were familiar with the struggles of keeping sheep.[40] The shepherd's presence is understood in everyday practice and, in this sentence, as a mental image created by the inflection of *Schäferhündchen*.[41] In this case, the shepherd is also something of an oblique subject, binding subjects and objects in speech, which linguists consider to be a common German inheritance.[42]

This creates a challenge for the modern translator: how to combine the audience's experience in the poem's context? To assist 21st-century readers, an otherwise assumed shepherd is implied, as it surely was to anyone familiar with rural life. The shepherd (*Schäfer*) is specifically mentioned in the second stanza. Other examples also help to demonstrate some common pitfalls of translation.

Friedrich speaks of his children leaping with the lambs. He uses a word, *hüpften*, that implies a sense of prancing or frolicking—two English words that are frivolously poetic and miss the cadence and tone of the original. Anyone familiar with sheep, as is this translator, knows that they do not customarily jump from a standing position. They run and leap: a small point but one that matters a great deal to the imagery of the poem. This translation clarifies just what sort of leaping, or frolicking, the poet had in mind.

In this same line, Rückert uses a word with two meanings. A shepherd and his dog would unquestionably drive (*treiben*) their flock home in the evening, yet this same word also means "drifting" or floating. The latter usage has significance in the second stanza and must be included. Having the children "drift" home with the flock, in English translation, combines both meanings while foreshadowing the poem's poignant closing line. It also clarifies the rather obvious point that a hired shepherd and his dog would not "drive" his employer's children anywhere, nor would their father be likely to think of his little ones being so herded (except, perhaps, by himself).

The second stanza invites readers into the heart of grief. Friedrich's use of the word *verschlafen*, literally "oversleep," suggests the poet's awareness that the scene he describes could never be repeated. The children, who never lie in, *continue* to sleep. Still, the English "oversleep" is jarring in a way that the German word is not. It implies morning, not evening, and a willful choice or an unintended act that could be remedied. None of these applies to this poem. The children did not choose to die. Friedrich knows there is no remedy, as the end of the poem makes plain, and so "you still sleep, missing it" better communicates the father's daily, painful reality.

Finally, the poet speaks of the rosy or glowing (*ros'gen*) clouds. This seemingly simple translation is made challenging by the very specific clouds in question. The German word for cirrocumulus clouds, *Schäfchenwolken*, is alternately translated as "fleecy clouds," "cotton wool clouds" or "little lamb clouds." Friedrich spins this word round, calling the high-altitude clouds *Wolkenlämmern*, or "cloud lambs." Rückert was fond of this type of verbal sleight of hand. He found ways to communicate multiple levels of meaning without resorting to the crass sentimentality associated with more direct words, such as, in this case, the implied "heaven." By avoiding clichés, the poet transformed old ideas into living grief. Puffy white clouds that were so often used in art to represent the peace of heaven became, in Friedrich's hands, a field of little lambs where his children continued to play. Descriptors like "rose-tinted" or "rosy" fail to communicate the poet's understated allusion. Instead, this translation precedes the closing couplet with one of Rückert's favorite images, "the red of dusk."

In this weather, in this gale / *In diesem Wetter, in diesem Braus* , KTL, 341. Most of the translations of this and other Rückert songs set to music are available in liner notes to accompany recordings. These same translations were often adapted for programs, surtitles during live performances and subtitles for video release. A libretto translator works under distinct requirements that affect how the words are rendered in English. For the most part, the translations are designed to accommodate the music in as literal a fashion as necessary. There are two reasons.

One, so readers may mentally "sing along" in their minds, adapting the translation as best possible as they listen to the original being sung. This has a surprising impact. For example, the same poem set to music by, say, Schumann or Grieg, may have a significantly different rendering in English to match the anatomy of the human vocal apparatus, high/low pitches, stress, prosodic and intonational patterns, rhyme, etc., of the musical setting.[43]

Such concerns also affect the translator's choices in another way. While libretto translators attempt to communicate as many subtle nuances as possible, their primary focus is to allow the composer's settings and the performers' interpretations to communicate the many and varied aspects of a piece. The translation, then, has a triple emphasis: music, drama and words, with words a distant third on the list.[44] Liner notes and performance surtitles/subtitles are designed to enhance the music. The dramatic flow of the music, legibility and clarity are primary concerns, even when such clarity must take liberties with the original (replacing pronouns with names is a common example). The end result is not only music, performance or words, but all three combined in what is called a form of "additive translation."[45]

For example, in the last two lines of the first stanza, a subtitle translator for one video release used a succinct rendering: "Someone took them, took them out. / I hadn't any say in it." This fits on the screen and follows mezzo-soprano Claire Brua's briskly-paced phrasing. What it loses in nuance it gains in legibility. We focus on the performers and the music.

Thomas Hampson's audio recording, on the other hand, is a bit slower, with a careful, meditative quality. The liner note translation is designed to be read along with the baritone's steady delivery: "They were dragged out. / I was not allowed to say anything against it." Mezzo-soprano Agni Baltsa's recording, in comparison, makes use of her exceptional diction. This is reflected in a translation that follows her verbal stress points: "But they were taken out. / And I could say nothing about it."[46]

None of these translations is better or worse than the other. Each was crafted to accommodate the specific requirements of its venue. The many English translations of "In this weather" were usually designed with these criteria in mind. My rendering labors under different constraints.

Rückert's original poem has a certain *storminess* in the phrasing, pauses and cadence. Read aloud, its rough-hewn tumult is steeped in the terrors of weather and the poet's internal struggles. As the original uses *words alone* to communicate a world of meaning, my translation is concerned solely with replicating the experience of those words in all their potent, jarring, lyrical beauty. As Henry Staten, professor of English and philosophy at the University of Washington, observed, "The translator, like the poet, is trying to write the best poem she can."[47]

I weigh this / *Wie ich reiflich*, KTL, 355–6. Here the poet seems to be reveling in the form "*–flich*" in slightly jarring combinations: *reiflich / unbegreiflich / bezweifl'ich / unbegreiflich / handgreiflich / unabstreiflich / umschweiflich.* Finally, Rückert ends with an oddly out-of-place word: *unauschleiflich*, which means a scratch or notch that can never be buffed out or filled in. To demonstrate Friedrich's faltering attempt at word play, this translation uses terms that also seem to stumble over each other: *hair / pair, obvious / oblivious, true / untrue, altered / altar*, etc. To replicate the repetition of the sound *-flich*, common English language prefixes are used throughout the poem, *in*conceivable / *in*comprehensible / *im*possible, ending with a word that equals the quirky *unauschleiflich*—*in*delible.

Ah, tell me this, and this alone / *Ach, nur eines möcht' ich wissen*, KTL, 364. In the original, Friedrich rhymes each line in an unenthusiastic, repetitive cadence, almost out of habit. My translation offers a hint of repetition (*this/this; them/them; smiles/joys*) but too much rhyme would detract from the poet's point.

Ah, my physical eyes are (Lyric) / *Ach, dies leiblich schwache Auge (Text)*, KTL, 381–2. The first edition of *Kindertodtenlieder*, based on the original manuscript, used Rückert's perfunctory title, *Text*, translated here as "Lyric."[48] Friedrich's rhyme scheme (*enge dunkle Rohr / enge dunkle Thor*) is a rather overt reference to Paul's phrasing as translated in the Luther Bible, "einem dunklen Worte." Rückert's use of *Rohr* (tunnel or tube) and *Thor* (funnel, eyeglass or pipe) are near-rhymes with the Luther Bible's *Worte* (word), to be sure, but the poet also understood that the Greek expression refers to a dark mystery. This translation replicates his rhyme, which in this piece seems important to the poet, with *tunnel / funnel*. In the two final lines, Friedrich contrasts the sun (as viewed by astronomers) with his children, repeating *Hell / heller*, which I replicate with *bright / brighter*, emphasizing that their brightness with an angelic choir is brighter still.

You need something to love / *Etwas brauchest du zu lieben*, KTL, 391. Rückert is speaking to himself: *du / dir*, alternatively in the nominative and the dative case, are prominently used in this poem. A literal translation of the second line is problematic: *Wär's auch nur ein einzig Haupt*, or "if it were only a single head." The subjective implications of the line are adequately communicated with a simple "if only" rather than a belabored "if it were," which is cumbersome in a way that Rückert is not.

Similarly, the English word *remain* serves double tense duty in this poem. The Perfekt past tense of *sind geblieben* (remained) is clearly intended as a present tense "remain." This is a common aspect of Perfekt in speech that literalists frequently ignore. After all, "It would be enough for more heads to have remained," comes off as more than a little silly. The poet uses the words *head / heads* (*haupt / häupter*), hinting at the crass nature of "counting heads." He then segues to another use of the same word: *haupt* can also refer to the main point, the central meaning. *What part of love was taken with that face*, he asks: *the face he remembers, so many faces his children made, so many expressions of who they were; from these faces, death can take nothing*.

As the lower branches of a / *Wie der Baum der indianischen Feige*, KTL, 403–4. In Rückert's day, the name *indianischen Feige* (*Opuntia ficus-indica*; Indian fig or cactus pear) was frequently used to indicate the banyan tree. Early European botanists preferred to call the cactus by that name, but it had already been applied to the banyan (now identified as *Ficus benghalensis*).[49] From the context of this poem, it is clear that Friedrich was thinking of the banyan tree. Today, to botanists' relief, *indianischen Feige* refers to the cactus, and the more utilitarian *bengalische Feige* is used for the banyan tree. Friedrich also writes that he would not have the tree tops be lowered (and buried) in grief (*Nicht den Wipfel will ich traurig senken*), but instead would prefer to find some small joy in his severed or cut-short thoughts (*Sondern froh der abgetrennten denken*), translated here as finding some quiet memories in absence.

I did not want so many / *Ich habe ja nicht soviele gewollt*, KTL, 404. *Mir blieb, was Gott gewollt*. A literal translation, "what remains, is God's will (or desire)," veers close to sounding pious, hopeless or resigned, yet this was not the poet's intent. Friedrich found a way to spin a tired cliché into an endearing expression of true gratitude: "God left me these, thank God."

Do not speak to me of this earthly vale of tears / *Sagt mir nichts von Erden Jammerthalen*, KTL, 408. Rückert refers to Matthew 25:14–30, using the word *Pfunde*, or pound, in the final sentence: *Wuchernd mit dem anvertrauten Pfunde*, or literally "increasing the pounds entrusted." Such a literal translation, however, fails to communicate the poet's intent. He is using a common idiomatic expression—*Pfunde* *wuchern*, meaning "to make the most of one's talents"—as a personal statement as well as an allusion to his children and to the famous parable. Bible translators of Matthew use "talents" or "bags of gold," among other phrases, for the prosaic coins. We know that Rückert's wife, Luise, read the Luther Bible in common use in 1834 (see the introduction). Luther's translation used *Zentner*, meaning quintal, centner or simply hundredweight.[50] As with the word pound, any of these terms are cumbersome and, in English, disrupt the line's message. In this translation of Rückert's poem, "increasing the *treasures* entrusted/to me, returning them with gratitude," most effectively communicates the poet's multiple meanings while honoring the cadence and pacing of the original. Friedrich's allusion to living pictures (*lebende bilder*) is more subtle, referring to Luise and Ernst as *zwei Himmelsbilder*, two heavenly pictures.

On days like today (As the years pass since my children died) / *Grad in diesen Tagen* **(***Als sich der Tod meiner Kinder bejährte***)**, RW-1, 210–1. An earlier draft used the phrase *Tod meines Kindes* (my child died) in the title, which the poet later changes to *Tod meiner Kinder* (my children died).[51]

Acknowledgments

My daughter, Jess, died on 16 January 2015 of a fentanyl-laced heroin overdose. She was twenty-six. A few months later, I came across Philip Yancey's thoughts on Friedrich Rückert's *Songs on the Death of Children* in his book *The Question That Never Goes Away*.

Less than a month later, I discovered a double-disc set of Gustav Mahler's setting of Rückert's songs in *Kindertotenlieder* as sung by the remarkable Christa Ludwig, with the Berlin Philharmonic under Herbert Von Karajan. It cost a mere fifty cents at a thrift shop that benefits half-way houses for ex-cons. Later I learned just how hard that particular recording is to come by. I have since listened to many other recordings of the Mahler settings, but Ludwig's interpretation is still my favorite, and the one I return to in moments of great need.

These events led me to download a copy of Rückert's complete 1872 book, *Kindertodtenlieder*. In it I discovered a communion of grief that I dared not imagine could exist. I translated one of his best, "Over All Graves," and sent it to Philip on a whim. He dubbed the piece "very fine" and kindly encouraged me to render into English more songs from this classic. "Over All Graves" and nine other Rückert laments appeared in my first book on grief, *Wounded in Spirit: Advent Art and Meditations* (Paraclete Press, 2018).

Songs on the Death of Children has been a companion of solace through many years of sorrow. For this, and for your calm, gentle support of a broken friend, thank you, Philip.

Two anonymous single-blind peer reviewers examined this manuscript. They offered keen insights and a lively discussion that contributed to the book a great deal. I am indebted and grateful.

To Johannes Wilkes and the Erlanger Rückert-Kreis; the staff of the Chester County Library; Timothy Jones; Lee Warren; the staff of McFarland; and Elaine: thank you all.

"You need something to love," "Holly-tree," "I thought to teach my little girl weaving," "My role, I think, is done," "Over all graves grass must grow," "What is dying? What is dead?," "Lift me above," "Nature is unsettled," "Never did I see you wake," and "Now the sun will rise as bright" from *Wounded in Spirit* by David Bannon. Copyright © 2018 by David Bannon. Reprinted by permission of Paraclete Press. All rights reserved.

"If the very air we breathe might kill us" by John Donne, as paraphrased by Philip Yancey, first appeared on pages 71 and 72 of *A Companion in Crisis: A Modern Paraphrase of John Donne's Devotions*, ed. and paraphrased by Philip Yancey (Illumify, 2021) and is reprinted by permission of Philip Yancey. Copyright © 2021 Philip Yancey. All rights reserved.

"Baseline 4-5-93" by Kimberlyn Blum-Hyclak first appeared on pages 17 and 18 of *In the Garden of Life and Death: A Mother and Daughter Walk* (Main Street Rag Publishing 2014) and is reprinted here with permission of Kimberlyn Blum-Hyclak. Copyright © 2014 Kimberlyn Blum-Hyclak. All rights reserved.

Quotations from Beopjeong originally appeared in *Meditations of a Zen Master*, ed. and tr. David Bannon (Bilingual Library, 2012). Translation copyright © 2012 David Bannon. Reprinted by permission. All rights reserved.

Certain passages are quoted for purposes of research, scholarship, review, comment and illustration. Pursuant to 17 U.S. Code § 107, certain uses of copyrighted material "for purposes such as criticism, comment, news reporting, teaching (including multiple copies for classroom use), scholarship, or research, is not an infringement of copyright." The passages are indicated with proper citation in the notes.

"Friedrich Rückert, 1833," an engraving created by Carl Barth made in the fall of 1833, first appeared in *Deutscher Musenalmanach für die Jahr 1834*, eds. Adelbert von Chamisso and Gustav Schwab (Weidmannsche Buchhandlung, December 1833): i. The pastel portraits of Luise Rückert and Ernst Rückert were painted by Carl Barth at the same time and now hang in the Rückert house (*Nattermannshof*) in Coburg-Neuses. All images in this book are exact, faithful photographic reproductions of two-dimensional, public domain works of art. The works of art themselves are in the public domain. Every attempt has been made "to reproduce the underlying works with absolute fidelity" in accordance with the United States District Court for the Southern District of New York ruling that "exact photographic copies of public domain works of art would not be copyrightable under United States law because they are not original." The images in this book are "'slavish' copies of public domain works of art" as defined by the court's ruling; as such, "Copyright is not available in these circumstances." [Bridgeman Art Library, Ltd., Plaintiff v. Corel Corporation, 36 F. Supp. 2d 191 (S.D.N.Y. 1999); https://www.law.cornell.edu/copyright/cases/36_FSupp2d_191.htm. See also Bridgeman Art Library v. Corel Corp., 25 F.Supp.2d 421 (S.D.N.Y. 1998)] "There is no copyright in photographic reproductions of two-dimensional works of art in the public domain," wrote Grischka Petri in "The Public Domain vs. the Museum: The Limits of Copyright and Reproductions of Two-dimensional Works of Art," *Journal of Conservation and Museum Studies* 12(1) (2014) p. Art. 8; https://www.jcms-journal.com/articles/10.5334/jcms.1021217/. "Bridgeman Art Library, Ltd. v. Corel Corp. set a precedent establishing reproductive images of two-dimensional artworks as not copyrightable…. The Southern District of New York has twice ruled that reproductive photography is most likely the only case in which a photograph is not copyrightable.... The copyright itself was found to be invalid," observed Katherine L. Kelley in "The Complications of 'Bridgeman' and Copyright (Mis)use," *Art Documentation: Journal of the Art Libraries Society of North America 30*(2) (Fall 2011): 38–42; https://www.jstor.org/stable/41244063. "It's not a gray area. If they make an unadorned photo of the public domain image, that photo can't be copyrighted—period!" according to Christopher Sprigman, instructor of intellectual property law at the University of Virginia Law School, interviewed by Bernard Starr, "Must You Pay to Use Photos of Public Domain Artworks? No, Says a Legal Expert," *Huffington Post* (12 November 2012): https://www.huffingtonpost.com/bernard-starr/museum-paintings-copyright_b_1867076.html.

Notes

Overture

1. Luise Rückert, Diary, March/April 1834, in KTL-W, 556.
2. In the poem "The maid brings news of their sister's," this collection.
3. The 1872 edition of *Songs on the Death of Children* used the now archaic spelling, *Kindertodtenlieder*. Throughout this book, I retain this spelling to differentiate from the song cycle by Gustav Mahler, which uses the modern spelling (without the "d"), *Kindertotenlieder*.
4. Luise Rückert, Diary, March/April 1834, in KTL-W, 556.
5. Job 19:25 KJV.
6. Luise Rückert, Diary, March/April 1834, in KTL-W, 556.
7. Orlinsky, 239–68; see 248, 249 for citations of the other linguists that discuss this problematic passage.
8. Linton, 16–7.
9. Luise Rückert quote the passage verbatim in Diary, March/April 1834, in KTL-W, 556. "Aber ich weiß, daß mein Erlöser lebet; und er wird mich hernach aus der Erde auferwecken," Hiob 19:25, *Die Bibel* [1834], German tr. Martin Luther, 491. Emphasis added. The German Luther Bible has been critically examined for centuries. Other translations suffer the same fate, some justifiably derided for their theological slant, others unfairly condemned without proper understanding of the translation process. Luther, for one, was not shy in announcing that his was a theologically-shaped translation of scripture: "But because various wild interpretations and prefaces have so confused Christians that one no longer even knows what 'Gospel' or 'law,' 'new' or 'old testament' means, necessity demands a notice and prefaces to be placed [in this book] so that the simple person will be led from his old delusion on to the right way and instructed in what he should expect in this book so that he not seek commandments and laws where he should be seeking Gospel and the promises of God." (Edwards, 110–1, tr. Mark Edwards; 167.) He was as good as his word. The Luther Bible is skillfully presented to highlight the views Luther felt were theologically important. (Wim François, "The Early Modern Bible between Material Book and Immaterial Word," in Jurkowlaniec, et al., 129–43.) Still, Luther and his staff did not appear to be willfully misrepresenting Job 19:25; they merely struggled with a passage that has vexed translators for centuries.
10. Knowles, 29.
11. Taylor, *Atlantic*, 33
12. Jenkins, 80.
13. Volker Hesse, "Kindstod im 19. Jahrhundert: Betrachtungen zu Friedrich Rückerts Kindertodtenliedern aus medizinischer Sicht," in LEB, 182.
14. Ibid.
15. Peter Revers, "'...the heart-wrenching sound of farewell': Mahler, Rückert, and the *Kindertotenlieder*," in Painter, ed., 173.
16. Volker Hesse, "Kindstod im 19. Jahrhundert: Betrachtungen zu Friedrich Rückerts Kindertodtenliedern aus medizinischer Sicht," in LEB, 182.
17. Ibid., 185.
18. Rückert to Albrecht Fischer, 1 April 1834, Coburg, in KTL-W, 535.
19. Rückert to Salomon Hirzel, 14 April 1834, Erlangen, in KTL-W, 537.
20. Rückert to Schnyder von Wartensee, 25 October 1834, KTL-W, 544.
21. The *Nattermannshof*; KTL-W, 608.
22. "...es nicht über fich gewinnen..." in Heinrich Rückert's preface to KTL, iii. See also "Friedrich Rückert's *Kindertodtenlieder (Aus feinem Nachlaffe.*)," 13 February 1873, *Augsburger Postzeitung*, 39–40.
23. Erdmann, 234.
24. Known as *bildungsweg*.
25. Benes, 61.
26. Gritt Klinkhammer, "The Emergence of Transethnic Sufism in Germany," in Geaves, et al., 130.
27. Bobzin, 173.
28. Galatians 3:28.
29. de Lagarde, "es sei unbegreiflich...," 18.
30. Bialystok, 229–35.
31. Klass and Goss, 547–67.
32. Quoted in Forssman, "Gastlichkeit im Hause Rückert," 18 March 2019.
33. *Die Verwandlungen des Ebu Seid von Serûg oder die Makâmen des Hariri*, in freier Nachbildung (the first one-volume edition was published in 1826); *Rostem und Suhrab*; *Die Weisheit des Brahmanen*.

34. La Grange, 283.
35. Uhland, v2, 9.
36. Muncker, 68.
37. Pfizer, 52. In the same essay, Pfizer was also highly critical of Rückert; but Friedrich was in good company. The following year, Pfizer would level a similar attack on Heinrich Heine.
38. Nordmeyer, 629.
39. Rückert, *Brahmanen*, Bd. 4 von 6, 257.
40. Müller, 4; Goethe's *West–östlicher Divan* was a collection of lyrical poems inspired by the Persian poet Hafez, alternately written in English as Ḥāfeẓ, Hafiz or Ḥāfiẓ.
41. Montefiore, 515–6.
42. Rückert, quoted in Scherliess, 7; translated by John Coombs.
43. *grossen persönlichen Erlebnissen*
44. Beyer, 67.
45. Neeff, vi.
46. Schimmel, 7.
47. Taylor, *Atlantic*, 33; also Taylor, *Essays*, 92.
48. Rückert, Hariri, ed. Schimmel (1966), 3.
49. König, ix–x.
50. I am influenced in this view by Ronald Taylor, who takes a pragmatic approach to the many myths surrounding Romantics in *The Romantics in the Romantic Tradition in Germany*.
51. Tymms, 2–3.
52. Surat Al-Kahf 18:60–82; Jung, v5, 193; MacCarthy, 35–6)
53. Rückert, "Chidher" (Khiḍr the Wanderer), *Gesammelte Gedichte*, v2 (Heyder, 1836), 53–4.
54. Jane Brown, "In the Beginning was Poetry," in Parsons, ed., 14, 24.
55. Beddoes to Thomas Forbes Kelsall, Hamburg, 29 September 1825; Beddoes, 74–5.
56. Matthews, 1.
57. *Armored Sonnets* (*Geharnischte Sonette*) was first published in *Deutsche Gedichte*, 1814. The term for "armored" in the title, *Geharnischt*, serves double duty as an adjective for something that is armor-clad, or particularly *sharply-worded*. Such dual meanings were common currency for Rückert throughout his career.
58. *Was schmiedst du, Schmied? »Wir schmieden Ketten, Ketten!«*, Sonnet 3, *Geharnischte Sonette, Rückerts Werke*, 16.
59. Planert, 692, 693.
60. Küpper, *Cultural Net*, 32, 238–9; Wilfried van der Will, "The functions of 'Volkskultur,' mass culture and alternative culture," in Kolinsky and Will, eds., 153–71.
61. Glaser, *Spiesser-Ideologie*, 37, 125; for Ernest Menze's English translation, see Glaser, *The Cultural Roots of National Socialism*, 52, 56n., 185.
62. Rolf Selbmann, "Der Dichter und Seine Vaterstadt: Die Wirkungsgeschichte Friedrich Rückerts in Schweinfurt," in Prang, 132.
63. Alexandra Gerstner, Gregor Hufenreuter and Uwe Puschner, "Völkischer Protestantismus: die Deutschkirche und der Bund für deutsche Kirche," in Grunewald and Puschner, eds., 409–35.
64. Quoted in Berkhof, 227.
65. Quoted in Eriksen, 85–6.
66. *Eroberer der arisch-östlichen Kultur*. From Stadtmuseum Erlangen, "Rückert-Stadt Erlangen," *Kultur & Freizeit*, retrieved 12 October 2021: https://www.erlangen.de/desktopdefault.aspx/tabid-1725/963_read-33318/.
67. Jenkins, 213; see also James Bentley, *Martin Niemöller* (Oxford University Press, 1984), passim.
68. Quoted in Stroud, 86–7.
69. Martin Niemöller, "A Sermon about the Relevance of Christianity in Nazi Germany," in Stroud, 85–93.
70. Verse five from "Dein König kommt in niedern Hüllen" (In lowly guise thy King appeareth).
71. Weiss, 168.
72. Mann, Golo, *Über Rückert: Einen der Liebenswertesten unter den deutschen Dichtern*, 3rd rev. ed. (Ergon, 2018). See also Fuhrmann, 121.
73. Rolf Selbmann, "Der Dichter und Seine Vaterstadt: Die Wirkungsgeschichte Friedrich Rückerts in Schweinfurt," in Prang, 132–4.
74. Schimmel, 121.
75. Tymms, 11.
76. Jacqueline Arnold, "'Spielwerk' des Biedermeier?: Friedrich Rückerts Sprachkonzeption in dessen Dissertatio philologico-philosophica de idea philologiae als poetologische Konstitutive," in LEB, 367.
77. Immoos, "ein ungekrönter König...," quoted in Schimmel, 121. See also Immoos, 1962.
78. Astrid Köhler, "Cultural and Intellectual Trends," in Breuilly, 82–3.
79. Rückert, "Haus–und Fahrslieder," *Gesammelte Gedichte*, v5, 21.
80. Herdt, 6.
81. Amrine, 2.
82. *Ibid.*, 10.
83. Eckhart was writing in the Middle High German. See Boes, *Formative Fictions*, 47. Boes also helpfully mentions Ernst Liechtenstein's informative conceptual history, *Zur Entwicklung des Bildungsbegriffs von Meister Eckhart bis Hegel* (Quelle & Meyer, 1966), 46n5.
84. Eckhart, *Essential Sermons*, tr. Colledge and McGinn, 59–60.
85. Herdt, 42, 240.
86. Deane, 174, 176.
87. Redfield, viii.
88. Furst, 65.
89. Herdt, 16.
90. This combination of imagination (*Einbildungskraft*) and unity (*Ineinsbildung*) is an essential aspect of Schelling's ideal. For the quotation and discussion, see Gentry, overview, in Gentry and Pollok, eds., 3.
91. Herdt, 3.
92. Herdt, 8–9.
93. McGregor, 121.
94. Thoreau, 2 April 1852, in *Journal*, 381.
95. "Bildung," *Gedichte von Freidrich Rückert* (Sauerländer, 1841), 721.
96. Taylor, *Atlantic*, 33; also Taylor, *Essays*, 92.
97. *Ibid.*

98. Quoted by Charles Brooks, "Translator's Preface," in Rückert, *Brahmin*, xi.
99. John Scholte Nollen, "Introduction," in *Schiller's Poems*, xxxv; also Schiller, *Correspondence*, 362.
100. The German translation was issued in Hamburg two years later.
101. Harold Jantz, "Schiller's Indian Threnody: A Problem in the Aesthetics of the Classical Age," in Frey, ed., 58–65. Armand's version had been published in French and English in 1703 and in German in 1709. See also Blegen, 198–9.
102. Schiller, "Nadowessische Todtenklage," *Sämtliche Werke*, 164–5.
103. Quoted by Charles Brooks, "Translator's Preface," in Rückert, *Brahmin*, xi–xii.
104. *Leid und Lied*.
105. Michael Neumann, "Vom Furor der Formerfindung : Friedrich Rückerts 'Kindertodtenlieder,'" in LEB, 233–45.
106. *Ibid.*, 239–40.
107. *Ibid.*, 233.
108. Schimmel, 34.
109. Anderson and Foley, 117.
110. McCracken, 139–56.
111. Attig, *How We Grieve*, 15.
112. "Aus der Jugendzeit" and "Ich liebe dich." The figures are from Gernot and Stefan Demal, "Verzeichnis der Rückert-Vertonungen," in Erdmann, ed., 417–550.
113. Sandy, 1.
114. *großer Stilvirtuose*
115. Rückert, *Gesammelte Poetische Werke*, v7, 374.
116. Loges, 340; for an informative overview see Loges, 337–44.
117. Fellinger, 105.
118. *Getreidemarkt*; Fellinger, 105
119. Loges, 340–1; Schimmel, *Lebensbild und Einführung*, 62.
120. Loges, 338.
121. *Wiegenlieder meiner Schmerzen*; Beller-McKenna, 170.
122. Rückert, *Gesammelte Gedichte*, v1, 317.
123. Eda Sagarra, "Friedrich Rückert's *Kindertotenlieder*," in Avery, 154–68.
124. "Trost für Untröstliche," Wirth, 98.
125. "größte Totenklage der Weltliteratur," Achim Aurnhammer and Thorsten Fitzon, "Lyrische Trauernarrative. Aktualisierter und distanzierter Kindsverlust in Gedichtzyklen des 19. Jahrhunderts," in Scheidt, 223.
126. "verrückt wie Rückert," quoted in Andre Gingrich, "The German-Speaking Countries," in Barth, et al., 59–154.
127. Octavio Paz, in Honig, 154, 160; emphasis in original.
128. Torsten Voß, "Orientalismus als Paradigma lyrischer Produktivität und Phantasie? Friedrich Rückerts und August von Platens Ghaselen," in Czapla, ed., "*Weltpoesie allein ist Weltversöhnung*," 211.
129. "Art and Beauty," 18–9, *The Vision of God*, tr. William Hastie, 26.
130. See Wollschläger's painstaking notes in KTL-W, passim.
131. Johannes Wilkes to David Bannon, 1 December 2021, personal correspondence.
132. Jones, 47–58.
133. For thoughts on the importance of context and inflection when reading words first written decades ago, and the changing meaning of words on repeated readings, see Hughes-Warrington, 115.
134. Grollman, *Living When a Loved One Has Died*, 91. The good rabbi is borrowing from William Shakespeare's *Troilus and Cressida*, Act III, Scene iii. (Shakespeare, *Troilus and Cressida*, 93.) Ulysses, speaking to Achilles in a bitterly ironic speech, dismisses the human foible of embracing the flashy and new over the reliable and old: "One touch of nature makes the whole world kin; / That all with one consent praise new-born gawds, / Though they are made and moulded of things past, / And give to dust that is a little gilt / More laud than gilt o'er-dusted." Rabbi Grollman redeems this frequently misquoted passage: unlike gilt and glitter, grief does indeed unite us in a family of compassion.
135. Chobli, *Grief*, 1.
136. Renate Egger-Wenzel, "Sarah's Grief to Death," in Reif and Egger-Wenzel, eds., 193–4.

Songs on the Death of Children

1. Surpassing even the works of Rückert's contemporary, Joseph von Eichendorff (Ralf Georg Czapla, "Wiedererweckung in der Poesie?," in LEB, 60).
2. Bobzin, Hartmut, "Rückert as translator and imitator of Persian ghazal poetry," in Neuwirth, et al., eds., *Ghazal as World Literature II*, 285–94; Irani-Tehrani, Amir, "The Birth of the German Ghazal out of the Spirit of World Literature," in Abedinifard, et al., eds., *Persian Literature as World Literature*, 17.
3. Also called Jena Romanticism or *Frühromantiker*; Furst, 65.
4. Muir, *My First Summer*, 196.
5. Emerson, *Essays: The First and Second Series*, 166.
6. Hubert Zapf, "Ecological Thought and Literature in Europe and Germany," in Parham and Westling, eds., 275.
7. Kate Rigby, "Romanticism and Ecocriticism," in Garrard, 67; Rigby, 103.
8. "Conversations on Poetry," Schlegel, 59–60. The piece appeared in the third and final issue of *Athenaeum*, published in 1800; Hugo, 221.
9. Buell, 271.
10. Ralf Georg Czapla, "Wiedererweckung in der Poesie?," in LEB, 61.
11. Updike, 98.
12. Sascha Monhoff, "Die Poetologie von Totenklage und, Totenersatz" in Friedrich Rückerts Kindertodtenliedern," in LEB, 225, 226.
13. Michael Neumann, "Vom Furor der

Formerfindung: Friedrich Rückerts *Kindertodtenlieder*," in LEB, 234.

14. Caswell, 319–34.
15. McNeish, 190–203.
16. *verschrenken*.
17. Brophy, 129, 130.
18. Hall, 219–232.
19. Park and Halifax, "Religion and Spirituality," in Neimeyer, *Grief and Bereavement*, 359.
20. Schiff, 109–120.
21. Telushkin, 630–1.
22. Donin, 219.
23. *Langsam und schwermütig*.
24. *Wie ein Wiegenlied*.
25. Analysis from Stephen Hefling, "Song and symphony (II). From *Wunderhorn* to Rückert and the middle-period symphonies: vocal and instrumental works for a new century," in Barham, 108, 111–3. "quaking emotion" from Bekker, 178, 232–3.
26. Monahan, 41.
27. Krolow, 52f.
28. Czapla, Ralf Georg, "Wiedererweckung in der Poesie?" in LEB, 61. Michael Newmann observed that in this sixteen-verse poem, there are only four verses that are not repeated in one form or another. (Michael Neumann, "Vom Furor der Formerfindung: Friedrich Rückerts *Kindertodtenlieder*," in LEB, 240.)
29. Century Media, "Maroon: Order."
30. Brown, et al., *Global Metal Music and Culture*, 6.
31. *Ibid.*, 13.
32. Andy Brown, "Un(su)Stained Class? Figuring out the Identity Politics of Heavy Metal's Class Demographics," in Brown, et al., *Global Metal Music and Culture*, 192.
33. Rosemary Lucy Hill, "Masculine Pleasure? Women's Encounters with Hard Rock and Metal Music," in Brown, et al., *Global Metal Music and Culture*, 291n1.
34. Charles, 1.
35. Kärjä, 85–6.
36. Walser, 59.
37. Pavarotti quoted in Rizzo, 6 September 2007.
38. Quoted in Owen Coggins, "Transforming Detail into Myth: Indescribable Experience and Mystical Discourse in Drone Metal," in Brown, et al., *Global Metal Music and Culture*, 311.
39. Simon Poole, "Retro Rock and Heavy History," in Brown, et al., *Global Metal Music and Culture*, 305–8.
40. Schimmel, 124.
41. Monhoff, Sascha, "Die Poetologie von Totenklage und "Totenersatz" in Friedrich Rückerts *Kindertotenliedern*," in LEB, 228, 229.
42. Volker Hesse, "Kindstod im 19. Jahrhundert: Betrachtungen zu Friedrich Rückerts Kindertodtenliedern aus medizinischer Sicht," in LEB, 208.
43. Marcel, 152.
44. Astell, 20, 70, 96.
45. Ariel Hirschfeld, "Is the Book of Job a Tragedy?" in Batnitzky and Pardes, eds., 24–5. For concise philological notes on *dust*, see also Mitchell, *The Book of Job*, 103, 128–9.
46. Monhoff, Sascha, "Das Totenbuch der Natur: Die "Lesbarkeit der Welt" in Friedrich Rückerts Kindertodtenliedern," in LEB, 252, 255.
47. Martison et al., 259–267; also Seigal, 10, 12.
48. Spratt, 299–306.
49. See McCoyd, 20–2.
50. Schiff, 55; Rosof, 261; also, "Anna Perkin's Priorities," in Finkbeiner, 198–206.
51. Neimeyer, *Behaviour Change*, 65–79; see also Neimeyer, *Meaning Reconstruction* (APA, 2001).
52. Beopjeong, 48.
53. Linton, *Poetry*, 98, 113.
54. Dyregrov, 45–8.
55. A common practice by the 18th century. Litovkina points out that there was a tradition of transforming common proverbial expressions with biting effect, notably by Lichtenberg, Kant, Schiller and Goethe. Anna Litovkina, "Anti-proverbs," in Hrisztova-Gotthardt and Varga, 328.
56. Job 21:34 CJB
57. Jedan, et al., 1.
58. Libera Pisano, "Silence, Translation, and Grammatical Therapy: Some Features of Linguistic Scepticism in the Thought of Rosenzweig and Wittgenstein," in Rebiger, ed., 129.
59. Rosenzweig, *The Star of Redemption*, tr. Barbara Galli, 327.
60. Kidorf, 44.
61. *Ibid.*, 45.
62. Klass, "Solace and Immortality," 343–68.
63. Wittgenstein, *Philosophical Investigations*, quoted in Hagberg, 60. Translated by Garry Hagberg.
64. Bakker, 207, 210; emphases in original.
65. Safranski, 233–4.
66. Goethe, "Wandrers Nachtlied, Ein gleiches," known as *Wandrers Nachtlied II, Goethes Werke: Vollständige Ausgabe letzter Hand*, v1, 99.
67. Safranski, 26.
68. Burnham, 189.
69. Romanoff, 697–711.
70. Jacobsen, xiii.
71. Hühn, 17.
72. Hühn, 8.
73. Eichendorff, 195.
74. Earl Grollman, "Spiritual Support after Sudden Loss," in Doka, ed., *Living with Grief: After Sudden Loss*, 187. Rabbi Grollman used the Hebrew text for his count.
75. Psalms 10, 22 and 74.
76. See Kristin De Troyer, "'Sounding Trumpets with Loud Shouts'—Emotional Responses to Temple Building: Ezra and Esdras," in Reif and Egger-Wenzel, eds., *Ancient Jewish Prayers*, 45. Also Deuteronomy 1:45; Job 2:12; Isaiah 30:19; Lamentations 1:2, 16.
77. Lamentations 3:8 CJB.
78. Rilke, "Wer, wenn ich schriee, hörte mich

denn aus der Engel Ordnungen?," *Duineser Elegien*, 7.

79. Rilke to Witold Hulewicz, 13 November 1925, Sierre, *Briefe*, v2, 484.

80. See Elaine Boney's commentary on *Duinesian Elegies* (1975), 72.

81. Werner Hamacher, "Bemerkungen zur Klage," in Ferber and Schwebel, 92.

82. Klass, "Solace and Immortality," 343–68.

83. Zapata, 154.

84. Philologist Heinz Rölleke noted that this poem influenced German novelist Wilhelm Raabe's final fragmentary work, *Altershausen*, which has rhyme schemes that are "tellingly close" to Rückert's, particularly verses 13–16. See Rölleke, 66–77; Raabe, 196.

85. Benedict Taylor, 277.

86. *himmlischem geleit.*

87. Moules, 142–66.

88. Gregory, v1, Book II.xvi.28, 87.

89. Astell, 84.

90. Often an important role of Asian and Middle Eastern mythologies: Campbell, 144.

91. O'Donohue, 226.

92. Luby was chief of psychiatry at Lafayette Clinic in Detroit when he was interviewed by Schiff in *The Bereaved Parent*, 23.

93. Rando, "The Unique Issues and Impact of the Death of a Child," in Rando, ed., *Parental Loss of a Child*, 14–5.

94. Rosenblatt, *Journal of Personal and Interpersonal Loss* 5(4), 343–60.

95. Ibid.

96. Kissane and Bloch, 729, 733.

97. Rosenblatt, *Journal of Personal and Interpersonal Loss* 5(4), 343–60.

98. Kissane and Bloch, 728, 731; Rando, "The Unique Issues and Impact of the Death of a Child," in Rando, ed., *Parental Loss of a Child*, 34.

99. "An die Kleingebliebenen," *Gedichte von Friedrich Rückert* (Sauerländer, 1841), 720.

100. Knapp, *Beyond Endurance*, 200, 202. Emphasis in original.

101. Boelen and Smid, *BMJ 357* (2017).

102. Knapp, 178–179; Klass, "Solace and Immortality," 343–368; Musaph, 175–9; Holland and Neimeyer, 103–20.

103. Valentine, *Bereavement Narratives*, 3–4.

104. Shear, et al., *BMJ 358* (2017).

105. Jakoby, 679–711.

106. Stroebe, et al., *Journal of Consulting and Clinical Psychology*, 479–82.

107. Freud to Ludwig Binswanger, 12 April 1929, *Letters*, tr. Tania & James Stern, 386; Zandvoort, 34–5.

108. Terry Martin and Kenneth Doka, "Masculine Grief," in Doka, ed., *Living with Grief: After Sudden Loss*, 170, 171.

109. Valentine, *Bereavement Narratives*, 3–4.

110. Fitzgerald, 119–20; Worden, *Counseling*, 123.

111. Stroebe, "Poetry of Grief," 92.

112. Lewis, *A Grief Observed*, 61.

113. Hayles, 31–2.

114. Certeau, Michel de, "History and Mysticism," tr. Arthur Goldhammer, in Revel and Hunt, eds., *Histories*, v1, 437–47. Emphasis added.

115. *Schicksalsschlag.* See KTL-W, 575.

116. Matthee, 449–62.

117. Schimmel, *A Two-Colored Brocade*, 5.

118. ADONAI, EL RAḤUM VE-ḤANNUN (Heb. יְהוָה, יְהוָה, אֵל רַחוּם וְחַנּוּן; Adonai is God, merciful and compassionate; Ex. 34:6–7 CJB. James Kugel, Professor Emeritus in the Bible Department at Bar Ilan University in Israel and the Harry M. Starr Professor Emeritus of Classical and Modern Hebrew Literature at Harvard University, provides a thoughtful discussion in Kugel, *The God of Old*, 129–30.

119. Muhawi and Kanaana, 325.

120. Goethe to Johann Kaspar Lavater, 8 October 1779, in *Goethes Briefe*, v4, 73–4. For Goethe's views on God and fate, see Safranski, 235; for the influence of Hafez and the Qur'an on Goethe, see Safranski, 469–71. See also Annemarie Schimmel's interview on Radio Germany, *Tehran Times* (23 September 2001): https://www.tehrantimes.com/print/72187/Hafez-From-the-View-of-Goethe.

121. This phrasing, whether seen as fate or an Act of God, is usually associated with Exodus 21:13; see Loimer, et al., 104.

122. Heschel, *Man Is Not Alone*, 76.

123. KTL-W, 576.

124. Thuné-Boyle, et al., 151–64.

125. Abernethy, et al., 456–63.

126. Browning, "Isobel's Child," X, 178–84; 25. Emphasis in original.

127. *des Tods Triumphe.*

128. Cantor, 121.

129. Schimmel, 129; see also Schimmel, *Alman Dili ve Edebiyatı Dergisi*, 9–10; and Maidt-Zinke, *Frankfurter Anthologie*.

130. Rückert, *Poetisches Tagebuch*, 1850–1866, 286.

131. J.D. Rolleston, 928.

132. Alan Swedlund and Alison Donta, "Scarlet fever epidemics of the nineteenth century: A case of evolved pathogenic virulence?" in Herring, 159–177.

133. Brown, *Journal of Hygiene*, 1–13.

134. Rolleston, 928.

135. Kittlinger, also recorded as Küttlinger. Volker Hesse, "Kindstod im 19. Jahrhundert: Betrachtungen zu Friedrich Rückerts Kindertodtenliedern aus medizinischer Sicht," in LEB, 186.

136. Chavassee, 336.

137. Kollock, 334–5.

138. Lindemann, "Symptomatology," 141–8.

139. Therese Rando, "Complications in Mourning Traumatic Death," in Doka, *Sudden Loss*, 146.

140. William Fish, "Differences of Grief Intensity in Bereaved Parents," in Rando, *Parental Loss*, 223, 417, 426.

141. Denis Forasacco, "'In ihrem großen Leib [...] waren zwei Früchte: ein Kind und ein Tod," in LEB, 155–6.

142. "Rückerts Qual, sein Mitgefühl, sein Hilflosigkeit..." in Volker Hesse, "Kindstod im 19.

Jahrhundert: Betrachtungen zu Friedrich Rückerts Kindertodtenliedern aus medizinischer Sicht," in LEB, 198.
143. Coelho, et al., 693–703.
144. Pusey, 228–9.
145. Gorer, 70.
146. Bullock, 193–200.
147. KTL-W, 580.
148. Linda Dowdney, "Children Bereaved by Parent or Sibling Death," in Skuse, et al., 151.
149. *Book of Health*, 40, 41.
150. *Ibid.*, 152, 169.
151. *Ibid.*, 40.
152. Volker Hesse, "Kindstod im 19. Jahrhundert: Betrachtungen zu Friedrich Rückerts Kindertodtenliedern aus medizinischer Sicht," in LEB, 186.
153. Luise Rückert, Diary, March/April 1834, in KTL-W, 555.
154. Humphry Rolleston, 501.
155. "Die Einreibungen am Kopf mit Quecksilber litt er ungern, er war aber des Vaters und meiner Stimme gehorsam bis zum Tod und ließ es geschehen." Luise Rückert, Diary, March/April 1834, in KTL-W, 555.
156. Luise Rückert, Diary, March/April 1834, in KTL-W, 555.
157. *risse.*
158. John 17:24 NIV; Johannes 17:24, *Die Bibel* [1834], *Neue Testament*, German tr. Martin Luther, 118.
159. Luise Rückert, Diary, March/April 1834, in KTL-W, 554–6.
160. Erdmann, 233.
161. *wechselwirkend.*
162. Judy Dunn, "Siblings and the Development of Social Understanding in Early Childhood," in Zukow, 106.
163. Dunn, "Sibling Relationships" in *Child Development*, 787–811.
164. Debra Pepler, Carl Corter and Rona Abramovitch, "Social Relations Among Children: Comparison of Sibling and Peer Interaction" in Rubin and Ross, 209–27.
165. Karen Ann Watson-Gegeo and David Gegeo, "The Role of Sibling Internation in Child Socialization" in Zukow, 54.
166. Thomas Weisner, "Comparing Sibling Relationships Across Cultures," in Zukow, 11.
167. Rittenour, et al., 169–83.
168. Edwards, et al., 46–7.
169. Susan Ervin-Tripp, "Sisters and Brothers" in Zukow, 184.
170. Judy Dunn, "Sibling Relationships," in Smith and Hart, 223–4.
171. Marecki, et al., 418–23.
172. *Messerchen und Gäbelchen.*
173. Heinzelmann, 105.
174. *jugendliche stürme.*
175. *jungen wilden.*
176. *geier.*
177. Weiss, Robert, "The Nature and Causes of Grief," in Stroebe, et al., eds., *Handbook of Bereavement Research and Practice*, 29–44.

178. See Charles Brooks, "Translator's Preface," in Rückert, *Brahmin*, xi–xii.
179. Malkinson and Bar-Tur, 110–1.
180. Adams, *Catharine*, 25–6.
181. Thuné-Boyle, et al., 151–64.
182. The well-known expression: "Totgesagte leben länger." Wilkes, 299–310.
183. Luise Rückert, Diary, March/April 1834, in KTL-W, 554–5.
184. Luise and Ernst rest in the Neustädter Friedhof in Erlangen. (Czapla, Ralf Georg, "Wiedererweckung in der Poesie?" in LEB, 60.)
185. Lindemann, "Symptomatology," 141–8; also Liston Mills, "Pastoral Care of the Dying and the Bereaved," in Mills, ed., *Perspectives*, 266.
186. "Denn ein begrebnis solt ja bilich ein feiner stiller ort sein, der abgesondert were von allen oertern, darauff man mit andacht gehen und stehen kuendte, den tod, das Juengst gericht und aufferstehung zu betrachten und zu beten." Luther, *Ob man vor dem Sterben fliehen möge* (1527), in *Werke* v23, 375.
187. Hauke Kenzler, "Religion, Status and Taboo. Changing Funeral Rites in Catholic and Protestant Germany," in Tarlow, ed., 151.
188. Douglas Davies, "Death's Impossible Date," in McCorristine, ed., 109, 115.
189. Paiuk, 12 January 2014.
190. Yancey, *Memoir*, 6.
191. *Ibid.*
192. Therese Rando, "Complications in Mourning Traumatic Death," in Doka, *Sudden Loss*, 146.
193. Yancey, *Memoir*, 3–6.
194. Douglas Davies, "Death's Impossible Date," in McCorristine, ed., 115.
195. Little angel (*engelchen*); little devils (*bengelchen*).
196. Douglas Davies, "Death's Impossible Date," in McCorristine, ed., 110–1; see the full report in Davies and Alastair Shaw, *Reusing Old Graves: A Report on Popular British Attitudes* (Shaw & Sons, 1995).
197. Valentine, *Bereavement Narratives*, passim.
198. Gershom Scholem, *Lament* (*Klage*), in Sigrid Weigel, "The Role of Lamentation for Scholem's Theory of Poetry and Language," in Ferber and Schwebel, 194, tr. Joel Golb.
199. Scholem, *Diogenes*, 164–94; tr. Simon Pleasance. See also Sigrid Weigel, "The Role of Lamentation for Scholem's Theory of Poetry and Language," in Ferber and Schwebel, 188, tr. Joel Golb.
200. Lewis, *A Grief Observed*, 73.
201. Koch and Sackett, 198–205.
202. *Ich wünsche euch ein glückseliges Neues Jahr. Langes Leben. Gesündheit. Fried und Einigkeit. Und nach dem Tod, ewig Glückseligkeit.* Koch and Sacket, 200.
203. Russ, 34–6.
204. *leichenfrau.*
205. This was common practice by the 19th century. See Fischer, 48.
206. Hauke Kenzler, "Religion, Status and

207. KTL-W, 552.
208. Linton, *Daphnis*, 281–306.
209. Linton, *Poetry*, 161–2, 163.
210. Jonson wrote "On My First Son" in 1603 after his eldest son, Benjamin, died at the age of seven. Jonson, 18.
211. Erlin, 54; Sieveking, 171.
212. *Bestattungstänze*.
213. Freitag, 85; Balogh, 1–14.
214. Backman, 136.
215. Tennyson, *In Memoriam*, Section LVII, 64, 186.
216. Linton, *Poetry*, 3, 6, 7.
217. *leichenschmaus*.
218. Stephenson, 199; Kenneth Doka, "The Power of Ritual," in Doka, *Children and Adolescents*, 289. See also Boss, 39; Bowlby, *American Journal of Orthopsychiatry* 52(4), 664–78.
219. Paul and Beernink, 153–69.
220. Leming and Dickinson, 480.
221. *leichenfrau*.
222. Herbert, 215.
223. Eden, 256, 259.
224. KTL-W, 608.
225. James Miller, "Grief Tips," in Dickinson, 235.
226. Grollman, *Living*, 23.
227. *erschrecke*.
228. Unamuno, Miguel de, "Fe que no duda es fe muerta," in *La Agonía del Cristianismo*, 22; this English translation is in *Selected Works*, v5, 10.
229. Burke, et al., 268–81.
230. David Thompson and Edward Holland, "Meaning Making in the Wake of Public Tragedy," in Doka and Lattanzi-Light, eds., *Living with Grief: Coping with Public Tragedy*, 173.
231. Paul Irion, "Ritual Responses to Death," in Doka and Davidson, eds., *Living with Grief at Work*, 163.
232. Davis, et al., 561–74.
233. Hess, 223, 227.
234. Tennyson, "In Memoriam A.H.H.," 1849, in *In Memoriam*, 114.
235. Taylor, 525–34.
236. C.S. Lewis to Vera Gebbert, 23 March 1953, *Collected Letters*, v3, 311.
237. Schimmel, 34.
238. Phillip Powers to his wife, 15 May 1864, on the death of James Ewell Brown "Jeb" Stuart, in Blaisdell, ed., 165.
239. Lincoln to Fanny McCullough, 23 December 1862, *Speeches and Letters*, 226.
240. From the funeral booklet for Maria Sophia Mayer (1657–8), quoted in German in Linton, *Poetry*, 123.
241. Psalm 88:18 NLT.
242. Kushner, 86.
243. Enez, 269–79.
244. Weidner, 13–4.
245. Hopkins, 68. See also Mariani, 223–8.
246. Subsequent research has confirmed her account as accurate and surprisingly self-effacing. See Denise Counihan's dissertation, *The Life of Corrie Ten Boom: A Psychobiography*, University of Johannesburg, 2019: https://ujcontent.uj.ac.za/vital/access/manager/Repository/uj:35783 and Cornelia Arnolda Johanna "Corrie" ten Boom, with John and Elizabeth Sherrill, *The Hiding Place* (Chosen Books, 1971).
247. Job 2:9 CJB.
248. Excerpted and adapted from Bannon, *Hevria*, 17 July 2019.
249. Schwab, 445–68.
250. Lyngstad, 79–86.
251. Bernstein, 101–6.
252. Nicole Baur, "Families, Stress and Mental Illness in Devon, 1940s to 1970s," in Jackson, ed., 32–3.
253. Rosof, 104–5.
254. Job 1:21 NIV.
255. Job 3:24 and 26; Job 6:2, Mitchell translation; Mitchell, 21.
256. Ezekiel 14:14. There is no question that the passage refers to the famous Noah and Job as we know them in the Bible. The identity of Daniel, or Danel, remains a contested topic. The accepted academic position identifies the character as the Danel that appears in the Ugaritic *Tale of Aqhat*. New scholarship posits that the Daniel in Ezekiel may be a different biblical character altogether. (Klein, 231–41.) Whatever the identity of this Daniel, he was certainly in fine company.
257. Swenson, 206.
258. Buechner, 70.
259. Nouwen, March 29.
260. Robert Rosenblum, "The Abstract Sublime," in Pipes, ed., 239–44.
261. Denis Forasacco, "'In ihrem großen Leib [...] waren zwei Früchte: ein Kind und ein Tod," in in LEB, 155.
262. Taylor, *Atlantic*, 33; tr. James Clarence Mangan.
263. Brunner, 11, 15–6, 91; Miles, 271–2; Flanders, 28–30.
264. Groeschel, 39–40.
265. Heller, 268–70.
266. Wernecke, 21.
267. Dickens, "A Christmas Tree," 1, 7.
268. Dickens, "What Christmas is, as we grow older," 3.
269. Carr, et al., 113–122.
270. Dickens, "What Christmas is, as we grow older," 2.
271. Klass and Marwit, "Toward a Model of Parental Grief," 31–50.
272. Shear, Katherine, Bonnie Gorscak, and Naomi Simon, "Treatment of complicated grief following violent death," in Rynearson, ed., *Violent Death*, 157–74; Cohen and Mannarino, 219–27.
273. Knapp, *Beyond Endurance*, 138; Schiff, *Parental Bereavement*, 110–1.
274. Volker Hesse, "Kindstod im 19. Jahrhundert: Betrachtungen zu Friedrich Rückerts Kindertodtenliedern aus medizinischer Sicht," in LEB, 200.
275. Blum-Hyclak, "Baseline 4-5-93," 18. Reprinted with permission of the author.

276. Chamisso and Schwab, eds., *Deutscher Musenalmanach für die Jahr 1834*, 7–105. Friedrich calls this *Der neuste Almanach*, the latest almanac.
277. West, *Music & Letters 67*, 37–49.
278. Chamisso and Schwab, eds., i.
279. KTL-W, 575. Rückert dedicated a poem, written in late summer, 1834, to his friend, spelling his name "Carl" Barth, which I have used in this book; KTL-W, 515, 608.
280. Forssman, "Gastlichkeit im Hause Rückert," 18 March 2019.
281. Chamisso and Schwab, eds., 106–7.
282. Brown, *Poets, Patrons, and Printers*, 61.
283. *Liebesfrühling*.
284. Rückert, *Gesammelte Gedichte* (1834), 404; Schimmel, 34; Reuter, 10.
285. From "Home Burial" in Frost, 28.
286. Rückert, "1834," *Gesammelte Gedichte* (1834), 406.
287. *Blätter für literarische Unterhaltung 1835* (63) (4 March 1835), 257; reviewing Rückert's *Gesammelte Gedichte*, v1 (Heyder, 1834).
288. Erdmann, 234.
289. Schiff, 39.
290. Miles and Demi, 299–314.
291. Jones, *Sigmund Freud*, 20.
292. Finkbeiner, 17.
293. Wright and Strawn, 156.
294. Schiff, 43.
295. Zandvoort, 41.
296. *Funfzig Fabeln für Kinder*.
297. Blamires, 321–2.
298. Pagels, xv.
299. Davis Bush (Prend), 77.
300. Attig, *Heart*, 39.
301. Klass, *New Directions*, 54.
302. David, 3–6.
303. Cook, 182, 211.
304. Davies, *Funerary Rites*, 229; Cleiren, 129; Hay, 83; Stroebe et al., 44(3), 143–158.
305. From Longfellow, "Footsteps of Angels," *Poems*, 4–5.
306. Klass, "Solace and Immortality," 343–68.
307. Redfern, 197–214; Al-Chokhachy; Toom, 1–13.
308. *Ruhestättchen*.
309. *ausgeschlüpft*.
310. *Silfettchen*.
311. Lewis to Vera Mathews on the death of her father, 27 March 51, *Letters*, vIII, 103–4.
312. Charles Brooks, "Translator's Preface," in Rückert, *Brahmin*, xi.
313. Schimmel, 58.
314. Rückert, "Amerika," *Illustrirte Dorfzeitung des Lahrer hinkenden Boten*, v4, n9, 72.
315. The material about Lincoln and his son's death is excerpted from Bannon, "Grief in the White House," *History Magazine*, 31–5. Readers may refer to that periodical for source notes.
316. Lincoln, Abraham, "The Return," *Quincy Whig 10*(3) (5 May 1847): 1. In the fall of 1844, Lincoln visited the graves of his mother and sister in southern Indiana. This poem, now known as "My childhood-home I see again," was the result. Lincoln sent the piece to Andrew Johnston in two letters, 18 April 1846 and 6 September 1846, though it may have been written as early as 25 February 1846. Johnston subsequently published it in the *Quincy Whig* under the title, "The Return." Lincoln requested that the poem be published anonymously. We reprint it here as it first appeared in the *Whig*. A slightly different version, edited by historian Roy Basler, is in Lincoln, *Collected Works*, 366–7.
317. Bannon, *Wounded in Spirit*, 9.
318. Cholbi, "Why Grieve?," in Chobli and Timmerman, eds., 185–6.
319. Cholbi, *Grief*, 11, 12, 13; emphasis in original.
320. KTL-W, 604–5.
321. ὁ τρώσας ἰάσεται; Moore, 195, 202. Although Rückert may well have read the Greek, translations were also readily available. The same line in a German translation of Euripides: *Wer da verletzt hat, wird auch heilen*. See KTL-W, 604–5.
322. "Nur eine Waffe taugt:—die Wunde schließt der Speer nur, der sie schlug," *Parsifal*, Act 3, Scene 2. See Möhn, 50–4.
323. Apollodorus, 189.
324. Apollodorus, 189n. Emphasis added.
325. Psalm 32:4 CJB. This is also noticeable in the Luther Bible translation of the same passage. Rückert wrote " dessen Hand auf dir ist schwer," echoing the Luther Bible rendering of Psalm 32:4—"deine Hand war Tag und Nacht schwer auf mir." *Die Bibel* [1834], German tr. Martin Luther, 519.
326. "Even today my complaint is bitter; his hand is heavy in spite of my groaning," Job 23:2 NIV; Hiob 23:2; *Die Bibel* [1834], German tr. Martin Luther, 494.
327. Job 6:10–11, CJB; "So hätte ich noch Trost... Was ist meine Kraft, daß ich möge beharren?" Hiob 6:10–1; *Die Bibel* [1834], German tr. Martin Luther, 483; informing Rückert's line "Wer kann dir Trost ertheilen?"
328. Taylor, *Atlantic*, 33; tr. Bayard Taylor.
329. Horace, 459.
330. KTL-W, 575.
331. Taylor, *Atlantic*, 33; also Taylor, *Essays*, 92.
332. In the same discussion, Schmidt couples chastisement with guilt, "Züchtigung und Schuldgefühl," Schmidt, 81–2.
333. Goethe, quoted by Thomas Mann in his introduction (tr. Gustav Arlt), *The Permanent Goethe*, xxxiv.
334. Romanoff, 697–711.
335. Weeks, O. Duane, "Using Funeral Rituals to Help Survivors," in Doka, ed., *Living with Grief: After Sudden Loss*, 133.
336. *Ibid*., 134.
337. Winkel, 67–79.
338. Hume, 166–82.
339. Monhoff, Sascha, "Die Poetologie von Totenklage und "Totenersatz" in Friedrich Rückerts Kindertotenliedern," in LEB, 230.
340. Oka, "'Grief is love': Understanding Grief

through Self-help Groups Organised by the Family Survivors of Suicide," in Drautzburg and Oldfield, 75–86. The groups were first formed in 2006 as part of the Basic Act on Suicide Countermeasures.

341. Tolstoy, 100.
342. Thompson and Neimeyer, 6.
343. Rückert to Albrecht Fischer, 1 April 1834, Coburg, in KTL-W, 535.
344. Ibid.
345. Finkbeiner, 109–10.
346. Volker Hesse, "Kindstod im 19. Jahrhundert: Betrachtungen zu Friedrich Rückerts Kindertodtenliedern aus medizinischer Sicht," in LEB, 207.
347. Thompson and Berger, "Grief and Expressive Arts Therapy," in Neimeyer, *Grief and Bereavement*, 304; Malchiodi, ix; Neimeyer, *Lessons*.
348. Gebirol, tr. Israel Abrahams, in Abrahams, 99–100.
349. The tree was a common European white or silver birch (*Betula pendula*). Ralf Georg Czapla, "Wiedererweckung in der Poesie?," in LEB, 52; Wilkes, 299–310.
350. "Abschied von der Rückert-Birke," (Nürnberger Presse, 19 February 2016): https://www.nordbayern.de/erlangen-abschied-von-der-ruckert-birke-1.5002211.
351. I am grateful to Johannes Wilkes for information about the history and final disposal of the tree. Personal correspondence, Johannes Wilkes to David Bannon, 1–2 November 2021.
352. Leyk, "Neustädter Friedhof," 2020. The Evangelisch-Lutherische Kirchengemeinde Erlangen-Neustadt serves the community and the university. Pfarrer Dr. Wolfgang Leyk works with the church council and the committee that maintains the cemetery. For a delightful travelogue of the Erlangen Rückert Circle, see http://www.rückert-kreis.de/rueckert-kreis-alte-Veranstaltungen.html. See also Forssman, "Gastlichkeit im Hause Rückert," 18 March 2019.
353. Volker Hesse, "Kindstod im 19. Jahrhundert: Betrachtungen zu Friedrich Rückerts Kindertodtenliedern aus medizinischer Sicht," in LEB, 207.
354. Gibson, 312–4; Galinsky, 351.
355. Ralf Georg Czapla, "Wiedererweckung in der Poesie?," in LEB, 51.
356. Linton, 75.
357. Hess, 50, discussing Schleiermacher's well-known *Hermeneutics: The Compendium of 1819* (Manuscript 3). For the full text in English, see Schleiermacher, 157–70.
358. Ziolkowski, 4.
359. Wheatley, introduction, in Wheatley, ed., ix–x.
360. Risinger, 13.
361. "Character of the Happy Warrior," Wordsworth, 32.
362. Ziolkowski, 5.
363. Ibid., 14.
364. Schlegel, "Durch alle Töne tönet," from the final stanza of "Die Gebüsche" in the cycle *Abendröte* (1801), in Schlegel, *Sämmtliche Werke*, v7, 171.
365. Nassar, 2.
366. Ibid., 5.
367. Schonberg, 438.
368. Mahler's four-year-old daughter: Maria Anna, called Putzi, 3 November 1902–5 July 1907. See Gartenberg, Mahler, 115, 119; Lebrecht, *Why Mahler?*, 124, 145; Wildhagen, "Das Lied von der Erde," tr. Jeremy Barham and Trefor Smith, in Barham, *Mahler*, 135.
369. Mahler to Max Marschalk, 26 March 1896, quoted in Reik, 252.
370. Robinson, 9.
371. Ibid., 6.
372. Stein, 191.
373. Parkes, *Bereavement Care 17*, 21–3; John Seymour, "Integrated Play Therapy with Childhood Traumatic Grief," in Malchiodi and Crenshaw, eds., 259; Robinson, 1.
374. Dickinson, *Complete Poems*, 312–3.
375. Denhup, 345–60.
376. Lichtenthal, et al., 791–812.
377. Rolf Selbmann, "Der Dichter und Seine Vaterstadt: Die Wirkungsgeschichte Friedrich Rückerts in Schweinfurt," in Prang, 134.
378. Following a description of Romantic poets by Bowra, 292.
379. Volker Hesse, "Kindstod im 19. Jahrhundert: Betrachtungen zu Friedrich Rückerts Kindertodtenliedern aus medizinischer Sicht," in LEB, 207.
380. Octavio Paz, in Honig, 157.
381. Schwartz-Borden, 239–48.
382. O'Donohue, *Anam Cara*, 95.
383. Ralf Georg Czapla, "Kindstod als Pop-Spektakel," in LEB, 335.
384. Adler, 185.
385. "Lass uns weinen!.... / Seelenvoller und himmlischer / ein Strom der Wehmuth // Nie spricht lauter die Lipp " als wenn sie bebt / Unaussprechlich bebt im Seufzen!," Herder, 501.
386. *Bessonnenheit*; Zammito, et al., 672. For Herder's unquestioned influence on 19th-century intellectual and literary life, see Ronald Taylor's informative chapter on the philosopher in *The Romantic Tradition in Germany*.
387. Schiller, "Nicht Fleisch und Blut, das Herz macht uns zu Vätern und Söhnen," Act 1, Scene 1, *Die Räuber*, 9.
388. Bleeker, 9, 17.
389. Ibid., 2; from a German translation of the tomb writing by Lüddeckens, 165.
390. Wickett, *Quaderni Di Studi Arabi 7*, 153; Wickett, *For the Living and the Dead*, 259.
391. Wilce, 61, 66.
392. Helmut Koopmann, "Die Vorteile des Sprachverfalls. Zur Sprache der Lyrik im 19. Jahrhundert," in Wimmer, 315, 318–21.
393. Ibid., 318.
394. Susan Cadell, "Stress, Coping, Growth, and Spirituality in Grief," in Groen, et al., 226–7.
395. The final stanza of "The Dying Flower" (*Die sterbende Blume*), *Gesammelte Poetische Werke*, v7, 273.

396. Morris, *Wanderers*, 49, 55.
397. Coleridge, *Biographia*, 174.
398. Wordsworth, *Poems*, v2, 49–50. For the reference to 175,000 miles, see Morris, *Wanderers*, 51.
399. Muir, *The Yosemite*, 256.
400. Colby, 7; Johnson, Daphins, 189–221
401. Linton, *Poetry*, 126–8.
402. Hardin, 76–6; Cathy Shrank, "Answer Poetry and Other Verse 'Conversations,'" in Bates, ed., 376–88.
403. Flesch, William, "The Poetics of Speech Tags," in Rasmussen, ed., 159–84.
404. Eichenberger, 543, 546.
405. Carrdus, *Modern Language Review*, 411.
406. Dufrechou, 357–78.
407. Davis Bush, 78.
408. Rückert's second line reads: "Wo die Todten ihre Todten legen." This is a slight variation on the Luther Bible that was in the Rückert home in 1834. In both Matthew and Luke, the passage reads "die Todten ihre Todten begraben." (Matthäus 8:22; *Luther Bibel* [1834], Neue Testament, 10; Lucas 9:60, *Luther Bibel* [1834], Neue Testament, 74.)
409. Mieder, Wolfgang, "Origins of Proverbs," in Hrisztova-Gotthardt and Varga, 35.
410. Matthew 12:34, King James Version; *Ex abundantia cordis os loquitur.*
411. "Weß das Herz voll ist, deß gehet der Mund über," Matthäus 12:34; *Luther Bibel* [1834], Neue Testament, 15.
412. Mieder, Wolfgang, "Origins of Proverbs," in Hrisztova-Gotthardt and Varga, 36. Mieder described the Luther translation of Matthäus 12:34 as "folksy."
413. ליקוט עצמות.
414. Reif, Stefan, "A Response to Professor Paxton's Paper," in Reif, et al., *Death in Jewish Life*, 47.
415. Crossan, *Essential Jesus*, 164.
416. Meyers, 95–6, 105, 107.
417. Crossan, *Essential Jesus*, 69.
418. Conte, 60.
419. Hoffmann von Fallersleben, 200–1.
420. *Böckchen*
421. Bolton and Camp, 49–59.
422. Worden, *Counseling*, 42.
423. Murphy, et al., *Death Studies 27*, 39–61.
424. Paul Irion, "Ritual Responses to Death," in Doka and Davidson, *Living with Grief at Work*, 157.
425. Ibid., 157, 163; Raphael, 281.
426. Reimers, 147–66.
427. Rubin, Simon Shimshon and Ruth Malkinson, "Parental Response to Child Loss across the Life Cycle: Clinical and Research Perspectives," in Stroebe, et al., eds., *Handbook of Bereavement Research*, 222.
428. Simms, "The Streamlet," X, XIII, XV, in *Poems*, 294, 295. See Matthew Brennan's discussion of the poem and its place in Romantic verse, 108–11.
429. "...das Kind die einzige Interpretation, die hier für den Trauernden sinnstiftend sein kann," Monhoff, Sascha, "Das Totenbuch der Natur: Die "Lesbarkeit der Welt" in Friedrich Rückerts Kindertodtenliedern," in LEB, 257.
430. Goodkin, Karl, Baldewicz, Teri T. Blaney, Nancy T. Asthana, Deshratn Kumar, Mahendra Shapshak, Paul Leeds, Barbara Burkhalter, Jack E. Rigg, David Tyll, Mary D. Cohen, Joshua Zheng, Wen Li, "Physiological Effects of Bereavement Support Group Interventions," in Stroebe, et al., eds., *Handbook of Bereavement Research*, 672.
431. Peale, 41–2.
432. Worden, 85–6.
433. Stepakoff, 105–13.
434. Knapp, 208; emphases in original.
435. Raphael, 281.
436. Schiff, 124, 132.
437. Hood, 572.
438. Rückert, "Vierzeilen" (Quatrains), quatrain 32, *Fünftes Bruchstück, Zahme Xenien* (Gentle Gifts), in *Gedichte von Friedrich Rückert* (Sauerländer, 1886), 80. The word for cabbage, *Kohl*, is also commonly used for rubbish or nonsense, as in the expressions "Kohl reden" (talking trash), "aufgewärmter Kohl" (a warmed over or rehashed story) and "Red keinen Kohl" (Don't talk nonsense). Double meanings were seldom lost on Rückert, whose line could easily be read as "for the *nonsense* you've grown (or spouted)."
439. Lee, et al., 291–305.
440. O'Neill, "Speaking to the Dead," conference paper, 27–9 October 2006.
441. "...spürte ich, wie die dumpfe Traurigkeit, die wie ein Stein in mir heruntergesunken war, immer wieder überspült wurde von einer wilden Hoffnung, wie sie sich wandelte und sich seltsam damit vermischte, wie eines zum andern wurde, die Traurigkeit, die Hoffnung, der Wind, der Abend ... ja, ich hatte einen Augenblick lang plötzlich das sonderbare Empfinden, als ob erst das wirklich und in einem sehr tiefen Sinne das Leben sei und vielleicht sogar das Glück: Liebe mit so viel Schwermut, Furcht und schweigendem Wissen," Remarque, *Drei Kameraden*, 356.
442. Giselinde Kuipers, "Where was King Kong when We Need Him?," in Gournelos and Greene, eds., 24.
443. Haig, 39, 129.
444. Giselinde Kuipers, "Where was King Kong when We Need Him?," in Gournelos and Greene, eds., 25.
445. Grollman, *Living*, 54.
446. Shrock, 254.
447. Leaver, 119.
448. Tony Walter, "Facing Death without Tradition," in Howarth and Jupp, eds., 193–204.
449. Psalm 119:73 CJB.
450. Goethe, "Staub soll er fressen, und mit Lust," Faust: Elne Tragödie (Cotta, 1862), 15. "Und mit Lust," is often translated as "and with zeal," or "and with enthusiasm." These are serviceable solutions but they fail to capture the chortling glee of Mephistopheles. It is nearly an aside, a throwaway line, adding insult to injury—precisely the intent of a similar aside in English, "and he'll like it."
451. Safranski, 529.

452. Dickinson, *Complete Poems*, 323–4.
453. Mitchell, *The Book of Job*, 88. For a discussion of Job's progression from sitting in dust to being dust, see Ariel Hirschfeld, "Is the Book of Job a Tragedy?" in Batnitzky and Pardes, eds., 24–5; and the entry in this volume for "Encircled by mountain."
454. "Quintessential" from Weber, 495. *Faust Part I* was published in 1808. Finishing *Part II* was an important focus of Goethe's final years. He finished it on 22 July 1831 but returned to it six months later. "New excitement about *Faust*," he wrote on 24 January 1832, "with regard to greater elaboration of the main motifs…" Goethe died on 22 March 1832 at the age of eighty-two. *Faust Part II* was published later that same year. See Safranski, 523–5.
455. Goethe, "Wie meine Muhme, die berühmte Schlange," *Faust: Elne Tragödie* (Cotta, 1862), 15.
456. Psalm 103:13–14 CJB.
457. David Thompson and Edward Holland, "Meaning Making in the Wake of Public Tragedy," in Lattanzi-Light and Doka, eds., *Living with Grief: Coping with Public Tragedy*, 173.
458. Earl Grollman, "Spiritual Support after Sudden Loss," in Doka, ed., *Living with Grief after Sudden Loss*, 187.
459. Lao Tzu, "On Being Uncommon," *Tao Te Ching* 20:3–4; the passage in Chinese, https://www.daodejing.org/20.html.
460. "Wer fliegt, der fliegt!" in Erman, 26. Translated from the pyramid texts into German by Erman, who was concerned that the language of the oldest Egyptian poetry was "extremely archaic, and so our understanding of it is fraught with tremendous challenges," (Erman, 26); I used Erman's German text for this translation.
461. Safranski, 200.
462. "Alles geben Götter die unendlichen, / Ihren Lieblingen ganz / Alle Freuden die unendlichen Alle Schmerzen die unendlichen ganz." Goethe to Auguste zu Stolberg, 17 July 1777, in Goethe, *Briefe an die Gräfin Auguste zu Stolberg*, 63. Cornelia died on 8 June 1777, three weeks after delivering her second child. (Safranski, 199.) *Unendlichen* is often translated as *infinite*, but here Goethe's phrasing allows a pleasing opportunity to match the German term with a similar English word, *endless*. *Ganz*, on the other hand, is replete with possible word choices in translation: *wholly, completely, fully,* etc. The poet's imagery is powerful, but his meaning can seem elusive for those unaccustomed to his phrasing. For example, a less structured rendering gains in clarity what it loses in similitude (this is also my translation): *The endless gods give without / reserve to those they love: / all our endless joys; all our / endless pain; without reserve.* In both versions, Goethe's use of *ganz* sneaks up on us, whether rendered as *without reserve* or "our pains, endless, entire."
463. Knapp, *Beyond Endurance*, 138.
464. Schiff, 110–1.
465. For an accessible and useful overview of the psalms of lament, see Davis, *Getting Involved with God*, 14–22.
466. Heschel, "On Prayer," (1970), 7.
467. Ralf Georg Czapla, "Wiedererweckung in der Poesie?," in LEB, 59–61. This short list is not intended to be comprehensive. The Rückerts were keen gardeners. We may reasonably assume that they kept other plants as well. (Consider his allusion to cabbages in "You need no market quote," translated in the grief note for "You five rose thorns."). Along with "You five rose thorns," another poem in this collection, "In the sacred silence of the wood I see my children," adds to the grieving father's moving tally of flowers that speak to him in new ways.
468. Buckley, 304; Rutherford, 146–55.
469. Fortlage, 13–4.
470. Gershom Scholem, "On Lament and Lamentation," from Scholem's essay, "Über Klage und Klagelied," 1917–1918, tr. Lina Barouch and Paula Schwebel, in Ferber and Schwebel, eds., *Lament in Jewish Thought*, 313, 317; emphasis in original.
471. Donne, paraphrased in Yancey, *A Companion in Crisis*, 71, 72. Reprinted with permission of the paraphrase author, Philip Yancey.
472. Stephenson, 133.
473. Jellinek, et al., 121–3.
474. Worden, *Counseling*, 30, 31.
475. Averill, 721–48.
476. *Luther on Women*, 199, 200.
477. *-chen* is a High German diminutive suffix used to create diminutive forms of name. Friedrich's referring to young Luise as "Luischen" is a term of endearment and, perhaps, a convenient, loving way to differentiate between his daughter and her mother, also named Luise. See Rückert to Albrecht Fischer, 1 April 1834, Coburg, in KTL-W, 535.
478. Peppers, 47–50.
479. Edmondston, 108.
480. Shakespeare, *King Richard II*, Act IV, scene i, 93.
481. Ano and Vasconcelles, 461–80; Neimeyer, *Behaviour Change 33*, 65–79; Park, *Journal of Social Issues 61*, 707–29; Shuchter and Zisook, 295–305; Calhoun and Tedeschi, *Posttraumatic Growth*, 7–13; Robert Neimeyer and Barbara Thompson, "Meaning Making and the Art of Grief Therapy," in Thompson and Neimeyer, eds., 6.
482. Castle and Phillips, 41–71.
483. Fromm, 108; emphasis in original.
484. Blum, 95–6. Emphasis in original.
485. James, *Human Immortality*, 9.
486. James, *Psychology*, v2, 308.
487. Quoted in Suckiel, 3. For a discussion of James's transformation in the context of his philosophical views, see Ward, 89.
488. Bergstraesser, et al., 128–38.
489. Henry Abramovitch, "The Influence of Martin Buber's Philosophy of Dialogue on Psychotherapy: His Lasting Contribution," in Mendes-Flohr, 169, 170.
490. Buber, 142.

491. Rückert to Albrecht Fischer, 1 April 1834, Coburg, in KTL-W, 535.
492. Gilovich, 379–95.
493. Minna Rozen, "Romans in Istanbul. Part 1: Historical and Literary Introduction," in Reif, et al., 305–6.
494. Spargo, 4, 143.
495. Schiff, 43.
496. Fromm, 108; emphasis added.
497. Bacon, "Of Parents and Children," *Essays*, 36.
498. Hauke Kenzler, "Religion, Status and Taboo. Changing Funeral Rites in Catholic and Protestant Germany," in Tarlow, ed., 165.
499. *Ibid.*, 156.
500. Malkinson, 289–305.
501. Gorer, 84, 85, 121–122; Buckle and Fleming, 1; Tedeschi, *Helping*, 13.
502. Knapp, *Beyond Endurance*, 206–7.
503. Leick and Davidsen-Nielsen, *passim*.
504. Irving, 304.
505. Attig, "Disenfranchised Grief Revisited," *OMEGA*, 197–215.
506. Greenspan, xiii.
507. *Ibid.*, xii.
508. Gamlin and Kinghorn, 33–5.
509. Goethe, "Und wenn der Mensch in seiner Qual verstummt, / Gab mir ein Gott, zu sagen wie ich leide," *Torquato Tasso*, 221.
510. Merrill, 328–9.
511. Moshe Halbertal, "Job, the Mourner," in Batnitzky and Pardes, 4; Genesis 23:9, 17–9.
512. *Leichenfrauen*, Hillard, 255.
513. *klügeln*
514. Gamino, et al., 79–92.
515. Black, et al., *Omega*, OnlineFirst.
516. Adams and Hyde, 58–67.
517. Steinsaltz, 54–6. See Genesis 37:1–36, 39:1–48:22, and 50:1–26.
518. Aberbach, *Surviving Trauma*, 44–70.
519. Aberbach, *International Review of Psycho-Analysis 14*, 509–26.
520. Aberbach, *Harvard Theological Review 86*, 321.
521. Terry Martin and Kenneth Doka, "Masculine Grief," in Doka, *Sudden Loss*, 163, 165.
522. James, Etta, Ellington Jordan and Billy Foster, "I'd Rather Go Blind" (Cadet Records 5578, 1967).
523. Adam Ferguson to David Bannon, 20 January 2019, personal correspondence.
524. Edwards and Luscombe, cover, 28–9.
525. Dickinson, *Poems* (1998), 552–3.
526. Gorer, 121–2.
527. Weiss, "Loss and Recovery," 48.
528. Worden, *Counseling*, 18.
529. Spargo, 177.
530. Darlene Fozard Weaver, "Sorrow Unconsoling and Inconsolable Sorrow: Grief as a Moral and Religious Practice," in Fagan, ed., 34.
531. Gorer, 121–2.
532. Emerson to Margaret Fuller, 28 January 1842, in *Letters*, 263.
533. 6 April 1842, in *Emerson's Letters*, 178.
534. Emerson, "Threnody," *Poems*, 134, 135.
535. *Ibid.*, 130.
536. Emerson, *Essays*, 52–3; for a discussion of grief, see Fruzińska, 160–1.
537. Saito, 133–4.
538. Cavell, 109.
539. Pastan, *Chicago Review 28*(4) (1977), 129; upper-case emphasis in original. This was changed to lower-case in Pastan's book, *The Five Stages of Grief*, 62.
540. Pastan, *Chicago Review 42*(3) (1996), 194.
541. Bolton and Camp, 343–52.
542. Joseph Bottum, "All That Lives Must Die," in Neuhaus, ed., 171, 172. Bottum's essay first appeared in a longer form in *First Things 63* (May 1996): 28–32.
543. Doka, *Grief Is a Journey*, 101.
544. *Ibid.*, 44, 85, 128.
545. Interviewed in Hendin, 175, 181.
546. Szanto, et al., 233–9; Simon, et al., 1105–10; McMenamy, et al., 375–89; Prigerson, et al., 194–207.
547. Lewis, 3.
548. Edelstein, 47–9.
549. Rosof, 45.
550. Schaal, et al., 476–81.
551. Gegieckaite and Kazlauskas (2020).
552. Knapp, *Beyond Endurance*, 36.
553. Klass, "Solace and Immortality," 343–68.
554. Bernstein, 210, 212.
555. Greeley, 813–835.
556. Benore, 1–22; Klugman, 249–262; Robert Weiss, "The Attachment Bond," in Parkes, *Attachment*, 74, 75.
557. Tedeschi, *Helping*, 8, 9, 10, 13.
558. Buechner, *Secrets*, 171.
559. Tournier, 171, 172.
560. O'Donohue, *Eternal Echoes*, 170, 178–9.
561. Richard Rohr, "Utterly Humbled by Mystery," in *This I Believe II*, Jay Allison, et al., eds., 193. Air date: 18 December 2006 on *NPR's Morning Edition*.
562. Rosof, 14–5.
563. Merton, "Creative Silence," in *Love and Living*, 40, 42.
564. For Berger's spiritual interests, see Borck, 117. The family connections are detailed by Ingeborg Forssman, ed., in Luise Rückert, "*Liebster Rückert!*" "*Geliebte Luise!*," 228f; and by Volker Hesse, "Kindstod im 19. Jahrhundert: Betrachtungen zu Friedrich Rückerts Kindertodtenliedern aus medizinischer Sicht," in LEB, 202.
565. Borck, 30, 30n11.
566. Laskow, *The Atlantic* (23 November 2014).
567. Millet, 522–42; Berger, *Psyche*, passim.
568. Kaplan, 174.
569. Borck, 43.
570. Hans Berger, "Über das Elektrenkephalogramm des Menschen (On the EEG in humans), *Archive für Psychiatre und Nervenkrankheiten* (1929).
571. Borck, 14.
572. Newman, 186.
573. Kaplan, 178–9.

574. Baumann, et al., 14–41; Ginzberg, 367, 371.
575. Posthumous nominations in 1942 and 1947 were not considered; Gerhard, et al., 156–60.
576. Borck, 73–4.
577. Kaplan, 178–9.
578. Ginzberg, passim.
579. Millet, 522–3
580. Rückert, "Ungereiht Perlen" (Unordered Pearls), quatrain 54, in *Gedichte von Friedrich Rückert* (Sauerländer, 1886), 573.
581. Ecclesiastes 3:11 CJB.
582. Kierkegaard, *Purity of Heart*, 35.
583. Thomas, Heywood, 33–40.
584. Shear, et al., *BMJ 358* (2017).
585. Attig, *Death Studies*, 389.
586. *Ibid.*, 390–2.
587. Stein and Spillman, 202, 256n11.
588. Tedeschi, *Helping*, 8, 9, 10, 13; Attig, *Heart of Grief*, 36–7, 255.
589. "Migrantes ex hac vita non amittimus, sed præmittimus. Non obeunt, sed abeunt." A version of this passage is listed in the *Index in Omnia Opera Sancti Augustini*, XLVI, column 0450. Johannes Teutschmann, the pastor of St. Bernhardin in the Silesian city of Breslau, quoted this passage in a sermon he delivered on 20 July 1621. Teutschmann had lost his young son to an outbreak of smallpox in February 1621. See Teutschmann, 164–5. The quotation first appeared in German funeral literature in 1623, according to Anna Linton. See her notes and this English translation in Linton, *Poetry*, 42.
590. Vögele, 2010.
591. Eckhart, "Das Licht leuchtet in der Finsternis ... dann werden sie das Licht sehen," *Reden der Unterweisung*, 26, 27.
592. Neimeyer, "Developmental Theory," in Neimeyer, *Techniques*, 9.
593. Ferguson, 33.
594. Hanh, 136, 142–143.
595. Terry Martin and Kenneth Doka, "Masculine Grief," in Doka, *Sudden Loss*, 163, 165.
596. Lindemann, Erich, "Symptomatology and Management of Acute Grief," in Williamson, 192.
597. Weiss, "The Attachment Bond," in Parkes et al., *Attachment*, 74, 75; See also Weiss, "Loss and Recovery," 48–9; Lehman, et al., 218–231.
598. Earl Grollman, "Spiritual Support After Sudden Loss," in Doka, *Living with Grief: After Sudden Loss*, 185–7.
599. Shakespeare, *King John*, Act IV, scene ii, 84.
600. *Ibid.*, Act III, scene iv, 72–3.
601. Mercer, Dorothy, "The role of religious affiliation and activity in recovery from drunk driving bereavement and injury," unpublished manuscript (1991); cited in Doka, ed., *Living with Grief: After Sudden Loss*, 36.
602. Janice Harris Lord, "America's Number One Killer: Vehicular Crashes," in Doka, ed., *Living with Grief: After Sudden Loss*, 36.
603. Haugk, 40.
604. Excerpted from my essay for *Broadview Magazine*, "Grieving at My Own Pace/A Time to Weep," (May 2020).
605. Jackson, 35.
606. Linton, *Poetry*, 41.
607. Nowatzki and Kalischuk, 91–111.
608. Translated by William Woodward in Woodward, 34.
609. Lotze, "The Divine Personality," (*Mikrokosmus* (1854–6), in Reardon, 137; tr. Elizabeth Hamilton and Constance Jones.
610. Joachim Pissarro, "The Formation of Crepuscular and Nocturnal Themes in van Gogh's Early Writings," in van Heugten, et al., 55.
611. The four poems Vincent inscribed: "Abendfeier," "O wie mild der Abendrauch," "Das Abendlied vom Turme" and "Abendstille." Pabst, 64; Baumann, 158; De Leeuw, 57.
612. Kōdera, 21; Haranburu Oiharbide, 5.
613. Baumann, 121.
614. Soth, 188.
615. Veldhorst, 70–1.
616. Pabst, 16.
617. There are many indirect references in the letters. These seven specifically name Rückert or quote from him: 15 July 1875; 24 July 1875; 1 September 1875; 12 September 1875; 18 September 1877; 3 April 1878; 10 April 1882.
618. Vincent also sent Rückert's "Aus der Jugendzeit" in the same letter. Vincent to Theo, 24 July 1875, *Vincent van Gogh: The Letters*, Van Gogh Museum, http://vangoghletters.org/vg/letters/let039/letter.html.
619. *Weltschmerz*.
620. My translation here uses the text as published in *Gedichte Von Friedrich Rückert* (Sauerländer, 1886), 389–90, which varies slightly from the well-known libretto of Mahler's *lied*, set to music by the composer in 1899. See also Rückert, "Um Mitternacht," in *Ausgewählte Werke*, v1, 234–5.
621. Goedeke, 162.
622. *Hirtenlied*.
623. Lenau to J. Kerner, mid-January 1835, in Goedeke, 163.
624. Gillies, et al., 61–74.
625. Parkes and Prigerson, xv.
626. Lenau to Schurz, 22 February 1835, in Goedeke, 163.
627. The Rückert Archives still hold letter from Frothingham (dated 1837), in which the reverend discusses his translation with the poet.
628. Horton, *Harper's Magazine* (19 July 2009).
629. Neumann, 80–90.
630. Horton, *Harper's Magazine* (19 July 2009).
631. Le Grange, 299.
632. Walter, 166; translated by Henry-Louis de La Grange in La Grange, 367.
633. When Natalie left that summer, Mahler gave her three of his *Kindertotenlieder*, which would ultimately be numbers 1, 3 and 4 in the composer's song cycle (Poems 300, 56 I & II, and 368 in Rückert's *Songs on the Death of Children*). These are likely the same pieces he played for her. (La Grange, 368n191.) In 1904, Mahler wrote

numbers 2 and 5 (Poems 68 and 336 in Rückert). (La Grange, 827.)
634. La Grange, 368.
635. Cushman, 4. There are many similarities, the most striking being the first of Mahler's *Kindertotenlieder* and the Funeral March in his Fifth Symphony: La Grange notes bars 313–15 especially. (La Grange, 368–9n191.)
636. Baumann, 121.
637. Stephen Hefling, "The Genesis of "Ich bin der Welt abhanden gekommen,"" in Kaplan, ed., 21
638. Vedder, et al., 48.
639. Kovarsky, 86–96.
640. Snauwaert, DOI: 10.1080/03069885.2021.1951661.
641. Morrison, 15–16.
642. Yancey, *Question*, 138–9.
643. See Heinrich Rückert's preface to KTL, iii. Also, an excellent discussion in KTL-W.
644. Hamman, 199.
645. For a concise discussion of survivor syndrome among bereaved parents, see Knapp, *Beyond Endurance*, 32.
646. 2 Samuel 18:33 (NRSV)
647. Brueggemann, 263–75.
648. Mother Teresa to Father Joseph Neuner, April 1961, in Mother Teresa, 210.
649. Sanders, 40.
650. Nancy Boyd Webb, "Play Therapy to Help Bereaved Children," in Doka, *Children and Adolescents*, 269, 278.
651. Bauer, 40, 51–2.
652. Paul Rosenblatt, "A Social Constructionist Perspective on Cultural Differences in Grief," in Stroebe, et al., eds., *Handbook of Bereavement Research*, 285–300.
653. Robert Neimeyer, "The Language of Loss: Grief Therapy as a Process of Meaning Reconstruction," in Neimeyer, ed., *Meaning Reconstruction*, 261.
654. Hühn, 10.
655. Muncker, "In der gesamten Natur...," 50; see also a useful discussion on empathy, a term of German coinage, in Boddice.
656. Bowra, 9.
657. Morten Solvik, "The literary and philosophical worlds of Gustav Mahler," in Barham, 29. See also Hefling in *ibid..*, 109.
658. "Ich hatte Anlass die geniale Verständnisfähigkeit des Mannes zu bewundern," Freud to Theodor Reik, 1 April 1935, in Reik, 343.
659. Steindl-Rast, 20, 23.
660. Mother Teresa to Father Joseph Neuner, 6 March 1962, in Mother Teresa, 1.
661. O'Donohue, *Anam Cara*, 94.
662. *La vida es sueño*; Cruickshank, 78.
663. Calderón, *Life Is a Dream (La vida es sueño)*, Act I, scene ii, in *Calderon's Dramas*, tr. Denis Florence MacCarthy, 15.
664. *El Principe constante*; Küpper, *Discursive "Renovatio,"* 293.
665. Behler, 437–60; *The Constant Prince* in German, *Der standhafte Prinz (El principe constante)*, in Calderón, *Schauspiele von Don Pedro Calderon de la Barca*, v2, translated into German by August Schlegel (Julius Eduard Hitzig, 1809): 1–162. Goethe to Schiller, "Ja, ich möchte sagen, wenn die Poesie ganz von der Welt verloren ginge, so könnte man sie aus diesem Stück wieder herstellen," 28 January 1804, in Goethe, *Gedenkausgabe der Werke*, XX: 964f. The Romantic Era use of *Poesie* is not interchangeable with the modern word, *Literatur*, but the intent is the same in this context; see "History as Divine Pageant," in Kluge, 170. For more on Poesie, see the translator note for "In loss it is difficult to begin."
666. Calderón, "Que eran cobardes, decia un sabio, por parecerle Que nunca andaba una sola," 45. The verse translation: Calderón, *Life is a Dream (La vida es sueño)*, Act II, scene xii, in *Calderon;s Dramas*, tr. Denis Florence MacCarthy, 67.
667. Ekanayake, et al., 71.
668. Tedeschi, *Helping*, 8, 9, 10, 13; Worden, *Counseling*, 30, 31; Hendin, 183.
669. Wieseltier, 166.
670. *Durchsichtige Saffieren*, a blue-transparent gemstone. See KTL-W, 605.
671. Ludger Lieb and Ricarda Wagner, "Dead Writing Matters? Materiality and Presence in Medieval German Narrations of Epitaphs," in Berti, et al., eds., 19.
672. "ein tiwer rubîn ist der stein / ob sîme grabe, dâ durch er schein," in Lachmann, 60.
673. Andrea Schindler, "*ein ritter allenthalben rôt*: Die Bedeutung von Farben im *Parzival*, Wolframs von Eschenbach," in Bennewitz and Schindler, eds, 471.
674. Poets, artists and musicians report the most vivid experiences. For an engrossing discussion, see Goss and Klass, 6–7.
675. Peng-Keller, 6.
676. Rilke to Countess Margo Sizzo-Noris-Crouy, 23 January 1924, Macy, February 27; Cholbi, *Grief*, i.
677. 1 Corinthians 13:12 KJV.
678. 1 Korinther 13:12, *Die Bibel* [1834], *Neue Testament*, German tr. Martin Luther, 183. See translator note for this poem.
679. Gill, 427, 428.
680. Behm, 315–42.
681. Paraphrased from Gill, 429.
682. DuBose, 367–74.
683. Parker, 257–83.
684. Burke, et al., 268–81.
685. La Grange, 783.
686. Dirk Vanderbeke, "Überlegungen zur Ästhetik in der Literatur und in den Naturwissenschaften," in Heydenreich, et al., eds., *Quarks and Letters*, 117.
687. For the Good Samaritan example, see Borg and Crossan, 34. For a fascinating discussion on the manner in which knowledge guarantees truth, and can therefore be linguistically factive (i.e., a verb that assigns the status of an established fact to its object) see Johannes Stern, "Belief, Truth, and Ways of Believing," in Nicolai and Stern, eds., 151–81; especially 151, 174–6.
688. Gilson, 45.

689. Heisenberg, "Die Bedeutung des Schönen in den exakten Naturwissenschaften," in *Schritte über Grenzen*, 289.
690. Gilson, 44.
691. *Ibid.*, 144.
692. Jeff Gates, "Knowledge, Understanding, Wisdom: A Biblical Model of Information Literacy," in Trott, ed., 106.
693. Dreisbach, 531–2.
694. Quoted by Pauck, 20–1, 23, 24. The same essay discusses Tillich's famous observation: *Der Glaube ist das Ergriffensein von dem was einen unbedingt angeht* (Faith is the state of being grasped by that which concerns one unconditionally.) Pauck's discussion of *Ergriffensein* and *angeht* in the context of Tillich's statement is particularly illuminating.
695. Jenkins, 80, 83.
696. For a different translation, see Arthur Waley's fine discussion in *The Way and Its Power* (Evergreen, 1958): 155.
697. Rückert, "Etwas wünschen und verlangen. / Etwas hoffen muß das Herz, / Etwas zu verlieren bangen, / Und um etwas fühlen Schmerz." The first stanza of a piece commonly referred to as *Wünsch* (*Wish*), from "Neue Lieder April-Mai 1832," strophe 16, *Gesammelte Gedichte*, v3 (Sauerländer, 1843), 9. Czech composer Zdeněk Fibich set *Wünsch* to music in 1865.
698. Klass, "Grief, Consolation, and Religions," 5–6.
699. Murphy, et al., *Journal of Nursing Scholarship 35*, 359–64; Neimeyer, "Searching for the Meaning of Meaning," 541–58.
700. Wolterstorff, 98.
701. Kuntsch, *Bemüht euch nicht mir Tröstung zu zusprechen / Kein Wunder wär es möcht das Band zerbrechen / Daß meinen Leib mit seiner Seel' verbind*, "Das blutende Mutter=Hertz," lines 31–3, in Carrdus, Anna, ed., *Das "weiblich Werk" in der Residenzstadt Altenburg : 1672–1720: Gedichte und Briefe von Margaretha Susanna von Kuntsch und Frauen in ihrem Umkreis* (Olms, 2004): 127; cited in Linton, 1, 4.
702. Milton, *Paradise Lost*, ix, 1101–7; 79. Emphasis in original. I have tacitly edited this well-known passage for modern readers. Malabar refers to India's western or southwestern coast; Deccan, the southern part or the whole of the peninsula. See Milton, 79n1103.
703. In India the tree is called *vata*.
704. Ram, 127.
705. Radwanska-Williams, 11–8.
706. Ram, 127.
707. As did the eastern influences of Goethe. See Georg Langenhorst, "Interreligiöses Lernen mit literarischen Texten? Theologisch-literarische Perspektiven—Beispiel Islam," in von Stosch and Hofmann, eds., 109–35; Sprenger, 187–9; Elke Segelcke, "'Occident and Orient': Poetics of Movement" in the Works of Zafer Şenocak," in Brinker-Gabler and Shea, eds., 115–26.
708. The final lines of Rückert's song, *mehr weiß ich nicht, weil alle meine Zweige / tief unten ruhn und nur im Winde winken* seem to have influenced Rilke's poem, which reads: "In den Boden senkt die untern Zweige, / Und die obern wiegt im Sonnenschein."
709. Bly, in Rilke, *Selected Poems*, tr. Robert Bly, 5.
710. Rilke, "Doch wie ich mich auch in mich selber neige," *Das Stunden-Buch*, 4.
711. Buckle, Jennifer and Stephen Fleming, "Parenting Challenges After the Death of a Child," Neimeyer, *Grief and Bereavement*, 93, 97.
712. *Dein Konig kommt in niedern Hüllen*.
713. Dufrechou, 357–78.
714. Bacon, "Of Regiment of Health," *Essays*, 178.
715. Addison, 102.
716. Beopjeong, 102.
717. Knapp, 183.
718. *Ibid.*, 184.
719. Rittgers, 257–8.
720. God's wrath: *Gottes Zorn*.
721. Kowalik, 109.
722. Job 9:16 CJB.
723. Moshe Halbertal, "Job, the Mourner," in Batnitzky and Pardes, eds., 42, 43.
724. Wilkes, 299–310.
725. Frankl, 39.
726. While the biblical passage refers to a geographic location, Friedrich uses the common symbolic interpretation of the phrase. The Hebrew in this biblical passage, עֵמֶק הַבָּכָא, with which language Rückert was conversant, is referring to the dry Baka Valley. The word Baka (בָּכָא) means "weeping," and so this geographic name translates literally as "the valley of weeping" or "vale of tears." (Bouchard, 41n7.) This passage is listed in most English-language Bibles as 84:6. Luther followed the traditional Hebrew numbering, listing it as 84:7. Psalm 84:7, *Die Bibel* [1834], German tr. Martin Luther, 544.
727. Matthew 25:14–30.
728. McIsaac, 152–3.
729. Buechner, *Secrets in the Dark*, 117–8.
730. Buechner material excerpted from Bannon, "Family Secrets," https://philipyancey.com/family-secrets.
731. Bonanno, 19.
732. Jaffee, in Morgan, ed., *Ethical Issues*, 283–96.

Supplemental Poems

733. Rückert to Albrecht Fischer, 1 April 1834, Coburg, in KTL-W, 535.
734. Forssman, "Gastlichkeit im Hause Rückert," 18 March 2019. Albrecht was Luise's adoptive father. Her biological father, Karl Friedrich Wiethaus, had died on 21 March 1799 at the age of twenty-five. Luise was one year and four months old. Four years later, her mother married Albrecht Fischer. When Albrecht died in 1836, he left his Neuses estate to Friedrich and Luise. Her mother lived with them for a time.
735. Anna Luise Magdalene Rückert (Witthaus-

Fischer), 17 November 1797–26 June 1857; KTL-W, 608.
736. Holland and Neimeyer, 80.
737. Shankar, et al., 103–11.
738. McCown and Davies, 41–53.
739. Kroen, 54.
740. Packman, et al., 817–41.
741. Nigel Field, "Whether to relinquish or maintain a bond with the deceased," in Stroebe, et al., *Handbook*, 113–32.
742. Byron, "Epistle to Augusta," 20.
743. Ralf Georg Czapla, "Kindstod als Pop-Spektakel," in LEB, 337–8.
744. Ralf Georg Czapla, "Kindstod als Pop-Spektakel," in LEB, 339.
745. Hall, 219–32.
746. *kindchen*.
747. Davis Bush (Prend), 80.
748. Jacob, 20–4.
749. Boelen and Smid, *BMJ 357* (2017).
750. Rostila, et al., 239–47.
751. Bowlby-West, 279–94.
752. "Sie erkennt in der Kindheit eine mythisch-zauberhaft Zeit, in der Traum und Endloses, Naives un Göttliches harmonisch nebeneinander bestehen," Ortrud Gutjahr, "Auf dem Schauplatz eines frühen Selbst. Inszenierungsformen von Kindheit in der Literatur," in Lange-Kirchheim, et al., eds., *Kindheiten*, 35–56.
753. Denis Forasacco, "In ihrem großen Leib [...] waren zwei Früchte: ein Kind und ein Tod," in in LEB, 153.
754. Dickinson, *Poems* (1998), 1064.
755. Raphael, 173–80.
756. Bendaña, 54–6.
757. Weeks, *Illness, Crisis & Loss*, 113–25.
758. From Longfellow, "Holidays," in *Sonnets*, 20.
759. Knapp, 178–179; Klass, "Solace and Immortality," 343–368; Gorer, 49.
760. Musaph, 175–9.
761. Holland and Neimeyer, 103–20.
762. Kugel, *The God of Old*, 190–191. Emphases in original.
763. Jürgen Thym, "Crosscurrents in Song: Six Distinctive Voices," in Hallmark, ed., 180–7; Gorrell, 10–1.
764. Paton, 29.
765. Quoted in Paton, 29.
766. Murphy, et al., *Death Studies 27*, 39–61.
767. Schiff, *Bereaved Parent*, 135–6.

Coda

1. John Hollander, in Honig, 36.
2. Magarshack quoted in McAteer, 89–90.
3. Attridge and Staten, 202, 203.
4. Sylvia Jaki, "*Sie haben feuchte Nüsse*—The Translation of Verbal Humour in German Subtitles of U.S. American Sitcoms," in Knospe, et al., eds., 361, 375–6.
5. Angelika Zirker, "Language Play in Translation: Character and Idiom in Shakespeare's *The Merry Wives of Windsor*," in Knospe, et al., eds., 302.
6. Leal, 102–3.
7. Hayles, 35.
8. Midgley, 35.
9. Nadeau, 25–6.
10. Sören Stumpf, "Free usage of German unique components: Corpus linguistics, psycholinguistics and lexicographical approaches," in Arndt-Lappe, et al., eds., 73; also Michael Hamburger, in Honig, 169.
11. For a discussion on translating cultural concepts, see my essay in *Translation Journal 12*(1).
12. Zhang Longxi, "Translation, Communication, and East-West Understanding," in Lee, ed., 251.
13. For a thorough discussion, see Jim Feist's *Significance in Language: A Theory of Semantics* (Taylor & Francis, 2022).
14. Svea Schauffler, "Wordplay in Subtitles Films—An Audience Study," in Zirker and Winter-Froemel, eds., 230.
15. Michael Hamburger, in Honig, 179; emphasis in original.
16. Octavio Paz, in Honig, 154, 155.
17. *Ibid.*, 155.
18. Edwin Honig, Introduction, in *Ibid.*, 3.
19. Ernst Wendland, "Translating 'translation': What do translators 'translate'?" in Faiq, ed., 12, 18.
20. Johns, 44, 45.
21. "On Translating: An Open Letter, 1590," tr. Charles Jacobs, rev. E. Theodore Bachmann, in Bachmann, ed., *Luther's Works* v35, 189.
22. Rückert quotation and textual observations from Michael Cooperson, "Note on the Translation," in al-Hariri, *Impostures*, xxxiv–xxxvi.
23. Schimmel, 30.
24. Rückert, *Makamen*, v.

Translator Notes

1. Rowley, 161–82.
2. Lindgren, *passim*; Christopher Sapp's discussion of the decline of the preterite tense in favor of the present perfect tense in Early New High German is particularly illuminating: Sapp, 419–50.
3. Klein, 359n2.
4. Martin Durell, "Mit der Sprache ging es immer schon bergab Dynamik, Wandel und Variation aus sprachhistorischer Perspektive," in Plewnia and Witt, 21–2.
5. Non-German speakers may enjoy Bruce Duncan's informative, accessible overview, "The Present Perfect Tense (*das Perfekt*)," http://www.dartmouth.edu/~deutsch/Grammatik/perfect/Perfect.html.
6. Klein, 359, 381.
7. Sascha Monhoff, "Das Totenbuch der Natur: Die "Lesbarkeit der Welt" in Friedrich Rückerts Kindertodtenliedern," in LEB, 251, 252.
8. Geurts and Nouwen, 549, 550.

9. Buchheim, in *Schiller's Wallenstein: Part II—Wallensteins Tod* (1896), 494–5n12.
10. Schiller, *Wallenstein*, Act V, scene 3, 138.
11. Crisman, 132.
12. Coleridge, in *Friedrich Schiller's Works* (1903), 345n1. Emphasis in original.
13. PW 3:205.
14. BL 2:142; cf BL 1:23.
15. Burwick, 108.
16. Hayward, "Preface to the Second Edition of the Translation," in *Faust* (1834), xvi–xvii.
17. Ernest Hartley Coleridge, grandson of Samuel and a scholar in his own right, note to *The Death of Wallenstein*, in *Complete Poetical Works* (1912), 796.
18. Schiller, *Wallenstein* (1827), tr. George Moir, 271.
19. Schiller, *Wallenstein's Death*, tr. Francis Lamport, in *The Robbers & Wallenstein* (1979), 454. This passage is quoted for purposes of research, scholarship, review, comment and illustration. Pursuant to 17 U.S. Code § 107, certain uses of copyrighted material "for purposes such as criticism, comment, news reporting, teaching (including multiple copies for classroom use), scholarship, or research, is not an infringement of copyright."
20. Kohl, 40–1.
21. Goethe, "Dichtung und Wahrheit," *Goethes Werke in zwei Bänden* (1891), 320; emphasis in original.
22. Goethe, *The Auto-biography of Goethe* (1848), tr. John Oxenford, 451; emphasis in original.
23. *Empfindung*.
24. Translated and discussed in Schreiber, 46.
25. Michael Neumann, "Vom Furor der Formerfindung: Friedrich Rückerts *Kindertodtenlieder*," in LEB, 240–1.
26. Ovid, *Tristia*, book 1, elegy 1, tr. into German, Kirchhof, 6.
27. Ovid, *Tristia*, book 1, elegy 1, tr. into English, Wheeler, 7–9.
28. Goethe, *Hermann und Dorothea*, 3–4.
29. Ibershoff, 78–9.
30. KTL-W, 598.

31. Klein, 359, 381.
32. Friedberg, 190–1.
33. Mueller, 107.
34. Ferber, 2.
35. Beiser, 1–2, and in fairness to the author's excellent thematic approach, passim.
36. Geurts and Nouwen, 549, 550.
37. La Grange, 783.
38. Geurts and Nouwen, 549.
39. Mitzman, 65.
40. Schwartz, 143–150; Fischer, Andreas, Gisbert Schalitz and Christoph Behling, "Breed-specific classification potentials of sheep in different grassland biotopes in the German federal state of Brandenburg," in Vliegher and Carlier, 568–71. Both works provide historical and contemporary overviews of sheepherding patterns and practices across the Germany, particularly Fischer, et al.
41. For a detailed study of mental representations and inflected words in German, see Clahsen and Eisenbeiss, 511, 521, 533–4.
42. Eythórsson and Barðdal, 847, 824–81.
43. Gorlée, 235–70.
44. *Ibid*.
45. Johan Wijnants, "Opera Surtitles: a New Text Between Libretto, Score, Translation, and Performance," in Cavagna and Constantino, eds., 39–40.
46. Claire Brua, soloist, *Kindertotenlieder*, conductor Amaury du Closel, G.B. Productions, March 1997. This DVD release used subtitles from an earlier Decca release, © 1960, liner notes, *Mahler: Symphony No. 9—Kindertotenlieder*, Christa Ludwig, Herbert von Karajan, Deutsch Grammophon, 1975, 12. Thomas Hampson, liner notes, *Kindertotenlieder*, with Wolfram Reiger, EMI Classics, 1997, 12. Agni Baltsa as Agnes Baltsa, liner notes, *Mahler: Symphony 3—Kindertotenlieder*, Lorin Maazel, CBS, 1987: 46.
47. Attridge and Staten, 144.
48. KTL-W, 605.
49. Griffith, 1915.
50. *Die Bibel* [1834], *Neue Testament*, German tr. Martin Luther, 31.
51. KTL-W, 609.

Bibliography

Papers, Journals, Periodicals, Documents, Audio/Video and Internet Sources

Aberbach, David, "Grief and Mysticism," *International Review of Psycho-Analysis 14* (1987): 509–26.

_____, "Mystical Union and Grief: The Ba'al Shem Tov and Krishnamurti," *Harvard Theological Review 86*(3) (July 1993): 309–21.

Abernethy, Alexis D., H. Theresa Chang, Larry Seidlitz, James S. Evinger, and Paul R. Duberstein, "Religious Coping and Depression Among Spouses of People with Lung Cancer," *Psychosomatics 43*(6) (2002): 456–63.

Adams, Kate, and Brendan Hyde, "Children's grief dreams and the theory of spiritual intelligence," *Dreaming 18*(1) (2008): 58–67.

Ano, Gene, and Erin Vasconcelles, "Religious Coping and Psychological Adjustment to Stress: A Meta-analysis," *Journal of Clinical Psychology 61*(4) (October 2004): 461–80.

Arndt-Lappe, Sabine, Angelika Braun, Claudine Moulin, and Esme Winter-Froemel, *Expanding the Lexicon: Linguisitc Innovation, Morphological Productivity, and Ludicity* (de Gruyter, 2018).

Attig, Thomas, "Disenfranchised Grief Revisited: Discounting Hope and Love," *OMEGA—Journal of Death and Dying 49*(3) (2004): 197–215.

_____, "The Importance of Conceiving of Grief as an Active Process," *Death Studies 15*(4) (1991): 385–393.

Augsburger Postzeitung, "Friedrich Rückert's Kindertodtenlieder (*Aus ſeinem Nachlaſſe*)," 13 February 1873 (Haas & Grabherr, 1873): 39–40.

Averill, James, "Grief: Its nature and significance," *Psychological Bulletin 70*(6, Pt.1) (1968): 721–48.

Balogh, Joseph: "Tänze in Kirchen und auf Friedhöfen," *Niederdeutsche Zeitschrift für Volkskunde 6* (1928): 1–14.

Bannon, David, "Family Secrets," *PhilipYancey.com* (23 August 2020): https://philipyancey.com/family-secrets.

_____, "Grief in the White House," *History Magazine* (Winter 2020/21): 31–5.

_____, "Grieving at My Own Pace/A Time to Weep," *Broadview Magazine* (May 2020): https://broadview.org/church-grief-response/.

_____, "$#*! My Translator Says: Cursing in Subtitles," *The ATA Chronicle (American Translators Association) 15*(1) (2011): 30–4.

_____, "The Surprising Faith of Job's Wife," *Hevria Magazine* (17 July 2019): https://hevria.com/davidbannon/the-surprising-faith-of-jobs-wife/.

_____, "Unique Korean Cultural Concepts in Interpersonal Relations," *Translation Journal 12*(1) (2008): http://www.translationjournal.net/journal/43korean.htm.

Bauer, Thomas, "Communication and Emotion: The Case of Ibn Nubātah's *Kindertotenlieder*," *Mamlūk Studies Review 7*(1) (2003): 49–95.

Baumann, Timo, Frank Sparing, Michael Martin, and Heiner Fangerau, "Neurophysiologen im Nationalsozialismus—Hans Berger, Paul Hoffmann, Richard Jung und Alois E. Kornmüller" ("Neurophysiologists and National Socialism—Hans Berger, Paul Hoffmann, Richard Jung and Alois E. Kornmüller"), *Klinische Neurophysiologie 51*(1) (2020): 14–41.

Behler, Ernst, "The Reception of Calderón Among the German Romantics," *Studies in Romanticism 20*(4) (Winter, 1981): 437–60. Presented at the symposium, "Calderón in Context," University of Wisconsin, 27–28 March 1981.

Behm, D.J., "Das Bildwort von Spiegel I Korinther 13, 12," *Rheinhold Seeburg Festschrift I* (1929): 315–42.

Bendaña, Ana, "Coping with Grief During the Holidays," *Nursing 47*(11) (November 2017): 54–6.

Benes, Tuska, "Transcending Babel in the Cultural Translation of Friedrich Rückert," *Modern Intellectual History 8*(1) (April 2011): 61–90.

Benore, Ethan, and Crystal Park, "Death-Specific Religious Beliefs and Bereavement: Belief in an Afterlife and Continued Attachment," *The International Journal for the Psychology of Religion 14*(1) (2004): 1–22.

Bergstraesser, Eva, Susanne Inglin, Rainer Hornung, and Markus A. Landolt, "Dyadic Coping of Parents After the Death of a Child," *Death Studies 39*(3) (2015): 128–38.

Bialystok, Ellen, "Reshaping the Mind: The Benefits of Bilingualism," *Canadian Journal of Experimental Psychology/Revue canadienne de psychologie expérimentale 65*(4): 229–35.

Black, Joshua, Kathryn Belicki, Robert Piro, and Hannah Hughes, "Comforting Versus Distressing Dreams of the Deceased: Relations to Grief, Trauma, Attachment, Continuing Bonds, and Post-Dream Reactions," *OMEGA—Journal of Death and Dying*, OnlineFirst (9 February 2020): https://doi.org/10.1177/0030222820903850.

Bleeker, C. Jouco, "Isis and Nephthys as Wailing Women," *Numen* 5(1) (1958): 1–17.

Blegen, Theodore, "A Note on Schiller's Indian Threnody," *Minnesota History* (Spring 1965).

Bobzin, Hartmut, "Friedrich Rückert (1788–1866): Ein vergessener Alttestamentler und Hebräist," *Zeitschrift für die Alttestamentliche Wissenschaft* 101(2) (01 January 1989): 173–84.

Boelen, Paul A., and Geert E. Smid, "Disturbed Grief: Prolonged Grief Disorder and Persistent Complex Bereavement Disorder," *BMJ: British Medical Journal* 357 (2017).

Bolton, Christopher, and Delpha Camp, "Funeral Rituals and the Facilitation of Grief Work," *Omega—Journal of Death and Dying* 17(4) (1986–87): 343–52.

———, and ———, "The Post-Funeral Ritual in Bereavement Counseling and Grief Work," *Journal of Gerontological Social Work* 13(3–4) (1989): 49–59.

Bonanno, George, "Laughter During Bereavement," *Bereavement Care* 18(2) (1999): 19–22.

Boss, Pauline, "Ambiguous Loss in Families of the Missing," *The Lancet* 360 (Special Issue) (01 December 2002): 39–40.

Bouchard, Gary, "Robert Southwell's 'A Vale of Tears' as a Critique of Pastoral Poetry," *Studies: An Irish Quarterly Review* 107(425) (Spring 2018): 28–42.

Bowlby, John, "Attachment and Loss: Retrospect and Prospect," *American Journal of Orthopsychiatry* 52(4) (1982): 664–78.

Bowlby-West, Lorna, "The Impact of Death on the Family System," *Journal of Family Therapy* 5(3) (1983): 279–94.

Brophy, Seán, "Reviewed Work: Redemption Road: Grieving on the Camino by Brendan McManus," *Studies: An Irish Quarterly Review* 105(417) (Irish Province of the Society of Jesus, 2016): 127–30.

Brown, W., and V. Allison, "Infection of the Air of Scarlet-Fever Wards with Streptococcus Pyogenes," *Journal of Hygiene* 37(1) (1937): 1–13.

Brueggemann, Walter, "The Formfulness of Grief," *Interpretation: A Journal of Bible and Theology* 31(3) (1977): 263–75.

Bullock, Michael, "The Grief-Relief Process: Coping with the Life and Death of Physically and Mentally Disabled Children," *Orthopedic Clinics of North America* 12(1) (January 1981): 193–200.

Burke, Laurie, Robert Neimeyer, Amanda Young, Elizabeth Piazza Bonin, and Natalie Davis, "Complicated Spiritual Grief II: A Deductive Inquiry Following the Loss of a Loved One," *Death Studies* 38(4) (2014): 268–81.

Burnham, Scott, "The Stillness of Time, the Fullness of Space: Four Settings of Goethe's 'Wandrers Nachtlied.'" *19th-Century Music* 40(3) (2017): 189–200.

Burwick, Frederick, "Coleridge's Art of Translation," *The Wordsworth Circle* 38(3) (2007): 108–12.

Bybee, Joan, "From Usage to Grammar: The Mind's Response to Repetition," *Language* 82(4) (December 2006): 711–33.

Carr, Deborah, John Sonnega, Randolph Nesse, and James S. House, "Do Special Occasions Trigger Psychological Distress Among Older Bereaved Spouses? An Empirical Assessment of Clinical Wisdom," *The Journals of Gerontology Series B: Psychological Sciences and Social Sciences* 69B(1) (January 2014): 113–122.

Carrdus, Anna, "Consolatory Dialogue in Devotional Writings by Men and Women of Early Modern Protestant Germany," *The Modern Language Review* 93(2) (April 1998): 411–27. First delivered at the Conference of University Teaches of German in Great Britain and Ireland, 10–12 April 1995.

Castle, Jason, and William Phillips, "Grief Rituals: Aspects That Facilitate Adjustment to Bereavement," *Journal of Loss and Trauma* 8(1) (2003): 41–71.

Caswell, Glenys, "Beyond Words: Some Uses of Music in the Funeral Setting," *OMEGA—Journal of Death and Dying* 64(4) (2012): 319–34.

Century Media, "Maroon: Order" release notes (17 April 2009). https://www.centurymedia.com/artist.aspx?IdArtist=125 Retrieved 05 July 2021.

Chamisso, Adelbert von, and Gustav Schwab, eds., *Deutscher Musenalmanach für die Jahr 1834* (Weidmannsche Buchhandlung, December 1833).

Charles, Ray, Liner Notes, *Ray Charles: The Music That Matters To Him* (Hear Music, 2002).

Chavassee, Pye H., "Treatment of Scarlatina Anginosa," *Southern Medical and Surgical Journal* 12(6) (June 1856).

Clahsen, Harald, and Sonja Eisenbeiss, "The Mental Representation of Inflected Words: An Experimental Study of Adjectives and Verbs in German," *Language* 77(3) (September 2001): 510–43.

Cleiren, Marc, René Diekstra, Ad Kerkhof, and Jan van der Wal, "Mode of Death and Kinship in Bereavement: Focusing on 'Who' Rather Than 'How,'" *Crisis* 15(1) (1994): 22–36.

———, Onja Grad, Anka Zavasnik, and Rene Diekstra, "Psychosocial Impact of Bereavement after Suicide and Fatal Traffic Accident: A Comparative Two-country Study," *Acta Psychiatrica Scandinavica* 94(1) (July 1996): 37–44.

Coelho, Alexandra, Maja de Brito, Pedro Teixeira, Pedro Frade, Luísa Barros, and António Barbosa, "Family Caregivers' Anticipatory Grief: A Conceptual Framework for Understanding Its Multiple Challenges," *Qualitative Health Research* 30(5) (April 2020): 693–703.

Cohen, Judith A., and Anthony P. Mannarino, "Trauma-Focused CBT for Traumatic Grief in

Military Children," *Journal of Contemporary Psychotherapy* 41(4) (2011): 219–27.

Crick, Joyce, "Some Editorial and Stylistic Observations on Coleridge's Translation of Schiller's Wallenstein," *English Goethe Society: Papers Read before the Society 1983–84* (1985): 37–75.

Crisman, William, "Coleridge's 'Wallenstein' Translations as a Guide to His Dejection Ode," *The Wordsworth Circle* 18(3) (1987): 132–6.

Cushman, Robert, "Walter Plays Mahler," liner notes, *Mahler Symphony No. 5*, Bruno Walter and the New York Philharmonic, *Masterworks Portrait*, recorded 10 February 1947 (Sony Classical, 1991).

David, Stacy, "Appearances of the Resurrected Jesus and the Experience of Grief," *unpublished paper*, Jesus Seminar, Santa Rosa, CA. (1995).

Davis, Christopher G., Susan Nolen-Hoeksema, and Judith Larson, "Making Sense of Loss and Benefiting from the Experience: Two Construals of Meaning," *Journal of Personality and Social Psychology* 75(2) (August 1998): 561–74.

Davis, Ellen, *Getting Involved with God: Rediscovering the Old Testament* (Rowman & Littlefield, 2001).

Denhup, Christine Yvonne, "A New State of Being: The Lived Experience of Parental Bereavement," *OMEGA—Journal of Death and Dying* 74(3) (February 2017): 345–60.

Dickens, Charles, "A Christmas Tree," *Household Words* 2(39) (21 December 1850): 1–7.

———, "What Christmas Is, as We Grow Older," *Household Words* (Christmas, 1851): 1–3.

Dreisbach, Donald, "Essence, Existence, and the Fall: Paul Tillich's Analysis of Existence," *The Harvard Theological Review* 73(3/4) (1980): 521–38.

DuBose, J. Todd, "The Phenomenology of Bereavement, Grief, and Mourning," *Journal of Religion and Health* 36 (1997): 367–74.

Dufrechou, Jay, "We Are One: Grief, Weeping, and Other Deep Emotions in Response to Nature as a Path Toward Wholeness," *The Humanistic Psychologist* 32(4) (September 2004): 357–378.

Duncan, Bruce, "Grammar Review," http://www.dartmouth.edu/~deutsch/Grammatik/Grammatik.html. Non-German speakers interested in an introductory overview of German tenses could do worse than this clear, concise and accessible review from Bruce Duncan, Dartmouth Professor of German Language Emeritus.

Dunn, Judy, "Sibling Relationships in Early Childhood," *Child Development* 54(4) (August 1983): 787–811.

Edwards, Haley Sweetland, and Belinda Luscombe, "United by Grief," *TIME Magazine* (10 December 2018): 28–35.

Ekanayake, Samanthika, Martin Prince, Athula Sumathipala, Sisira Siribaddana, and Craig Morgan, "'We Lost All We Had in a Second': Coping with Grief and Loss After a Natural Disaster," *World Psychiatry* 12(1) (February 2013): 69–75.

Enez, Özge, "Complicated Grief: Epidemiology, Clinical Features, Assessment, and Diagnosis," *Psikiyatride Güncel Yaklaşımlar* 3 (October 2018): 269–79.

Erlanger Rückert-Kreis, "Eindrücke vergangener Veranstaltungen" (2019), http://www.rückert-kreis.de/rueckert-kreis-alte-Veranstaltungen.html.

Eythórsson, Thórhallur, and Jóhanna Barðdal, "Oblique Subjects: A Common Germanic Inheritance," *Language* 81(4) (December 2005): 824–81.

Fellinger, Imogen, "Brahms-Studien, Band 11," *Die Musikforschung* 53(1) (2000): 104–6.

Forssman, Ingeborg, "Gastlichkeit im Hause Rückert," lecture, Stadtbibliothek Erlangen, 18 March 2019; http://www.rückert-kreis.de/PDF/2019-03-18_Gastfreundschaft%20im%20Hause.pdf.

Friedberg, Lilian, " Verbrechen, Die Ich Meine...': 'Manners of Death' as Thickly Descriptive Translation of 'Todesarten,'" *Monatshefte* 94(2) (2002): 189–208.

Fruzińska, Justyna, "'I Grieve That Grief Can Teach Me Nothing': Emerson, Grief, and the Annihilation of History," *AAA: Arbeiten Aus Anglistik Und Amerikanistik* 44(2) (2019): 159–66.

Fuhrmann, Horst, "Gedenkworte für Golo Mann," *Orden Pour le mérite für Wissenschaften und Künste*, v24 (Lambert Schneider, 1993–94): 115–21.

Gamino, Louis, Larry Easterling, Linda Stirman, and Kenneth Sewell, "Grief Adjustment as Influenced by Funeral Participation and Occurrence of Adverse Funeral Events," *OMEGA—Journal of Death and Dying* 41(2) (October 2000): 79–92.

Gamlin, Ryan, and S. Kinghorn, "Using hope to cope with loss and grief," *Nursing Standard* 9(48) (1995): 33–5.

Gegieckaite, Goda, and Evaldas Kazlauskas, "Fear of Death and Death Acceptance Among Bereaved Adults: Associations with Prolonged Grief," *OMEGA—Journal of Death and Dying* (April 2020): doi:10.1177/0030222820921045.

Gerhard, U.J., A. Schönberg, and B. Blanz, "'Hätte Berger das Ende des zweiten Weltkrieges noch erlebt—gewiss wäre er ein Anwärter auf den Nobelpreis geworden'—Hans Berger und die Legende vom Nobelpreis" ("'If Berger had Survived the Second World War—He Certainly would have been a Candidate for the Nobel Prize.' Hans Berger and the Legend of the Nobel Prize"), *Fortschritte der Neurollogie—Psychiatrie* 73(3) (2005): 156–60.

Geurts, Bart, and Rick Nouwen, "*At Least*, et al.: The Semantics of Scalar Modifiers," *Language* 83(3) (September 2007): 533–59.

Gibson, G.J., "Horace, Carm. 3.30.1–5," *The Classical Quarterly* 47(1) (1997): 312–4.

Gill, David, "Through a Glass Darkly: A Note on 1 Corinthians 13:12," *The Catholic Biblical Quarterly* 25(4) (1963): 427–9.

Gillies, James, Robert Neimeyer, and Evgenia

Milman, "The Grief and Meaning Reconstruction Inventory (GMRI): Initial Validation of a New Measure," *Death Studies* 39(2) (2015): 61–74.

Gilovich, Thomas, and Victoria Husted Medvec, "The Experience of Regret: What, When, and Why," *Psychological Review* 102(2) (April 1995): 379–95.

Ginzberg, Raphael, "Three Years with Hans Berger: A Contribution to His Biography," *Journal of the History of Medicine and Allied Sciences* 4(4) (Autumn, 1949): 361–71.

Gorlée, Dinda, "Intercode Translation: Words and Music in Opera," *Target: International Journal of Translation Studies* 9(2) (2 January 1997): 235–70.

Greeley, Andrew, and Michael Hout, "Americans' Increasing Belief in Life After Death: Religious Competition and Acculturation," *American Sociological Review* 64(6) (December 1999): 813–835.

Griffith, M. Patrick, "The Origins of an Important Cactus Crop, Opuntia ficus-indica (Cactaceae): New Molecular Evidence," *American Journal of Botany* 91(11): 1915–21.

Guillot, Marie-Noëlle, "Cross-Cultural Pragmatics and Audiovisual Translation," *Target: International Journal of Translation Studies* 28(2) (January 2016): 288–301.

Hall, M. Elizabeth Lewis, "Suffering in God's Presence: The Role of Lament in Transformation," *Journal of Soul Formation and Soul care* 9(2) (1 Nov 2016): 219–32.

Haranburu Oiharbide, Mikel, Nekane Balluerka Lasa, Arantxa Gorostiaga Manterola, and Jesús Guerra Plaza, "Rasgos Psicopatológicos de Vincent van Gogh," paper presented at XVII Congreso Virtual Internacional de Psiquiatria, 29 February 2016.

Hardin, James, "Reviewed Work: Gedichte des Barock by Ulrich Maché, Volker Meid," *Monatshefte* 75(1) (Spring, 1983): 74–6.

Harms, Viktoria, "Sympathy for a Villain? Suffering Men and Angelic Women in the Novels of Caroline Auguste Fischer (1764–1842)," *Women in German Yearbook* 29 (2013): 41–66.

Heller, Hartmut, "'O Tannenbaum': Textkontrafakturen über konstanter Melodie," *Matreier Gespräche—Schriftenreihe der Forschungsgemeinschaft Wilheminenberg* (2008): 268–77.

Heller, Reinhold, "Kandinsky and Traditions Apocalyptic," *Art Journal* 43(1) (1983): 19–26.

Heschel, Abraham, "On Prayer," *Conservative Judaism* 25(1) (Fall, 1970): 1–12. From a speech delivered on 28 August 1969 at an inter-religious convocation for the U.S. Liturgical Conference, Milwaukee, Wisconsin, USA.

Holland, Jason, and Robert Neimeyer, "An Examination of Stage Theory of Grief among Individuals Bereaved by Natural and Violent Causes: A Meaning-Oriented Contribution," *OMEGA—Journal of Death and Dying* 61(2) (1 Oct 2010): 103–20.

Hood, Thomas, "The Death-bed," *The Englishman's Magazine* 1(5) (August 1832): 572.

Horton, Scott, "Rückert/Mahler—Um Mitternacht," *Harper's Magazine* (19 July 2009): https://harpers.org/2009/07/ruckertmahler-um-mitternacht/.

Hugo, Howard, "An Examination of Friedrich Schlegel's 'Gespräch über die Poesie,'" *Monatshefte* 40(4) (April 1948): 221–31.

Hume, Janice, "'Portraits of Grief,' Reflectors of Values: *The New York Times* Remembers Victims of September 11," *Journalism & Mass Communication Quarterly* 80(1) (March 2003): 166–82.

Ibershoff, C.H., "On a Passage of Friedrich Rückert," *Modern Language Notes* 24(3) (1909): 78–9.

Jacob, Susan, "Facing It Alone: Preholiday Grief," *Journal of Psychosocial Nursing and Mental Health Services* 29(11) (1991): 20–4.

Jakoby, Nina, "Grief as a Social Emotion: Theoretical Perspectives," *Death Studies* 36(8) (2012): 679–711.

Jellinek, Michael, Paul Goldenheim, and Michael Jenike, "The Impact of Grief on Ventilatory Control," *The American Journal of Psychiatry* 142(1) (January 1985): 121–3.

Johnson, Lathrop, "Theory and Practice of the Baroque Echo Poem," *Daphnis* 19(2) (03 Jan 1990): 189–221.

Jones, Logan, "The Psalms of Lament and the Transformation of Sorrow," *Journal of Pastoral Care & Counseling* 61(1–2) (March 2007): 47–58.

Keppler, Kurt, "Origin and Authorship of the *Divan*-Poem 'Nimmer Will Ich Dich Verlieren,'" *Modern Language Notes* 70(6) (1955): 433–7.

Kidorf, Irwin W., "The Shiva: A Form of Group Psychotherapy," *Journal of Religion and Health* 5(1) (1966): 43–6.

Kissane, D.W., and S. Bloch, "Family Grief," *The British Journal of Psychiatry* 164 (1994): 728–40.

Klass, Dennis, "Grief, Consolation, and Religions: A Conceptual Framework," *OMEGA—Journal of Death and Dying* 69(1) (August 2014): 1–18.

———, "Solace and Immortality: Bereaved Parents' Continuing Bond with Their Children," *Death Studies* 17(4) (July/August 1993): 343–68.

———, and Robert Goss, "Spiritual Bonds to the Dead in Cross-Cultural and Historical Perspective: Comparative Religion and Modern Grief," *Death Studies* 23(6) (1999): 547–67.

———, and Samuel Marwit, "Toward a Model of Parental Grief," *Omega* 19(1) (1988–1989): 31–50.

Klein, Reuven Chaim (Rudolph), "Identifying the Daniel Character in Ezekiel," *Jewish Bible Quarterly* 46(4) (2018): 231–41.

Klein, Wolfgang, "An Analysis of the German Perfekt," *Language* 76(2) (June 2000): 358–82.

Klugman, Craig, "Dead Men Talking: Evidence of Post Death Contact and Continuing Bonds," *Omega* 53(3) (2006): 249–262.

Kohl, Katrin, "Wir Wollen Weniger Erhoben, und

Fleissiger Gelesen Sein," *Publications of the English Goethe Society* 60(1): 39–62.

Kollock, P.M., "Health of the City of Savannah During the Winter and Spring of 1856," *Southern Medical and Surgical Journal* 12(6) (June 1856).

Kovarsky, Roslyn, "Loneliness and Disturbed Grief: A Comparison of Parents Who Lost a Child to Suicide or Accidental Death," *Archives of Psychiatric Nursing* 3(2) (1989): 86–96.

Krechel, Ursula, "Mittelwärts," *Monatshefte* 84(2) (1992): 137–40.

Krolow, Karl: Mein Gedicht,—In: *Westermanns Monatshefte* N.F. 26 (April 1974), H. 4, S. 52f. Rückerts "Du bist ein Schatten am Tage...."

Laskow, Sarah, "The Role of the Supernatural in the Discovery of EEGs," *The Atlantic* (23 November 2014): https://www.theatlantic.com/health/archive/2014/11/the-role-of-the-supernatural-in-the-discovery-of-eegs/382838/.

Leaver, Robin, "The Funeral Sermon for Heinrich Schütz, *Bach* 25(2) (1994): 115–29.

Lee, Sherman, Laurin Roberts, and Jeffrey Gibbons, "When Religion Makes Grief Worse: Negative Religious Coping as Associated with Maladaptive Emotional Responding Patterns," *Mental Health, Religion & Culture* 16(3) (2013): 291–305.

Leeuw, Ronald de, "Henry Boughton and the "Beautiful Picture" in Van Gogh's 1876 Sermon," *Van Gogh Museum Journal 1995* (Waanders, 1995): 49–62.

Lehman, Darrin, Camille Wortman, and Allan Williams, "Long-Term Effects of Losing a Spouse or Child in a Motor Vehicle Crash," *Journal of Personality and Social Psychology* 52(1) (1987): 218–231.

Leyk, Wolfgang, "Neustädter Friedhof," Evangelische Gemeinde Erlangen Neustadt, Stadt + Universitäts (2020): https://www.erlangen-neustadt-evangelisch.de/neustaedter-friedhof/.

Lichtenthal, Wendy, Joseph Currier, Robert Neimeyer, and Nancy Keesee, "Sense and Significance: A Mixed Methods Examination of Meaning Making After the Loss of One's Child," *Journal of Clinical Psychology* 66(7) (July 2010): 791–812.

Lindemann, Erich, "Symptomatology and Management of Acute Grief," *The American Journal of Psychiatry* 101(2) (1944): 141–8.

Linton, Anna, "Der Tod als Brautführer: Bridal Imagery in Funeral Writings," *Daphnis* 29(1–2) (2000): 281–306.

Loimer, Hermann, Mag Driur, and Michael Guarnieri, "Accidents and Acts of God: A History of the Terms," *American Journal of Public Health* 86(1) (01 January 1996): 101–7.

Long, Rose-Carol Washton, "Kandinsky's Abstract Style: The Veiling of Apocalyptic Folk Imagery," *Art Journal* 34(3) (1975): 217–28.

Lyngstad, Torkild Hovde, "Bereavement and Divorce: Does the Death of a Child Affect Parents' Marital Stability?" *Family Science* 4(1) (2013): 79–86.

MacCarthy, Anne, "'Cityful Passing Away': Joyce's Version of Mutability Contrasted with Mangan's 'The World's Changes,'" *Papers on Joyce* 15 (2009): 31–47.

Maidt-Zinke, Kristina, "Friedrich Rückert: 'Der Reigen dreht ohn" Unterlaß,'" *Frankfurter Anthologie* (07 October 2020): https://www.faz.net/aktuell/feuilleton/buecher/frankfurter-anthologie/frankfurter-anthologie-der-reigen-dreht-ohn-unterlass-von-friedrich-rueckert-16854825.html.

Malkinson, Ruth, "Cognitive-Behavioral Grief Therapy: The ABC Model of Rational-Emotion Behavior Therapy," *Psihologijske teme* 9(2) (2010): 289–305.

———, and Liora Bar-Tur, "Long Term Bereavement Processes of Older Parents: The Three Phases of Grief," *OMEGA—Journal of Death and Dying* 50(2) (01 March 2005): 103–129.

Marecki, Marsha, Powhatan Wooldridge, Ann Dow, Jacqueline Thompson, and Clarice Lechner-Hyman, "Early Sibling Attachment," *Journal of Obstetric, Gynecologic and Neonatal Nursing* 14(5) (September 1985): 418–23.

Martison, Ida, Betty Davies, and Sandra McClowry, "Parental Depression Following the Death of a Child," *Death Studies* 15(3) (1989): 259–67.

Matthee, Rudi, "The Imaginary Realm: Europe's Enlightenment Image of Early Modern Iran," *Comparative Studies of South Asia, Africa and the Middle East* 30(3) (2010): 449–62.

McCown, Darlene, and Betty Davies, "Patterns of grief in young children following the death of a sibling," *Death Studies* 19(1) (1995): 41–53.

McCracken, Janet, "Falsely, Sanely, Shallowly: Reflections on the Special Character of Grief," *International Journal of Applied Philosophy* 19(1) (Spring, 2005) 139–56.

McIsaac, Peter, "Rethinking *Tableaux Vivants* and Triviality in the Writings of Johann Wolfgang Von Goethe, Johanna Schopenhauer, and Fanny Lewald," *Monatshefte* 99(2) (2007): 152–76.

McGregor, Robert Kuhn, "Deriving a Biocentric History: Evidence from the Journal of Henry David Thoreau," *Environmental Review: ER* 12(2) [Oxford University Press, American Society for Environmental History, Forest History Society, Forest History Society and The American Society for Environmental History] (1988): 117–26.

McMenamy, Jannette, John Jordan, and Ann Mitchell, "What do Suicide Survivors Tell Us They Need? Results of a Pilot Study," *Suicide and Life-Threatening Behavior* 38(4) (2008): 375–89.

McNeish, David, "Grief is a Circular Staircase: The Uses and Limits of Models of Grief in the Pastoral Care of the Bereaved," *Practical Theology* 6(2) (2013): 190–203.

Merrill, Selah, "The Cave of Machpelah," *The Old and New Testament Student* 11(6) (December 1890): 327–35.

Meyers, Eric M., "The Theological Implications of

an Ancient Jewish Burial Custom," *The Jewish Quarterly Review* 62(2) (1971): 95–119.

Miles, Margaret Shandor, and Alice Sterner Demi, "Toward the Development of a Theory of Bereavement Guilt: Sources of Guilt in Bereaved Parents," *OMEGA—Journal of Death and Dying* 14(4) (1984): 299–314.

Millett, David, "Hans Berger: From Psychic Energy to the EEG," *Perspectives in Biology and Medicine* 44(4) (2001): 522–42.

Mitzman, Arthur, "Anti-Progress: A Study of the Romantic Roots of German Sociology," *Social Research* 33(1) (Spring, 1966): 65–85.

Möhn, Rudolf, "Die Wunde schließt der Speer nur, der sie schlug—medizinische Bemerkungen zu einigen Werken Richard Wagners," *Aktuelle Dermatologie* 40(1/2) (2014): 50–4.

Monahan, Seth, "Negative Catharsis as Rotational Telos in Mahler's First 'Kindertotenlied,'" *Intégral* 28/29 (2014): 13–51. From a paper delivered at the annual meeting of the Society for Music Theory, 01 November 2013, Charlotte, North Carolina, USA.

Moore, Christopher, "Chaerephon, Telephus, and Diagnosis in the *Gorgias*," *Arethusa* 45(2) (2012): 195–210.

Morgan, Bayard, "On Translations of Goethe's Works," *Monatshefte für Deutschen Unterricht* 24(3/4) (March-April 1932): 103–6.

Morrison, Danny, "Dear Future," *Kunapipi* 20(2) (1998).

Mortazavi, Seyede Salehe, Shervin Assari, Amirali Alimohamadi, Mani Rafiee, and Mohsen Shati, "Fear, Loss, Social Isolation, and Incomplete Grief Due to COVID-19: A Recipe for a Psychiatric Pandemic," *Basic and Clinical Neuroscience* 11(2) (2020): 225–32.

Moules, Nancy, "Legitimizing Grief: Challenging Beliefs That Constrain," *Journal of Family Nursing* 4(2) (May 1998): 142–66.

Murphy, Shirley, L. Clark Johnson, and Janet Lohan, "Challenging the Myths About Parents' Adjustment After the Sudden, Violent Death of a Child," *Journal of Nursing Scholarship* 35(4) (2003): 359–64.

———, L. Clark Johnson, Lang Wu, Juan Juan Fan, and Janet Lohan, "Bereaved Parents' Outcomes 4 to 60 Months After Their Children's Deaths by Accident, Suicide, or Homicide: A Comparative Study Demonstrating Differences," *Death Studies* 27(1) (2003): 39–61.

Musaph, Herman, "Anniversary Reaction as a Symptom of Grief in Traumatized Persons," *Israel Journal of Psychiatry and Related Sciences* 27(3) (1990):175–9.

Neimeyer, Robert, "Meaning Reconstruction in the Wake of Loss: Evolution of a Research Program," *Behaviour Change* 33(2) (June 2016): 65–79.

———, "Searching for the Meaning of Meaning: Grief Therapy and the Process of Reconstruction," *Death Studies* 24(6) (2000): 541–58.

Neumann, Peter Horst, "Gustav Mahler und Friedrich Rückert-eine Mesalliance?" *Musik & Ästhetik* 11(41) (2007): 80–90.

Newman, Barclay Moon, "Electrical Rhythms of the Human Brain," *Scientific American* 159(4) (1938): 186–8.

Nordmeyer, Henry Waldemar, review of "Friedrich Rückert als Lyriker der Befreiungs-Kriege," *The Journal of English and Germanic Philology* 15(4) (1916): 625–32.

Nowatzki, Nadine, and Ruth Grant Kalischuk, "Post-Death Encounters: Grieving, Mourning, and Healing," *Omega—Journal of Death and Dying* 59(2) (October 2009): 91–111.

O'Neill, Mary, "Speaking to the Dead," conference paper, *Constructions of Death, Mourning, and Memory*, Woodcliff Lake, New Jersey, USA (27–9 October 2006).

Orlinsky, Harry, "Studies in the Septuagint of the Book of Job: Chapter III (Continued)," *Hebrew Union College Annual* 32 (1961): 239–68.

Packman, Wendy, Heidi Horsely, Betty Davies, and Robin Kramer, "Sibling Bereavement and Continuing Bonds," *Death Studies* 30(9) (2006): 817–41.

Paiuk, Cara, "Mourning the Father I Never Knew," *Modern Loss*, 12 January 2014, https://modernloss.com/mourning-father-never-knew/.

Park, Crystal, "Religion as a Meaning-Making Framework in Coping with Life Stress," *Journal of Social Issues* 61(4) (December 2005): 707–29.

Parker, Julie, "Extraordinary Experiences of the Bereaved and Adaptive Outcomes of Grief," *OMEGA—Journal of Death and Dying* 51(4) (2005): 257–83.

Parkes, Colin Murray, "Traditional Models and Theories of Grief," *Bereavement Care* 17(2) (1998): 21–23.

Pastan, Linda, "The Five Stages of Grief," *Chicago Review* 28(4) (Spring, 1977): 128–9.

———, "The Five Stages of Grief," Fifty Years: A Retrospective Issue, *Chicago Review* 42(3) (1996): 194–6.

Pauck, Wilhelm, "To Be or Not to Be: Paul Tillich on the Meaning of Life," *Bulletin of the American Academy of Arts and Sciences* 33(2) (1979): 9–25.

Paul, Norman, and K.D. Beernink, "The Use of Empathy in the Resolution of Grief," *Perspectives in Biology and Medicine* 11(1) (Autumn 1967): 153–69.

Planert, Ute, "From Collaboration to Resistance: Politics, Experience, and Memory of the Revolutionary and Napoleonic Wars in Southern Germany," *Central European History* 39(4) (2006): 676–705.

Prigerson, Holly, Katalin Szanto, Patricia Houck, Lin Ehrenpreis, and Charles Reynolds III, "Suicidal Ideation in Elderly Bereaved: The Role of Complicated Grief," *Suicide and Life-Threatening Behavior* 27(2) (Summer, 1997): 194–207.

Radwanska-Williams, Joanna, "The banyan tree: a story of language gain," *English Today* 17(2) (2001): 11–8.

Ram, H.Y. Mohan, "A Leaf from Nature," *India International Centre Quarterly 36*(1) (2009): 122–31. Adapted from the 26th Dr. C.D. Deshmukh Memorial Lecture, *The Traditional Knowledge of Plants in India*, delivered at the IIC, New Delhi, 14 January 2009.

Raphael, Beverley, "The Management of Pathological Grief," *Australian and New Zealand Journal of Psychiatry 9*(3) (1975): 173–80.

Reimers, Eva, "Death and Identity: Graves and Funerals as Cultural Communication," *Mortality 4*(2) (1999): 147–66.

Rittenour, Christine, Scott Myers, and Maria Brann, "Commitment and Emotional Closeness in the Sibling Relationship," *Southern Communication Journal 72*(2) (2007): 169–83.

Rizzo, Alessandra, "Italian Tenor Pavarotti Has Died at Age 71, His Manager Says," The Associated Press (6 September 2007).

Rölleke, Heinz, "Kommentierungen zu Wilhelm Raabes 'Altershausen,'" *Jahrbuch der Raabe-Gesellschaft 49* (2009): 66–77.

Rolleston, Humphry, "Irregular Practice and Quackery," delivered before the Oxford Medical Society, 12 November 1926, *The Canadian Medical Association Journal 17*(5) (May 1927): 501–8.

Rolleston, J.D., "The History of Scarlet Fever," *The British Medical Journal 2* (24 Nov 1928): 926–9. A paper read in the Section of History of Medicine at the Annual Meeting of the British Medical Association at Cardiff, 1928.

Romanoff, Bronna, "Rituals and the Grieving Process," *Death Studies 22*(8) (1998) 697–711.

Rosenblatt, Paul, "Protective Parenting After the Death of a Child," *Journal of Personal and Interpersonal Loss 5*(4) (2000): 343–60.

Rostila, Mikael, Jan Saarela, Ichiro Kawachi, and Anders Hjern, "Testing the Anniversary Reaction: Causal Effects of Bereavement in a Nationwide Follow-up Study from Sweden," *European Journal of Epidemiology 30*(3) (2015): 239–47.

Rowley, Anthony, "Das Präteritum in den Heutigen Deutschen Dialekten," *Zeitschrift Für Dialektologie Und Linguistik 50*(2) (1983): 161–82.

Rückert, Friedrich, "America," *Illustrirte Dorfzeitung des Lahrer hinkenden Boten*, v4 (J.H. Geiger, 1866).

Rutherford, Kay, "Mobilizing the Healing Emotions: Nature Experiences in Theory and Practice," *The Journal of Humanistic Counseling 33*(4) (June 1995): 146–55.

Sapp, Christopher, "Syncope as the Cause of *Präteritumschwund*: New Data from an Early New High German Corpus," *Journal of Germanic Linguistics 21*(4) (2009): 419–50.

Schaal, Susanne, Anne Richter and Thomas Elbert, "Prolonged Grief Disorder and Depression in a German Community Sample," *Death Studies 38*(7) (2014): 476–81.

Scherliess, Volker, liner notes, *Mahler Symphony No. 9, Kindertotenlieder, Rückert-Lieder*, tr. John Coombs (recorded and written, 1979/80) (Deutsche Grammophon, 1997).

Schimmel, Annemarie, "Friedrich Rückert: Dichter und Orientalist," *Alman Dili ve Edebiyatı Dergisi—Studien zur deutschen Sprache und Literatur 3* (1956): 1–18.

Schlegel, Friedrich, "Gespräch über die Poesie," *Athenaeum 3*, Eine Zeitschrift (1800): 58–121.

Scholem, Gershom, "The Name of God and the Linguistic Theory of the Kabbala: (Part 2)," tr. Simon Pleasance, *Diogenes 20*(80) (December 1972): 164–94.

Schwab, Reiko, "A Child's Death and Divorce: Dispelling the Myth," *Death Studies 22*(5) (1998): 445–468.

Schwartz-Borden, Gwen, "Metaphor—Visual Aid in Grief Work," *OMEGA—Journal of Death and Dying 25*(3) (November 1992): 239–48.

Shankar, Sarah, Lizette Nolte, and David Trickey, "Continuing Bonds with the Living: Bereaved Parents' Narratives of Their Emotional Relationship with Their Children," *Bereavement Care 36*(3) (2017): 103–11

Shear, M. Katherine, Stephanie Muldberg, and Vyjeyanthi Periyakoil, "Supporting Patients Who Are Bereaved," *BMJ: British Medical Journal 358* (2017).

Shuchter, Stephen, and Sidney Zisook, "Treatment of Spousal Bereavement: A Multidimensional Approach," *Psychiatric Annals 16*(5) (1986): 295–305.

Sieveking, Georg Heinrich, "Fragment über Luxus, Burger-Tugend und Bürger-Wohl, für hamburgische Bürger, die das Gute wollen und können," *Verhandlungen und Schriften der Hamburgischen Gesellschaft zur Beförderung der Künste und nützlichen Gewerbe 4* (1797): 163–82.

Simon, N.M., M.H. Pollack, D. Fischmann, C.A. Perlman, A.C. Muriel, C.W. Moore, A.A. Nierenberg, and M.K. Shear, "Complicated Grief and Its Correlates in Patients with Bipolar Disorder," *The Journal of Clinical Psychiatry 66*(9) (31 Aug 2005):1105–10.

Snauwaert, Maïté, "Grief Memoirs & the Reordering of Life. On Resilience, Loneliness, and Writing," *British Journal of Guidance & Counselling* (2021), DOI: 10.1080/03069885.2021.1951661.

Soth, Lauren, "Vincent van Gogh Addendum," *Word & Image 22*(2) (2006): 188.

Spratt, Mary, and Douglas Denney, "Immune Variables, Depression, and Plasma Cortisol Over Time in Suddenly Bereaved Parents," *Journal of Neuropsychiatry and Clinical Neurosciences 3*(3) (August 1991): 299–306.

Sprenger, Hans, "Das europäische Sonett," *Zeitschrift Für Religions- Und Geistesgeschichte 56*(2) (2004): 187–9.

Stadtmuseum Erlangen, Martin-Luther-Platz 9, 91054 Erlangen; https://www.stadtmuseum-erlangen.de/ and https://www.erlangen.de/

Stepakoff, Shanee, "From Destruction to Creation, from Silence to Speech: Poetry Therapy Principles and Practices for Working with Suicide

Grief," *The Arts in Psychotherapy* 36(2) (2009): 105–13.

Stroebe, Margaret, "The Poetry of Grief: Beyond Scientific Portrayal," *OMEGA—Journal of Death and Dying* 78(1) (2018): 67–96.

Stroebe, Wolfgang, Margaret Stroebe, and Günther Domittner, "Individual and Situational Differences in Recovery from Bereavement: A Risk Group Identified," *Journal of Social Issues* 44(3) (Fall, 1988): 143–158.

_____, Margaret Stroebe, and Henk Schut, "Does 'grief work' work?" *Journal of Consulting and Clinical Psychology* 59(3) (1991): 479–82. An edited and slightly updated version of this paper appeared in *Bereavement Care* 22(1) (2003): 3–5.

Szanto, K., K. Shear, P.R. Houck, C.F. Reynolds, III, E. Frank, K. Caroff, and R. Silowash, "Indirect Self-Destructive Behavior and Overt Suicidality in Patients With Complicated Grief," *The Journal of Clinical Psychiatry* 67(2) (2006): 233–9.

Tang, Suqin, and Zhendong Xiang, "Who Suffered Most After Deaths Due to COVID-19? Prevalence and Correlates of Prolonged Grief Disorder in COVID-19 Related Bereaved Adults," *Global Health* 17(19) (2021): https://doi.org/10.1186/s12992-021-00669-5

Taylor, Bayard, "Friedrich Rückert," *Atlantic Monthly* 18(105) (July 1866). Also collected in *The Atlantic Monthly*, v18 (Ticknor & Fields, 1866).

Taylor, P.G., "Exploring the Roles of Grief and Grieving in Coping with Lifelong Change," *International Journal of Lifelong Education* 19(6) (2000): 525–34.

Thomas, Heywood, "Kierkegaard's View of Time," *Journal of the British Society for Phenomenology* 4(1) (1973): 33–40.

Thuné-Boyle, Ingela C., Jan A. Stygall, Mohammed R. Keshtgar, and Stanton P. Newman, "Do Religious/Spiritual Coping Strategies Affect Illness Adjustment in Patients with Cancer? A Systematic Review of the Literature," *Social Science & Medicine* 63(1) (2006): 151–64.

Toom, Victor, "Finding Closure, Continuing Bonds, and Codentification After the 9/11 Attacks," *Medical Anthropology: Cross-Cultural Studies in Health and Illness* (June 2017): 1–13.

Updike, John, "Facing Death," *American Heritage* 43(3) (May/June 1992): 98–105.

Van Gogh Museum, *Vincent van Gogh: The Letters*, http://vangoghletters.org/vg/letters.html.

Vedder, Anneke, Kathrin Boerner, Jeffrey E. Stokes, Henk A.W. Schut, Paul A. Boelen, and Margaret S. Stroebe, "A systematic review of loneliness in bereavement: Current research and future directions," *Current Opinion in Psychology* 43 (2021): 48–64.

Venuti, Lawrence, "Translation as Cultural Politics: Regimes of Domestication in English," *Textual Practice* 7(2) (1993): 208–23.

Verdery, Ashton, Emily Smith-Greenaway, Rachel Margolis, and Jonathan Daw, "Tracking the Reach of COVID-19 Kin Loss with a Bereavement Multiplier Applied to the United States," *PNAS: Proceedings of the National Academy of Sciences of the United States of America* 117(30) (10 July 2020): 17695–17701.

Walter, Bruno, "Mahlers Weg: ein Erinnerungsblatt," *Der Merker* 3(5) (March 1912): 166–71.

Weber, Christian, "Review of *Goethe's Faust: Theatre of Modernity*," *Seminar: A Journal of Germanic Studies* 48(4) (2012): 494–6.

Weeks, O. Duane, "Comfort and Healing: Death Ceremonies That Work," *Illness, Crisis & Loss* 12(2) (2004): 113–25.

Weiss, Robert, "Loss and Recovery," *Journal of Social Issues* 44(3) (1988): 37–52.

West, Ewan, "The Musenalmanach and Viennese Song 1770–1830," *Music & Letters* 67(1) (1986): 37–49.

Wickett, Elizabeth, "The Aesthetics and Poetics of Upper Egyptian Funerary Lament in Performance," *Quaderni Di Studi Arabi* 7 (2012): 145–68.

Wilce, James, "Traditional Laments and Postmodern Regrets: The Circulation of Discourse in Metacultural Context," *Journal of Linguistic Anthropology* 15(1) (June 2005): 60–71.

Wilkes, Johannes, "Friedrich Rückert: Über die Fähigkeit zu trauern," *Schriftenreihe der Deutschen Gesellschaft für Geschichte der Nervenheilkunde* 9, eds. G. Nissen and G. Holdorff (2003): 299–310.

Winkel, Heidemarie, "A Postmodern Culture of Grief? On Individualization of Mourning in Germany," *Mortality* 6(1) (2001): 67–79.

Wirth, Mathias, "Trost für Untröstliche? Friedrich Rückerts Kindertotengedichte in eschatologischer Perspektive," *Zeitschrift für Theologie und Kirche* 115(1) (2018): 98–123.

Wright, Ronald, and Brad Strawn, "Grief, Hope, and Prophetic Imagination: Psychoanalysis and Christian Tradition in Dialogue," *Journal of Psychology and Christianity* 29(2) (2010): 149–57.

Zammito, John, Karl Menges, and Ernest Menze, "Johann Gottfried Herder Revisited: The Revolution in Scholarship in the Last Quarter Century," *Journal of the History of Ideas* 71(4) (2010): 661–84.

Zandvoort, Albert, "Living and Laughing in the Shadow of Death: Complicated Grief, Trauma and Resilience," *The British Journal of Psychotherapy Integration* 9(2) (2012): 33–44.

Zhai, Yusen, and Xue Du, "Loss and Grief amidst COVID-19: A Path to Adaptation and Resilience," *Brain, Behavior, and Immunity* 87 (2020): 80–1.

Books

Abedinifard, Mostafa, Omid Azadibougar, and Amirhossein Vafa, eds., *Persian Literature as World Literature* (Bloomsbury, 2021).

Aberbach, David, *Surviving Trauma: Loss, Literature and Psychoanalysis* (Yale University Press, 1989).

Abrahams, Israel, *Festival Studies: Being Thoughts on the Jewish Year* (MacMillan and Co., 1906).

Adams, Nehemia, *Catharine* (J.E. Tilton and Co., 1859).

Addison, Jospeh, *Essays on the Pleasures of the Imagination*, ed. Hugh Blair (Duverger, 1828).

Adler, Frederick Henry, *Herder and Klopstock* (University of Illinois, 1913).

Al-Chokhachy, Elissa, *Our Children Live On: Miraculous Moments for the Bereaved* (Llewellyn, 2012).

Al-Hariri, *Impostures*, tr. Michael Cooperson (New York University Press, 2020).

Allison, Jay, and Dan Gediman, eds., *This I Believe II* (Henry Holt, 2008).

Amrine, Frederick, *Goethe and the Myth of the Bildungsroman: Rethinking the Wilhelm Meister Novels* (Cambridge University Press, 2020).

Anderson, Herbert, and Edward Foley, *Mighty Stories, Dangerous Rituals: Weaving Together the Human and the Divine* (John Wiley & Sons, 1998).

Andrews, William Page, *Goethe's Key to Faust* (Houghton Mifflin, 1913).

[Anon.], *Zur Geschichte Friedrichs I. und Friedrich Wilhelms I. von Preußen* (De Gruyter, 2019).

Apollodorus, *The Library*, v2, tr. James George Frazer (William Heinemann, 1921).

Astell, Ann, *Job, Boethius, and Epic Truth* (Cornell University Press, 1994).

Attig, Thomas, *The Heart of Grief: Death and the Search for Lasting Love* (Oxford University Press, 2000).

———, *How We Grieve: Relearning the World* (Oxford University Press, 1996).

Attridge, Derek, and Henry Staten, *The Craft of Poetry: Dialogues on Minimal Interpretation* (Routledge, 2015.)

Augustine Aurelius (Augustine of Hippo), *Index in Omnia Opera Sancti Augustini [...]*, [Editores], VIII, 558, in Jacques Paul Migne, *Patrologia cursus completus. [...] Series Latina [...]*, 221 vols. (Migne, 1844–65).

Avery, Gilian, and Kimberley Reynolds, eds., *Representations of Childhood Death* (Palgrave Macmillan UK, 1999).

Bachmann, E. Theodore, ed., *Luther's Works: Word and Sacrament I*, v35 (Muhlenberg Press, 1960).

Backman, E. Louis, *Religious Dances in the Christian Church and in Popular Medicine* (Allen & Unwin, 1952).

Bacon, Francis, *Bacon's Essays*, ed. Sydney Humphries (A & C Black, 1912).

———, *Essays* (Woodward & Co., 1893). First published in 1612.

Bakker, Egbert, *Poetry in Speech: Orality and Homeric Discourse* (Cornell University Press, 2018).

Bannon, David, *Wounded in Spirit: Advent Art and Meditations* (Paraclete Press, 2018).

Barham, Jeremy, ed., *The Cambridge Companion to Mahler* (Cambridge University Press, 2007).

Barth, Fredrik, Andre Gingrich, Robert Parkin, and Sydel Silverman, *One Discipline, Four Ways: British, German, French, and American Anthropology* (University of Chicago Press, 2010).

Bates, Catherine, ed., *A Companion to Renaissance Poetry* (John Wiley & Sons, 2018).

Batnitzky, Leora, and Ilana Pardes, eds., *The Book of Job: Aesthetics, Ethics, Hermeneutics* (de Gruyter, 2015).

Baumann, Lukas, *Zyklus und Serie: Van Goghs Ansichten des ummauerten Feldes in Saint-Rémy* (Universitätsverlag Göttingen, 2018).

Beddoes, Thomas Lovell, *The Letters of Thomas Lovell Beddoes*, ed. Edmund Gosse (Elkin Mathews & John Lane; Macmillan & Co., 1894).

Beiser, Frederick, *The Romantic Imperative: The Concept of Early German Romanticism* (Harvard University Press, 2003).

Bekker, Paul, *Gustav Mahlers Sinfonien* (Schuster & Loeffler, 1921; repr. Schneider, 1969.

Beller-McKenna, Daniel, *Brahms and the German Spirit* (Harvard University Press, 2004).

Benjamin, Walter, *Illuminations: Essays and Reflections*, ed. Hannah Arendt, tr. Harry Zohn (Schocken Books, 2007).

Bennewitz, Ingrid, and Andrea Schindler, eds., *Farbe im Mittelalter: Materialität—Medialität—Semantik* (Akademie Verlag, 2012).

Beopjeong, *Meditations of a Zen Master*, ed. and tr. David Bannon (Bilingual Library, 2012).

Berger, Hans, *Psyche* (Fischer, 1940).

Berkhof, Hendrikus, *Christian Faith: An Introduction to the Study of the Faith*, rev. ed., tr. Sierd Woudstra (Eerdmans, 1986).

Bernstein, Judith, *When the Bough Breaks: Forever After the Death of a Son or Daughter* (Andrews and McMeel, 1997).

Berti, Irene, Katharina Bolle, Fanny Opdenhoff, and Fabian Stroth, eds., *Writing Matters: Presenting and Perceiving Monumental Inscriptions in Antiquity and the Middle Ages* (De Gruyter, 2017).

Beuchner, Frederick, *Telling the Truth* (Harper & Row, 1977).

Beyer, Konrad, *Friedrich Rückert, Ein biographisches Denkmal* (Sauerländer, 1868).

———, *Friedrich Rückert's Leben und Dichtungen* (G. Sendelbach, 1866).

Die Bibel: oder Die ganze Heilige Schrift des Alten und Neuen Testaments, 12th ed., also known as the *Luther Bibel*, German tr. Martin Luther and staff (Gedruckt für die Amerikanische Bibel-gesellschaft bey G.W. Mentz und sohn, 1834). It seems reasonable to infer that the Rückerts had a *Bibel* very much like this one in their home. Friedrich occasionally references Hebrew phrasing; at other times his poems are informed by German expressions from the Luther translation of the Bible that was in print during his lifetime. We know with a fair amount of certainty that Luise Rückert read a *Luther Bibel* (see the introduction), in light of certain passages that are unique to the Luther translation.

Bielschowsky, Albert, *The Life of Goethe: Volume III, 1815–1832, From the Congress of Vienna to the Poet's Death*, tr. William Cooper (G.P. Putnam's Sons, 1908).

Blaisdell, Bob, ed., *Civil War Letters: From Home, Camp and Battlefield* (Dover, 2012).

Blamires, David, *Telling Tales: The Impact of Germany on English Children's Books 1780–1918* (OpenBook, 2009).

Blum, Deborah, *Ghost Hunters: William James and the Search for Scientific Proof of Life After Death* (Penguin, 2006).

Blum-Hyclak, Kimberlyn, *In the Garden of Life and Death: A Mother and Daughter Walk* (Main Street Rag, 2014).

Boddice, Rob, *The History of Emotions* (Manchester University Press, 2018).

Boes, Tobias, *Formative Fictions: Nationalism, Cosmopolitanism, and the Bildungsroman* (Cornell University Press, 2012).

———, *Thomas Mann's War: Literature, Politics, and the World Republic of Letters* (Cornell University Press, 2019).

Bonhoeffer, Dietrich, *Dietrich Bonhoeffer Werke, Widerstandund Ergebung: Briefe und Aufzeichnungenaus der Haft*, v8, eds. Christian Gremmels, Eberhard Bethge, Renate Bethgein, with Ilse Tödt (Gütersloher Verlagshaus, 1998, 2011).

The Book of Health: A Compendium of Domestic Medicine (Richardson, Lord and Holbrook, 1830).

Borck, Cornelius, *Brainwaves: A Cultural History of Electroencephalography*, tr. Ann Hentschel (Routledge, 2019).

Borg, Marcus, and John Dominic Crossan, *The First Christmas: What the Gospels Really Teach About Jesus's Birth* (HarperOne, 2007).

Bowlby, John, *Attachment and Loss: Vol. 1, Attachment* (Basic Books, 1969).

———, *Attachment and Loss: Vol. 2, Separation: Anxiety and Anger* (Basic Books, 1973).

———, *Attachment and Loss: Vol. 3, Loss: Sadness and Depression* (Basic Books, 1980).

———, *A Secure Base: Parent-Child Attachment and Healthy Human Development* (Basic Books, 1988).

Bowra, C. Maurice, *The Romantic Imagination* (Oxford University Press, 1961).

Brennan, Matthew, *The Poet's Holy Craft: William Gilmore Simms and Romantic Verse Tradition* (University of South Carolina Press, 2010).

Breuilly, John, ed., *Nineteenth-Century Germany: Politics, Culture, and Society 1780–1918*, 2nd ed. (Bloomsbury, 2020).

Brinker-Gabler, Gisela, and Nicole Shea, eds., *The Many Voices of Europe: Mobility and Migration in Contemporary Europe* (De Gruyter, 2020).

Brown, Andy, Karl Spracklen, Keith Kahn-Harris, and Niall Scott, eds., *Global Metal Music and Culture: Current Directions in Metal Studies* (Routledge, 2016).

Brown, Cynthia, *Poets, Patrons, and Printers: Crisis of Authority in Late Medieval France* (Cornell University Press, 1995).

Browning, Elizabeth Barrett, *The Complete Poetical Works of Mrs. Browning* (Houghton Mifflin, 1900).

Bruford, Walter Horace, *The German Tradition of Self-Cultivation: "Bildung" from Humboldt to Thomas Mann* (Cambridge University Press, 1975).

Brunner, Bernd, *Inventing the Christmas Tree*, tr. Benjamin Smith (Yale University Press, 2012).

Buber, Martin, *I and Thou*, tr. Ronald Gregor Smith (Charles Scribner's Sons, 1958).

Buckle, Jennifer, and Stephen Fleming, *Parenting After the Death of a Child: A Practitioner's Guide* (Routledge, 2010).

Buckley, Kelly, *Gratitude in Grief* (AuthorHouse, 2010).

Buechner, Frederick, *Secrets in the Dark: A Life in Sermons* (HarperSanFrancisco, 2006).

Buell, Lawrence, *Literary Transcendentalism: Style and Vision in the American Renaissance* (Cornell University Press, 1973).

Byron, George Gordon, *Byron's Poetry: Authoritative Texts, Letters and Journals, Criticism, Images of Byron*, ed. Frank McConnell (W.W. Norton & Co., 1978).

Calderón de la Barca, Pedro, *Calderon's Dramas: The Wonder-Working Magician; Life Is a Dream; The Purgatory of Saint Patrick*, tr. Denis Florence MacCarthy (Kegan Paul, Trench & Co., 1887).

———, *La vida es sueño* (Insel-Verlag, 1900).

Calhoun, Lawrence, and Richard Tedeschi, *Posttraumatic Growth in Clinical Practice* (Routledge, 2013).

———, eds., *Handbook of Postraumatic Growth: Research and Practice* (Psychology Press/Taylor & Francis, 2006).

Campbell, Joseph, *The Masks of God: Oriental Mythologies* (Viking Compass, 1962).

Cantor, Norman, *In the Wake of the Plague: The Black Death and the World It Made* (Perennial, 2002).

Cavagna, Mattia, and Costantino Maeder, eds., *Philology and Performing Arts: A Challenge* (Presses universitaires de Louvain, 2014).

Cavell, Stanley, *This New Yet Unapproachable America: Lectures After Emerson After Wittgenstein*, 1987 Frederick Ives Carpenter Lectures (Living Batch Press, 1989).

Chamberlain, Timothy, ed., *Eighteenth-Century German Criticism: Herder, Lenz, Lessing, and others*, rev. ed. (Bloomsbury, 1992).

Cholbi, Michael, and Travis Timmerman, eds., *Exploring the Philosophy of Death and Dying: Classical and Contemporary Perspectives* (Routledge, 2021).

———, *Grief: A Philosophical Guide* (Princeton University Press, 2022).

Cleiren, Marc, *Adaptation After Bereavement: A Comparative Study of the Aftermath of Death from Suicide, Traffic Accident, and Illness for Next of Kin* (Leiden University Press, 1991).

Colby, Elbridge, *The Echo-Device in Literature* (New York Public Library, 1920).

Coleridge, Samuel Taylor, *Biographia Literaria* (Clarendon, 1907).

———, *The Complete Poetical Works of*

Samuel Taylor Coleridge, v2, ed. Ernest Hartley Coleridge (Oxford University Press, 1912).

Conte, Gian Biagio, *Stealing the Club from Hercules: On Imitation in Latin Poetry* (De Gruyter, 2017).

Cook, Christopher, *Hearing Voices, Demonic and Divine: Scientific and Theological Perspectives* (Routledge, 2019).

Crossan, John Dominic, *The Birth of Christianity: Discovering What Happened in the Years Immediately After the Execution of Jesus* (HarperCollins e-books, 1998).

_____, *The Essential Jesus: What Jesus Really Taught* (HarperSanFrancisco, 1994).

Cruickshank, Don, *Don Pedro Calderón* (Cambridge University Press, 2009).

Czapla, Ralf Georg, ed., *"...euer Leben fort zu dichten.": Friedrich Rückerts "Kindertodtenlieder" im literatur- und kulturgeschichtlichen Kontext* (Rückert-Studien 21) (Ergon-Verlag, 2016).

_____, ed., *"Weltpoesie allein ist Weltversöhnung": Friedrich Rückert und der Orientalismus im Europa des 19. Jahrhunderts* (Rückert-Studien 22) (Ergon-Verlag, 2021). Symposium papers delivered in Schweinfurt, 2016.

Davies, Douglas, *Death, Ritual and Belief: The Rhetoric of Funerary Rites*, 3rd ed. (Bloomsbury Academic, 2017).

Davis Bush, Ashley (published under Ashley Davis Prend), *Transcending Loss: Understanding the Lifelong Impact of Grief and How to Make it Meaningful* (Berkley, 1997).

Deane, Jennifer Kolpacoff, *A History of Medieval Heresy and Inquisition* (Rowman & Littlefield, 2011).

de Lagarde, Paul, *Erinnerungen an Friedrich Rückert: Ueber einige Berliner Theologen, und was von ihnen zu lernen ist* (Druck der Dieterichschen Universitäts-Buchdr, 1897).

Dickinson, Emily, *The Complete Poems of Emily Dickinson*, ed. Thomas Johnson (Little, Brown & Co., 1890, 1960).

_____, *The Poems of Emily Dickinson*, v2, ed., Ralph W. Franklin (The Belknap Press of Harvard University Press, 1998).

Dickinson, George, Michael Leming, and Alan Mermann, *Dying, Death, and Bereavement 98/99* 4th ed. (McGraw-Hill, 1998).

Döblin, Alfred, *Berlin Alexanderplatz: Die Geschichte vom Franz Biberkopf* (Fischer, 1929; Suhrkamp, 1961).

_____, *Berlin Alexanderplatz: The Story of Franz Biberkopf*, tr. Eugene Jolas (Continuum, 2004).

_____, *Berlin Alexanderplatz*, tr. Michael Hofmann (New York Review Books, 2018).

Doka, Kenneth, ed., *Disenfranchised Grief: New Directions, Challenges, and Strategies for Practice* (Research Press, 2002).

_____, ed., *Disenfranchised Grief: Recognizing Hidden Sorrow* (Lexington, 1989).

_____, *Grief Is a Journey: Finding Your Path through Loss* (Atria, 2016).

_____, and Terry Martin, *Grieving Beyond Gender: Understanding the Ways Men and Women Mourn*, rev. ed. (Routledge ebook, 2010).

_____, ed., *Living with Grief: After Sudden Loss* (Taylor & Francis/Hospice Foundation of America, 1996).

_____, and Joyce Davidson, eds., *Living with Grief at Work, at School, at Worship* (Taylor & Francis/Hospice Foundation of America, 1999).

_____, ed., *Living with Grief: Children, Adolescents, and Loss* (Routledge, 2000).

_____, ed., *Living with Grief: Loss in Later Life* (Hospice Foundation of America, 2002).

_____, and Marcia Lattanzi-Light, eds., *Living with Grief: Coping with Public Tragedy* (Routledge/Hospice, 2003).

_____, and Amy Tucci, eds., *Living with Grief: Children and Adolescents* (Hospice Foundation of America, 2008).

Donin, Hayim Halevy, *To Pray as a Jew: A Guide to the Prayer Book and the Synagogue Service* (Basic Books, 1980).

Donne, John, *A Companion in Crisis: A Modern Paraphrase of John Donne's Devotions*, ed. and paraphrased by Philip Yancey (Illumify, 2021).

Drautzburg, Anita, and Jackson Oldfield, *Making Sense of Suffering: A Collective Attempt* (Brill, 2019).

Dyregrov, Kari, and Atle Dyregrov, *Effective Grief and Bereavement Support: The Role of Family, Friends, Colleagues, Schools and Support Professionals* (Kingsley, 2008): 45–8.

Ebner-Eschenbach, *Krambambuli* and A Oscar Klaussmann, *Memoiren eines Offizierburschen*, ed. Arnold Werner Spanhoofd (American Book Company, 1896.)

Eckhart, Meister (Eckhart von Hochheim), *Reden der Unterweisung* (Insel-Verlag, 1963). This and other readily available versions use a standard rendition from the Middle High German to German.

_____, *Meister Eckhart: The Essential Sermons, Commentaries, Treatises, and Defense*, ed. and tr. Edmund Colledge and Bernard McGinn (Paulist Press, 1981).

Edelstein, Linda, *Maternal Bereavement: Coping with the Unexpected Death of a Child* (Praeger, 1984).

Eden, Barbara, with Wendy Leigh, *Jeannie Out of the Bottle* (Crown Archetype/Random House, 2011).

Edmondston, Catherine Ann Devereux, *Journal of a Secesh Lady: The Diary of Catherine Ann Devereux Edmondston, 1860–1866*, eds. Beth Gilbert Crabtree and James Patton (University of North Carolina Press, 2018).

Edwards, Mark U., Jr., *Printing, Propaganda, and Martin Luther* (University of California Press, 1994).

Edwards, Rosalind, Lucy Hadfield, Helen Lucey, and Melanie Mauthner, *Sibling Identity and Relationships: Sisters and Brothers* (Routledge, 2006).

Eichenberger, Nicole, *Geistliches Erzählen: Zur deutschsprachigen religiösen Kleinepik des Mittelalters* (de Gruyter, 2015).

Eichendorff, Joseph (Karl Benedikt) Freiherr von,

Geschichte der poetischen Literatur Deutschlands, v2 (Schöningh, 1857).
Ellis, John, *Heinrich Von Kleist: Studies in the Character and Meaning of His Writings* (University of North Carolina Press, 2020).
Emerson, Ralph Waldo, *Essays: The First and Second Series* (Houghton Mifflin, 1883).
———, *Essays: Second Series—Emerson's Complete Works*, v3 (Waverley, 1883).
———, *The Heart of Emerson's Journals*, ed. Bliss Perry (Houghton Mifflin, 1926).
———, *Poems—Emerson's Complete Works*, v9 (Waverley, 1883).
———, *The Selected Letters of Ralph Waldo Emerson*, ed. Joel Myerson (Columbia University Press, 1997).
Erdmann, Jürgen, ed., *200 Jahr Friedrich Rückert 1788–1866, Dichter und Gelehrter: Katalog der Ausstellung* (Landesbibliothek, 1988).
Eriksen, Robert, *Theologians Under Hitler: Gerhard Kittel, Paul Althaus and Emanuel Hirsch* (Yale University Press, 1985).
Erlin, Matt, *Necessary Luxuries: Books, Literature, and the Culture of Consumption in Germany, 1770–1815* (Cornell University Press, 2014).
Erman, Adolf, *Die Literatur der Aegypter* (J.C. Hinrichs'sche Buchhandlung, Leipzig, 1923).
Fagan, Andrew, ed., *Making Sense of Dying and Death* (Rodopi, 2004).
Faiq, Said, ed., *Discourse in Translation* (Routledge, 2019).
Ferber, Ilit, and Paula Schwebel, eds., *Lament in Jewish Thought: Philosophical, Theological, and Literary Perspectives* (de Gruyter, 2014).
Ferber, Michael, *Poetry and Language: The Linguistics of Verse* (Cambridge University Press, 2019).
Ferguson, George, *Signs & Symbols in Christian Art* (Oxford University Press, 1954, 1961).
Finkbeiner, Ann, *After the Death of a Child: Living with Loss Through the Years* (Johns Hopkins University Press, 1996).
Fischer, Christian August, *Margarethe, ein Roman* (Mohr and Zimmer, 1812).
Fischer, Norbert, *Geschichte des Todes in der Neuzeit* (Sutton, 2001).
Fitzgerald, Helen, *The Mourning Handbook* (Simon & Schuster, 1994).
Flanders, Judith, *Christmas: A Biography* (Thomas Dunne, 2017).
Forssman, Ingeborg, *Luise Rückert geb. Wiethaus-Fischer "Mein guter Geist, mein beßres Ich!": ein Lebensbild der Frau des gelehrten Dichters* (Mönau-Verlag, 2016).
Fortlage, Karl, *Friedrich Rückert und Seine Werke* (Sauerländer, 1867).
Frankl, Viktor, *The Unheard Cry for Meaning: Psychotherapy and Humanism* (Simon & Schuster, 1978).
Freitag, Barbara, *Sheela-na-gigs: Unravelling an Enigma* (Routledge, 2004).
Freud, Sigmund, *Letters of Sigmund Freud*, ed. Ernst L. Freud, tr. Tania & James Stern (Basic Books, 1960, 1970).

Frey, John, ed., *Schiller 1759/1959: Commemorative American Studies* (University of Illinois Press, 1959).
Fromm, Erich, *Psychoanalysis and Religion* (Yale University Press, 1950).
Frost, Robert, *Robert Frost's Poems*, ed. Louis Untermeyer (St. Martin's, 2002).
Furst, Lilian, *Romanticism in Perspective*, 2nd ed. (MacMillan, 1979).
Galinsky, Karl, *Augustan Culture: An Interpretive Introduction* (Princeton University Press, 1996).
Garrard, Greg, ed., *Oxford Handbook of Ecocriticism* (Oxford: Oxford University Press, 2014).
Gartenberg, Egon, *Mahler: The Man and His Music* (Schirmer, 1978).
Geaves, Ron, Markus Dressler, and Gritt Klinkhammer, eds., *Sufis in Western Society: Global Networking and Locality* (Routledge, 2009).
Gentry, Gerad, and Konstantin Pollok, eds., *The Imagination in German Idealism and Romanticism* (Cambridge University Press, 2019).
Gillespie, Stuart, and David Hopkins, eds., *The Oxford History of Liteary Translation in English, Volume 3: 1660–1790* (Oxford University Press, 2005).
Gilson, Étienne, *God and Philosophy*, 2nd ed.(Yale University Press, 1941, 2002). From Gilson's Powell Lectures on Philosophy at Indiana University.
Glaser, Hermann, *The Cultural Roots of National Socialism*, tr. Ernest A. Menze (University of Texas Press, 1978; Routledge, 2019). This is *Spiesser-Ideologie* in a tactful translation that loses some of Glaser's vitriol.
———, *Spiesser-Ideologie* (Rombach, 1964).
Goedeke, Karl, with Edmund Goetze, *Grundriss zur Geschichte der deutschen Dichtung aus den Quellen*, v8 (Ehlermann, 1905).
Goethe, Johann Wolfgang von, *The Auto-biography of Goethe—Truth and Poetry, from my own life*, thirteen books, v1, tr. John Oxenford (H.G. Bohn, 1848).
———, *The Complete Works of Johann Wolfgang von Goethe: Volume V, Poems* (P.F. Collier & Son, 1839).
———, *Faust* (Halle, 1900).
———, *Faust*, tr. Bayard Taylor (Brockhaus, 1876).
———, *Faust: A Dramatic Poem*, 2nd ed., tr. Abraham Hayward (Moxon, 1834).
———, *Faust: A Dramatic Poem*, 7th ed., tr. Abraham Hayward (Moxon, 1860).
———, *Faust, I & II*, tr. Charles Passage (Bobbs-Merrill, 1965).
———, *Faust Parts One and Two*, trans. Georgeo Madison Priest (Britannica, 1952).
———, *Gedenkausgabe der Werke, Briefe und Gespräche*, ed. Ernst Beutler (Artemis. 1948–54).
———, *Goethe: The Collected Works—Faust I & II*, v2, ed. and tr. Stuart Atkins (Princeton University Press, 1984).
———, *Goethes Briefe*, v4, 01 Januar 1779–07 November 1780 (Hermann Böhlau, 1889).
———, *Goethes Briefe an die Gräfin Auguste zu*

Stolberg, *Verwitwete Gräfin Von Bernstorff* (Brockhaus, 1881).

―――, *Goethe's Faust*, tr. Walter Kaufmann (Doubleday/Anchor, 1961/63).

―――, *Goethes Sämtliche Werke*, v5, ed. Franz Schultz (Theodor Knaur Nachf, c.1920).

―――, *Goethes Werke in zwei Bänden*, ed. Gerhard Stenzel (Bergland-Buch, 1891).

―――, *Goethes Werke: Vollständige Ausgabe letzter Hand*, v1 (J.G. Cotta'sche Buchhandlung, 1827).

―――, *Hermann und Dorothea* (Grote'sche Verlagsbuchhandlung, 1881).

―――, *The Permanent Goethe*, ed. Thomas Mann (Dial Press, 1958).

―――, *Torquato Tasso* (Göschen, 1790).

―――, *West-östlicher Divan* (In der Gottaischen Buchhandlung, 1819).

―――, *Wilhelm Meister's Apprenticeship*, ed. and tr. Eric Blackall, *Goethe: Collected Works*, v9 (Princeton University Press, 1995).

Gorer, Geoffrey, *Death, Grief, and Mourning* (Doubleday, 1965).

Gorrell, Lorraine, *The Nineteenth-century German* Lied (Amadeus, 1993).

Goss, Robert, and Dennis Klass, *Dead but Not Lost: Grief Narratives in Religious Traditions* (AltaMira/Rowman & Littlefield, 2005).

Gournelos, Ted, and Viveca Greene, eds., *A Decade of Dark Humor: How Comedy, Irony, and Satire Shaped Post-9/11 America* (University Press of Mississippi, 2011).

Greenspan, Miriam, *Healing Through the Dark Emotions: The Wisdom of Grief, Fear and Despair* (Shambhala, 2003).

Greenspoon, Leonard, ed., *Authority and Dissent in Jewish Life* (Purdue University Press, 2020).

Gregory I, Pope (St. Gregory the Great), *Morals on the Book of Job*, v. I, parts I & II, tr. members of the English Church (John Henry Parker, 1844).

Groen, Janet, Diana Coholic, and John Graham, eds., *Spirituality in Social Work and Education: Theory, Practice, and Pedagogies* (Wilfrid Laurier University Press, 2012).

Groeschel, Benedict, *Behold, He Comes: Meditations on the Incarnation* (St. Anthony Messenger Press, 2001).

Grollman, Earl, ed., *Concerning Death: a Practical Guide for the Living* (Beacon, 1975).

―――, *Living When a Loved One Has Died* (Beacon Press, 1977).

Grunewald, Michel, and Uwe Puschner, eds., *Das evangelische Intellektuellenmilieu in Deutschland, seine Presse und seine Netzwerke (1871–1963)*, conference proceedings (Peter Lang, 2008).

Hagberg, Garry, *Meaning & Interpretation: Wittgenstein, Henry James, and Literary Knowledge* (Cornell University Press, 1994.)

Haig, Robin, *The Anatomy of Grief: Biopsychosocial and Therapeutic Perspectives* (Charles C. Thomas, 1990).

Hallmark, Rufus, ed., *German Lieder in the Nineteenth Century: Routledge Studies in Musical Genres* (Routledge, 2010; first published by Schirmer, 1996).

Hamman, Adalbert-G., *Early Christian Prayers* (H. Regnery Co., 1961).

Hammett, Dashiell, *The Maltese Falcon, The Thin Man, Red Harvest* (Alfred A. Knopf, 1929, 2000).

Hanh, Thich Nhat, *Answers from the Heart: Practical Responses to Life's Burning Questions* (Parallax, 2009).

Haugk, Kenneth, *Experiencing Grief: Journeying through Grief—Book Two* (Stephen Ministries, 2004).

Hay, David, *Religious Experience Today: Studying the Facts* (Mowbray, 1990).

Hayles, N. Katherine, *Chaos Bound: Orderly Disorder in Contemporary Literature and Science* (Cornell University Press, 1990).

Heinzelmann, Ursula, *Food Culture in Germany* (Greenwood, 2008).

Heisenberg, Werner, *Schritte über Grenzen: Gesammelte Reden Und Aufsatze* (R. Piper & Co., 1997).

Hendin, David, *Death as a Fact of Life* (W.W. Norton & Co., 1973).

Herbert, George, *The Poetical Works of George Herbert*, ed. Alexander Balloch Grosart (George Bell and Sons, 1886).

Herder, Johann Gottfried von, *Herders sämmtliche Werke*, v29 (Weidmannsche Buchhandlung, 1889).

Herdt, Jennifer, *Forming Humanity: Redeeming the German Bildung Tradition* (University of Chicago Press, 2019).

Herring, D. Ann, and Alan Swedlund, eds., *Human Biologists in the Archives: Demography, Health, Nutrition and Genetics in Historical Populations*, Cambridge Studies in Biological and Evolutionary Anthropology (Cambridge University Press, 2002).

Heschel, Abraham, *Man is Not Alone* (Farrar, Straus and Giroux, 1951).

Hess, Scott, *Authoring the Self: Self-Representation, Authorship, and the Print Market in British Poetry from Pope through Wordsworth* (Routledge, 2005).

Heugten, Sjraar, Joachim Pissarro, and Chris Stolwijk, *Van Gogh and the Colors of the Night* (The Museum of Modern Art, 2008).

Hey, Wilhelm, *Funfzig Fabeln für Kinder* (Friedrich Perthes, 1833).

Heydenreich, Aura, Christine Lubkoll, und Klaus Mecke, eds., *Quarks and Letters: Literatur und Naturwissenschaften*, v2 (De Gruyter, 2015).

Hillard, Derek, Heikki Lempa, and Russell A. Spinney, eds., *Feelings Materialized: Emotions, Bodies, and Things in Germany, 1500–1950* (Berghahn Books, 2020).

Hoffmann, von Fallersleben, and August Heinrich, *Gedichte von Hoffman von Fallersleben* (G. Grote'sche, 1887).

Honig, Edwin, *The Poet's Other Voice: Conversations on Literary Translation* (University of Massachusetts Press, 1985).

Hopkins, Gerard Manley, *Poems and Prose* (David Campbell, 1995).
Horace (Quintus Horatius Flaccus), *Satires, Epistles and Ars Poetica*, tr. Henry Rushton Fairclough (Harvard University Press, 1942).
Howarth, Glennys, and Peter Jupp, *Contemporary Issues in the Sociology of Death, Dying and Disposal* (Palgrave Macmillan, 1996).
Hrisztova-Gotthardt, Hrisztalina, and Melita Aleksa Varga, eds., *Introduction to Paremiology: A Comprehensive Guide to Proverb Studies* (De Gruyter Open Poland, 2015).
Hughes-Warrington, Marnie, with Anne Martin, *Big and Little Histories: Sizing Up Ethics in Historiography* (Routledge 2021, 2022).
Hühn, Peter, *Facing Loss and Death: Narrative and Eventfulness in Lyric Poetry* (De Gruyter, 2016).
Immoos, Thomas, *Friedrich Rückerts Aneignung des Shiking* (Theodosius-Buchdr, 1962).
Irving, Washington, *The Sketch Book of Geoffrey Crayon* (John Miller, 1820).
Jackson, Edgar, *The Christian Funeral: Its Meaning, Its Purpose, and Its Modern Practice* (Channel Press, 1966).
Jacobsen, Thorkild, *The Harps That Once ... Sumerian Poetry in Translation* (Yale University Press, 1987).
Jackson, Mark, ed., *Stress in Post-war Britain, 1945–85* (Routledge, 2015).
James, William, *Human Immortality: Two Supposed Objections to the Doctritne*, 3rd ed. (Archibald Constable & Co., 1899).
―――, *The Principles of Psychology*, v2 (MacMillan & Co., 1922).
Jedan, Christoph, Avril Maddrell, and Eric Venbrux, eds., *Consolationscapes in the Face of Loss: Grief and Consolation in Space and Time* (Routledge, 2018).
Jenkins, Philip, *The Great and Holy War: How World War I Became a Religious Crusade* (HarperOne, 2014).
Johns, Alessa, *Bluestocking Feminism and British-German Cultural Transfer, 1750–1837* (University of Michigan Press, 2014).
Jones, Ernest. *The Life and Work of Sigmund Freud*, v3 (Basic Books, 1957).
Jonson, Ben, *The Oxford Poetry Library: Ben Jonson*, ed. Ian Donaldson (Oxford University Press, 1995).
Jung, Carl, *The Collected Works of C.G. Jung*, v5, ed. and tr. Gerhard Adler and R.F.C. Hull (Princeton University Press, 1970).
Jurkowlaniec, Grażyna, Ika Matyjaszkiewicz, and Zuzanna Sarnecka, eds., *The Agency of Things in Medieval and Early Modern Art: Materials, Power and Manipulation* (Routledge, 2019).
Kant, Immanuel, *Abhandlungen nach 1781, Immanuel Kant: Werke*, v8 (de Gruyter, 1971).
Kaplan, Gilbert, ed., *Gustav Mahler—Ich Bin der Welt Abhanden Gekommen: Facsimile Edition of The Autograph Manuscripts* (Kaplan Foundation, 2015).
Kaplan, Robert, *The Exceptional Brain and How It Changed the World* (Allen & Unwin, 2011).

Kärjä, Antti-Ville, *The Popular and the Sacred in Music* (Routledge, 2021).
Kierkegaard, Søren, *Purity of Heart Is to Will One Thing*, tr. Douglas Steere (Harper Torchbooks, 1956.)
Klass, Dennis, *Parental Grief: Solace and Resolution* (Springer, 1988).
―――, Phyllis Silverman, and Steven Nickman, eds., *Continuing Bonds: New Understandings of Grief* (Taylor & Francis, 1996).
―――, and Edith Steffen, eds., *Continuing Bonds in Bereavement: New Directions for Research and Practice* (Routledge ebook, 2017).
Kleist, Heinrich von, *H. v. Kleists Werke, im Verein mit Georg Minde-Pouet und Reinhold Steig herausgegeben von Erich Schmidt*, 5 vols. (Leipzig, 1904–05; 2nd ed. rev. by Georg Minde-Pouet, 7 vols., 1936–38).
―――, *The Marquise of O—And Other Stories*, tr. David Luke and Nigel Reeves (Penguin, 1978).
Kluge, Sofie, *Literature and Historiography in the Spanish Golden Age: The Poetics of History* (Routledge/Taylor & Francis, 2022).
Knapp, Ronald, *Beyond Endurance: When a Child Dies* (Schocken Books, 1986).
Knospe, Sebastian, Alexander Onysko, and Maik Goth, eds., *Crossing Languages to Play with Words: Multidisciplinary Perspectives* (De Gruyter, 2016).
Knowles, Frederic Lawrence, "Grief and Joy," *On Life's Stairway* (L.C. Page & Co., 1901).
Koch, William, and Samuel John Sackett, *Kansas Folklore* (University of Nebraska Press, 1961).
Kōdera, Tsukasa, *Vincent van Gogh: Christianity versus Nature* (J. Benjamins Pub. Co., 1990).
Kolinksy, Eva, and Wilfried van der Will, eds., *The Cambridge Companion to Modern German Culture* (Cambridge University Press, 1999).
König, Christoph, *Philologie der Poesie: Von Goethe bis Peter Szondi* (De Gruyter, 2014).
Kowalik, Jill Anne, *Theology and Dehumanization: Trauma, Grief, and Pathological Mourning in Seventeenth and Eighteenth-Century German Thought and Literature*, ed. Gail Hart (Peter Lang, 2009).
Kroen, William, *Helping Children Cope with the Loss of a Loved One: A Guide for Grownups* (Free Spirit, 1996).
Krüger, Peter, ed., *Das europäische Staatensystem im Wandel* (Oldenbourg Wissenschaftsverlag, 2009).
Kübler-Ross, Elisabeth, and David Kessler, *Life Lessons* (Scribner's, 2000).
Kugel, James, *The God of Old: Inside the Lost World of the Bible* (Free Press, 2003).
Küpper, Joachim, *The Cultural Net: Early Modern Drama as a Paradigm* (De Gruyter, 2018).
―――, *Discursive "Renovatio" in Lope de Vega and Calderón* (de Gruyter, 2018).
Kurzke, Hermann, *Thomas Mann: Life as a Work of Art—A Biography*, tr. Leslie Willson (Princeton University Press, 2002).
Kushner, Harold, *The Lord Is My Shepherd: Healing Wisdom of the Twenty-third Psalm* (Knopf, 2003).

Lachmann, Karl, ed., *Wolfram von Eschenbach* (Reimer, 1891).

La Grange, Henry-Louis de, *Gustav Mahler Vol. 2—Vienna: The Years of Challenge (1897–1904)* (Oxford University Press, 1995).

Lange-Kirchheim, Astrid, Joachim Pfeiffer, and Petra Strasser, eds., *Kindheiten*, Pamphlet Freiburger Literaturpsychologische Gespräche (Königshausen & Neumann, 2011).

Leal, Alice, *English and Translation in the European Union: Unity and Multiplicity in the Wake of Brexit* (Routledge, 2021).

Lebrecht, Norman, *Why Mahler? How One Man and Ten Symphonies Changed Our World* (Pantheon, 2010).

Lee, Chin-Chuan, ed., *Internationalizing "International Communication"* (University of Michigan Press, 2015).

Leick, Nini, and Marianne Davidsen-Nielsen, *Healing Pain: Attachment, Loss, and Grief Therapy*, tr. David Stoner (Routledge, 1991).

Leming, Michael, and George Dickinson, *Understanding Dying, Death, and Bereavement*, Fourth Edition (Holt, Rinehart & Winston, 1998).

Lewis, Clive Staples (C.S.), *The Collected Letters of C.S. Lewis, vIII: Narnia, Cambridge, and Joy 1950–1963*, ed. Walter Hooper (HarperCollins, 2007).

_____, *A Grief Observed* (HarperOne, 1961, 1996).

Lincoln, Abraham, *Abraham Lincoln's Speeches and Letters: 1832–1865*, rev. ed., ed. Paul Angle (Dutton & Co., 1957).

_____, *The Collected Works of Abraham Lincoln*, v1, ed. Roy Basler (Rutgers University Press, 1953).

Lindgren, Kaj Brynolf, *Über den oberdeutschen Präteritumschwund* (Suomalainen Tiedeakatemia, 1957).

Linton, Anna, *Poetry and Parental Bereavement in Early Modern Lutheran Germany* (Oxford University Press, 2008.

Loges, Natasha, *Brahms and His Poets: A Handbook* (Boydell Press, 2017).

Longfellow, Henry Wadsworth, *Poems of Henry Wadsworth Longfellow* (Crowell, 1901).

_____, *The Sonnets of Henry Wadsworth Longfellow*, ed. Ferris Greenslet (Houghton, Mifflin & Co., 1907).

Lüddeckens, Erich, *Untersuchungen über religiösen Gehalt, Sprache und form der ägyptischen Totenklagen*, Mitteilungen des Deutschen Instituts für Ägyptische Altertumskunde in Kairo, Band II, Heft I, 2 (Reichsverlagsamt, 1943).

Luther, Martin, *Luther on Women: A Sourcebook*, tr. Susan Karant-Nunn Merry Wiesner-Hanks (Cambridge University Press, 2003).

_____, *D. Martin Luthers Werke, Kritische Gesamtausgabe*, v23 (Hermann Böhlaus Nachfolger, 1901).

Macy, Joanna, and Anita Barrows, trans. and eds., *A Year with Rilke: Daily Readings from the Best of Rainer Maria Rilke* (HarperOne, 2009).

Malchiodi, Cathy, *The Art Therapy Sourcebook*, 2nd ed. (McGraw-Hill, 2006).

_____, and David Crenshaw, eds., *Creative Arts and Play Therapy for Attachment Problems* (Guilford Press, 2014).

Marcel, Gabriel, *Creative Fidelity*, tr. Robert Rosthal (Fordham University Press, 2002).

Mariani, Paul, *A Commentary on the Complete Poems of Gerard Manley Hopkins* (Cornell University Press, 1970).

Matthews, Samantha, *Poetical Remains: Poets' Graves, Bodies, and Books in the Nineteenth Century* (Oxford University Press, 2004).

Mawdudi, Sayyid Abul A'la, *Towards Understanding the Qu'ran: Abridged version of Tafhim al-Qur'an*, tr. and ed. Zafar Ishaq Ansari (The Islamic Foundation, 2007).

McAteer, Cathy, *Translating Great Russian Literature: The Penguin Russian Classics* (Routledge, 2021).

McCorristine, Shane, ed., *Interdisciplinary Perspectives on Mortality and Its Timings: When Is Death?* (Palgrave MacMillan, 2017).

McCoyd, Judith, and Carolyn Ambler Walter, *Grief and Loss Across the Lifespan: A Biopsychosocial Perspective*, 2nd ed. (Springer, 2016).

Meister Eckhart, see Eckhart, Meister (Eckhart von Hochheim).

Mendes-Flohr, Paul, ed., *Dialogue as a Transdisciplinary Concept: Martin Buber's Philosophy of Dialogue and its Contemporary Reception* (De Gruyter, 2015).

Merton, Thomas, *Love and Living*, eds. Naomi Burton Stone, Patrick Hart (Harvest/HBJ, 1979).

Midgley, Mary, *The Myths We Live By* (Routledge, 2003).

Miles, Clement, *Christmas in Ritual and Tradition, Christian and Pagan* (Unwin, 1912).

Mills, Liston, ed., *Perspectives on Death* (Abdingdon Press, 1969).

Milton, John, *Paradise Lost Books IX and X*, ed. R.E.C. Houghton (Oxford University Press, 1969).

Mitchell, Stephen, *The Book of Job*, tr. Stephen Mitchell (Harper Perennial, 1987). Published by Doubleday in 1979 as *Into the Whirlwind* and revised in 1987 by North Point Press.

Montefiore, Claude Goldsmid, ed. with commentary, *The Book of Psalms* (MacMillan and Co., 1901).

Morgan, John, ed., *Ethical Issues in the Care of the Dying and Bereaved Aged* (Routledge, 1996).

Morris, David Brown, *Wanderers: Literature, Culture and the Open Road* (Routledge, 2022).

Moser-Rath, Elfriede, ed., *Predigtmärlein der Barockzeit* (De Gruyter, 2019).

Mother Teresa, *Come Be My Light: The Private Writings of the "Saint of Calcutta,"* ed. Brian Kolodiejchuk (Doubleday, 2007).

Mueller, Adeline, *Mozart and the Mediation of Childhood* (University of Chicago Press, 2021).

Muhawi, Ibrahim, and Sharif Kanaana, *Speak, Bird, Speak Again: Palestinian Arab Folktales* (University of California Press, 1989).

Muir, John, *My First Summer in the Sierra* (Houghton Mifflin, 1911).

_____, *The Yosemite* (The Century Company, 1912).

Müller, Friedrich Max, *India: What Can it Teach Us?: A Course of Lectures Delivered Before the University of Cambridge* (Longmans, Green, and Co., 1883).

Muncker, Franz, *Friedrich Rückert* (Buchnersche Verlagsbuchhandlung, 1890).

Nadeau, Ray, *A Modern Rhetoric of Speech-communication*, 2nd ed. (Addison-Wesley, 1972).

Nassar, Dalia, *The Romantic Absolute: Being and Knowing in Early German Romantic Philosophy, 1795–1804* (University of Chicago Press, 2014).

Nathan, Emmanuel, and Anya Topolski, eds., *Is there a Judeo-Christian Tradition?: A European Perspective* (De Gruyter, 2016).

Neeff, Gotthold August, *Vom Lande des Sternenbanners: Eine Blumenlese deutscher Dichtungen aus Amerika* (Carl Minter's Universitätsbuchhandlung, 1905).

Neimeyer, Robert, *Lessons of Loss: A Guide to Coping* (Center for the Study of Loss and Transition, 2006).

_____, ed., *Meaning Reconstruction & the Experience of Loss* (American Psychological Association, 2001).

_____, ed., *Techniques of Grief Therapy: Assessment and Intervention* (Routledge, 2015).

_____, Darcy Harris, Howard Winokuer, and Gordon Thornton, eds., *Grief and Bereavement in Contemporary Society: Bridging Research and Practice* (Routledge, 2011).

Neuhaus, Richard John, ed., *The Eternal Pity: Reflections on Dying* (University of Notre Dame Press, 2000).

Neuwirth, Angelika, Michael Hess, Judith Pfeiffer, and Börte Sagaster, eds., *Ghazal as World Literature II—From a Literary Genre to a Great Tradition: The Ottoman Gazel in Context* (Ergon-Verlag, 2016).

Nicolai, Carlo, and Johannes Stern, eds., *Modes of Truth: The Unified Approach to Truth, Modality, and Paradox* (Routledge, 2021).

Nouwen, Henri, *Bread for the Journey: A Daybook of Wisdom and Faith* (HarperOne, 1997).

O'Donohue, John, *Anam Ċara* (HarperCollins, 1997).

_____, *Eternal Echoes* (HarperCollins, 1999).

Ovid, *Tristia—Ex Ponto*, tr. into English, Arthur Leslie Wheeler (Harvard University Press/William Heinemann, 1939).

_____, *Versuch einer Uebersetzung der fünf Trauerbücher des ehemaligen Römischen Ritters und Poeten Publius Ovidius Naso nebst Anmerkungen und der Lebensbeschreibung des Dichters*, tr. into German Johann Heinrich Kirchhof (J.P.C. Reuss, 1777).

Pabst, Fieke, ed., *Vincent van Gogh's Poetry Albums*, Cahier Vincent 1 (Waanders, 1988).

Pagels, Elaine, *The Origin of Satan* (Vintage, 1995).

Painter, Karen, ed., *Mahler and His World* (Princeton University Press, 2020).

Parham, John, and Louise Westling, eds., *A Global History of Literature and the Environment* (Cambridge University Press, 2017).

Parkes, Colin, and Holly Prigerson, *Bereavement: Studies of Grief in Adult Life*, 4th ed. (Routledge, 2009).

_____, Joan Stevenson-Hinde, Peter Marris, eds., *Attachment across the Life Cycle* (Routledge, 1991).

Parsons, James, *The Cambridge Companion to the Lied* (Cambridge University Press, 2004).

Pastan, Linda, *The Five Stages of Grief* (W.W. Norton & Co., 1978).

Paton, John Glenn, *Gateway to German Lieder: An Anthology of German Song and Interpretation* (Alfred Music, 2000).

Peale, Norman Vincent, *The Healing of Sorrow* (Inspiration Book Service/Doubleday, 1966).

Peng-Keller, Simon, *Sinnereignisse in Todesnähe: Traum- und Wachvisionen Sterbender und Nahtoderfahrungen im Horizont von Spiritual Care* (De Gruyter, 2017).

Peppers, Larry, and Ronald Knapp, *Motherhood & Mourning: Perinatal Death* (Praeger, 1980).

Pfizer, Gustav, *Uhland und Rückert: Ein kritischer Versuch* (J.G. Cotta, 1837).

Pinsky, Robert, *The Figured Wheel: New and Collected Poems 1966–1996* (Noonday/Farrar Straus & Giroux, 1996).

Pipes, Richard, ed., *Reading Abstract Expressionism* (Yale University Press, 1991).

Plewnia, Albrecht, and Andreas Witt, eds., *Sprachverfall?: Dynamik—Wandel—Variation* (De Gruyter, 2014).

Prang, Helmut, ed., *Rückert-Studien IV* (Schweinfurt, 1982).

Purdy, Daniel, *On the Ruins of Babel: Architectural Metaphor in German Thought* (Cornell University Press, 2011).

_____, *Chinese Sympathies: Media, Missionaries, and World Literature from Marco Polo to Goethe* (Cornell University Press, 2021).

Pusey, Edward Bouverie, *Private Prayers*, ed. H.P. Liddon (Rivingtons, 1883).

Raabe, Wilhelm, *Altershausen* (Otto Janke, 1911).

Rando, Therese ed., *Parental Loss of a Child* (Research Press, 1986).

Raphael, Beverly, *The Anatomy of Bereavement* (Aaronson, 1983, 1994).

Rasmussen, Mark, *Renaissance Literature and Its Formal Engagements* (Palgrave Macmillan, 2002).

Reardon, Bernard, *Religious Thought in the Nineteenth Century* (Cambridge University Press, 1966).

Rebiger, Bill, *Yearbook of the Maimonides Centre for Advanced Studies 2017* (De Gruyter, 2017).

Redfern, Suzanne, and Susan Gilbert, *The Grieving Garden: Living with the Death of a Child* (Hampton Roads, 2008).

Redfield, Marc, *Phantom Formations: Aesthetic Ideology and the Bildungsroman* (Cornell University Press, 2018).

Reif, Stefan, Andreas Lehnardt, and Avriel Bar-Levav, eds., *Death in Jewish Life: Burial and*

Mourning Customs Among Jews of Europe and Nearby Communities (de Gruyter, 2014).

———, and Renate Egger-Wenzel, eds., *Ancient Jewish Prayers and Emotions* (de Gruyter, 2015).

Reik, Theodor, *The Haunting Melody: Psychoanalytic Experiences in Life and Music* (Farrar, Straus and Young, 1953).

Remarque, Erich Maria, *Drei Kameraden* (Kiepenheuer & Witsch, 1964, 1991).

Reuter, Fritz, *Friedrich Rückert in Erlangen und Joseph Kopp* (Seippel, 1888).

Revel, Jacques, and Lynn Hunt, eds., *Histories: French Constructions of the Past, Postwar French Thought*, v1 (New Press, 1995).

Richards, Robert, *The Romantic Conception of Life: Science and Philosophy in the Age of Goethe* (University of Chicago Press, 2002).

Rigby, Kate, *Topographies of the Sacred: The Poetics of Place in European Romanticism* (University of Virginia Press, 2004).

Rilke, Rainer Maria, *Briefe*, 2 vols. (Insel, 1950).

———, *Duineser Elegien* (Insel-Verlag, 1923).

———, *Duinesian Elegies*, 2nd ed., tr. Elaine Boney (University of North Carolina Press, 1975).

———, *Selected Poems of Rainer Maria Rilke*, tr. Robert Bly (Harper & Row, 1981).

———, *Das Stunden-Buch* (Insel-Verlag, 1907).

Risinger, Jacob, *Stoic Romanticism and the Ethics of Emotion* (Princeton University Press, 2021).

Rittgers, Ronald, *The Reformation of Suffering: Pastoral Theology and Lay Piety in Late Medieval and Early Modern Germany*, Oxford Studies in Historical Theology (Oxford University Press, 2012).

Robinson, Peter, *The Sound Sense of Poetry* (Cambridge University Press, 2018).

Rosenzweig, Franz, *The Star of Redemption*, tr. Barbara Ellen Galli (University of Wisconsin Press, 2005).

Rosof, Barbara, *The Worst Loss: How Families Heal from the Death of a Child* (Henry Holt, 1994).

Rubin, Kenneth, and Hildy Ross, eds., *Peer Relationships and Social Skills in Childhood* (Springer-Verlag, 1982).

Rückert, Friedrich, *Aus Friedrich Rückert's Nachlass*, ed. Heinrich Rückert (Salomon Hirzel, 1867).

———, *Briefe*, 2 vols., ed. Rüdiger Rückert and Christa Kranz (Rückert-Gesellschaft, 1977); v3, *Spezial-Register und Nachtrag* (Rückert-Gesellschaft, 1982).

———, *Gedichte von Friedrich Rückert* (Sauerländer, 1841).

———, *Gedichte von Friedrich Rückert* (Sauerländer, 1886).

———, *Gedichte von Friedrich Rückert: Auswahl des Verfassers* (Sauerländer, 1872).

———, *Gesammelte Gedichte*, v1–6 (Heyder, 1834–1838).

———, *Gesammelte Gedichte*, v1–3 (Sauerländer, 1843).

———, *Gesammelte Poetisches Werke*, v1–12 (Sauerländer, 1868–69).

———, *Gesammelte Poetische Werke*, v1–12, ed. Konrad Beyer (Sauerländer, 1882).

———, *Kindertodtenlieder*, ed. Heinrich Rückert (Sauerländer, 1872).

———, *Kindertodtenlieder und andere Texte des Jahres 1834*, Historisch-kritische Ausgabe/»Schweinfurter Edition«, eds. Rudolf Kreutner and Hans Wollschläger (Wallstein Verlag, 2007).

———, *Leid und Lied: Neue Ausgabe [der Kindertodtenlieder]*, ed. Marie Rücker (Sauerländer, 1881).

———, *Liebesfrühling* (Sauerländer, 1844).

———, *Poetisches Tagebuch, 1850–1866*, ed. Marie Rückert (Sauerländer, 1888).

———, *Rückerts Werke*, ed. Georg Ellinger, v1–2 (Bibliographisches Institut, 1897).

———, *Rückert-Studien: Ungedruckte, vereinzelte Gedichte*, ed. Robert Borberger (Friedrich Andreas Berthes, 1878).

———, *Die Verwandlungen des Abu Seid von Serug, oder die Makamen des Hariri*, 4th ed. (Cottaschen, 1864).

———, *Die Verwandlungen des Abu Seid von Serug, 24 Makamen, aus dem Arabischen übertragen von Friedrich Rückert*, ed. Annemarie Schimmel (Reclam, 1966).

———, *The Vision of God as Represented in Rückert's Fragments*, ed. and tr. William Hastie (MacLehose and Sons for the University of Glasgow, 1898).

———, *Die Weisheit des Brahmanen*, Viertes Bändchen (Bd. 4 von 6) (Weidmann 1838).

———, *The Wisdom of the Brahmin: A Didactic Poem*, v1–6, tr. Charles Brooks (Roberts Brothers, 1882).

Rückert, Luise, *Erinnerungen von Luise Rückert und ihrer Tochter Anna Berger*, ed. Ingeborg Forssman (Mönau-Verlag, 2002).

———, *"Liebster Rückert!" "Geliebte Luise!" Braut- und Ehebriefe aus den Jahren 1821 bis 1854*, Rückert zu Ehren, eine Schriftreihe der Rückert-Gesellschaft, Band 12, ed. Ingeborg Forssman (Ergon, 2002).

———, *"Mein liebstes Geschäft ist, euch zu schreiben" : Der Briefwechsel zwischen Luise Rückert und ihren Eltern Albrecht und Luise Fischer*, ed. Ingeborg Forssman (Mönau-Verlag, 2020).

Russ, Jennifer, *German Festivals & Customs* (Humanities Press, 1980).

Rynearson, Edward, ed., *Violent Death: Resilience and Intervention Beyond the Crisis* (Routledge, 2006).

Safranski, Rüdiger, *Goethe: Life as a Work of Art*, tr. David Dollenmayer (Liveright/W.W. Norton, 2017). Originally published in Germany as *Goethe: Kunstwerk des Lebens: Biographie* (Carl Hanser, 2013).

Saito, Naoko, *The Gleam of Light: Moral Perfectionism and Education in Dewey and Emerson* (Fordham University Press, 2019).

Sanders, Catherine, *Surviving Grief… and Learning to Live Again* (John Wiley & Sons, 1992).

Sandy, Mark, *Romanticism, Memory and*

Mourning (The Nineteenth Century) (Routledge, 2014).
Scheidt, Carl, Gabriele Lucius-Hoene, Anja Stukenbrock, and Elisabeth Waller, eds., *Narrative Bewältigung von Trauma und Verlust* (Schattauer, 2015).
Schiff, Harriet Sarnoff, *The Bereaved Parent* (Penguin, 1977).
Schiller, Johann Christoph Friedrich von, *Correspondence between Schiller and Goethe from 1795 to 1805*, tr. George Calvert (Wiley and Putnam, 1845).
_____, *Friedrich Schiller's Works: The Piccolomini; The Death of Wallenstein; Wallenstein's Camp*, tr. Samuel Taylor Coleridge (Nimmo, 1903).
_____, *Die Räuber* (Frankfurt und Leipzig: 1781).
_____, *The Robbers & Wallenstein*, tr. Francis Lamport (Penguin, 1979).
_____, *Sämtliche Werke: Gedichte* (Commission der Wagner'schen Buchhandlung, 1826).
_____, *Schiller's Poems*, ed. John Scholte Nollen (Holt and Co., 1905).
_____, *Schiller's Wallenstein: Part II—Wallensteins Tod*, ed. and notes by Carl Buchheim (Bell, 1896).
_____, *Wallenstein*, v2, ed. Johann Wilhelm Schaefer (J.G. Cotta'sche Buchhandlung, 1892).
_____, *Wallenstein: A Dramatic Poem*, v2, tr. George Moir (Cadell and Co., 1827).
Schimmel, Annemarie, *Friedrich Rückert: Lebensbild und Einführung in sein Werk* (Wallstein Verlag, 2015).
_____, *A Two-Colored Brocade: The Imagery of Persian Poetry* (University of North Carolina Press, 1992).
Schlegel, Friedrich, *Friedrich Schlegel, 1794–1802: Seine Prosaischen Jugendschriften*, v2, ed. J. Minor (Carl Konegen, 1882).
_____, *Sämmtliche Werke*, v7 (J. Mayer, 1822).
Schleiermacher, Friedrich, *Friedrich Schleiermacher: Pioneer of Modern Theology*, tr. John Oman, ed. Keith Clements (Fortress Press, 1991).
Schmidt, Hans-Peter, *Schicksal Gott Fiktion: Die Bibel als literarisches Meisterwerk* (Brill, 2005).
Schonberg, Harold, *The Lives of the Great Composers* (W.W. Norton, 1970).
Schreiber, Elliott, *The Topography of Modernity: Karl Philipp Moritz and the Space of Autonomy* (Cornell University Press, 2012).
Schwartz, Barbara, *Wanderschäferei und Landschaftspflege im Pfälzerwald* (Verlag der Pfälzischen Gesellschaft zur Förderung der Wissenschaften in Speyer, 1996).
Seigal, Catherine, *Bereaved Parents and their Continuing Bonds: Love after Death* (Kingsley, 2017).
Selbmann, Rolf, *Friedrich Rückert und sein Denkmal: eine Sozialgeschichte des Dichterkults im 19. Jahrhundert* (Königshausen & Neumann, 1989).
Seung, Thomas Kaehao, *Goethe, Nietzsche, and Wagner: Their Spinozan Epics of Love and Power* (Lexington/Rowman & Littlefield, 2006).

Shakespeare, William, *King Richard II* (University Society, 1901).
_____, *Troilus and Cressida* (University Society, 1901).
_____, *A Winter's Tale/King John* (University Society, 1901).
Shrock, Dennis, *Choral Repertoire* (Oxford University Press, 2009).
Simms, William Gilmore, *Poems: Descriptive, Dramatic, Legendary and Contemplative*, v2 (John Russell, 1853).
Skuse, David, Helen Bruce, and Linda Dowdney, eds., *Child Psychology and Psychiatry: Frameworks for Clinical Training and Practice*, 3rd ed. (Wiley-Blackwell, 2017).
Slunitschek, Matthias, *Hermann Kurz und die "Poesie der Wirklichkeit"* (De Gruyter, 2017).
Smith, Peter, and Craig Hart, eds., *Blackwell Handbook of Childhood Social Development* (Blackwell, 2002).
Spargo, R. Clifton, *The Ethics of Mourning: Grief and Responsibility in Elegiac Literature* (Johns Hopkins University Press, 2004).
Stein, Deborah, and Robert Spillman, *Poetry into Song: Performance and Analysis of* Lieder (Oxford University Press, 1996).
Stein, Kevin, *Poetry's Afterlife: Verse in the Digital Age* (University of Michigan Press, 2010).
Steindl-Rast, David, and Sharon Lebell, *Music of Silence: A Sacred Journey Through the Hours of the Day* (Seastone, 1998, 2002).
Steinsaltz, Adin, *Biblical Images: Men & Women of the Book*, tr. Yehuda Hanegbi and Yehudit Keshet (Maggid, 2010).
Stephenson, John, *Death, Grief, and Mourning: Individual and Social Realities* (Free Press, 1985).
Stern, David, *Complete Jewish Bible* (Messianic Jewish Publishers, 1998).
Steven, Hugh, *Translating Christ: The Memoirs of Herman Peter Aschmann, Wycliffe Bible Translator* (William Carey, 2011).
Stroebe, Margaret, Wolfgang Stroebe, Robert Hansson, and Henk Schut, eds., *Handbook of Bereavement Research: Consequences, Coping, and Care* (American Pyschological Association, 2001).
_____, Robert Hansson, Henk Schut, and Wolfgang Stroebe, eds., *Handbook of Bereavement Research and Practice: Advances in Theory and Intervention* (American Psychological Association Press, 2008).
Stroud, Dean, *Preaching in Hitler's Shadow: Sermons of Resistance in the Third Reich* (Eerdmans, 2013).
Suckiel, Ellen Kappy, *Heaven's Champion: William James's Philosophy of Religion* (University of Notre Dame Press, 1998).
Suphan, Bernhard, *Friedrich Rückert* (Hermann Böhlau, 1888). From a lecture delivered in Weimar, 16 May 1888.
Swenson, Kristin, *Living Through Pain: Psalms and the Search for Wholeness* (Baylor University Press, 2005).

Tarlow, Sarah, ed., *The Archaeology of Death in Post-medieval Europe* (de Gruyter, 2015).

Taylor, Bayard, *Critical Essays and Literary Notes* (Putnam's Sons, 1880).

Taylor, Benedict, *The Melody of Time: Music and Temporality in the Romantic Era* (Oxford University Press, 2016).

Taylor, Ronald, *The Romantic Tradition in Germany: An Anthology with Critical Essays and Commentaries* (Routledge, 2020).

Tedeschi, Richard, and Lawrence Calhoun, *Helping Bereaved Parents: A Clinician's Guide* (Routledge, 2003).

Telushkin, *Jewish Literacy* (William Morrow, 1991).

Tennyson, Alfred, *In Memoriam*, ed. William Rolfe (Houghton Mifflin, 1895).

Teutschmann, Johannes, *Geistliches Wischtüchlein Fromer [...]* (Privately published by Johannes Teutschmann with Johann Bösemesser, printer, 1623).

Thompson, Barbara, and Robert Neimeyer, eds., *Grief and the Expressive Arts: Practices for Creating Meaning* (Routledge, 2014).

Thoreau, Henry David, *Journal of Henry D. Thoreau* (Houghton Mifflin, 1949).

Thym, Jürgen, ed., *Of Poetry and Song: Approaches to the Nineteenth-Century Lied* (University of Rochester Press, 2010).

Tolstoy, Leo, *Childhood, Boyhood, Youth*, tr. Rosemary Edmonds (Penguin, 1964).

Tournier, Paul, *The Person Reborn*, tr. Edwin Hudson (Heinemann, 1966).

Trott, Garrett, ed., *The Faithful Librarian: Essayы on Christianity in the Profession* (McFarland, 2019).

Tymms, Ralph, *German Romantic Literature* (Methuen & Co., 1955).

Uhland, Ludwig, *Ludwig Uhland Werke*, 2 vols., ed., Hans-Rüdiger Schwab (Insel, 1983).

Unamuno, Miguel de, *La Agonía del Cristianismo* (Editorial Losada, 1938).

_____, *Selected Works of Miguel de Unamuno, Volume 5: The Agony of Christianity and Essays on Faith*, tr. Anthony Kerrigan (Princeton University Press, 2015).

Valentine, Christine, *Bereavement Narratives: Continuing Bonds in the Twenty-first Century* (Routledge, 2008).

Vaughn, William, *Caspar David Friedrich: 1774–1840*, exhibition catalogue (Tate Gallery, 1972).

Veldhorst, Natascha, *Van Gogh and Music: A Symphony in Blue and Yellow*, tr. Diane Webb (Yale University Press, 2018).

Vliegher, A. de, and L. Carlier, eds., *Proceedings of the 14th Symposium of the European Grassland Federation, Ghent, Belgium, 3–5 September 2007* (European Grassland Federation, 2007).

Vögele, Wolfgang, *Wer die Glocken hört [Who Hears the Bells]* (Agentur Des Rauhen Hauses, 2010).

von Stosch, Klaus, and Michael Hofmann, eds., *Islam in der deutschen und türkischen Literatur* (Schöningh, 2012).

Walser, Robert, *Running with the Devil: Power, Gender, and Madness in Heavy Metal Music* (Wesleyan University Press, 1993).

Ward, Roger, *Conversion in American Philosophy: Exploring the Practice of Transformation* (Fordham University Press, 2019).

Weidner, Stefan, *Fluchthelferin Poesie: Friedrich Rückert und der Orient* (Wallstein, 2017).

Weiss, Andrea, *In the Shadow of the Magic Mountain: The Erika and Klaus Mann Story* (University of Chicago Press, 2008).

Wernecke, Herbert, *Christmas Customs Around the World* (Westminster John Knox Press, 1959.)

Wheatley, Kim, ed., *Romantic Periodicals and Print Culture* (Frank Cass & Co., 2003).

Wickett, Elizabeth, *For the Living and the Dead: The Funerary Laments of Upper Egypt, Ancient and Modern* (Bloomsbury, 2010).

Wieseltier, Leon, *Kaddish* (Vintage, 1998).

Williamson, John, and Edwin Shneidman, eds., *Death: Current Perspectives* (Mayfield, 1995).

Wimmer, Rainer, ed., *Das 19. Jahrhundert: Sprachgeschichtliche Wurzeln des heutigen Deutsch* (Walter de Gruyter, 1991).

Wolterstorff, Nicholas, *Lament for a Son* (Eerdmans, 1987).

Woodward, William, *Hermann Lotze: An Intellectual Biography* (Cambridge University Press, 2015).

Worden, J. William, *Children and Grief: When a Parent Dies* (Guilford, 2001).

_____, *Grief Counseling & Grief Therapy: A Handbook for Mental Health Practitioners*, 2nd ed. (Springer, 1991).

Wordsworth, William, *Poems in Two Volumes* (Longman, Hurst, Rees and Orme, 1807).

Yancey, Philip, *The Question That Never Goes Away* (Zondervan, 2013).

_____, *Where the Light Fell: A Memoir* (Convergent, 2021).

Zapata, Celia Correas, *Isabel Allende: Life and Spirits*, tr. Margaret Sayers Peden (Arte Público Press, 2002).

Ziolkowski, Theodore, *The Classical German Elegy, 1795–1950* (Princeton University Press, 1980).

_____, *German Romanticism and Its Institutions* (Princeton University Press, 1990).

Zirker, Angelika, and Esme Winter-Froemel, *Wordplay and Metalinguistic/Metadiscursive Reflection: Authors, Contexts, Techniques, and Meta-Reflection* (De Gruyter, 2015.)

Zukow, Patricia Goldring, *Sibling Interaction Across Cultures: Theoretical and Methodological Issues* (Springer-Verlag, 1989).

Zurita, Raúl, *Purgatory: A Bilingual Edition*, tr. Anna Deeny (University of California Press, 2009).

Index of First Lines in English and German

From *Songs on the Death of Children* and supplemental poems

A letter from a friend arrives / *Freundesbrief, zu guter Stunde* (KTL, 332) 119

A light shines on me / *Mir ist ein Licht erschienen* (KTL, 360) 126

A precious life gone too soon / *Der Liebe Leben ist schnell vollbracht* (*Gesammelte Poetisches Werke*, v2 [Sauerländer, 1868], 66–7) 142

A tree would buckle under the weight / *Der Baum ertrüge selbst nicht die Beschwerden* (KTL, 392) 91

A year is now gone as you / *Ein Jahr ist nun geschwunden* (RW-1, 214–5) 140

Ah, if only a child / *Ach daß ohne Wehen* (KTL, 32) 90

Ah, my physical eyes are (Lyric) / *Ach, dies leiblich schwache Auge* (*Text*) (KTL, 381–2) 130

Ah, tell me this, and this alone / *Ach, nur eines möcht' ich wissen* (KTL, 364) 128

All our laments do not / *Alles Klagen frommt nicht* (KTL, 154) 32

All that is in heaven / *Alles Irdische muß haben* (KTL, 365) 50

And why shouldn't I curse the custom / *Und soll ich nicht der Sitte fluchen* (KTL, 43) 53

Angels hover round us / *Engel umschweben uns* (KTL, 345–6) 131

As the lower branches of a / *Wie der Baum der indianischen Feige* (KTL, 403–4) 134

As the poor hen / *Wie's der armen Henne* (KTL, 171–2) 34–5

Astonishing, how the heart endures / *Unglaublich, wie erträgt ein Herz* (KTL, 156) 45

At first I accompanied poetry / *Pflegte stets die Poesie* (KTL, 14) 78–9

Because you were the smallest / *Weil ihr wart die Kleinsten* (KTL, 279–80) 89

Blight has fallen / *In meinen Blumengarten ist* (KTL, 39) 98

By all appearances / *Wie den Anschein es gewann* (KTL, 89) 106

Carry on, go ahead, but / *Sie haben nun ihre Possen* (KTL, 41) 50

Christmas—fresh and healthy / *Weihnachten frisch und gesund* (KTL, 64) 3

Colors float before my eyes / *Dem Auge schweben Farben vor* (KTL, 385) 81

Consider a man alone / *Einen einzlen Mann, der wehrlos* (KTL, 377–8) 128

Dark premonitions / *Trauriger Ahnung Gedanken* (KTL, 30) 40

Deep in the wood / *Tief im Waldesgrund* (KTL, 206–7) 83–4

Do not speak to me of this earthly vale of tears / *Sagt mir nichts von Erden Jammerthalen* (KTL, 408) 137

Doctors are ruled by the dictum / *Ärzte wissen nach den Regeln* (KTL, 36–7) 40–1

Earliest, tiny golden bowls (Primula Veris) / *Goldne Himmelsschlüsselchen* (*Primula Veris*) (KTL, 217–8) 87

Encircled by mountain / *Von Gebirg umschlossen* (KTL, 242–3) 29

Enough, enough pain! / *Nun genug, genug der Pein!* (KTL, 402) 42

Fifty Fables for Children / *Funfzig Fabeln für Kinder* (KTL, 286–8) 66–7

Flowers exposed, dead / *Die Blumen, die erfrieren* (KTL, 380–1) 129

Four come to you (The children's birthday wish for their mother) / *Heut kommen deine Vier* (*Der Kinder Geburtstagswunsch an ihre Mutter*) (RW-1, 215) 138

From our happy moments you are missing / *Zur heiteren Stunde fehlet ihr* (KTL, 161–2) 59

From the silver bloom of morning / *Aus des Morgens Silberflor* (KTL, 405–6) 135

Go! you cannot stay / *Geh! du kannst ja doch nicht bleiben* (KTL, 102) 44

God has granted you a task / *Nun hat euch Gott verliehen* (KTL, 336) 88

Good night and good morning / *Gute Nacht und guten Morgen* (KTL, 395) 84

He who finds rest, as I do / *Wer gewohnt ist wie ich zu thun* (KTL, 255–7) 36

Here rests in this chest / *Hier lieg' in der Truhe* (KTL, 279) 89

Holly-tree / *Holly-tree* (KTL, 13) 8

How your five brothers doted / *Von fünf Brüdern, o beneidenswerthe* (KTL, 79) 93

"I ask only a hint" / *Nur ein wenig hätt' ich gern* (KTL, 367–8) 93–4

I asked God / *Ich habe Gott gebeten* (KTL, 166) 108

I carry this grief each day / *Uebertags kann ich den Kummer* (KTL, 139) 107

I casually listened / *Ich hab' in läß'gen Ohren* (KTL, 74–5) 103

I did not want so many / *Ich habe ja nicht soviele gewollt* (KTL, 404) 135

I did not want to grieve (A Mother Speaks) / *Ich wollte*

Index of First Lines in English and German

gar nicht Klagen (*Die Mutter spricht*) (KTL, 168) 112

I found a wondrous plant / *Ich fand eine Wunderpflanze* (KTL, 319) 105

I have covered you with roses / *Ich habe so mit Rose* (KTL, 44) 53–4

I loved you so, my little girl! / *Ich hatte dich lieb, mein Töchterlein!* (KTL, 47–8) 42

I repeat as I heard them / *Nicht allein zu Schmerzerbeutung* (KTL, 37–8) 46–7

I thought to pick a bud / *Ich wollt' eine Knospe pflücken* (KTL, 196) 81

I thought to teach my little girl weaving / *Ich wollte mir erziehn eine Spinnemädchen* (KTL, 70) 121

I weigh this / *Wie ich reiflich* (KTL, 355–6) 126

I would have an ancient / *Ein leichenbalsamirender* (KTL, 18) 81

If only I slept / *Ich wollte, daß ich schliefe* (KTL, 167–8) 125

If our dead are not with us / *Wenn dir nicht deine Todten leben* (KTL, 392–3) 33

In a milder, softer climate / *In mildem lauem Klima* (KTL, 16) 79

In loss it is difficult to begin / *Im Verluste zu gewinnen* (KTL, 10) 73

In prose and poetry / *In Gesichten und Gedichten* (KTL, 15) 79

In the first leaf of spring / *Das erste Frühlingsblatt* (KTL, 239) 87–8

In the sacred silence of the wood I see my children / *In des Waldes heil'gem Schweigen werd' ich meine Kinder sehn* (KTL, 243–4) 23

In this weather, in this gale / *In diesem Wetter, in diesem Braus* (KTL, 341) 123

Inseparables now, alas, separated by death (Inséparables) / *Unzertrennliches, ach vom Tod getrenntes* (*Inseparables*) (KTL, 157–9) 45–6

Is it only now at her / *Hab' ich jetzt erst eingesehn* (KTL, 7–8) 72

It wasn't just you that died / *Ihr nicht seid mir gestorben allein* (KTL, 313–4) 118

"It's too hard, what I've got" / *Es ist zu schwer, was ich erlitt* (KTL, 156–7) 56

Let me join them in sleep / *Laß mich nur entschlafen* (KTL, 189) 125

Life and death are the / *Wie übel ist's auf dieser Welt* (KTL, 125–6) 106

Lift me above / *Hebt mir von des Himmels Ecken* (KTL, 185–6) 113

Little May Bells / *Maienglöckchen* (KTL, 209–11) 86

Muses, my old friends, you / *Musen, meine Freundinnen* (KTL, 11–3) 74

My angel, my little angel, come and play but not / *Mein Engelchen, mein Engelchen, Ach hol dir zum Gespielen* (KTL, 78–9) 48

My angel, my little angel, you hope to fly away / *Mein Engelchen, mein Engelchen, Du willst gewiß entfliegen* (KTL, 40) 51

My homespun tunes / *In meine häuslichen Lieder* (KTL, 5) 71–2

My little ones could not / *Es waren meine Kindchen* (KTL, 335) 121

My role, I think, is done / *Meine Rolle, denk' ich, ist nun ausgespielt* (KTL, 153) 112

Nature is unsettled / *Unruhig ist's in der Natur* (KTL, 198) 82

Never did I see you wake / *Niemals anders sah ich dich erwachen* (KTL, 74) 61

Now for the dark days, a / *Entgegen geh' ich nun den trüben Tagen* (RW-1, 211) 139

Now I know why the flame in your eyes / *Nun seh' ich wohl, warum so dunkle Flammen* (KTL, 70) 102

Now the sun will rise as bright / *Nun will die Sonne so hell aufgehn* (KTL, 369) 25

O Christmas tree / *O Weihnachtsbaum* (KTL, 154–5) 62

Oft I think, they're out and about / *Oft denk' ich, sie sind nur ausgegangen* (KTL, 311) 117

Oh sad wintering tears / *O du traurig winternde Thräne* (KTL, 163) 54

On days like today (As the years pass since my children died) / *Grad in diesen Tagen* (*Als sich der Tod meiner Kinder bejährte*) (RW-1, 210–1) 143

Once I held the reality of you / *Als Gestalten hab' ich euch besessen* (KTL-W, 521) 54

Once I was out of town for / *Als ich einen Monat einst* (KTL, 334) 120

Over all graves grass must grow / *Über alle Gräber* (KTL, 153) 30

Perhaps it was desecration / *Ich fürcht', es war Entweihung* (KTL, 9–10) 64

Shepherdess, oh how tenderly (Tender Burial) / *Schäferin o wie haben* (*Süßes Begräbnis*) (*Gesammelte Gedichte*, v2 [Sauerländer, 1843], 76) 143

Sighs, as you float / *Seufzer, die ihr wehet* (KTL, 55) 99

Sitting on your mother's knee / *Wenn du an das Knie dich setztest* (KTL, 45–6) 47

Spare me these delights / *Rathet mir nicht zum Vergnügen* (KTL, 142) 108

Sprigs of birch (from One Hundred Tercets) / *O Birkenreiser* (*from Dreizeilen-Hundert*) (KTL-W, 288) 76

Spring buds would / *Frühlingsblumen müßten* (KTL, 390–1) 68–9

Still in my words I obey their / *Immer that ich ihren Willen* (KTL, 13–4) 75

Summer flowers were a comfort / *Im Sommer war es mir ein Trost, mit Blüten* (RW-1, 211–2) 141

Surrounded by old extravagance / *Von Freuden floß um mich vorzeiten* (KTL, 17–8) 80

That I should drink and eat / *Daß ich trinken soll und essen* (KTL, 59–60) 101

The death and life of a person / *Menschentod und Menschenleben* (KTL, 403) 16–7

The house is empty / *Das Haus ist leer* (KTL, 180–1) 15

The maid brings news of their / *Es bringt die Magd die Todeskunde* (KTL, 39–40) 24

The New Year's revelers arrive / *Da sind die Neujahrsgratulanten* (KTL, 41–2) 50–1

The raucous cries of sheer joy / *Der grelle Schrei der rohen Lust* (KTL, 42) 51

The spear that struck my wound / *Der Speer, der meine Wunde schlug* (KTL, 373) 70

The sun sets each evening / *Untergeht die Sonn' am Abend* (KTL, 146–7) 60

There are your beds / *Seh' ich eure Bettchen* (KTL, 316) 68

They forgot to / *Sie haben dir die Augen* (KTL, 60–2) 103

This is my sole consolation / *Das sei mein Trost allein* (KTL, 131–2) 109–10

Those who did no harm on / *Die kein Weh gethan auf Erden* (KTL, 36) 97

To be dead must be bliss / *Gestorben sein, muß eine Wonne sein* (KTL, 43–4) 52

We abolish many manners /

Index of First Lines in English and German

Abzuschaffen geschärfte Todesarten (KTL, 88) 63

What good, then, is sunshine / *Was hilft der Sonnenschein dann* (KTL, 45) 127

What is dying? What is dead? / *Was ist sterben? was ist todt sein?* (KTL, 143) 76

When I prayed over my child / *Wenn ich betet' über meinem Kinde* (KTL, 407) 58

When in the door / *Wenn zur Thür herein* (KTL, 59) 100

When she left, my little girl / *Als mein Seelchen schied* (KTL, 34–5) 95–6

When your heart dwells / *Wenn dein Herz Gedanken nachhängt* (KTL, 163) 55

When your mother / *Wenn dein Mütterlein* (KTL, 59–60) 100

Worse than being a patient / *Schlimmer als ein Kranker sein* (KTL, 80) 43

You are a shadow in the day / *Du bist ein Schatten am Tage* (KTL, 19) 27

You ask, "Where is God's hand" / *Sprichst du: wo ist Gottes Hand* (KTL, 406–7) 136

You did not see what you had / *Du hattest ein viel zu großes Glück* (KTL, 306) 115

You five rose thorns / *Ihr fünf Rosendorne* (KTL, 33–4) 91

You need something to love / *Etwas brauchest du zu lieben* (KTL, 391) 133

You stole them, Death / *Mir das schönste Paar zu rauben* (KTL, 402) 41–2

You who filled our home with (Preface) / *Ihr, denen, was mein Haus von stillem Glücke (Vorwort)* (KTL, 3) 38

Your children are lost now (Reunion) / *Deine Kinder, hier verloren (Wiedersehn)* (KTL-W, 527; *Gedichte von Friedrich Rückert: Auswahl des Verfassers* [Sauerländer, 1872], 534) 7

Your hurts, small as a child / *Wie du sonst dein kleines Leid* (KTL, 173) 89

Your life was so short there / *So kurz war euer Beider Leben* (KTL, 8) 73

Your spirits are not here (In the Churchyard) / *Eure Geister sind nicht hier zugegen (Auf dem Kirchhof)* (KTL, 390) 85

Index of First Lines and Authors

Poems and fragments that were not part of *Songs on the Death of Children*

A heart needs something to desire (Rückert) 133
Ah, my dear angry Lord (Bitter-Sweet) (Herbert) 53
At midnight (Rückert) 122
Children age as is their lot (To those who remain) (Rückert) 35–6
"Enlighten the world," easy to say (Rückert) 14
Farewell, thou child of my right hand, and joy (On My First Son) (Johnson) 52
500 years went by and then (Rückert) 11
Forlorn, alas: I am homeless (*Tao Te Ching*) 97
Grief fills the room up of my absent child (Shakespeare) 119
He shines through the ruby slab (Eschenbach) 130
He sought for nothing (Rückert) 69
He that flies, flies! He flies away from us, all of us (pyramid engraving) 97
Heart of the world, you continue (Rückert) 82
His grave is in the forest, and he sleeps (Simms) 88
I finished my race ere I knew how to run it (Mayer) 56–7
I measure every Grief I meet (Dickinson) 109
I saw her once, a little while, and then no more (Rückert) 61
I today (Calderón) 128
It is well, he is gone (Schiller) 16
Joy is a partnership (Grief and Joy) (Knowles) 4
Let us weep (Herder) 80
Lullabies of my sorrows (Rückert) 18
Misfortunes are cowards (Calderón) 128
More skilful in self-knowledge, even more pure (Wordsworth) 77

Much I make as make the others (Rückert) 72
My daughter is three months into her "very aggressive" (Blum-Hyclak) 64
My spirit and feelings are equal to 100 separate songs (Rückert) 9
No worst, there is none. Pitched past pitch of grief (Hopkins) 57–8
Not mine—I never called thee mine (Threnody) (Emerson) 110
O Lord of grace and faith (In lowly guise thy King appeareth) (Rückert) 13
Occasional poetry deserves no comment (Wisdom of the Brahmin) (Rückert) 9
Oh! memory—thou mid-way world (Lincoln) 70
Oh, take not, Lord, my babe away (Isobel's Child) (Browning) 40
One touch of nature makes the whole world kin (Shakespeare) 173n134
Over all peaks (Goethe) 32
Pain—has an Element of Blank (Dickinson) 95
Peace; come away: the song of woe (Tennyson) 52
Philologist and poet, neither entirely (Rückert) 9
Remembrance has a Rear and Front (Dickinson) 142
Say that again (Shakespeare) 100
Spare me your attempts at consolation (Kuntsch) 134
The Brain is just the weight of God (Dickinson) 78
The dance turns without ceasing (Rückert) 41
The figtree, not that kind for fruit renowned (Milton) 134
The Future comes unbidden (Rückert) 20

The gods, endless, give all (Goethe) 97
The holiest of all holidays are those (Longfellow) 142
The hyacinthine boy, for whom (Emerson) 110
The May Bells ring in the valley (Hoffmann von Fallersleben) 86
Things were different then (Good Times, Bad Times) (Rückert) 17
This anguish will be wearied down, I know (Schiller) 153
This show 'tween me and God fades in my Vision fair (Rückert) 20
Through all the tones and (Schlegel) 77
We align thirty spokes: a wheel (*Tao Te Ching*) 133
We each face an image (Rückert) 116
We watch'd her breathing thro' the night (Hood) 90–1
We were and are—I am, even as thou art (Byron) 139
What do you smith, smithee? We smith shackles, shackles! (Armored Sonnets) (Rückert) 11
When all without is dark (The Royal Crown) (Gebirol) 75
When man falls silent in torment (Goethe) 106
With a slow and noiseless footstep (Footsteps of Angels) (Longfellow) 68
With harp and flute they (Rückert) 65
Yet as much as I lean into myself (The Book of Hours) (Rilke) 135
You need no market quote (Rückert) 91

Index of Bible Verses

Genesis 23 107
2 Samuel 18 (33) 125
Job 1 (21) 59
Job 2 (9) 247
Job 3 (24, 26) 59
Job 6 (2, 10–11) 59, 71
Job 19 (25) 4
Job 42 (3, 5–6) 95
Psalm 13 (1–2) 100

Psalm 32 (4) 71
Psalm 84 (6) 137
Psalm 119 (25, 28, 73) 94
Psalm 103 (13–14) 95
Ecclesiastes 3 (11) 116
Isaiah 21 (11–12) 71
Jeremiah 10 (19–20) 27
Lamentations 3 (8) 33
Ezekiel 14 (14) 59

Matthew 8 (22) 85
Matthew 12 (34) 85
Matthew 25 (14–30) 137, 166
Luke 9 (60) 85
John 17 (24) 45
1 Corinthians 13 (12) 131
Galatians 3 (28) 7

Index

abandonment 43, 55, 91, 96, 97, 106, 109, 119, 125, 137, 139, 155; *see also* betrayal
Aberbach, David 108
Abraham 106–7
absence 27–9, 54, 56, 59–61, 67, 74, 90, 100–1, 110–2, 134–5, 166
Achilles 71, 173n134
Adams, Nehemia 48
Addison, Joseph 136
afterlife 93–6, 113–5, 121–3, 127–8, 131–3; *see also* reunion; sense of presence
al-Hariri 9, 17, 148
Allende, Isabel 34
Althaus, Paul 12
Ambrose of Milan 125
anger 34, 53, 98, 105, 120, 136, 139, 156
Anschütz, Ernst 62
Apollodorus 71
Armand, Louis, Baron de Lahontan 16
Armored Sonnets 11–2, 172n57
Attig, Thomas 17, 67, 106, 117
Attridge, Derek 146
Auden, W. H. 13
Augustine Aurelius (Augustine of Hippo) 117–8, 132
Aurnhammer, Achim 18

Bacon, Francis 105, 136
Bakker, Egbert 31–2
Banks, Lilian (Friedberg) 159
Bannon, Jessica Autumn "Jess" 4, 25, 27–9, 60–1, 63, 66, 90, 95, 120–1, 141, 143, 168
Barth, Carl (artist) 6, 64–5, 178n279
Barth, Karl 14
Battin, Delia 112
Bauer, Thomas 126
Bauer-Lechner, Natalie 123
Bavaria 11–2, 20
Beddoes, Thomas Lovell 11
Behm, D. J. 131
Beiser, Frederick 160
Beopjeong 30, 136
Berger, Anna (née Rückert; daughter) 115
Berger, Hans (grandson) 21, 115–7

Bernhard, Christoph 94
Bernstein, Judith 58
betrayal 63, 98, 106, 109, 111–2, 119, 153, 155; *see also* abandonment
Biedermeier 10–1, 13, 62
Bildung 13–5
blame 42–3, 58–9, 65–6, 97–8, 102
Blum-Hyclak, Kimberlyn 64
Bly, Robert 135
Boelen, Paul 141
Book of Job 4, 29–30, 58–9, 71, 95, 247
Brahms, Johannes 17–8
Brophy, Seán 25–6
Browning, Elizabeth Barrett 40
Buber, Martin 104
Buchheim, Carl Adolph 153–4
Buechner, Frederick 59, 113, 138
Bullock, Michael 43–4
Bush, Ashley Davis 67, 140
Byron, George Gordon 139

Calderón de la Barca, Pedro 128–9
Callenberg Castle 82
Carver, Jonathan 16
Cavell, Stanley 111
cemeteries 48–9, 85–6
Charles, Ray 27
Christmas 3, 5, 8, 61, 62–3, 120, 139–40
churches 3–4, 12, 28, 70, 96–7, 118, 119–20, 141
Coburg 3–4, 6, 49, 51, 62, 82, 86, 87, 115, 118, 134, 160, 163
Coleridge, Samuel Taylor 82–3, 153–4
continuing bonds 7–8, 38, 67–8, 74, 113, 139
Crossan, John Dominic 85
Czapla, Ralf Georg 27
Dachau 13
David, Stacy 68
Davies, Douglas 49–50
death anniversaries *see* memorial days
De Certeau, Michel 39
De Legarde, Paul 7
Demi, Alice 65
depression 37, 40, 99, 112–3, 129

despair 32–3, 53, 74–5, 106, 136–7, 140
De Unamuno, Miguel 56
Dickens, Charles 62–3
Dickinson, Emily 78, 95, 109, 142
Dietz, Johann Simon 45
divorce 58–9
Doka, Kenneth 38, 112
Donne, John 99
doubt *see* faith

Easter 3–4
Eckhart, Meister (Eckhart von Hochheim) 14, 118
Eden, Barbara 54
Egypt 81, 97, 181n460
Eichendorff, Joseph (Karl Benedikt) Freiherr von 33
electroencephalogram (EEG) *see* Berger, Hans
Emerson, Ralph Waldo 23, 110–1, 123
Erlangen 5, 48–9, 75, 82, 106–7, 118, 133, 179n352; *see also* University of Erlangen
Erman, Adolf 181n460
Eschenbach, Wolfram von 130
Euler, Ulf Svante von 116
Euripides 71

faith 12–3, 39, 40, 49, 55, 58–9, 96–8, 113, 115, 117, 120, 129, 132, 136–7, 185n694; *see also* spirituality
Faust 48, 94–5, 180n450, 181n454
fear 33–60, 40, 55, 72–3, 82, 92, 96, 106, 112–3, 139
Fechner, Gustav Theodor 127
Field, Nigel 139
Fifty Fables for Children (Funfzig Fabeln für Kinder) (book) 66–7
Fitzon, Thorsten 18
Fortlage, Karl 98
France 13, 137
Franck, Melchior 62
Frankl, Viktor Emil 137
Frazer, James George 71
Freud, Sigmund 37–8, 66, 93, 127
Frischmuth, Barbara 18
Fromm, Erich 101, 105
Frost, Robert 65

Index

Die Gelehrtenrepublik see Klopstock, Friedrich Gottlieb
German Muses Almanac of 1834 (*Deutscher Musenalmanach für die Jahr 1834*) 7, 64–5
Germany 11–13
ghazal 23, 39, 41, 61
Gill, David 131
Gilson, Étienne 132
Goethe, Johann Wolfgang von 9, 16, 32, 39, 73, 94–5, 97–8, 106, 123, 129, 137–8, 154–5, 157, 180n450, 181n454, 181n462
Goodkin, Karl 88–9
Gorer, Geoffrey 110
Greenspan, Miriam 106
Gregory I (St. Gregory the Great) 34
grief: acute 35, 48, 67, 73–4, 109, 113; complicated 68, 89–90, 112; siblings 7, 44–8, 138–9; stages 111; *see also* grief work
Grief Mean Time (GMT) 49; *see also* time
grief work 36–8, 93, 105, 110, 155
Groeschel, Benedict 61
Grollman, Earl 22, 54, 93, 96, 173n134
guilt 43, 63, 65–6, 90, 105–6, 109, 125, 142, 157–8
Gutjahr, Ortrud 142

Hahnemann, Samuel 41
Halifax, Roshi Joan 26
Hall, Elizabeth Lewis 140
Hamacher, Werner 33
Hammer-Purgstall, Joseph von 39
Hanh, Thich Nhat 119
Hariri's Maqam see al-Hariri
Harnack, Adolf von 12
Hayward, Abraham 154
Hefling, Stephen 123
Heisenberg, Werner 132
Herbert, George 53
Herder, Johann Gottfried von 11–2, 80, 160
Hermann und Dorothea 157
Herrick, Robert 76
Heschel, Abraham 39–40, 98
Hesse, Volker 43
Hey, Johann Wilhelm see *Fifty Fables for Children*
Hirschfeld, Ariel 29–30
Hitler, Adolf 12–3
Honig, Edwin 147
hope 4, 26, 32–3, 40, 48, 55, 67, 71, 88–93, 113, 117, 137–8
Horace (Quintus Horatius Flaccus) 72, 76

idealization 66, 94
Immoos, Thomas 13
Irion, Paul 56, 87
The Irish News 124
Irving, Washington 106

Jackson, Edgar 120
Jakoby, Nina 37
James, William 101–2
Jedan, Christoph 31
Job see *Book of Job*

Kaddish 26
Khidr 10–1
Kidorf, Irwin 31
Kierkegaard, Søren 116
Kindertotenlieder (musical setting) see Mahler, Gustav
King David 57, 125
King John see Shakespeare, William
King Richard II see Shakespeare, William
Kirchhof, Johann Heinrich 156
Kittlinger, Johann Friedrich 42, 45
Klein, Wolfgang 151, 158
Klopstock, Friedrich Gottlieb 154
Knapp, Ronald 36, 90, 136
Knowles, Frederic Lawrence 4
König, Christoph 10
Koopmann, Helmut 82
Krolow, Karl 27
Kugel, James 143, 175n118
Kuntsch, Margarethe Susanna von 133–4
kyrielle 24–5

La Grange, Henry-Louis de 161, 184n635
Lamport, Francis 154
Lao Tzu 96–7, 133
Lenau, Nicolaus 122
Lewis, Clive Staples (C. S.) 38, 50, 56, 68, 112
Lincoln, Abraham 56, 69–70,
Lindgren, Kaj 150
Longfellow, Henry Wadsworth 68, 142
Lord, Janice Harris 120
Lotze, Hermann 121
Luby, Elliot 35
Luther, Martin 48–9, 100, 131, 148, 171n9
Luther Bible (1834) 4, 7, 85, 131, 148, 165, 167, 171n9, 178n325, 180n408
Lyngstad, Torkild Hovde 58

MacCarthy, Denis Florence 129
Magarshack, David 145
Mahler, Gustav 1–2, 26, 78, 101, 102–3, 117, 123, 124, 127, 183–4n633
Mann, Golo 13
Marcel, Gabriel 29
Maroon 27–9
Martin, Terry 38
Martinson, Ida 30
Mayer, Maria Sophia 56–7
McCullough, Mary Frances "Fanny" 56
McNeish, David 24–5
memorial days 20, 36, 62–3, 76, 87, 105, 140–3
memorials 89–90

Merton, Thomas 115
Metamorphoses of Abou-Seyd of Serudj, The 8
Meyers, Eric 85
Miles, Margaret 65
Milton, John 134
Moir, George 154
Monhoff, Sascha 28–9, 88, 151
Montefiore, Claude Goldsmid 9
Moraweck, André see Maroon
Moritz, Karl Philipp 155
Morris, David Brown 82
Mother Teresa 125–6, 128
Moules, Nancy 34
Mourning and Melancholia see Freud, Sigmund
Muir, John 23, 83
Müller, Friedrich Max 8–9
Muncker, Franz 127

nature 10, 24, 32, 36, 61, 63–4, 82–5, 97–8, 108–9, 124, 136, 157
Nazi party (National Socialist German Workers' Party) 12–3
Neeff, Gotthold August 9
Neimeyer, Robert 127
Neumann, Michael 16, 155–6, 174n28
Neuses 5–6, 8, 48–9, 82, 98, 106–7, 115, 118, 185n734
New Voyages to North-America see Armand, Louis, Baron de Lahontan
New Year's Day 3, 5, 50–1, 140
New York 13, 95
Niemöller, Martin 12–3
Nordmeyer, Henry 8
Nouwen, Henri 61

O'Donohue, John 34, 80, 114, 128
O'Neill, Mary 92
Orlinsky, Harry 4
Ovid 156

Pagels, Elaine 67
Park, Crystal 26
Parsifal 71
Parzival 130
Pastan, Linda 111
Pavarotti, Luciano 28
Paz, Octavio 18, 79, 147
Peale, Norman Vincent 89
Pelian spear see Achilles
Peng-Keller, Simon 130
Pfizer, Gustav 8, 172n37
Planert, Ute 11
protectiveness 35–6
Pusey, Edward Bouverie 43

Raphael, Beverly 90
regret see guilt
relief 43–4
Remarque, Erich Maria 92–3
remorse see guilt
reunion 7, 26, 46, 56, 60, 88–90, 117; 137–8; *see also* afterlife; sense of presence
Rilke, Rainer Maria 33, 130, 135, 185n708

Index

ritual 26, 31, 53, 73, 74, 87, 94, 101–2, 105, 107, 120, 124, 141–3
Rohr, Richard 115
Romantic Era 10–5, 77; and grief 17, 76–8; poetry 88, 128–9, 133, 142, 153, 155
Rosem and Suhrab 8
Rosenzweig, Franz 31
Rückert, Anna (daughter) *see* Berger, Anna
Rückert, Anna *Luise* Magdalene Rückert (Witthaus-Fischer) 3–4, 5–6, 8, 48, 65, 75, 86, 93–4, 100–1, 103–5, 112–3, 124, 135, 138–9; *see also* scarlet fever
Rückert, August (son) 3, 5
Rückert, Emilie Therese *Luise* (daughter) 3, 5, 6; funeral 3, 24–5, 51–3, 74–5, 105–7; *see also* scarlet fever
Rückert, *Ernst* Wilhelm Moriz (son) 3, 5, 6; *see also* scarlet fever
Rückert, Friedrich 4–5, 7, 8–18, 64–66, 145–8
Rückert, Heinrich (son) 3, 5, 6–7, 8, 16, 19, 20, 39, 54, 137
Rückert, Karl (son) 3, 5
Rückert, Leo (son) 3, 5
Rückert, Marie (daughter) 15–6; and Brahms 17–8

Sachsenhausen camp *see* Niemöller, Martin
Sammenhaber, David 62
scarlet fever 5, 75, 78, 98–9, 102, 110; treatment 41–5
"Schatten" *see* Maroon
Schelling, Friedrich Wilhelm Joseph 14, 160, 172n90
Schiff, Harriet Sarnoff 26, 66, 90
Schiller, Johann Christoph Friedrich von 15–6, 81, 123, 129, 162; *see also* Wallenstein
Schimmel, Annemarie 9, 16, 28, 56
Schlegel, August 129, 138
Schlegel, Friedrich 24, 77, 160
Schleiermacher, Friedrich 76, 133

Schmidt, Hans-Peter 72–3
Scholem, Gershom 50, 99
Schubert, Franz 2
Schumann, Clara 1, 17, 164
Schumann, Robert 1, 17, 164
Schütz, Heinrich 94
Schwab, Reiko 58
Schweinfurt 4, 13, 18
Selbmann, Rolf 12
sense of presence 23–4, 34, 38, 48–50, 66–8, 83–9, 113–5, 117, 120–1, 130; *see also* afterlife; reunion
shadow grief 100–1
Shakespeare, William 69, 76, 100–1, 119, 173n134
Shear, M. Katherine 117
shiva *see* support
Simms, William Gilmore 88
Smid, Geert 141
Snauwaert, Maïté 124
Sorrow and Song (Leid und Lied) 16, 18
Spain 13, 128–9, 130
Spargo, R. Clifton 105
Speckter, Otto *see Fifty Fables for Children*
spirituality 8, 23, 34, 79, 127–8, 160, 162, 184n665; *see also* faith
Staten, Henry 165
Stein, Leo 12
Steindl-Rast, David 128
Steinsaltz, Adin 108
Stockmar, Christian von 8
Stroebe, Margaret 37, 38
suicide 74, 112, 115–7, 124, 125, 138
support 30–2, 40, 74, 111, 112, 119–20, 132
survivor syndrome *see* guilt

Tao Te Ching see Lao Tzu
Taylor, Bayard 15, 72
Telephus 71
Tennyson, Alfred 52, 55
Thoreau, Henry David 14
Tillich, Paul 133–4
time 19–20, 48, 79, 81–2, 111, 116, 143
Tolstoy, Leo 74
Tournier, Paul 114

traumatic death 66, 90, 94, 119–20, 122, 124, 128–9, 138
Travels Through the Interior Parts of North America see Carver, Jonathan
The Triumph of Death (des Tods Triumphe) 41
trust 109, 120, 125, 129, 136–7
Tu me manques (you are missing from me) *see* absence

Uhland, Ludwig 8
University of Erlangen 5, 12–13, 45
Updike, John 24

Valentine, Christine 38, 50
Van Gogh, Theo *see* Van Gogh, Vincent
Van Gogh, Vincent 121–3
Vögele, Wolfgang 118

Wagner, Richard 71
Wallenstein 153–4
Walser, Robert 28
Wangenheim, Karl August von 5, 8
Weeks, O. Duane 73
Weidner, Stefan 57
Weiss, Robert 119
West–östlicher Divan see Goethe, Johann Wolfgang von
Wiese, Benno von 12
Wieseltier, Leon 129
Wilce, Jim 81
Wilkes, Johannes 20, 75–6
Wirth, Mathias 18
Wisdom of the Brahmin (Weisheit des Brahmanen) 8–9, 17
Wittgenstein, Ludwig 31–2
Wollschläger, Hans 18, 20
Wolterstorff, Nicholas 133
Wool, John 69
Worden, J. William 109
Wordsworth, William 77, 82–3

Yancey, Philip 49, 124
Yeti the cat 104

Zandvoort, Albert 66
Zarnack, August 62